Hydroelectricity and Industrial Development

QUEBEC 1898–1940

Studies in Economic History
Published in Coöperation with the
Committee on Research in Economic History

Hydroelectricity and Industrial Development

QUEBEC 1898-1940

JOHN H. DALES

with a foreword by
Abbott Payson Usher

HARVARD UNIVERSITY PRESS
Cambridge, Massachusetts
1957

Distributed in Great Britain by Oxford University Press, London

Library of Congress Catalog Card Number 57–9074

Printed in the United States of America

ACKNOWLEDGMENTS

Over the long period during which this work has been in process, I have built up a considerable number of debts. The choice of topic for the doctoral dissertation which underlies this book arose out of a short conversation with Professor Usher; and the present volume deals with areas—such as industrial development, the economics of energy, and the economics of location—in which he has long-established mastery. He will surely have forgotten that discussion, but because it was the beginning of the work I am especially pleased that he has written a foreword to the finished product.

The early stages of research were greatly facilitated by a Social Science Research Council fellowship which I held during 1948–49. The fellowship was granted by the Committee on Research in Economic History (at that time affiliated with the Social Science Research Council, but now a separate organization), and it is that committee which has subsidized the publication of this volume. Professor A. H. Cole has been the Chairman of the Committee almost without a break since its inception, and to him personally I owe no inconsiderable debt for his help as reader, adviser, and skilled guide through the tortuous path from the beginning of doctoral research to page proofs. I am also grateful for the financial assistance given me by the Committee administering the Rockefeller Grant at the University of Toronto for the study of the economic, political, and social development of Canada; on several occasions that Committee has come to my aid with small grants to cover incidental expenses.

The final stages of research were done in Montreal while I was teaching at McGill University. Here my work was greatly facilitated by assistance extended by officers of the power companies, the development of which I was studying. I hope that the several people who took time to talk with me and answer my questions will not feel offended if I mention by name only Mr. J. A. Fuller and Mr. J. B. Challies of The Shawinigan Water and Power Company, who introduced me not only to experts in their own company, but also to high officials in other power companies. My research involved a study of the hydroelectric industry rather than a detailed study of hydroelectric firms. Accordingly, I requested of the companies information not about their internal policies and histories, but information that would permit me to "place" each company in the history of the industry—such things as the early history of the enterprise, statistics on the growth of capacity and load, and statistics of physical and dollar sales. With the exception of one company (fortunately a company of minor significance for my purpose), these data were readily given when they were available; for early periods they were sometimes missing, and of course different companies kept different breakdowns of their sales statistics.

Several friends and colleagues have been generous of their time in performing the essential functions of reading and criticizing portions of the manuscript at various stages. I appreciate their help very much. Making the usual virtue out of necessity, I cheerfully acknowledge that they bear no responsibility whatsoever for the book as it now stands.

Mrs. Anna E. Spang and Miss Martha Partridge, custodians of the Corporations Records Room in the Baker Library of the Harvard Business School, Miss Grace Hamlyn of the McGill library, and Miss E. S. Challies of The Shawinigan Water and Power Company library were most helpful. To Miss Ruth Crandall of Professor Cole's *atelier*, my debt is great. During the process of revision and publication she has piloted the manuscript along its way with skill and care. The work of the staff of Harvard University Press, and especially Mrs. C. A. Pitha's exemplary editorial work on the typescript, has been much appreciated.

The deepest obligations inhibit words. The late Professor H. A. Innis was my teacher in Economic History. Elizabeth Dales, my wife, has shared in this book.

J. H. Dales
Department of Political Economy
University of Toronto

November 1956

CONTENTS

TABLES, CHARTS, AND MAPS

Tables

Charts

Maps

Foreword

The emergence of atomic energy as a source of primary power and concern over the development of backward areas have given new importance to the long-range analysis of economic resources. The characteristic features of the general problem are vividly presented by the hydroelectric development in central Canada. The study of this area affords an illustration of the impact of new power resources upon the economy of an area poorly supplied with fuel. The technique of analysis is applicable to other areas and to power derived from atomic energy.

The long-range problems of economic change are not happily approached through current theoretical models. The space dimensions of the economy are almost completely ignored. The time dimensions are arbitrary, incompletely specified, and inadequate for concrete historical analysis. The spatial dimension requires a sound understanding of the location of energy resources, primary fuels, and metals. The time dimension of the economy is notably, but not exclusively, associated with the emergence of new patterns of social and entrepreneurial action; new concepts in the sciences and in law; and the diffusion of these various novelties. When these space-time problems are ignored, or sophisticated by formal abstractions, there emerges a concept of a world economy in which regional differentiation seems to be a temporary and incidental feature of social life. The equalization of opportunity, which is set up as an ideal, is accepted as an achievement that is just around the corner.

Early reports of the study by the California Institute of Technology (May 1956), "Resources of the World: A Speculative Projection," suggest that this important research project falls into the statistical trap set up by world totals and averages. The statistical summary presents us with a world economy that has no dimension in space. It is the market point of the pure theorists. Although theoretical analysis of the space economy has made a great advance in the past thirty years, we have not yet achieved a comprehensive theory of location of specific activities within a region; and, still less, a theory of the distribution of economic activity among the differentiated regions that enter into the world economy. For the present, it is necessary to be content with the analysis of particular problems. Much has been done on the iron industries, both in major industrialized areas, and in areas without adequate fuel close to the ores. Studies of power systems have emphasized the development of scale in producing units and interconnection. Little attention has been given to the specific effects of hydroelectric power systems upon the economy of a region. Hydroelectric power presents the problem of energy that can be economically utilized only as power, since electricity is not an economical source of heat. A region supplied primarily by energy from water power is not able to choose freely between energy used as heat or as power. Industries using large amounts of energy in the form of heat are not suited to such a region. Industrial development, therefore, will be dominated by the cumulative selection of industries using a minimum amount of heat.

The actual position of regions dependent upon hydroelectric energy has latterly become clear as a matter of record, though there has been little sustained analysis. In this study, a careful historical account of power development in central Canada is completed by a stimulating analysis in terms of locational theory. We have, therefore, a full case history of an episode of commanding importance, together with a technique of analysis that can be applied generally.

The immediate significance of this general analysis lies in its applicability to the problems of regions that will be dependent exclusively upon atomic energy. In these regions, heat can be supplied in large quantities only under special circumstances. Furthermore, large investments of capital will be required. At the present time, it is presumed that atomic power plants will be integrated into general power systems. The choices between power and heat will be closely similar to the choices in the hydroelectric system in regions without mineral fuel.

The history of central Canada enables us to foresee many of the consequences of the introduction of atomic energy in regions inadequately supplied with fuel. Regional differentiation does not cease to be important, though it does become more complex.

Abbott Payson Usher

Harvard University

HYDROELECTRICITY AND INDUSTRIAL DEVELOPMENT

QUEBEC, 1898–1940

Introduction:
Problems and Approaches

Application of electrical knowledge has been the channel through which the physicist and the engineer have exerted perhaps their greatest influence on society during the last hundred years. The first socially significant application of electricity, the telegraph, became commercially feasible in the decade after 1840. This invention proved to be the beginning of an electrical revolution in communications: it was followed by the development of the telephone after 1876, radio telegraphy after 1900, radio broadcasting after 1920, and by the beginnings of television in the 1930's. While social and political relations were being thus subjected to a series of shocks by successive applications of electrical science to the development of new techniques of communication, economic life was being modified by another series of electrical inventions that led eventually to profound changes in the power basis of modern industrial economies. It is with the development based on this second set of inventions, and in particular with their repercussions on the economy of the Canadian province of Quebec, that this book is concerned.

In both aim and approach the book is frankly a mixture of history and theory. It provides an historical account of the rise of the hydroelectric industry in Quebec, but it also seeks to illuminate the relationship between hydroelectric growth and the growth of secondary manufacturing industry in the province. In the latter endeavor it becomes a study in the theory of economic development, and we hope that this aspect of the work will have some relevance, or at least suggestiveness, for areas far beyond the confines of a Canadian province.

The late Professor H. A. Innis of the University of Toronto formulated what has become the main view of Canadian economic history. In that view, Canadian economic history is to be interpreted in terms of continual adjustments to a series of staple industries which have bulked large in Canadian history, from cod-fishing in the sixteenth century to wheat-growing and newsprint production in the twentieth. The products of these industries, raw or semi-processed materials, have always found their main markets abroad, usually in the more highly industrialized countries of England and the United States. Canadian economic development, therefore, has been primarily that of a primary-producing area closely dependent on more highly developed areas, both for markets and for the techniques with which it exploits its natural resources.

Manufacturing industry finds but a small place in this interpretation of Canadian development, and this accords with the small part which it has in fact played in the Canadian economy until very recent times. During the present century, however, partly under the impulses transmitted to the economy by two world wars, a large manufacturing development has taken place in Canada, and since the outbreak of World War II the growth of manufacturing has been proceeding more rapidly than ever before. Certainly the Canadian economy can no longer be interpreted purely in terms of staple products. To a large extent, the growth of manufacturing in Canada has been associated with hydroelectric power; and the hydroelectric industry, it may be suggested, has played a dual role in Canadian economic development.

From the point of view of supply, the industry conforms closely to Professor Innis's summary of the main trend of Canadian economic development, "the application of mature techniques to virgin natural resources." The organization of this book, indeed, follows the suggestion of this phrase. Thus a brief historical account of the maturing of electrical technology in the United States during the last quarter of the nineteenth century, in Chapter 1, is followed by a survey of Quebec's water-power resources and their utilization in Chapter 2. Chapters 3 to 7 present a more detailed account of the development of the industry by individual companies, the organization by companies having been chosen in preference to an organization by time periods, or by some other horizontal division such as "stages" of development, because of the individuality of the firms in the industry. As will become abundantly clear, the major power companies in Quebec have faced such different problems and have developed along such different lines that it has seemed unwise to try to fit them into common molds—even the rather flexible molds of the historian.

But if the production of hydroelectricity conforms to the "staple" theory of Canadian development, its consumption does so only partially and imperfectly. Canadian staples, as we have noted, have traditionally found their major markets abroad. A large part of Canada's electrical output (almost 50 per cent of firm power sales in Quebec) has indeed been used in the production of pulp and paper and of base metals, and since the great bulk of these products is sold abroad it can reasonably be argued that in the main, hydroelectricity conforms, though at one remove, to the "export" character of the classic Canadian staples. But this is not the whole story. A significant proportion of Canadian electricity (roughly 30 per cent of firm power sales in Quebec) has been consumed at home by general manufacturing industries, and in this respect hydroelectricity has definitely *not* been a staple product. Indeed, it is argued here that arithmetic seriously understates the economic significance of that part of hydroelectric output which is sold to manufacturing industry, and that the new hydroelectric technology, applied to Canada's virgin water-power resources, has played a major role in deflecting Canada from its accustomed narrow path of primary production to the broader road of a more diversified economic life.

It is here that our study trenches on the subject of economic development, and accordingly takes a more theoretical turn. A word of warning and explanation is necessary. "Economic growth," "industrial development," and similar phrases, often used synonymously, are convenient but vague expressions. In this essay we assign to them a moderately precise meaning. We use them to refer especially to the growth of manufacturing, and even this word is used in a relatively narrow sense. We are interested mainly in secondary manufacturing, in general manufactures, from breakfast foods to bulldozers, and are much less interested in primary manufacturing, i.e., the early stages of transforming raw materials into semi-finished products. When we speak of manufacturing, therefore, we are thinking of furniture factories rather than sawmills, of food products rather than flour mills, of metal-working plants rather than metal refineries. Now much of the hydroelectric development in Quebec has been closely allied with two primary manufacturing industries—pulp and paper production and nonferrous metal refining, particularly aluminum reduction—and yet in this essay both these industries are slighted. We do so on the grounds that the interrelations of these heavy power consumers with the hydroelectric industry are well understood,[1] and that their great importance in the Quebec economy can safely be taken for granted. Our main concern is with the more difficult problems posed by the less direct relationship between hydroelectric development and the growth of general manufacturing industry. Thus we have made no study of the Northern Quebec Power Company, which serves the northern mining area of the province, and have given short shrift to the Saguenay River installations, because they have developed almost entirely in response to the pulp and paper and aluminum reduction industries.[2] In the southern areas of the province, notably in the St. Maurice region, the pulp and paper load is less easily separable from the general load since the power companies are not specialized to one market; here the pulp and paper industry has been treated as an integral part of the general development of industry in the province, but no special attention has been devoted to it.

The subject of the relationship between hydroelectricity and general manufacturing fairly bristles with problems. Does water power provide an energy base sufficient to support a large-scale growth of manufacturing? Or is it merely a supplement to coal, the energy resource which, in the past, has been the *sine qua non* of an industrial economy? If hydroelectric power by itself (or, more realistically, water power combined with some fuel resources) is able to support an industrial structure, how will that structure differ from industrial structures based on coal? Is hydroelectric development an active agent in the industrializing process? If so, what is the mechanism involved? These questions lie just below the surface throughout our historical work, and they are brought out into the open and subjected to direct discussion in the last two chapters. Chapter 8 is an attempt to display analytically the relation between hydroelectricity and general manufacturing industry in Quebec, and Chapter 9 summarizes the ideas relating to this subject that have emerged from both the historical and the theoretical sections of the essay.

Surely few topics in recent economic history can be more important than that of showing how electric power has impinged on the latter-day course of the Industrial Revolution, and the subject should soon attract more scholarly effort than it has yet received. A study of the significance of hydroelectric power to economic growth, to make only one point, would be directly relevant to the modern problem of "backward areas." Professor Usher[3] has shown that many such areas, including the continents of Africa and South America, possess large supplies of water power but little coal; and it was he who suggested to the author that we badly needed a more precise idea of the type of industrial structure that might be reared on the basis of water power as distinct from the familiar coal-based industrial structures.

The whole problem of the relationship between coal, electricity, and manufacturing industry is surprisingly obscure — perhaps in large part because it is concerned with the technology of production, a subject towards which economists have long evinced a certain disdain.[4] Some basic points in the relationship are, however, clear. Virtually all manufacturing processes require energy both as motive power and as heat: in modern industry the former is supplied predominantly by electricity, the latter almost exclusively through the direct combustion of fuels. Technologically, heat and electricity may be transformed one into the other. Economically, however, the situation is different. The potential heat of coal can be economically transformed into electricity. But to transfer this electricity back again into heat involves a double transformation of energy that is wasteful physically (since there are energy losses at both stages of the process) and therefore expensive. For most purposes, therefore, the production of heat from thermal (i.e., fuel-produced) electricity is uneconomic as compared with the single process of releasing the heat of coal (or some other fuel) through direct combustion. And where hydroelectricity competes, even potentially, with thermal electricity, the price of the former will be adjusted to the price of the latter so that hydroelectric heating will also be uneconomic for most industrial purposes. (The reason for the qualifications, and exceptions to the general rule, will be noted in Chapter 8, where the whole subject is treated at length.) Since, as we have noted, virtually every industry requires heat as a factor of production, it appears that a good supply of coal (or some other fuel) is a necessary condition of industrial development.

This conclusion, however, is based on a discussion of the relationship between heat and electricity in "old" coal areas. The question remains as to what the relationship would be in a situation where fuel was very scarce (and therefore expensive) and hydroelectricity very abundant (and therefore cheap). Would hydroelectricity then provide a sufficiently cheap source of heat to support industrial growth? Or would new manufacturing techniques be developed that would reduce the total amount of heat required, and thus make electrical heating economic, even though on a per-B.T.U. basis its price might be high relative to that of fuel-produced heat in areas richly endowed with coal?[5] History offers few answers to these questions, for so far our experience with industrialization has been confined mainly to coal areas. In these areas, electricity is produced from coal and has thus provided a new power form without significantly affecting the areas' power resources. Needless to say, this is not conclusive evidence that industry cannot develop in water-power areas, where hydroelectricity has in effect created large new power resources: [6] it may be evidence only of a technological lag. The whole question of the possibility of industrialization in "new" areas possessing abundant water power, but deficient in fuels, is still an open one.

What light does the present study cast on the question of industrialization in a water-power area? At first glance, central Canada would seem to offer a most favorable setting for a study of this question, since Ontario and Quebec are well endowed with water power but have no fuel resources. But this is not necessarily so. The industry of this region is by no means entirely a creation of hydroelectricity since it has always been able to draw upon the Appalachian coal fields of the United States by way of the Great Lakes, and, in the case of Quebec, also upon the Nova Scotian fields by way of the St. Lawrence River. Thus industry in central Canada, like industry in the United States, has enjoyed a joint energy base, and this very fact makes it difficult to distinguish the contribution of each energy resource to economic development. In Quebec, for instance, many firms that chose to locate in the province partly on the basis of its excellent supply of hydroelectricity certainly would not have done so if imported coal had not also been readily available for process heating. Nevertheless the fact remains that industry in Quebec has been more dependent on water power than industry in most other regions of the world, and our study should yield at least some indications of the relationships between hydroelectric development and industrial growth.

Our plan, then, is to proceed by way of historical narrative to an analysis of the meaning of hydroelectricity for economic development. But historical narrative itself always requires some sort of analytical framework, however crude, as a guide in the ordering and interpreting of raw data. The economic characteristics of the hydroelectric industry have been used as such a guide and, precisely because they are only implicit in the body of the study, it is necessary that they be set out explicitly here. This exercise will also serve to forewarn the reader of a certain unorthodoxy in our approach to the industry. In many respects our essay is an "industry study," yet in it we make little use of many of the standard techniques for analyzing an industry. In particular, so central a concept as "price," usually the focus of any economic inquiry, plays a small role in our work. The peculiarities of our approach reflect the economic peculiarities of the hydroelectric industry itself, and these we discuss under three headings: the individuality of firms in the industry, the dominance of overhead costs, and the special "administered" nature of the "price" of electricity (i.e., electric rates). None of these characteristics is unique to the hydroelectric industry, of course. But when, as in most public utilities, it happens that each of these characteristics is pronounced and that all three are found in combination, they give a definite tone to an industry. The difference between public utilities as a group (and the hydroelectric industry in particular) and other industries is perhaps only a difference of degree, but that degree is so great that analytical techniques appropriate to ordinary industries are usually more or less inappropriate to public utilities.

The outstanding feature of the hydroelectric industry is the individuality of its component firms; each enterprise is in many respects unique and therefore not comparable to other enterprises. The point may be expressed analytically by saying that cost and revenue functions differ widely from one hydroelectric development to another. The cost of a hydroelectric plant depends to a large extent on such particulars as the flow characteristics of the stream that is being developed and the geographical and geological features of the power site to be harnessed, and these factors differ greatly from one power plant to another. Again, as we shall see, the revenue structure of a hydroelectric enterprise is exceedingly complex, and the revenue pattern of one firm serving one set of markets will be quite different from that of another firm exploiting a different set of marketing opportunities. It is the complexity and *ad hoc* character of hydroelectric economics that have at once impeded the study of the industry and provided fertile ground for polemical charges and refutations concerning the relative merits of different systems of electricity supply.[7]

Having emphasized the diversity that one must expect to find in hydroelectric affairs, we must nevertheless now stress the importance of one economic feature that is common to all hydroelectric firms, namely, a very high ratio of overhead (i.e., nonallocatable) costs to total costs. Costs in the industry are mainly the overhead costs of interest on plant and equipment (dams, power houses, transmission lines, distribution systems), rentals on power sites, depreciation, maintenance, and administration. Variable costs are usually negligible in the production and transmission of power and are still a small proportion of total costs in the distribution end of the industry. The resulting ratio of overhead to total costs is very large — usually, perhaps, over 90 per cent. This high ratio, incidentally, reflects one of the main economic differences between the hydroelectric industry and the thermal electric industry, where the corresponding ratio is considerably lower owing to a smaller investment in fixed plant and higher variable costs, chiefly the costs of fuel and firing.

The high proportion of overhead to total costs in the hydroelectric industry is mainly responsible for two of its most prominent features, regional monopoly and price discrimination. Heavy overhead costs mean that both average and marginal costs for the production of hydroelectricity fall over a wide range of output; they probably fall, indeed, right up to the point where output equals the physical capacity of the power site. Monopoly is the inevitable result. One power site is almost always exploited by one company, and in most cases the rule is "one river, one company."

Heavy overhead costs also create an enormous pressure on hydroelectric enterprises to utilize their capacity as fully as possible. This, plus the fact that power companies can easily prevent resale transactions and thus segment their market, results in an extraordinarily complex system of price discrimination in the industry.[8] In retail markets, electricity is generally sold under a three-part or four-part tariff with a minimum bill. Power sales to large industrial consumers are made by individual contract, and the contract itself is extremely complicated. The fee charged for the service will depend not only on the amount of electricity purchased, but also on the ratio of peak demand to average demand ("load factor"), on the time of day when the peak demand occurs and its duration ("diversity factor"),[9] and on the type of machinery for which the power is used (for on this depends the "power factor"[10] of the load). It would be impracticable to require publication of these individual contract rates with all the detailed conditions involved in each case, and, perhaps because of the absence of public regulation in this field, perhaps also because of the difficulty of compiling a meaningful average of industrial rates, not even a summary statement of such rates is ordinarily available to the public. It is apparent, then, that "the price of electricity," and especially "the price of industrial electricity," far from being a simple figure, is a complex thing of many dimensions, a concept more suitable as a weapon in the public- versus private-power controversy than as a tool of economic analysis.

The "price of electricity" is an unsatisfactory vantage point from which to analyze the hydroelectric industry, not only because "price" in this case is a complicated phenomenon about which essential information is unavailable, but also because electrical rates are primarily *administered* prices. Now an administered price and an ordinary price are fundamentally different things with very different economic meanings.

The "price" of traditional economic theory, that pure number which emerges from the interaction of supply and demand in a perfectly competitive market, is a thing to be marveled at. It is, among other things, a servo-mechanism, at once a transmitter of economic information and a regulator of economic action. On the one hand, it is a simple, one-figure summary of the host of factors which affect the supply of and demand for a commodity. On the other, it governs the actions of consumers and producers in such a way as to balance those very forces of supply and demand of which it is a summary. Thus a change in the conditions of demand or supply will be sensitively registered in a change in price, and this change of price in turn will lead to changes in consumption and production which will result in a new equilibrium of supply and demand. It is no wonder then that when an economist wishes to study an industry, his inquiry focuses on the nerve center of that industry, the price of its product. Changes in the price reflect the changing adaptation of the industry to its environment and thus put the student on the trail of the things he wants to know — how the industry has been affected by the outside world, and the outside world by it.

Unfortunately, very few industries conform to all the conditions of perfect competition, and as these conditions are violated prices become less efficient servo-mechanisms and begin to take on an "administered" character. In extreme cases, their roles are reversed and they become the servants rather than the masters of businessmen (though even then they still retain some of their old functions, for instance rationing of scarce goods). When this happens the significance of a commodity's price — for society, for the businessman, and for the student — has been drastically changed.

In any particular industry, of course, it is a nice question to what extent nonconformity with the postulates of perfect competition has altered the economic significance of price. Simple monopoly (a violation of the "large numbers" condition of perfect competition) does not, perhaps, greatly alter the character of price. If the monopolist wants to maximize profits, there is, after all, only one price he can charge to do so under given conditions of demand and supply; [11] he does not have much freedom of action and his "administration" of price is likely to be more illusory than real. The violation of other prerequisites of perfect competition, such as freedom of entry, a single, homogeneous product, divisibility of factors, and so on, may be more serious. And at the far end of the scale we could imagine an extreme case where the logically necessary assumption of equilibrium theory itself — the independence of supply and demand — would be breached. Thus if a monopolist had effective control over the demand for his product — if he could, perhaps, determine tastes through advertising, and income through control over government spending — his freedom to operate at whatever output and price he chose would be almost unlimited. Price would then be completely "administered," and traditional economic theory would be all but irrelevant.

Because of considerable interdependence between the supply and demand sides of the market, the electrical industry, like other public utilities, has certain disquieting overtones of this imaginary case. In its impact on society the electrical industry has displayed explosive tendencies, as is suggested by the political heat it has generated. The ordinary restraints of competition which serve to keep most industries under control seem to be unusually weak in this one. They are not, of course, altogether lacking, but one gets the impression that the effective limits to the expansion of an electrical enterprise take the form not so much of the shapes and slopes of cost and revenue curves but of resource limitations, governmental policy, public opinion, and the fighting ability of rival enterprises.

Price, at any rate, is unable to perform that regulatory role in the hydroelectric industry which is one of its chief functions in most industries. Thus indivisibilities of investment (the necessity in most cases of damming a whole river or not damming it at all, for example) make it impossible in practice to maintain a continuous balance between power supply and power demand. If price were allowed to try to perform the impossible, it would swing from one extreme to another through such a wide range, and impose such strains on both producers and consumers in the process, that the industry would no doubt succumb to its own instability. In practice, therefore, entrepreneurs attempt to stabilize their business through direct policies designed to equate, as well as may be, the supply of and demand for power. Thus the two sides of the market for electricity are related through entrepreneurial policy, especially in the long run. In the short run, the supply and demand sides of the market are in many respects independent of one another, so that we may properly speak of short-run power shortages or gluts, although even here one must be cautious: to speak of complete independence between supply and demand is always suspect in an industry where, as one writer has put it, "the consumer and the company are tied to each other physically by . . . cables."[12] In the long run, to speak of independence between supply and demand is definitely misleading, for both supply and demand are largely functions of entrepreneurial policy. Thus power companies will show great initiative in creating demand—through research and advertising, for example—if they find themselves with a stubborn surplus of power, and they can equally well take steps to choke off a growth in demand if for some reason it is deemed imprudent to expand—if, for instance, the market potentially available is considered too small or too unstable to warrant an addition to capacity.[13]

With its function of equating supply and demand rendered almost impossible by the technology of the industry, and its "natural equilibrium" character seriously weakened by the interdependence of supply and demand, the "price" of electricity becomes an administrative tool and therefore something quite different from an ordinary price—a fact which we instinctively recognize when we speak of electrical *rates* rather than the *price* of electricity. As an administrative instrument electrical rates can be used for a variety of purposes. Thus the amount of power demanded may be stimulated or dampened by rate reductions or increases, and, because of the many opportunities for price discrimination in the industry, the rate pattern may be altered so as to shift output from one market to another without affecting aggregate sales. Again, rate structures are designed to increase a firm's load factor (i.e., to match supply and demand in the short run), and thus to increase its profits. And of course rates may be set with many other ends in view—the promotion of an industry (or an area), the weakening of a rival, the wooing of the public (or the politicians), and so on.

Briefly, then, in the hydroelectric industry as in most public utilities, price plays the unaccustomed role of servant. For the purpose we have in view—the understanding of the historical dynamics of the industry—the price of electricity provides no central reference point around which to organize our material.[14] It is entrepreneurial policy, not price, which becomes the nerve center of the hydroelectric industry, and accordingly our essay focuses attention on the ways in which entrepreneurs have both utilized and overcome the special characteristics of their industry. How have the physical characteristics of hydroelectricity—its transportability, its nonstorability, its technological advantages and disadvantages over other forms of power[15]—affected the industry? How has the entrepreneur dealt with the problems posed by high overhead costs? How has he used rates? What markets has he gone after? Or has he, perhaps, in Professor Hicks' happy phrase, led a "quiet life"[16] and merely exploited the advantages of an entrenched position?

These are the questions we shall be asking of our historical material. And their discussion, we hope, will illuminate the analysis in Chapter 8 of the relationship between hydroelectricity and economic growth.

CHAPTER 1

The Beginnings of the Central Electric Station

1. *Technological Change, 1880–1895*[1]

The modern electrical age was born in the summer of 1895 when the Niagara Falls Power Company brought into operation a 5000-h.p. hydroelectric station at Niagara Falls, New York. Behind this event lay a decade and a half of very rapid technological change during which electricity moved from the laboratory to the market place; before it lay a half-century during which electrical technology would mature and electricity would become a major part of the energy base of modern economics. Behind it lay a multitude of small-scale, local, urban lighting utilities; before it stretched the age of the giant, regional, electrical power company.

The fifteen years before 1895 had seen no less than three distinct electrical technologies developed and applied. This outburst of invention and innovation was set off by the development in the 1870's of the electric generator, a machine by which continuous electrical current could be produced in commercial quantities. The principle of the generator, originally known as the dynamo or dynamo-electric machine, had been discovered by Faraday in 1831, but Faraday "characteristically declined to interest himself in designing a commercial machine,"[2] and it was only after Gramme, working in Paris, designed a superior machine in 1870 that the generator became an economic reality. Within a decade generators had evolved to the point where "electricity could be produced reliably, cheaply and in quantity" so that it then became possible "to commercialize many applications [of electricity] hitherto confined to mere laboratory experiments."[8] The first large-scale application of the generator came with the arc light. Commercial installations of arc lights were made in London and Paris in 1878, and in the following year Brush pioneered the American development with an installation of lamps of his own design in Cleveland. For a decade thereafter the industry boomed, but the commercial success of arc lighting was hardly warranted on technological grounds, for within a few years of its introduction the light was obsolete.

Arc-lighting systems had two serious limitations. First, the lamp itself was much too brilliant for domestic lighting purposes: it was occasionally used in large buildings, but its main market was found in street lighting. Second, arc-lighting systems were wired in series, which meant that all lights in the circuit had to be used at the same time; such inflexibility was of little consequence in street lighting, but rendered electric lighting impracticable in most other markets. These limitations of arc lighting were obvious to everyone, but it remained for Edison to transcend them. Edison had, indeed, started to work on an electrical system which would render arc lighting obsolete in 1877, a year or two before the latter became a commercial reality.

Edison's achievement is best described as the invention of the central electric station — a system whereby electricity, produced at one place, could be used at will by consumers in a number of different places for a number of different purposes. All his particular inventions were mere corollaries of his conception of the central station. To mention but three: his system of parallel wiring (which overcame the inflexibility of the series circuit) was necessary to allow consumers to use what lights they wanted when they wanted them; his variable-power generator was necessary to permit use of the parallel wiring system; and his incandescent lamp was designed to allow electricity to compete with gas lighting in the home as well as on the street. Edison's conception of electric lighting was fundamentally different from — and in many ways the opposite of — arc-lighting technology. The greatness of his invention lies in the novelty of his system — the central electric station. In the face of this achievement the controversy over the "originality" of the various components of his system stands revealed as niggling and technologically uninformed pedantry. Edison generalized electricity; he did for the electrical industry what the central exchange did for the telephone and what, at a later date, the broadcasting station did for radio.

Edison's station on Pearl Street in the New York financial district—the world's first central electric station—began operation on September 4, 1882, and immediately proved a resounding success. From the beginning of his work Edison had been alive to the profit potentialities of an electrical system that could compete with gas in the domestic lighting market, and following his Pearl Street success, he and his associates lost no time in pressing the advantages of being first in the field. The Edison system was promoted energetically at home and abroad, and Samuel Insull, who had come to America to take up a position as Edison's secretary in 1881, later wrote that "by 1890 upwards of sixty cities were equipped with the . . . [Edison] system, all of which . . . are today [1898] so remunerative their securities are considered among the most desirable local investments, especially in cities of the first and second rank."[4]

Most of Edison's work was of permanent value, but his system had one major shortcoming and, strange to say, like the arc-lighting systems, was obsolete within a few years of its introduction. The Edison system was based on direct-current electricity. Now the distance over which electricity can be economically transmitted varies directly with the voltage used. Since it was impossible to change the voltage of direct current once it was generated, direct-current systems had to operate on the same voltage throughout, from generator to lamp. Arc-lighting systems could use fairly high voltage and thus transmit their power some distance, because the public was never in contact with the electrical connections. But Edison, realizing that high-voltage electricity in the home would be dangerous, chose the low figure of 110 as the basic voltage for his system. The result was that the Edison system's effective radius of transmission was not much more than half a mile from the power house, and Edison had to plan on no fewer than thirty-six generating stations for New York City alone.

It was alternating current that overcame the narrow transmission limitation of the Edison direct-current system, and the key invention that made alternating-current systems practicable was the transformer. By means of the transformer, a simple piece of apparatus with no moving parts, the voltage of an alternating current could be increased or decreased at will. Thus an alternating current could first be raised to a high voltage for transmission, thereby greatly increasing the economical transmission distance, and then reduced to a low voltage for distribution. Long-distance transmission, in turn, laid the basis for the giant regional central electric station which could take full advantage of the very large economies to be gained by large-scale operations; it also valorized large water-power sites, commonly located in rough country remote from markets, for once the transmission problem had been solved these became potentially valuable sources of power.

Alternating current as such was no novelty, having long been used in European arc-lighting systems; but in America electricians had become firmly committed to direct current, especially after Edison's success in 1882. Consequently the pioneering work on alternating-current systems was done in Europe; in 1881 the first patent for a transformer was taken out by Gaulard, a Frenchman, and Gibbs, an Englishman. At this point, however, George Westinghouse became interested in the possibilities of alternating current, and the initiative in the new technology passed from Europe to the United States. Westinghouse imported a Gaulard-Gibbs transformer, set one of his associates to improving it, purchased the American rights to the Gaulard-Gibbs patent, and in 1886 founded the Westinghouse Electrical Company to promote alternating-current systems in the United States.

Despite this bold beginning, alternating-current technology was still in a very rudimentary state. Its main shortcoming was that no motor which could operate on alternating current had yet been invented, and this became a serious competitive weakness of the Westinghouse system when large numbers of direct-current motors for use on Edison lines began to appear on the market in the late eighties. Actually this deficiency was soon overcome as far as invention was concerned, for in 1887, the year in which Westinghouse made his first commercial installations, a patent for an alternating-current motor was filed at the United States Patent Office by Nikola Tesla, a Serbian who had come to the United States only three years earlier. Not until the early nineties, however, were the design and performance of alternating-current motors sufficiently improved to make them commercially practicable. Tesla's work was also significant in that it promoted the use of multiphase current. The first alternating-current systems used single-phase power, whereas Tesla based his solution to the problem of the motor on two- or three-phase current. It is not feasible to explain here the technical reasons for the superiority of three-phase electricity; it is enough to point out that Tesla was able to envision the complete system of generation, transmission, and distribution of three-phase alternating current which is in almost universal use today.

By the early nineties all the strategic inventions that underlie the modern central electric station had been made and had passed the test of practicability in hundreds of small installations throughout the United States and Canada. At the consumption end of the industry, too, technology was sketching out the future. The electric tramway boom got underway in the late eighties, the electric motor was beginning its long slow invasion of steam's monopoly in the market for industrial power, a number of inventors were experimenting with electrolytic processes that would soon result in the development of a whole new group of electroprocess industries, and electric irons and fans heralded the arrival of the home-appliance industry. Never has a major change in "the state of the arts" been conceived, applied, and elaborated so quickly. The contributions of the inventors and innovators to the amazing growth of the electrical industries in the years between 1880 and 1895 speak for themselves. But should we not also stress the contribution made by the consumers themselves? Only in a new country, surely, where people were untrammeled by tradition and were eager for novelty, could the industry have grown so rapidly. In Europe, where burgesses were more dignified and circumspect, the industry grew much more slowly. To an important extent the American consumer made it possible for the American innovator to harvest the crop which frequently had been sown, ironically, by European scientists and inventors.

But progress is never without its costs, and fifteen years of frenzied activity had been hard on both engineers and businessmen. On the one hand, the electrical systems of major American cities in the middle nineties presented scenes of unparalleled technological confusion; arc lighting, direct-current systems, alternating-current systems, mixed systems, different voltages, and a great variety of frequencies provided a visual history of the development of the industry from its inception. On the other hand, central-station entrepreneurs of the period had been so preoccupied with the short-run problem of survival in a situation where rapid technological change continually accentuated competition and threatened obsolescence that they had little time or energy to ponder the long-run business significance of the technological revolution in which they were embroiled. While inventors were opening new markets for electric power, central-system men still thought almost exclusively in terms of lighting; almost a decade after alternating current had made long-distance transmission and the regional utility a practical proposition, businessmen still thought of the central station as a purely local utility and of long-distance transmission as a few miles of line out to the residential suburbs. The Niagara Falls installation of 1895 was an education for electrical engineer and central-station executive alike.

II. *The Niagara Falls Power Company* [5]

The inauguration of the Niagara Falls plant was a landmark in electrical development of coördinate importance with Edison's first central station and Westinghouse's introduction of alternating current into the United States, but the achievement of its promoter, Edward Dean Adams, unlike those of his predecessors, was not based on any striking new invention or recently discovered scientific principle. The Niagara installation was a triumph in business and engineering rather than in science. In concept it differed from previous electrical enterprises in three main ways. It was intended to produce electricity on a scale never before attempted in a single station; it was conceived primarily as a power rather than a lighting project; and, since it was thought that the primary market for power would be found in Buffalo, twenty miles distant, a system of large-scale power transmission was planned as an integral part of the installation. The history of the Niagara Falls enterprise is full of interest as an example of the tentative, experimental nature of the founding of a new industry, and its successful completion full of significance because it immediately became a model for similar developments elsewhere—among others the pioneering installation of The Shawinigan Water and Power Company on the St. Maurice River in Quebec.

The Niagara Falls Power Company was originally formed in 1886 to execute a scheme advocated by Thomas Evershed, an engineer on the Erie Canal. The project—it now seems fantastic—was purely hydraulic. A tunnel, to be built under the town of Niagara Falls, would form the common tail-race for a large number of separate hydraulic installations that were to provide power for more than two hundred manufacturing plants. The water was to be led from the upper river by a network of canals, used to operate turbines sunk in vertical shafts, and then discharged by means of branch tunnels to the main tail-race. The original company obtained a charter with wide powers under a special act, secured options on land for the necessary rights-of-way, and then cast about for suitable financial backing. After an abortive attempt to sell the company to an English group was made in 1887, successful negotiations with a group of New York financiers were concluded in 1889.

Under the vigorous leadership of Edward Dean Adams, a New York banker who became president of the enterprise in 1890, the new group plunged into the task of harnessing Niagara Falls. It was immediately realized that the Evershed scheme was impracticable, if only because of the enormous expense of excavating from solid rock the required tunnels and wheel-pits. It soon became evident that what was required was some sort of *centralized* power production combined with a transmission and distribution system. Accordingly, the company began an intensive study of power

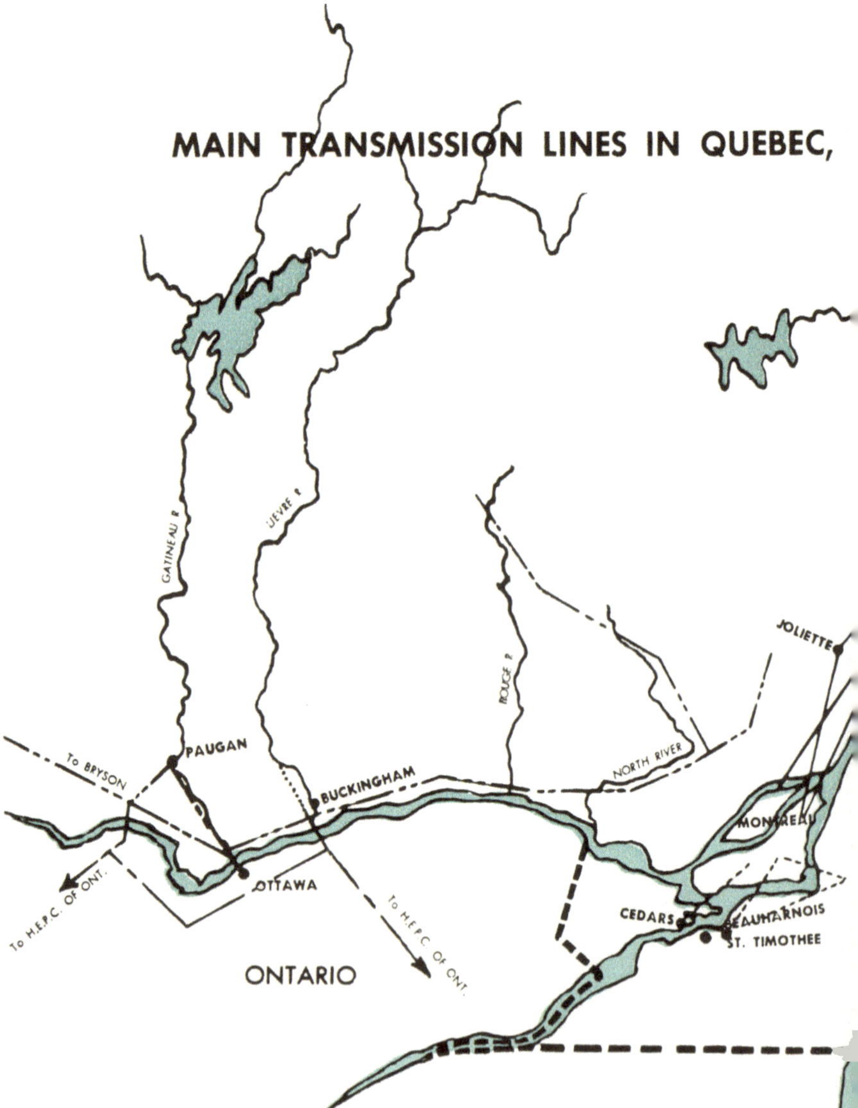

Figure 1. Map of Southern Quebec

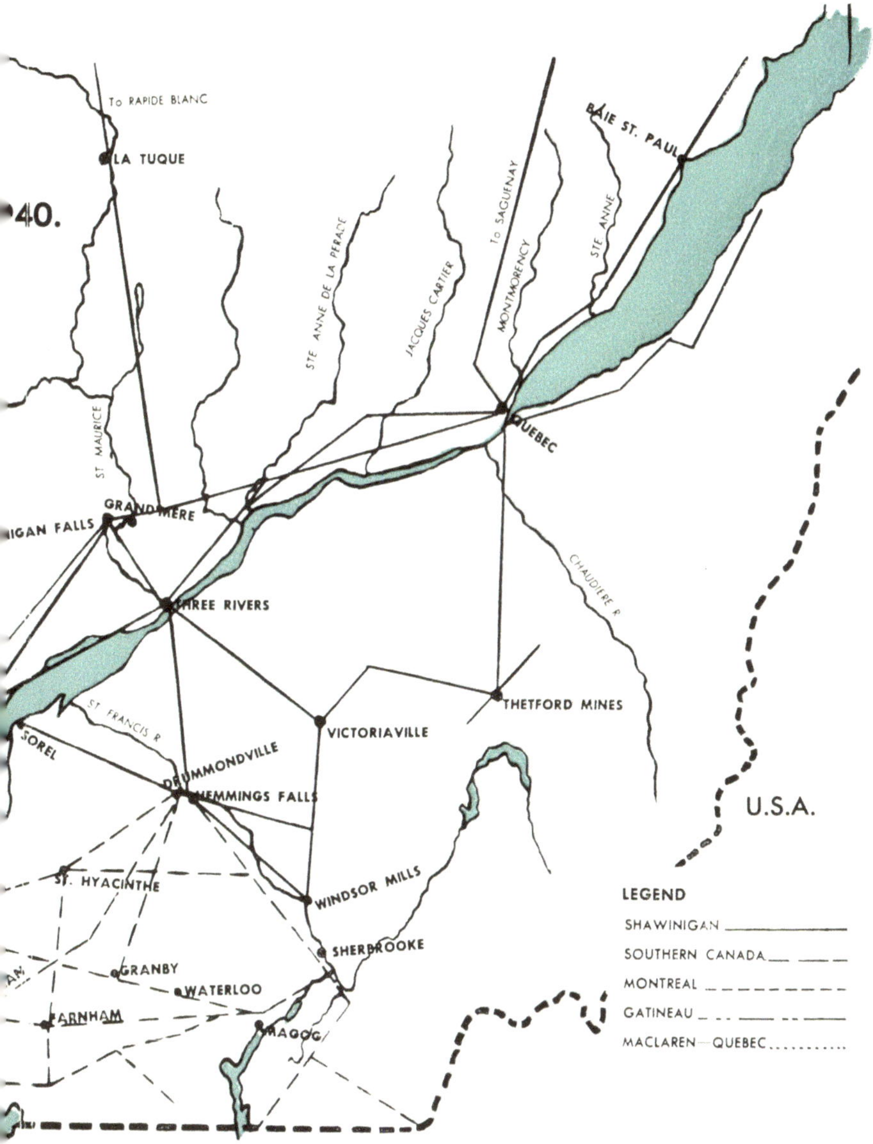

ng Main Transmission Lines, c. 1940.

developments and distribution systems in both the United States and Europe and sought the advice of experts in power engineering.[6]

In 1890 Adams made an extended personal investigation of power systems in France and Switzerland, and soon realized that Europe was far ahead of the United States in hydraulic technology and in experimental work with power transmission. He thereupon set up the International Niagara Commission through which the company offered cash prizes for the best hydraulic plans and schemes of power transmission submitted to it. The commission was headed by Lord Kelvin and included one outstanding engineer or physicist from Switzerland, France, and the United States. Numerous schemes were submitted to the commission in 1891, and it reveals much about the state of the electrical art at the time to note that of eight power-transmission proposals made four were for hydraulic or pneumatic transmission. The other four called for an electrical system, but of these only one proposed multiphase alternating current. Nevertheless the commission in its final report advocated the use of electricity in preference to other types of power distribution, and this, plus the success of the Lauffen-Frankfort line,[7] led the company to decide in favor of an electrical development at Niagara.

In December 1891, an invitation to submit plans for such an installation was sent to electrical companies in the United States and Switzerland, but the final decision to use multiphase alternating current was not made until May 1893, when the Westinghouse installation at the Chicago Exposition was successfully demonstrated. In August of that year, the primary contact between the Niagara Falls company and the Westinghouse company was made, and two years later the plant was successfully brought into operation.[8]

Adams had been wise to create world-wide interest in his project, for the technical excellence of the finished installation was due in part to the fact that it represented the best of both European and American engineering talent. Swiss firms were chosen to design the turbines, and the plans of Faesch and Piccard for a 5000-h.p. Fourneyron-type turbine were finally accepted. (The largest turbines in use anywhere at that time were probably less than 1000 h.p.) The turbine governors designed by this company, also superior units, were used at Niagara until 1910. This hydraulic installation, because of its size, efficiency, and reliability in operation, served as a model for hydraulic engineers and inaugurated the era of giant water-power developments.

Equally interesting was the electrical installation, requiring the construction of electrical apparatus in sizes then unheard of. The resulting machinery embodied many novel engineering features, most striking of which was, perhaps, the generating plant. The largest alternating-current generators in use in the United States in 1892 had a capacity of 150 h.p., so that the building of 5000-h.p. generators by the Westinghouse company was a considerable engineering accomplishment. The transmission line to Buffalo, built by the General Electric Company and completed in 1896, also represented a notable advance in engineering. Transformers of 1250-h.p. capacity were used on the line, whereas the largest transformers previously built had a capacity of only 10 h.p. The line transmitted power at 11,000 volts by overhead wires, and over a period of years much experience in transmission technique was gained by its operation.

The Niagara plant proved to be wonderfully flexible in operation. Part of the output, generated as two-phase alternating current, was transformed into three-phase alternating current and transmitted to Buffalo, where it was converted to direct current to supply the local distribution system. Another part was used locally, in both alternating and direct forms, at various voltages by the electroprocess plants that were soon located at Niagara Falls. Another part served the lighting system (both arc and incandescent) and the motor capacity at Niagara Falls, and, finally, still another part was converted to direct current to operate the Niagara Falls street railway. As one commentator put it, "Niagara was not only the birthplace of hydroelectric power, but it was also the first large-scale example of a comprehensive power system supplying power of all kinds from one circuit." [9]

It is interesting to note the role which the new electroprocess industries played in the early success of the Niagara Falls Power Company. Throughout the period of construction the promoters had assumed that Buffalo would be the main load center and that the local lighting and power load would be relatively small. This expectation proved wrong on two scores. Buffalo manufacturers were slow in changing over from the traditional steam engine to the new electric motor, and the growth in the Buffalo load was consequently small during the first few years of the company's operations. On the other hand, the Niagara Falls load grew rapidly, largely because of the great outburst of activity in the electroprocess industry, which in turn had been encouraged by the prospect of the large quantities of electricity that were to become available at Niagara.[10] By 1897 there were no less than five electrochemical concerns using Niagara power. The first arrival, the Pittsburgh Reduction Company (now the Aluminum Company of America), had moved there in 1895 and become the first customer of the new power plant. Manufacturers of artificial abrasives, carbide, and other chemicals followed within the next year, and these were soon joined by the electrometallurgical industries with their electric steel furnaces and new techniques for the electrolytic reduction of various ores. The rise of this group of industries contributed much to the early commercial success of the power company. It is remarkable that practically all of these new processes had been invented and developed commercially after 1886, the year that the Niagara Falls Power Company had obtained its charter: "Aluminum, artificial abrasives, calcium carbide, artificial graphite, ferro-alloys, and many other now common things were only laboratory curiosities when work was started upon the large-scale production of Niagara hydroelectric service. . ." [11]

Thus by a combination of the vigorous enterprise of a group of New York bankers, the hydraulic skill of Swiss engineers, the inventiveness of American and European electricians, and the coincident development of the electroprocess industries, again by Europeans and Americans, the Niagara power project became a scientific and commercial success, and proclaimed the arrival of the age of electric power.

III. *Economics, Politics, and Power Development*

It was Samuel Insull, the Englishman who had emigrated to America to become Edison's secretary at the very beginning of the electrical revolution, who perhaps read most clearly the business meaning of the new situation created by the Niagara triumph. His published speeches show a keen awareness of both the economic and political characteristics of the electrical industry. Early in his career as a central-station executive, he grasped the key significance of discriminatory pricing.[12] Discrimination according to quantity was a technique for increasing consumption by existing customers; discrimination between markets was a means of opening up new markets, thereby increasing load factor and reducing costs per unit. Reduced costs resulting from an increased load factor allowed one to lower prices, drive rivals out of business, increase load factor further by absorbing their markets, and end up with even smaller costs.[13] The industry was a perpetual motion machine. And what prevented further expansion? If load factors could be improved by monopolizing the business in one city, still more could they be improved by combining a number of cities into one large system. Then one could go on to collect several such systems, first tying them together by a holding company and later, perhaps, if they were not too far apart, by actual electric wires.

Insull appreciated that explosive character of the electrical industry already mentioned. He saw, too, that if economics dictated no limits to the size of the enterprise the forces of public opinion and political action would.[14] On the political front he argued incessantly that the industry should accept governmental regulation in exchange for a statutory monopoly of electrical distribution in a given area. To deal with public opinion he took the initiative in promoting that vast and infamous scheme of propaganda which the Federal Trade Commission unmasked in its investigations of the power industry in 1928. Insull must have been aware of the dangers involved in attempting to carry the economics of the power industry to their logical conclusion, but he could not resist the lure. In the end he was devoured by that very process of "getting into a larger way of business" of which he was one of the earliest and most articulate advocates and one of the most enthusiastic practitioners.

With the possible exception of its propagandistic component, it would be a mistake to view Insull's career as a case of entrepreneurial pathology, for his activities evinced a keen understanding of the economics of electric power. The internal economics of the central electric station indeed dictated monopoly as the only feasible long-run equilibrium position for the electric-power industry. But the path to that position and the political repercussions of the movement along that path have varied considerably from one region to another, and in each instance have reflected the power resource patterns and the political traditions of the particular region concerned. Before we turn our attention to the development of the industry in Quebec, it will be useful to illustrate this proposition — and thereby put the Quebec development in perspective — by very brief and impressionistic surveys of the industry's growth in other areas.

In the United States power resources were large, markets were ripe, and the economic forces were subject to only the weakest of political restraints until the depression of the 1930's. It was this setting that provided Insull with his opportunity. The result was a very rapid electrification of the economy, an entrenchment of private power interests, and a legacy of stubborn political problems that have only begun to be worked out with the valley authorities and the rural electrification policy. In England the strength of local governments and the tradition of local authorities imposed severe limits on large private power systems, and it proved difficult to arrange for large interconnected systems, even with the encouragement of national authorities. Electrification accordingly proceeded more slowly in England than in the United States, and perhaps the whole English economy slipped a step farther behind its American rival as a result. On the other hand, this measured economic pace minimized the political problems of electric power and permitted a more orderly development of public control in England than in the United States.

In Ontario the dominance of Niagara Falls as the major source of power, and the strength of the manufacturing interests in the smaller towns of western Ontario — interests which were reluctant to see Niagara's power monopolized by private firms for the benefit of the metropolitan center, Toronto — resulted in a drastic political solution to the electric-power problem at the very beginning of the industry's development. The towns made common cause against Toronto and called for public ownership as a weapon of defense, an appeal whose efficiency was enhanced by the public attention already focused on Niagara Falls as a tourist attraction and as the site of a public park. The result was the Hydro-Electric Power Commission of Ontario.

In Quebec the situation differed again. Political checks were weak. In contrast with the situation in Ontario, there was no vigorous manufacturing industry outside Montreal, and the province possessed a number of good power sites in the hinterlands rather than one Niagara on which public attention could be concentrated. Private enterprise accordingly became entrenched. But in Quebec the resource pattern was such that private monopoly has developed along somewhat different lines than it did in the United States.

The American electrical tradition was urban; when the industry began to expand in the United States, it moved from the city outwards. Moreover, the predominance of coal as the source of power, and the relative "evenness" with which coal was spread over large areas, meant that in its outward expansion a particular electrical enterprise did not experience any significant rise in costs; its geographical progress was hampered only by the strength of rival enterprises moving outward from other cities. In Quebec, with the exception of Montreal, expansion has taken place inwards from a few hinterland water-power sites to the urban, or town, markets, and in this expansion the enterprises have been checked not only by the strength of their rivals — although that may always be counted on as an effective force — but by other factors as well.

In the first place, when electrical development began in Quebec, there were really no urban markets for power which offered easy profits, again excepting Montreal. As a result, the power companies, although each laid claim to a geographical area of its own as soon as possible, could expand their revenues only by promoting the economic development of their respective territories. This was a relatively slow process and one which took a great deal of business energy. Secondly, the technical problems of harnessing a particular river are to a considerable extent unique to that river. The personnel of a hydroelectric enterprise based on the resources of one river tend to become specialized for that river basin, and a firm that attempts to expand to another river basin will probably experience rising costs in various parts of its organization — for example, in its engineering and sales departments. Moreover, as distance from a water-power site increases, the costs of transmission increase because higher voltage lines are required to keep power losses within economic bounds. For these reasons, the technical and economic costs of geographic expansion are usually greater in a water-power area than in a coal area. In the United States the power systems are sprawling affairs, and the power map has been formed by the outcome of corporate warfare. In Quebec the power systems are regional monopolies, and corporate boundaries follow reasonably closely the geographic boundaries of major watersheds. Since each enterprise has been preoccupied with the problems of its own river and watershed, firms in the industry have in the main lived in a state of mutual respect and even coöperation.

The Shawinigan Water and Power Company began operations on the St. Maurice River in 1898. The St. Maurice, a northern tributary of the St. Lawrence, was a strategic river from the point of view of hydroelectric development in Quebec. It was centrally located midway between Montreal and Quebec City; it had vast power potentialities; and its major power sites were located only a few miles from the St. Lawrence. South of the St. Lawrence there was a relatively "weak" power area, for none of the southern tributaries of *le fleuve* had large power potentials. In this setting the Shawinigan company proceeded to take command of the territory along both shores of the St. Lawrence and eventually organized the whole of the immediate river valley from Montreal to some distance below Quebec. (See Figure 1.) Montreal itself was marginal territory, for here the water power of the St. Maurice came up against the immense power potential of the St. Lawrence River above Montreal. The first significant exploitation of this potential was undertaken jointly by Shawinigan and the Montreal Light, Heat and Power Company, but as technology improved and became equal to the task of harnessing the full powers of the St. Lawrence, the Montreal company became dominant in Montreal and the region west of the city.

Across the river, Shawinigan thrust to the southeast, aiming at the asbestos load of the Eastern Townships, and in this direction it finally extended its network to the United States border. The Shawinigan company, however, neglected the agricultural region in the southwest section of the province (roughly the watershed of the St. Francis River), which then offered few prospects of a remunerative market for power. This territory was therefore left free for occupation by another enterprise, and after 1910 it was organized slowly by the Southern Canada Power Company on the basis of the power resources of the St. Francis River. The Shawinigan, Montreal, and Southern Canada enterprises thus laid claim to most of the settled area of the province. (See Figure 1.)

To the north of the St. Lawrence, in the thinly populated regions of the province, there remained two major power rivers which were not exploited until the late 1920's. The resources of the Saguenay River were developed by the Duke-Price interests and the Aluminum Company of America to provide power for pulp and paper mills and an aluminum reduction industry. The resources of the Gatineau River, a tributary of the Ottawa, were developed by International Paper Company interests through a subsidiary concern, the Gatineau Power Company. Part of the power from the Gatineau plants was used by the Canadian International Paper Company's pulp and paper mills in the region, while most of the remainder was sold to the Hydro-Electric Power Commission of Ontario. Although selling mainly to a few large customers, the Gatineau and Saguenay concerns also supply the general electricity requirements of the rather sparse populations in their respective regions.

CHAPTER 2

The Quebec Industry: A Preliminary Survey

1. *The Geographical Setting and its Significance*

"The Precambrian shield dominates the history as it dominates the landscape of Canada. It has set the terms and moulded the forms of Canadian life and having had the first word will, in its time, have the last." [1] The Precambrian, or Laurentian, shield and the river system which it has fashioned provide the favorable mold within which the hydroelectric power industry of Quebec has developed. The southern boundary of the shield is Quebec's "fall line." Moving westward, the line follows the St. Lawrence River to Quebec City where it arcs gently to the north. Rejoining the St. Lawrence, it sends a spur of granite across the river to form the rapids just west of Montreal. At no point are the Laurentian hills more than 100 miles from the north shore of the river, and thus the drainage from the immense area of northern Quebec thunders down from the ancient uplands directly into the fertile and populous St. Lawrence valley.[2] Virtually the entire settled portion of the province is within 100 miles from at least one of the large power sites on the north shore of the river.

Not only is the power favorably located: it is also conveniently concentrated. In the economically developed portion of the province, there are four rivers with massive power resources: the St. Lawrence itself, west of Montreal, where the Great Lakes empty over the Precambrian ledges into the open river; the Ottawa, and its main power tributaries, the Gatineau and the Lièvre, which join the St. Lawrence at Montreal; the St. Maurice, which divides into three mouths at Three Rivers, midway between Montreal and Quebec City; and the Saguenay River which empties into the St. Lawrence at Tadoussac some 150 miles below Quebec City. Together with several smaller sites, these four concentrations of water power form the natural power grid of Quebec.

The economic significance of this geographic setting may be made clear by a discussion of two general questions relating to the background of our study. Have the power resources of the province been adequate to the demands made upon them? Is the power cheap? The first question permits a categorical answer: for our period, up to the second world war, there was no question of a shortage of water-power resources in Quebec as a whole,[3] nor even of an individual company's suffering from a serious resource stringency. The Gatineau company and the Maclaren-Quebec Power Company, operating on the Lièvre River, had, it is true, developed most of their resources by the early thirties, but their power supplies were more than adequate during the depression years. The only company discussed in this study which did feel any tightness in its resource situation was the small Southern Canada Power Company located south of the St. Lawrence River. Experiencing a steady growth in demand, this company, toward the end of the period, found it cheaper to purchase more and more power from Shawinigan rather than to develop its own remaining sites. For the rest, in 1939 the Montreal, Shawinigan, and Saguenay companies all had immense undeveloped power still available to them. Indeed, despite a doubling of developed capacity since 1940, Quebec is today one of the two provinces of Canada — the other being British Columbia — which can still boast large undeveloped power resources. Truly the Laurentian shield has been lavish.

The second question, is Quebec power cheap?,[4] must be construed in a very general sense. As we have already pointed out, exact cost comparisons in the electric-power industry are all but impossible to make because of the complex nature of the costs involved. Nevertheless, it is important to have some approximate idea of the cost of producing power in Quebec, and what is really a complicated, controverted question here may receive a simple, dogmatic answer. Hydroelectric power in Quebec *has* been cheap: the real costs of supplying electricity in Quebec have been considerably lower than in the northeastern United States, and have also, probably, been somewhat lower than in Ontario. This judgment is based partly on impressions left after prolonged study of the industry in Quebec, and partly on a priori considerations.[5]

The cost of producing hydroelectricity is mainly that of servicing the investment involved in constructing the plant.[6] Now there are good geographical reasons why the cost of constructing hydroelectric plants in Quebec should be very reasonable. First, the rock of the Precambrian shield provides good footings for the required heavy powerhouses and dams, and this is very important, as engineers know. Secondly, the precipitation pattern in Quebec has helped to keep the unused capacity problem within bounds and thus to militate in favor of low-cost power. A glance at the meteorological records in the first chapter of the *Statistical Year Book* of Quebec will show that the precipitation in the province is moderately heavy (35 to 40 inches per year in most areas) and, more important for the present discussion, well distributed over the year. Huge forests in the shield act as storage for the heavy snowfall, which is thus released gradually in the spring,[7] and this too helps to keep the run-off pattern of the major rivers in Quebec more stable than in most regions where hydroelectric power is generated.

Physiography is favorable, but of course seasonal changes in stream flow do pose a serious problem for power companies in Quebec, as elsewhere.[8] In Quebec the spring flood comes in May, and stream flow is lowest toward the end of the summer and early autumn.[9] The ratio of maximum to minimum daily stream flow varies greatly between rivers. The ratio of 2:1 for the St. Lawrence is amazingly low because of the natural reservoir formed by the Great Lakes: for north shore tributaries Normandin gives average figures of 30:1 for large rivers and 50:1 for medium-sized rivers; and for south shore tributaries the ratio is even greater.[10]

The problem of variable flow has been very successfully met in Quebec by building storage dams which impound water during periods of heavy run-off and release it during the drier seasons. Since river control may either increase the power resources of a river or the use factor of a station of given capacity,[11] and customarily does both, it is thus a powerful force making for low-cost power in Quebec,[12] especially on the northern tributaries of the St. Lawrence. Their headwaters are usually strings of small lakes which offer good opportunities for creating large reservoirs at small expense through construction of strategic dams, and the land that must be flooded is of little alternative value. On the southern tributaries, regulation is much more expensive both because the terrain is less suitable for dam construction and because the land that would have to be condemned for flooding is much more expensive. Thus there are only two storage dams south of the river, both of them small structures built in 1917 by the Quebec Streams Commission at the headwaters of the St. Francis River. Although storage raised the minimum flow of this river from 300 c.f.s. to 1200 c.f.s., thus quadrupling the firm power available on the river, the ratio of maximum to minimum flow on the St. Francis is still high. On the northern rivers regulation has been most successful. It has been undertaken by the power companies in coöperation with the Quebec Streams Commission, a body created in 1910 to study flow conditions in the province and to regulate rivers when feasible. Although in most cases the storage works were built by the companies concerned, they are owned and operated by the Commission. (In the Saguenay district, however, except for the Kenogami storage, the works are owned and operated by private companies, under government supervision.[13]) The Streams Commission charges a royalty for the additional power resulting from regulation, and, where the Commission itself has financed the construction, it also levies an additional charge designed to amortize the investment over a thirty-year period. The Saguenay, the St. Maurice, the Gatineau, and the Lièvre are all controlled rivers, and in each case the minimum flow of the river has been raised to three or four times over that of its natural state.[14] The economic importance of this technological achievement is underlined by Normandin when he writes that "in general, without storage reservoirs, the cost of power at our plants would be almost double what it is." [15]

Still another reason for the low cost of power in Quebec is the proximity of the power sites to the demand centers, which helps to keep transmission costs low. Quebec consumes more power than Ontario, but the former province has less than half the high-tension transmission line mileage of the latter. From the point of view of costs the Quebec hydroelectric industry should be able to provide cheap power not only at the power site but also throughout the settled portions of the province.

In summary, the physical setting of the hydroelectric industry in Quebec has been propitious. Geology and geography, together with man-made geography in the form of river control, have provided the province with an abundance of water power which could be developed and transmitted at low cost. How were these potentialities developed and how did their development affect the Quebec economy?

II. *The Government and the Power Industry*

What was made of the physical potentialities for development in Quebec depended in part on the political and social environments in which they were exploited. The political environment is of particular concern to the hydroelectric industry, for a power company has to deal with political authorities at every step in its development—from the time it obtains a right to a waterfall, owned by the provincial government (and in certain cases subject also to Dominion jurisdiction), until it secures a permit to use a city street for distribution of electricity. By its nature the industry puts a premium on the exercise of political influence. In the United States, Lincoln Steffens pointed out that the public-utility companies succeeded the railways as the main agents of political corruption, and in Canada the Pacific Scandal of the 1870's was followed by the Beauharnois Scandal of the 1930's. In Quebec, the power companies have usually got what they wanted in their dealings with governments. Until recently, indeed, the hydroelectric industry in Quebec has been allowed to develop in an environment of unfettered private enterprise that public utilities seldom enjoy.

Granting, as even the apostles of private enterprise do, that "natural monopolies" should be subject to some sort of social control, there are at least three main ways in which the government of Quebec could have exercised such control. The companies could have been brought to terms at the resource level, when the water-power rights were first granted, by means of contracts analogous to those arranged between pulp and paper companies and the provincial government.[16] Second, the companies might have been regulated by a Public Service Board, the system favored in the United States. Third, they might have been subjected to competition by publicly owned enterprises. (Alternatively, of course, private enterprise might have been displaced more or less completely and the industry developed under public auspices, as it has been in Ontario.) What has been done along these lines in Quebec?

Until 1907 Quebec disposed of its water powers by outright sale, either through private contract or at public auction; since then concessions have been made by emphyteutic lease, usually of 50, 75, or 99 years' duration. It is easy today to criticize the ridiculously small sums paid by private companies for resources which now support large and profitable power concerns,[17] but it must be remembered that in 1907 a hydroelectric venture still represented a very speculative investment. Those who were willing to speculate got some fine bargains, however, and even when the properties were not developed immediately, the capital gains accruing to the purchasers must have been substantial. Many of the finest powers in the province had been alienated before 1907. On the Saguenay, the Shipshaw powers went for $10,000 in 1899, and the Grande Décharge site, at the outlet of Lake St. Jean, for $18,000 the following year. On the St. Maurice, Shawinigan Falls was sold to the promoters of The Shawinigan Water and Power Company for $60,000 in 1897, the falls at La Tuque to private individuals for $50,000 in

1905—exceptionally high prices—and the falls at Grand'Mère to the Laurentide Pulp Company for $5,000 in 1899. Similar grants were made on the upper Ottawa, while lumber interests obtained title to many power properties on the Gatineau and Lièvre rivers, most of these having been used for lumbering purposes for many years previously.[18]

Since 1907, with the technique of alienation by long lease, the government has been able to exercise a slightly greater control over water-power development. These leases usually contain conditions designed to ensure reasonably prompt development of the site and a cancellation clause for nonfulfillment of such conditions. An annual rent is charged and a royalty levied on the power developed. Nevertheless terms have been very moderate, with annual rentals (reduced to a horsepower basis) varying from a nominal sum to $1.00 per horsepower and royalties from 25¢ to $1.00 per horsepower.[19] Since 1926, following provincial legislation of that year, the leases have also included restrictions on the export of electricity,[20] but these regulations have probably hampered only the entrepreneurs interested in the development of water powers on the St. Lawrence and the lower Ottawa Rivers. On the whole, regulation at the resource level has been anything but cramping on the power companies in Quebec.[21]

Of social control by regulatory boards in Quebec, the most charitable thing one can say is that it has been minimal. A Public Utilities Commission was set up in 1909, and this body, renamed the Quebec Public Service Commission in 1920, exercised a general supervision over electrical as well as all other utilities until 1934. In that year a Provincial Royal Commission,[22] headed by the Hon. Ernest Lapointe, was appointed to study the electrical industry, probably in an attempt to slough off public discontent associated with the depression, which in part was taking the form of agitation for public ownership of electrical utilities.[23] After soberly discussing the merits and demerits of different possible forms of ownership of electric undertakings, the commissioners advocated private ownership regulated by a permanent Electricity Commission, and ended with the pious hope that this recommendation would "meet with the approval of the Government and the public."[24]

Accordingly, the Quebec Electricity Commission was set up in December 1935 with very wide powers of inquiry and regulation, and the old Public Service Commission was deprived of its jurisdiction over electrical utilities. This commission (and its successors) has admittedly done some good work in collecting statistical data[25] and other information pertaining to the power companies; but its usefulness as an effective regulatory body has been very small, in part because it immediately became a political plaything. The Quebec Electricity Commission of 1935 was replaced by the Provincial Electricity Board in 1937, which in turn was taken over by a refurbished general utilities commission under the name of the Public Service Board in 1940. The history of these institutions is best suggested by the unintended irony and humor of the language used in the first report of the first commission. The head office of the commission was set up in the Transportation Building in Montreal, near the head offices of the power companies, and "in order . . . to be properly situated to deal directly with the members of the Legislature whose duties frequently require their presence at the seat of the Government, a branch office was also provided in Quebec City, facing the Parliament Buildings on Grande Allée." [26]

If social control of the hydroelectric industry in Quebec has been weak, in that access to Crown resources has been relatively easy and public regulation largely ineffective, control through public ownership has not even been attempted until recently.[27] Of course there have always been a few municipally owned generating stations — 20 in 1921, 12 in 1928, and 16 in 1940 — but they have been small and have accounted for only an insignificant fraction of the total electrical output of the province. Public ownership, or the threat of public ownership, has on occasion been responsible for forcing rate reductions by the private companies,[28] but on the whole the municipal stations have been only a minor nuisance to private enterprise.[29] Since 1944, however, the situation has changed drastically. In that year the provincial government set up the Quebec Hydro-Electric Commission which took over ownership and operation of the Montreal Light, Heat and Power Consolidated. At present, therefore, the government is deeply involved in the hydroelectric industry, and public ownership in the province is now on trial.

III. *The Social Setting*

The hydroelectric industry, in its relationships with the people, shares a common position with nearly all other industry in Quebec: a minority of English-speaking industrialists do business in a predominantly French-speaking province which, until recently, has been an economically "backward" area. The impact of capital and the economic virtues on a population without capital and with noneconomic virtues sets off long-run social repercussions about which, in spite of their importance, we still know very little. In the short run, though, the economic repercussions are quite simple. The situation leads to what is usually called "exploitation," but which might more precisely and less emotionally be described simply as a situation making for high profits. High profits result naturally and directly from the situation. Entrepreneurs find an economy of low performance and a population with a low material standard of living. By their ventures they increase the output of goods and services. Of this increase, however, they need allocate only a small portion to the population, because its members will be satisfied with an improvement in their standard of living no matter how small that improvement may be in absolute terms: the rest of the increase in the social dividend can be retained by the entrepreneurs. In practice this apparently benevolent result of high profits for the entrepreneurs plus a higher standard of living for the population works out either through a pattern of low wages (as compared with the wage level in more highly industrialized areas) or high commodity prices. For the power companies in Quebec, low wages have been important directly in construction activities (though not in regular operating activities since labor costs are such a small proportion of total costs), and indirectly as an attraction to entice other industries to the area and thus to build up the demand for power. High prices have been important in the retail market for electricity (mainly a French-speaking market), and the revenue which the power companies have derived from this market is out of all proportion to the amount of electricity sold in it.

The situation is of course not stable. In general, the working of the system depends on continual increases in the standard of living for the population, and thus on gradual increases in wages or reductions in prices. At some "critical" point, perhaps, the pace of these developments increases sharply: the population seems suddenly to accept the economic values of a capitalist society, begins to demand larger and larger increments in its material standard of living, and campaigns for economic equality with populations in nonbackward areas.

Some such development has certainly been going on in Quebec. In the case of the hydroelectric industry, we can point to the gradual reduction of domestic electricity rates, however grudgingly conceded, over the last thirty years. Generally, more and more people have improved their standard of living, although perhaps only slightly, as they have left their farms and entered the expanding industry of the province. And since World War II, there has been an increasing number of indications that the "critical" point has been reached and that change is proceeding at an accelerated rate. Unionization is growing and will no doubt have the effect of reducing and eventually wiping out the historical discrepancy in wage levels between Quebec and Ontario.

An illuminating example of the trend of the times as it affects the hydroelectric industry is provided by the growth of rural electrification. A situation in which the Gatineau Power Company, as late as 1939, operated only seven miles of rural line[30] will no longer be tolerated, and the old explanations that rural electrification is unprofitable, especially in Quebec where the farmers show a deplorable lack of interest in newfangled gadgets, will no longer serve. After a series of commissions of inquiry and of feckless legislative gestures in the 1930's,[31] the government in 1945 finally created an effective Rural Electrification Bureau. From 1946 to the end of 1949, thirty-two coöperatives organized by the bureau built 3441 miles of rural line and provided service to 17,157 customers. Under this stimulus the private companies between 1945 and 1949 doubled the length of their rural lines (an addition of 7749 miles) and extended service to 57,400 new farm customers.[32] And it must be remembered that for private enterprise the provision of rural electrical service is very low-value, even unprofitable, business.

The short run is drawing to a close, and the days of abnormally high profits in Quebec are clearly numbered. The long-run social problems arising from the industrial growth of the province, however, must still be worked out. Unfortunately, social friction incidental to the economic development of "backward areas" does not necessarily diminish with the reduction of entrepreneurial profits and an increase in the standard of living of the general population. It may even increase.

In bold outline, then, we are dealing with an industry which has been well endowed geographically and, with reservations, favorably situated socially. Profit opportunities have been alluring, reflecting low costs as a result of the physical environment, high prices as a result of the socio-economic environment, and freedom of action resulting from a generous or careless governmental attitude toward the industry. In our period, too, the industry has been relatively secure. Although it has been concerned with the issue of public ownership, and the threat which sentiment in favor of that system posed to the survival of the private power industry; and although the English-speaking owners and managers of industry in a French-speaking province have probably always experienced a sense of vague uneasiness, neither of these problems seriously menaced the industry before the second world war.

IV. *A Statistical Survey of the Industry, 1931–1940*

The sheer size of Quebec's water-power development is impressive. The per capita output of hydroelectric energy in Quebec is higher than

TABLE 1

WATER-POWER DEVELOPMENT IN QUEBEC, ONTARIO, AND CANADA, 1900–1940

	Hydraulic turbine installation (1000's of h.p.) [a]				Primary power equipment in central electric stations — main plants only (1000's of h.p.) [b]		
Year	Quebec	Ontario	Canada	Year	Quebec	Ontario	Canada
1900	83	54	173	1920	632	800	1,897
1901	139	63	239	1921	662	827	1,978
1902	153	77	273	1922	758	972	2,258
1903	164	80	299	1923	788	1,100	2,424
1904	180	112	355	1924	957	1,286	2,849
1905	184	203	454	1925	1,415	1,461	3,569
1906	205	279	608	1926	1,523	1,461	3,769
1907	243	345	728	1927	1,753	1,548	4,173
1908	270	410	821	1928	2,058	1,564	4,628
1909	306	438	891	1929	2,218	1,604	4,926
1910	335	491	977	1930	2,322	1,731	5,401
1911	469	634	1,363	1931	2,518	1,775	5,707
1912	514	659	1,482	1932	2,917	1,870	6,344
1913	552	752	1,689	1933	3,063	2,004	6,616
1914	664	859	1,951	1934	3,304	2,005	6,854
1915	804	871	2,106	1935	3,476	2,079	7,104
1916	836	921	2,222	1936	3,355	2,205	7,120
1917	857	956	2,287	1937	3,513	2,225	7,342
1918	905	981	2,379	1938	3,571	2,252	7,477
1919	937	1,037	2,470	1939	3,633	2,256	7,607
1920	955	1,057	2,516	1940	3,883	2,263	7,936

[a] Source: *Canada Year Book*, 1939, p. 361. Note: See Appendix, Section 1.

[b] Source: *Central Electric Stations in Canada*, various years.

in any other Canadian province, while on the same measurement Canada ranks second only to Norway in the production of hydroelectric power. Table 1 shows the progress of water-power development in Quebec, Ontario,[33] and Canada. With large power developments at Niagara Falls in the early years of the century, Ontario became the leading province in hydroelectric development, but its margin over Quebec was never large. In the 1920's, with the rapid development of the pulp and paper industry, Quebec surged ahead, overtook Ontario, and became the leading power province in Canada in 1926. Since then the gap between Quebec and Ontario has steadily increased: accounting for about 40 per cent of the Canadian central electric station capacity in 1926, Quebec has improved its position until today it provides more than half of the Canadian total of installed hydroelectric capacity.

Production by Individual Companies

A more accurate idea of the Quebec industry is provided by Chart 1, which shows the total output of electricity in the province and also the production of the individual companies[34] considered here (except for the Maclaren-Quebec Power Company, the Chute à Caron plant of the Aluminum Company of Canada, and the Quebec Power Company, for which output figures are not available[35]). During the period covered, these companies have accounted for about 90 per cent of the total output of the province, and virtually all of this amount has been produced by four large concerns. Less than 10 per cent of the province's output has been accounted for by companies not considered in this book, including the Northern Quebec Power Company, which serves the mining area of northwestern Quebec; the Lower St. Lawrence Power Company operating in the Gaspé region; the municipal company in Sherbrooke; and a number of smaller concerns.

Chart 1 shows the relative importance of the different companies only as this is measured by output generated. A different comparison, based on power distributed by the various companies for consumption in Quebec, involves adjusting the "output generated" figures for intercompany sales and for exports. On this basis the Gatineau company's importance is considerably reduced since about half of its production is exported to Ontario. The Saguenay company's stature is also reduced (by approximately 650 million kwhs. per year) as a result of the 100,000 h.p. which it has sold to the Shawinigan company since 1927. Shawinigan's position as the leading power company in the province is somewhat enhanced by the new compari-

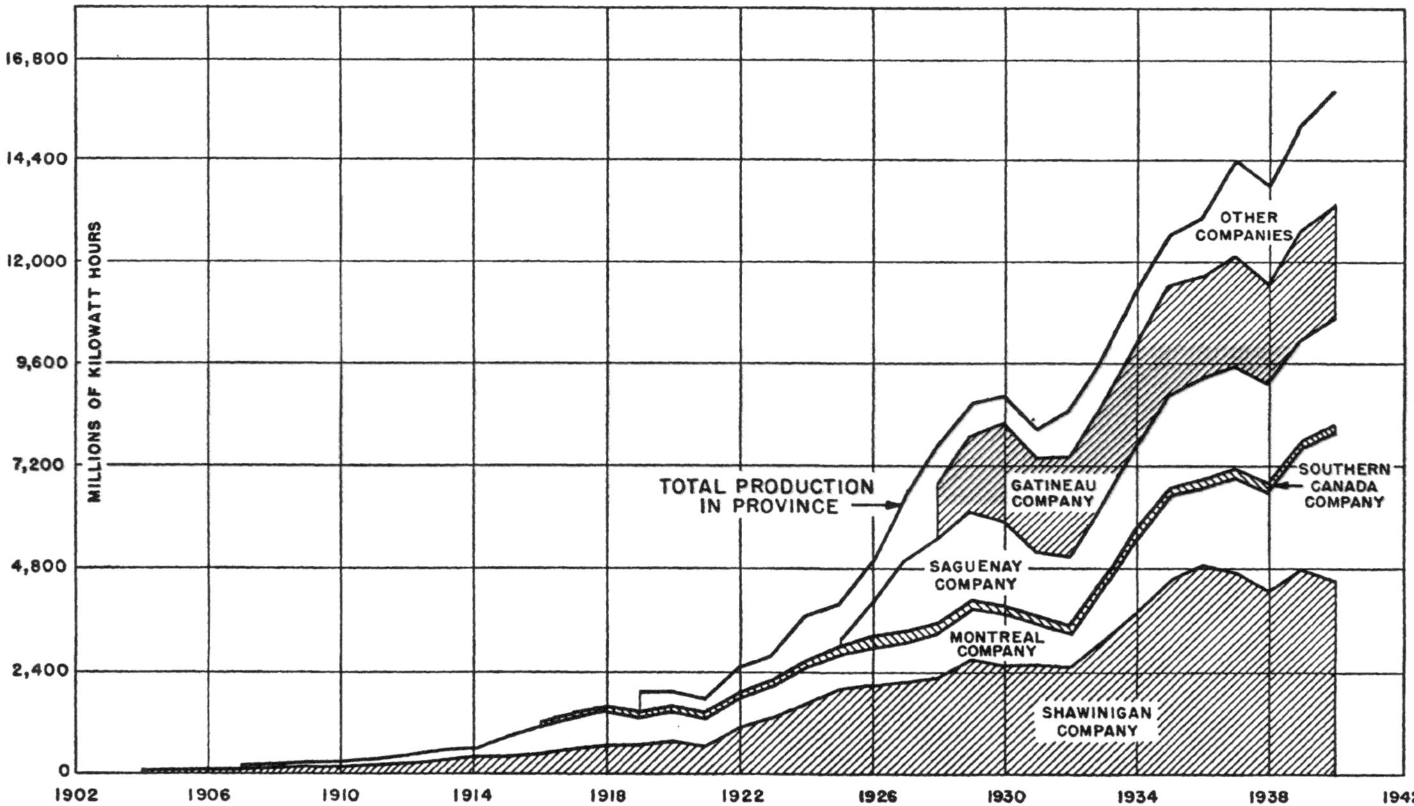

Chart 1. Hydroelectric Production by Companies

son, since its purchases from the Saguenay company have exceeded its sales to the Montreal company. The Montreal company's distributive standing in the province is raised by its purchases from Shawinigan, which, in approximate figures, rose from 70 million kwhs. in 1908 to 200 million by 1920, 400 million by 1930, and over 600 million by 1940; but this gain is more than offset by the export of some 300 to 400 million kwhs. to the United States since 1915, and by exports to Ontario which were 350 million kwhs. in 1934 and 1935, practically nothing in 1936 and 1937 (when the contracts were in dispute), 600 million kwhs. in 1938, and over 700 million kwhs. in 1939 and 1940. Southern Canada's significance on our present basis of comparison is slightly reduced, since it had a net balance of sales to the Shawinigan company up until 1940. Since then, however, this balance has been reversed, and Southern Canada now distributes more power than it generates.

A third, but much less objective, ranking emerges when we think of a company's "importance" or "size" in terms of the general extent of its business, as indicated by such things as territory covered, number of customers served, and diversity of business. Here Shawinigan again stands out clearly as the premier power company in Quebec. Centrally located, it does a large and diversified business throughout most of the settled portion of the province. Second in importance is the Montreal company. Although restricted in its operations to Montreal Island and the area along the St. Lawrence River to the west of Montreal, it provides electricity for domestic purposes to the large population of the metropolis and electric power to the heavy concentration of industries, large and small, heavy and light, which has been built up in the Montreal area. The Southern Canada company, comparatively unimportant on the basis of the first two criteria, figures more prominently — perhaps third — on our present scale. This company serves a sizable population in the western part of the Eastern Townships, roughly the area between the St. Francis and Richelieu Rivers. Its territory includes both prosperous farming country and a number of small to medium-sized towns in which are located a considerable number and variety of light manufacturing industries. The Gatineau, Maclaren-Quebec, and Saguenay companies are of relative insignificance on our third scale of importance. Although large producers of power, their output is sold almost exclusively in a few specialized markets. The first two companies export large amounts of power to Ontario and most of the rest of their production is used in pulp and paper mills. Only a small fraction of their output is required to supply the general domestic and industrial needs of the small population of the

Ottawa valley. The Saguenay company serves the sparse population of the Saguenay valley and Lake St. Jean districts, but nearly all of its production goes to the reduction works of the Aluminum Company of Canada and to pulp and paper mills in the vicinity.

Markets

Table 2 shows a breakdown of the demand for Quebec power as far as the available statistics permit. (For comparison, a similar breakdown of the Ontario figures is presented in Exhibit B of the Appendix.) It becomes apparent at once that most of Quebec's power is sold in a few specialized markets, and that the impressive hydroelectric development in the province has not necessarily resulted in the growth of a general industrial market for power impressive either in size or diversity. Let us try to get a rough idea of the amount of electricity used in Quebec for domestic, commercial, and general industrial purposes, for it is this magnitude which is relevant to an appraisal of the part played by electricity in general economic development. To arrive at this figure for Quebec there must be subtracted from total production three classes of sales: (1) exports; (2) secondary power; and (3) sales to the "special" industries of pulp and paper manufacturing and aluminum reduction. The rectitude of subtracting exports is obvious, but the other two deductions require some comment.

Secondary power is electricity sold by the power companies on an "if, as, and when available" basis. Delivery of secondary electricity may be cut off without notice by the power company concerned,[36] and deliveries are made only when the companies have power available that would not otherwise be used. Such power is sold at very low rates, which cover the marginal costs of production (sensibly zero), but certainly do not cover average costs of production.[37]

In brief, from the power companies' point of view, secondary power (also known as "boiler power") is surplus power, which may represent (a) power produced from generating capacity not being used because of the difference between the annual peak load for firm power (i.e., power which the power company is bound to deliver if, as, and when required) and the average yearly demand for power; (b) power generated from spring floods or summer rains by standby generating equipment; or (c) power produced by surplus generating capacity in the true sense of the word, that is, equipment which has been rendered excess by a fall in demand or which has been installed in anticipation of potential demands. The third type of excess capacity has been the important one in Quebec during our period. As ex-

TABLE 2

PRODUCTION AND SALES OF POWER IN QUEBEC, 1931–1940 [a]

(Millions of kwhs.; thousands of dollars)

Year	Produced		Exports		Secondary		Firm power used in province (1)−(3)−(5)	Firm power used in wood and paper industry	
	Kwhs. (1)	Revenue (2)	Kwhs. (3)	Revenue [b] (4)	Kwhs. (5)	Revenue [b] (6)	Kwhs. (7)	Kwhs. (8)	Revenue [c] (9)
1931	8,066	42,011	1,608	4,674	1,781	1,500	4,678	1,749	7,716
1932	8,491	44,720	1,640	6,374	2,542	2,150	4,303	1,649	7,545
1933	9,611	44,520	2,159	7,074	2,854	2,150	4,598	1,832	6,695
1934	11,336	46,818	2,164	8,774	3,901	2,900	5,271	1,854	7,927
1935	12,629	47,809	2,266	9,274	4,516	3,350	5,847	1,884	7,789
1936	13,020	45,938	1,882	5,474	5,306	4,250	5,832	1,736	8,068
1937	14,341	50,336	2,152	4,840	5,789	4,850	6,400	1,453	8,253
1938	13,707	53,260	2,816	7,174	4,299	3,700	6,592	1,434	8,022
1939	15,234	56,619	3,661	8,274	4,775	4,050	6,798	1,441	7,915
1940	16,011	61,737	4,070	8,874	3,642	3,640	8,299	2,071	8,559

Year	Nonferrous industries		Ordinary consumption (7) – (8) – (10)	Retail [e]		Small power		Losses	All other [f]	
	Kwhs. (10)	Revenue (11)	Kwhs. (12)	Kwhs. (13)	Revenue (14)	Kwhs. (15)	Revenue (16)	Kwhs.[d] (17)	Kwhs. (18)	Revenue (19)
1931	646	1,783	2,283	429	14,871	90[b]	2,429	823	940	9,048
1932	402	1,695	2,252	454	15,069	92[b]	2,307	850	856	9,580
1933	467	691	2,299	448	15,486	82	2,203	725	1,044	10,221
1934	486	732	2,931	452	14,546	86	2,187	871	1,522	9,752
1935	636	756	3,327	458	14,306	103	2,368	825	1,941	9,966
1936	807	546	3,289	494	15,243	93	2,305	833	1,869	10,052
1937	1,073	2,474	3,874	536	16,031	95	2,518	833	2,410	11,370
1938	1,661	3,451	3,497	575	16,986	108	2,464	800	2,014	11,463
1939	1,853	3,878	3,504	622	17,938	135	2,558	915	1,832	12,006
1940	2,220	5,148	4,008	662	18,922	122	2,452	960	2,264	14,142

[a] Sources: (1) *Central Electric Stations in Canada*, various years. (2) Statistics compiled by Dr. H. Massue.

[b] Estimated by Dr. H. Massue.

[c] These figures are based on the assumption that all secondary power was sold to the wood and paper products industries. They have been derived by subtracting from the figures of total consumption (and revenue) for these industries the figures for secondary power consumption (and revenues therefrom) for the province. The component figures are all Dr. Massue's.

[d] My estimate.

[e] Domestic, farm, commercial and street lighting.

[f] This is a residual category. It is made up primarily of general manufacturing industries, but also includes mines, electric railways, and items unaccounted for.

plained in the next chapter, the electric boiler, which makes secondary sales possible on a large scale, was developed in the early 1920's to provide a market for the generating capacity built during the first world war and rendered surplus by the disappearance of wartime demands. In the latter part of the 1920's there was again a large increase in power capacity, and the construction boom even carried over into the early years of the depression. This building program, plus the fall in demand during the depression years, resulted in a large amount of excess capacity in the industry, and the result, as shown by Table 2, was a tremendous increase in secondary power sales. With the second world war the demand for firm power increased, and consequently secondary power sales were "squeezed out" of the market.[38] The relatively small amounts of secondary power sold during the war years came primarily from sources (a) and (b) above. In our period, then, secondary power sales are generally indicative of excess capacity in the industry: secondary power is not sold in large quantities under normal circumstances, and for that reason it has little relevance to a discussion of electricity and economic development. When we subtract secondary power sales and export sales from the total production of electricity in Quebec, we obtain the consumption (including losses) of firm power in Quebec itself (Column 7 of Table 2).

From this figure we deduct sales to the pulp and paper industry and the aluminum industry[39] in order to arrive at a significant figure for relating hydroelectric development to general economic growth. As explained in the introduction, these two industries require exceptionally large amounts of power in their operations, and low-cost power is consequently an important factor in their location. When the power consumption of these "special" industries is deducted, we obtain the figures for "ordinary consumption" (Table 2, Column 12).

Having made all these deductions, we can see how the giant has shrunk. For the period 1931 to 1946 — a period covering both the years of abnormal depression and the war years of abnormal prosperity — the total consumption of electricity in Quebec, including losses, for domestic, farm, commercial, and general manufacturing purposes combined was very moderate, rising irregularly from 2.3 billion kwhs. in 1931 to 4.0 billion kwhs. in 1940. The Shawinigan company alone could easily have carried such a load — its installed capacity was, in fact, sufficient to provide for a firm power demand 50 per cent larger than this calculated load. It is apparent that such general manufacturing industry as has so far developed in Quebec could have been supported on a relatively small water-power base.

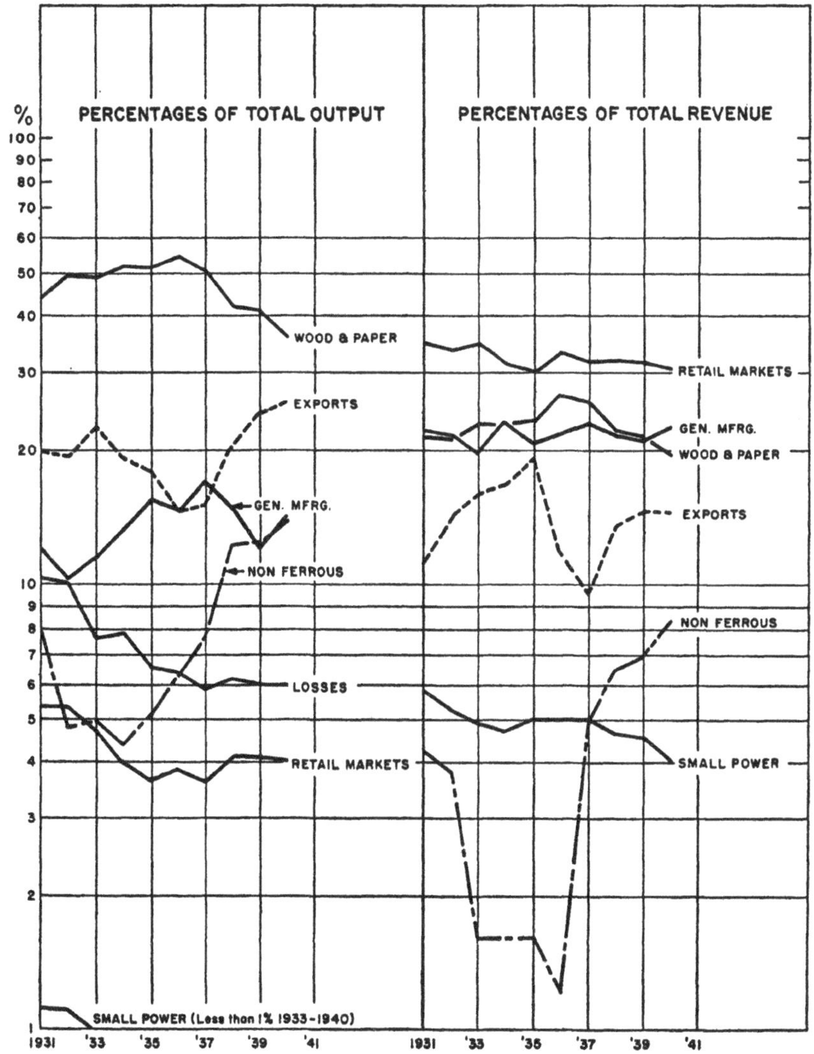

Chart 2. Sales of Electricity in Quebec: by Markets, 1931–1940

Quantities and Revenues

Electricity is sold in a number of well-separated markets, where it is used for many differentiated purposes; discriminatory pricing is therefore characteristic of the industry. Chart 2, which juxtaposes the physical and dollar sales to the different markets in Quebec, suggests the character and degree of this discrimination. The chart shows the percentages of total output sold to, and total revenue derived from, different markets. The simplifying assumption is made that all secondary power sales were made to the pulp and paper industry, so that the figures for this industry include both firm and secondary power. Actually some secondary power was sold to other industries, but such sales were small in relation to the deliveries of secondary power to pulp and paper mills. From the chart it is clear that lighting sales (for domestic, commercial, municipal, and farm use) and small power sales (i.e., sales to establishments with a connected load of less than 50 kilowatts) form the "high-value" portion of the power companies' business, while exports and sales to the pulp and paper and aluminum industries are in the "low-value" category. Sales to general manufacturing industry apparently [40] provide about "average" business, since this market's share of kilowatt-hour consumption is fairly close to its percentage contribution to revenue.

This picture of the industry is of course arbitrary, for its characteristics depend on the particular magnitudes — total output and total revenue — which were chosen as bases for calculating the percentages. An alternative picture of the industry is provided by calculating the percentages on the narrower base of the firm power utilized in the province, i.e., total power less secondary power and exports (Column 7, Table 2). Sales to the pulp and paper industry, now that only primary sales to the industry are considered, will of course occupy a less prominent place in the new picture; sales to other manufacturing industries and losses will bulk considerably larger.[41] In Table 3 the figures as calculated on both bases are presented in an abridged form, and for the sake of comparison the corresponding figures for Ontario are also listed. (For Ontario, "total power" is taken to be power generated plus imports from Quebec. "Firm power utilized" is taken to be this figure less secondary sales and exports to the United States, i.e., Column 7, Exhibit B, in the Appendix.)

Which of the two patterns (or what other pattern) one should emphasize depends mainly on the purpose in view. The "total power" pattern has been presented here partly because it emphasizes again the result of our preceding discussion, namely, that about three-quarters of Quebec's power production is either exported or sold to two large industries, and that only a minor part of the output is used for general purposes within the province; and partly because it highlights the importance of the pulp and paper industry to power development in the province. On the other hand, for the purpose of suggesting the role that the hydroelectric industry has played in the economic development of Quebec, it is desirable to exclude the

TABLE 3

PERCENTAGE DISTRIBUTION OF POWER SOLD TO AND REVENUE DERIVED FROM VARIOUS MARKETS[a]

Averages[b] for the Period 1931–1940

A. Percentages of Total Power

Markets	Quebec		Ontario	
	Kwhs. sold	Revenue	Kwhs. sold	Revenue
Retail[c]	4	30 – 35	22 →18	52 →50
Small power	1	5 → 4	2.5	6 – 7
General manufacturing[d]	12 – 15	20 – 23	27 – 33	28
Exports	20	15	13	5
Wood and paper	50→35	20 – 25	15 →28 →18	7 → 8.5→ 7
Nonferrous	5→13	1.5→ 8	3.5→ 6.5	2.4→ 4.5
Losses	6 – 7		10 – 11	

B. Percentages of Firm Power Utilized in the Province

Markets	Quebec		Ontario	
	Power used	Revenue	Power used	Revenue
Retail[c]	10 → 8.5	42 →40	26 →23	55 →53
Small power	1.5 – 2	6.5→ 5	3.5→ 3	7
General manufacturing[d]	25 – 30	25 – 30	33 – 38	28 – 30
Wood and paper	37 →21	22 →18	17 →14	7 → 6.5
Nonferrous	10 →26	5 → 2 → 9	4 → 8.5	2 → 4.5
Losses	12 – 14		13 – 14	

[a] Sources: The percentages on which this summary table is based were derived from the data presented in Table 2 and Exhibit B of the Appendix. Part A, of course, simply summarizes the information presented in Chart 2.

[b] The averages are only approximate, having been derived by simple inspection from the series calculated. Two figures separated by a dash, e.g., 12–15, indicate that the magnitude varied between these figures over the period. An arrow is used to indicate an apparent trend: thus 50 →35 is to be read as "percentage falling from 50 to 35 over the period."

[c] "Retail" includes residential, commercial, farm service and street lighting.

[d] "General Manufacturing" includes electric railways, mines, and also, being a residual category, items otherwise unaccounted for.

influence of exports and of secondary power from consideration, as has been done in Part B of the table. It is on this "firm power utilized" pattern, therefore, that we shall base our further comments.

The hydroelectric industries of Quebec and Ontario present a striking contrast, particularly in the categories of "retail," "wood and paper," and "nonferrous" sales. Retail sales account for less than 10 per cent of electricity sales in Quebec and about a quarter of all sales in Ontario. Sales to the wood and paper and nonferrous smelting industries together account for almost half of all sales in Quebec, but only about 20 per cent of sales in Ontario. Once again we see to what a large extent the hydroelectric industry in Quebec is associated with these two groups of industries which require such large quantities of power in their production processes.

The revenue side of the table, however, shows that the importance of markets cannot be judged by physical sales alone. In Quebec the least important markets for physical sales — the retail markets for lighting and small power — are seen to be by far the most important markets from a dollar point of view; they produce more than half as much revenue again as the wood-using and nonferrous metal industries combined, which between them consume about half of the firm power sold in the province. In both provinces, sales of electricity to general manufacturing industry are "average" business, in the sense that they are made at prices in the neighborhood of the average revenue received from all provincial sales — a little above the average in Quebec, and slightly below the average in Ontario.

Average Revenues

In the preceding discussion the categories of "high-value" and "low-value" business were suggestive of the different average rates charged for electricity in the different markets, but the absolute figures were not given and the percentage figures given in the above paragraphs do not, by themselves, indicate the relative levels of electricity rates in different markets or in the same markets in Quebec and Ontario. Table 4 presents this information, along with some data on American electricity revenues which are included for comparative purposes. It must be emphasized that the figures in Table 4 are not prices in the ordinary sense of the word: they are simply the average revenues received by the sellers (or the average costs to the buyers) in various markets.

In Table 4, the most striking feature at first glance is the level of American average revenues in relation to the level of the Quebec and Ontario series. Both residential and industrial rates for electricity in the United

TABLE 4

AVERAGE REVENUES FROM POWER SALES: SELECTED SERIES, 1931–1940

(Revenue in cents per kwh.)

Year	All sales		Secondary power		Nonferrous industries		Small power		Domestic and farm [a]		Residential U.S.A.[b]	General mfg.[c]		Commercial and industrial U.S.A.[b]
	Que.	Ont.	Que.	Ont.	Que.	Ont.	Que.	Ont.	Que.	Ont.		Que.	Ont.	
1931	.52	.75	.08	.08	.28	.80			3.62	1.78	5.8	.74	.60	2.20
1932	.53	.87	.08	.08	.42	.60			3.43	1.77	5.6	.74	.63	2.26
1933	.48	.79	.08	.08	.15	.43	2.7	1.9	3.25	1.77	5.55	.63	.76	2.07
1934	.41	.66	.07	.07	.15	.36	2.5	1.6	3.28	1.71	5.3	.57	.64	2.01
1935	.38	.63	.07	.08	.12	.33	2.3	1.6	3.22	1.68	5.0	.51	.56	1.93
1936	.35	.60	.08	.08	.07	.28	2.5	1.7	3.19	1.68	4.65	.48	.565	1.78
1937	.35	.58	.08	.08	.23	.36	2.7	1.7	3.06	1.51	4.3	.50	.51	1.73
1938	.39	.60	.09	.10	.21	.36	2.3	1.7	3.02	1.44	4.1	.545	.575	1.85
1939	.37	.56	.08	.08	.21	.41	1.9	1.7	2.94	1.43	4.0	.51	.53	1.72
1940	.39	.55	.10	.10	.23	.37	2.0	1.5	2.97	1.43	3.85	.52	.47	1.61

[a] From *Central Electric Stations in Canada*, various years.

[b] Based on the statistics published in *Historical Statistics of the United States 1789–1945*, series C229–233. The "Residential" series does not include farm customers.

[c] Based on Dr. Massue's statistics. The procedure has been to deduct from his total kwh. and revenue figures for manufacturing industry the analogous figures for the "wood and paper" and "nonferrous" industry groups. All other figures are derived from the data presented in Table 2 and Exhibit B in the Appendix.

States were almost certainly higher during the 1930's than those prevailing in central Canada:[42] the common impression that, relative to the United States,[43] Ontario and Quebec offer "cheap power" is apparently correct. Similarly, we can confidently infer from the figures presented that domestic electric rates have been considerably lower in Ontario than in Quebec, and that Ontario has also probably offered lower rates to small power consumers than has Quebec. The average revenue from sales to general manufacturing industry seems to have been roughly the same in both provinces. Secondary power sales in both provinces have been made at average revenues of less than one-tenth of a cent per kilowatt-hour. The average return from all sales has been lower in Quebec than in Ontario because of the proportionately larger quantities of secondary sales and bulk sales to large consumers made in the former province. Finally, the table illustrates clearly the distinction previously made between high-value and low-value business. In Quebec we have, in the former category, the lighting and small power markets; in the latter, in ascending order of normal average revenues, we have secondary power, sales to the nonferrous industry,[44] exports, and sales to the general industrial market, the average revenues from this latter market being somewhat higher in Quebec, and slightly lower in Ontario, than the average revenue from all sales.

v. *Summary*

The hydroelectric industry in Quebec has developed on a base of abundant water power in a geographic setting that has provided numerous opportunities for low-cost power developments. Furthermore, these opportunities have been exploited in a political and social setting that has also favored profitable investment by private enterprise. The lushness of the environment has been reflected both in the rate and pattern of the industry's growth. Making steady progress in the first fifteen years of the century, it grew rapidly during the first world war and then, after three quiet postwar years, boomed throughout the twenties.[45] Firm power sales faltered briefly in 1931 and again in 1936, and the rate of advance of the industry was somewhat reduced in the decade of the thirties. In general, however, the hydroelectric industry in Quebec has shown a considerable resistance to the downswing of the business cycle: profits have been reduced in depression years, but losses have been avoided and output has continued to expand.

To a large extent, this growth has responded to the demands of the pulp and paper industry, the aluminum industry, and the export market in Ontario. An unusually large proportion of Quebec's power is sold to these markets in wholesale quantities and at low rates. A minor portion of the output services general manufacturing industry in the province, and a very small proportion of the total goes to the retail markets for domestic and commercial lighting and for small power. Retail sales, however, provide high-value business. The retail markets, in fact, provide over 30 per cent of the total revenue from power sales and are the largest single source of revenue for the power companies.

Individual power companies in Quebec have developed in different ways. The Gatineau Power Company and the Maclaren-Quebec Power Company were built up after 1925 on the basis of the pulp and paper industry in the Ottawa Valley and the export market in Ontario. Development of the Saguenay River's power resources was started in 1925, partly to provide power for the pulp and paper industry in the Lake St. John region and partly to provide electricity for a new aluminum reduction plant. Since 1937, the expansion of the hydroelectric industry in this area has gone hand in hand with the expansion of the aluminum industry. The Montreal Light, Heat and Power Company, formed in 1901, lived off the Montreal market and later, with the development of power on the St. Lawrence River, began to export electricity to the Aluminum Company of America at Massena, New York, and to Ontario. The Southern Canada Power Company, since the first world war, has cultivated the retail and general industrial markets in the Eastern Townships. Only The Shawinigan Water and Power Company, the pioneer hydroelectric enterprise in the province, has shared in all these developments — providing power for the Montreal market, building up the aluminum and chemical industries at Shawinigan Falls, building and being built by the pulp and paper industry of the St. Maurice valley, and supplying electricity for domestic and general industrial purposes throughout a large portion of Quebec. It is to the history of that enterprise that we now turn.

CHAPTER 3

Early Years of The Shawinigan Water and Power Company, 1898-1914

1. *Beginnings, 1895–1905*

Interest in Quebec water powers as a source of electricity developed during the closing years of the nineteenth century. At Three Rivers the North Shore Power Company was formed by a local entrepreneur, Edouard Lacroix, and backed by a Sherbrooke banker, William Farwell, to exploit a waterfall at St. Narcisse on the Batiscan River some eighteen miles away. By 1897 this plant was in successful operation and is reputed to have been the first system in the British Empire to transmit electricity for any significant distance.

In 1895 another group from Three Rivers, led by A. Carignan and H. Mailhot, formed the Shawinigan Electric Light and Power Company Ltd. to exploit the enormous power potential of Shawinigan Falls. They gained the promise of financial support from a Montreal financier and assured themselves of a market for their proposed output by getting a contract for municipal lighting in Three Rivers. The next step was to obtain the right to use certain Dominion lands for the construction of the necessary structures. The government was willing, but its title to the lands in question was challenged by John Forman, a Montreal merchant, who claimed them as his own, and was also challenged by the Province of Quebec on the grounds

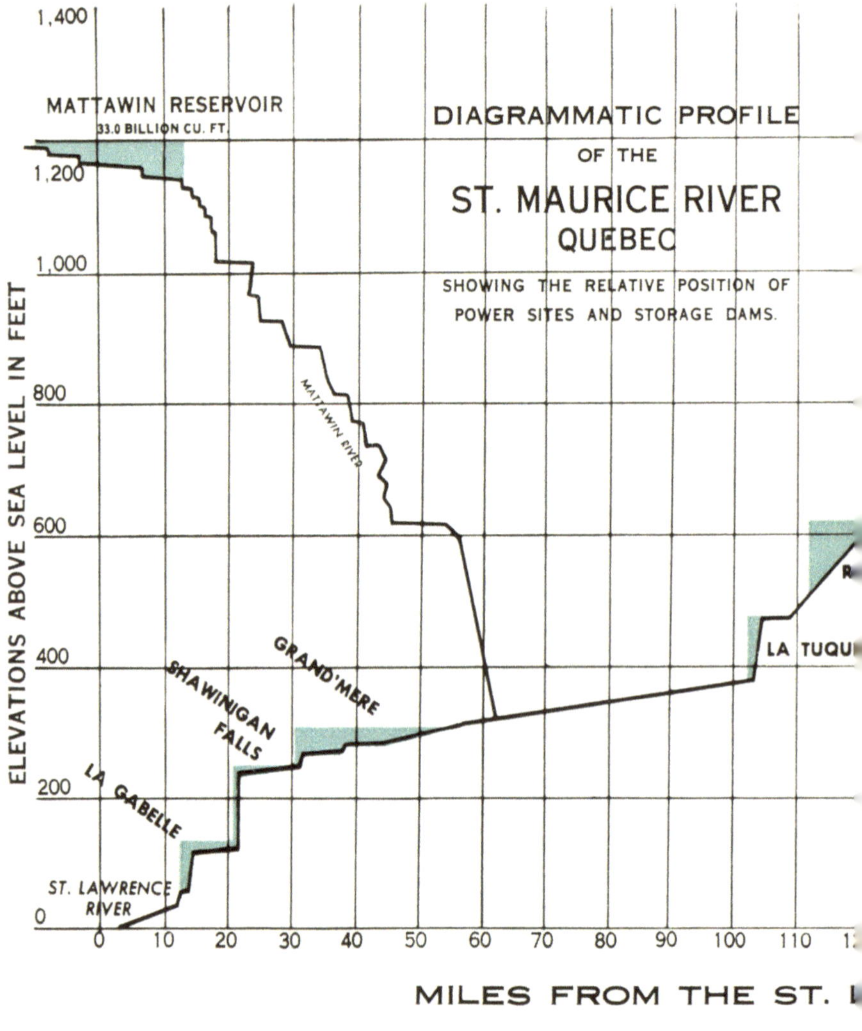

Figure 2. Profile and Plan Views of the Development of the St. Maurice River, Showi
plied by The Shawiniga

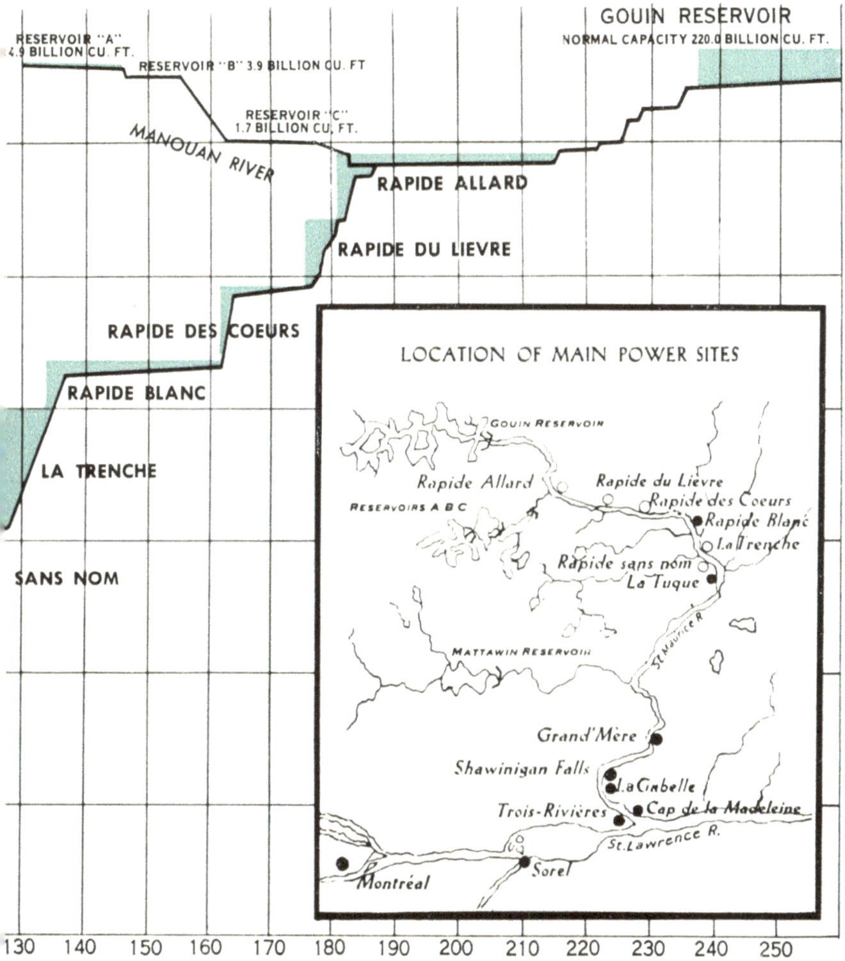

WRENCE RIVER

h Actual and Proposed Hydroelectric Stations (drawing prepared from materials sup-
r & Power Company).

that it owned all lands in the beds of navigable rivers. The dispute became the subject of litigation. Forman chose to sue the provincial government and lost his case. The dispute between the two governments was taken to the Privy Council, which in 1898 handed down a decision, still binding, to the effect that the beds of rivers which either are navigable or can be used for floating logs are the property of the provincial governments.

Meanwhile, Carignan and Mailhot had turned their attention to the provincial government and had arranged to buy Shawinigan Falls at auction on June 15, 1897, for $10,000. Fate intervened in May, however, in the form of an election, and the new government set new terms for the alienation of the waterfall. The auction was set forward to September 9, 1897, and the terms were stiffened. The successful bidder would now have to pay at least $50,000 for the site and also assume obligations to invest two million dollars within 18 months and a further two million in the next 12 months, spend $200,000 annually in wages, and bring the station into operation within 20 months.[1]

These terms were beyond the means of the local entrepreneurs, but the government was not deliberately pricing itself out of the market, for it had already heard that American capitalists were interested in the property. Would Shawinigan Falls have been developed by local enterprise if litigation and an election had not delayed proceedings and allowed time for foreign capital to become interested in the project? Probably not. Successful development of the immense power potential of Shawinigan Falls required monetary and engineering resources on a scale that was almost certainly beyond what the local group could have commanded.

The actual development of power at Shawinigan Falls was, apparently, the outgrowth of a scheme to manufacture calcium carbide. The scanty evidence about the formation of the Shawinigan company comes mainly from an early court case which the Privy Council finally disposed of in 1904.[2] The chain of events starts around 1896 in Boston with one John Joyce, a wealthy brewer of that city, who had recently acquired a patent on an electric furnace for the manufacture of calcium carbide. Joyce, it seems, wanted to set up a carbide plant in Canada;[3] in his search for assistance in this project he was introduced to Edwin Whitney of Manchester, New Hampshire. Whitney, an electrical engineer by profession (but who seems to have been a company promoter by temperament and avocation) went to Canada, and on visiting Shawinigan Falls was impressed with their power possibilities. At this time he was in contact with J. N. Greenshields, an outstanding corporation lawyer in Montreal, whom he had approached about incorporation of a carbide company, and whom he now retained as his personal counsel.[4] Plans were made to acquire the Falls, and Greenshields on behalf of Whitney negotiated their purchase on September 9, 1897, making a down payment of $1000.

Whitney's next task was to raise money for the final payment. After attempting unsuccessfully to interest the General Electric Company in the project, he asked Joyce to advance $10,000, the sum necessary to hold the property for a short time until he could raise the needed funds. Joyce went to Montreal and put up the $10,000 after he had received from Whitney a written document which gave Joyce the title to the property and Whitney an option to repurchase it if he could raise the money necessary to reimburse Joyce and make the final payment to the government. Whitney could do neither, and Joyce personally made the final payment to the province. Joyce had paid the piper and henceforth called the tune; Whitney was dropped.[5]

The site having been acquired, a company was immediately organized and a law for its incorporation was brought before the Quebec legislature in the fall of 1897. The charter was granted on January 15, 1898, giving the company wide powers to engage in the business of electrical production and distribution, with the right to purchase other electrical enterprises and to expropriate lands necessary to its business.

By this time, Mr. J. E. Aldred had become interested in the project. Aldred, a friend of Joyce, was the vice-president of the Puritan Trust Company in Boston. Having lived in Lawrence, Massachusetts, Aldred was alive to the possibilities of water power, and after investigating the Shawinigan site he apparently decided to devote his full time to the new venture, for he resigned from his position at the trust company in January, 1898. Aldred was the real entrepreneur in the Shawinigan development, and although very little is known of him, the subsequent history of The Shawinigan Water and Power Company bears eloquent testimony to his financial and business abilities.[6]

By early 1898 a loose group of capitalists had been formed to get the company started.[7] The three best-known members of the group were J. L. Forget, J. N. Greenshields, and H. S. (later Sir Herbert) Holt. Forget was a leading financier, associated with the Royal Trust Company of Montreal, a senator and an influential Conservative, and the president of the Montreal Tramways Company, the Dominion Cotton Mills, and a navigation company operating on the Richelieu River. Greenshields was perhaps the foremost lawyer in Quebec, having earned his reputation in part by defending Louis Riel a decade earlier. Politically, he complemented Forget, for he was a prominent Liberal and a financial backer of Israel Tarte, the influential journalist who was then supporting Laurier through the columns of his paper, *La Patrie*. Holt, an Irish engineer who had worked for the Canadian Pacific Railroad and had then become associated with Mackenzie and Mann, the railway builders, was on the threshold of his career as a financier. He was associated with the Royal Trust Company, dominated the Montreal Gas Company, and in a few years was to engineer a consolidation of all the power companies in Montreal to form the Montreal Light, Heat and Power Company. Other prominent men were also included in the group. From Montreal came William Wainwright, manager of the Grand Trunk Railway. Representing the Eastern Townships were William Mitchell, a large lumber merchant from Drummondville who had promoted a railway in Drummond county (of which J. N. Greenshields was then the president), and William Farwell of Sherbrooke who had financed the early hydroelectric plant at St. Narcisse. From Quebec City there was Thomas McDougall, general manager of the Bank of Quebec.[8]

The significance of this list of names is uncertain. These people were all of them either incorporators, directors, or officers of the company, but how many of them played an active role in providing funds and how many of them merely lent their names for window-dressing is not known. Holt, at any rate, proceeded to build up his own utility concern, the Montreal Light, Heat and Power Company, and the difficulty that Shawinigan later experienced in entering the Montreal market suggests that Holt was more a rival than a collaborator from Shawinigan's point of view. Forget, too, was probably more interested in the Montreal situation than in the Shawinigan project. With the exception of Greenshields and Joyce, who were officers of the company in its early years, none of these men played an important part in the company's development, although many of them were members of the board of directors at various times. And in spite of the impressive array of names, it is certain that Shawinigan's financial position was anything but easy for the first few years.[9] All in all, it seems as though Aldred had to make his way in the world without the benefit of unqualified support from St. James Street. The political capabilities of Greenshields, who was president of the company from its inception until 1904, may perhaps have been the most valuable contribution which the American promoters of Shawinigan received from Canadian men of affairs.

Construction began in the spring of 1899.[10] Aldred had succeeded in engaging as chief engineer for the project Wallace Johnson of Holyoke, Massachusetts, who at that time was working on the Niagara Falls power project. Furthermore, he had been able to interest a New York construction firm in his venture, and the Warren-Burnham Company undertook to do the job and accept payment in common stock of the Shawinigan company. Warren, the president of the construction company, was also appointed to Shawinigan's board of directors.

These matters having been attended to, Aldred immediately concerned himself with finding markets for his prospective power. In August 1889, his first contract was signed, with the Northern Aluminum Company, which agreed to purchase 5000 hydraulic h.p. from the company.[11] A year later a second contract for hydraulic power was signed with Belgian capitalists who were looking for a site for a pulp mill and were induced to locate at Shawinigan Falls. The first large contract for electrical power, however, was not signed until 1902, when the Shawinigan company was finally able to make an arrangement to sell power to the Montreal Light, Heat and Power Company. It thereby gained the opportunity to prove that it could deliver electricity at a pressure of 50 kv. over a distance of nearly 90 miles to Montreal — the longest transmission that had yet been attempted.[12]

The first delivery of Shawinigan power to Montreal, on March 1, 1903, marked a turning point in the company's fortunes. The feat served to draw public attention to the company, and financial men could now see for themselves that Shawinigan had promise. How the company had survived the preceding four years of spending, with but meager returns from sales of hydraulic power in the last two of them, is not known. Payments in stock probably accounted for the major part of the expenditure. With the Montreal contract honored, however, the company was able to float its first bond issue of $1.5 million, sold largely in New York and Boston. The next year, 1904, with a second line to Montreal and the first submarine transmission line across the St. Lawrence to its credit, the company was able to put its financing on a more stable basis by arranging for a $5-million bond issue through the Royal Trust Company in Montreal. These bonds were subsequently sold partly in the United States and partly in England. The financial corner had been turned.

In the search for markets, the carbide industry, which had first directed attention to Shawinigan, had by no means been forgotten. A hitch had developed in Joyce's early plans, however, because his patents promised to conflict with those of Thomas L. ("Carbide") Willson, the founder of the electrical process for the manufacture of calcium carbide.[13] Joyce had gone to see Willson's plant at Merriton, Ontario, and apparently attempted to get Willson interested in a scheme to set up a carbide plant at Shawinigan

Falls. It was not until the turn of the century, however, that Aldred arranged to license Willson's patents and set up a plant at Shawinigan. Since this was during the period of financial stringency, the power company could not itself finance the enterprise and it remained for a group of Montreal financiers to float the venture. Willson took an active part in the formation of the company, and became its first vice-president. The Shawinigan Carbide Company was organized in 1901, but not until 1904 did the plant begin operations and provide the fourth major market for Shawinigan power.

In spite of his preoccupation with financial and industrial problems, Aldred, New Englander that he was, did not forget that he was building a town as well as a company, and from the very first the Shawinigan company took an active part in town planning. The construction period, of course, had been chaotic. The land around the area was poor, and hundreds of underemployed farmers flocked to the new construction projects during the first few months of operations in the spring of 1899. In 1900 Shawinigan alone employed 1500 construction workers, and many others were working on the projects of the aluminum company and the pulp company. Many of the workers spent the winters of 1899 and 1900 in tents; the more fortunate found lodgings in the miserable hovels that mushroomed on the cheap land around the town.[14] In the town itself land was more expensive and development was more orderly. About 1100 acres had been bought by the company as the nucleus of the future settlement. Of this holding, some 500 acres were divided into lots to be sold for residential purposes — the company had already built some lodgings near the Falls for its employees — and the remainder was reserved for mill sites. Even during the first hectic years of construction,[15] the company had drawn up a plan for the future city,[16] and by 1905 it could boast that the town had been "built up along lines laid down after careful study and with the object in view of erecting a model manufacturing town . . . The development of the town has been under the direction of competent engineers and is now complete with excellent streets, substantial buildings and all the necessary features of a modern manufacturing community."[17]

II. *The Development of Markets, 1905–1914*

By 1905 the Shawinigan company had gained a foothold in the new industrial world of electrical power, base metals, and chemicals. It was even then a profitable firm and in 1907 declared its first dividend at the annual rate of 4 per cent. In the next decade it consolidated its position and experienced a steady but moderate growth in its business. In this period the foundations were laid for the wartime expansion of the company's load and for the tremendous boom that it was to enjoy in the 1920's.

Only one of the policies that had been adopted at the very beginning of the company's history was abandoned — the sale of hydraulic power. This policy had been followed because it would yield quick returns on a minimum investment. Sale of hydraulic power required only waterworks and did not have to await the construction of expensive electrical equipment; it was thus an ideal means of providing the company with at least a small amount of immediate revenue. Hydraulic power was cheap power and in the first years of the century was probably meant to induce plants to locate in Shawinigan Falls. An early brochure of the company [18] indicated that Shawinigan's hydraulic development was capable of "furnishing water to factories desiring to install their own water wheels in their mills. . ." But except for the two plants already mentioned, the inducement was unavailing. It soon became evident that Shawinigan would have to go to the customer in order to dispose of its power, and in any event once the company was financially established it did not have to depend on sales of cheap power from simple waterworks.

By 1905 the Shawinigan company had two separate developments, a combined electrical [19] and hydraulic station and a purely hydraulic plant. From the first development, one penstock led directly to a powerhouse owned by the Northern Aluminum Company, which used the water to generate direct current electricity for its aluminum reduction process. The second development had two 12-foot penstocks, one to the aluminum plant, and the other to the mill of the Belgo-Canadian Pulp and Paper Company. The aluminum company, first of its kind in Canada, had built both a reduction plant and a fabricating plant at Shawinigan Falls, the latter turning out rods, bars, wires, cables, and structural shapes.[20] With a large expansion in its plant and equipment in 1906, the company became one of the largest producers of aluminum in the world. Its consumption of Shawinigan's hydraulic power rose from 5000 h.p. in 1901 to 10,000 h.p. in 1905, 20,000 h.p. in 1906, and 30,000 h.p. in 1909.

The pulp company had got off to a bad start. During the construction of the plant the Belgian bank that was financing it ran short of capital, decided to liquidate the project, and sent Mr. H. Biermans out to Canada to salvage what he could from the venture. Fortunately for the Shawinigan company, Biermans instead persuaded his principals to raise further funds in Belgium, and a groundwood plant was completed.[21] The company was unprofitable at first, but matters probably improved somewhat after a newsprint mill was added in 1904.[22] Further extensions to the plant in 1906 raised its daily capacity to 150 tons of groundwood pulp and 86 tons of paper. Few figures are available for Belgo-Canadian's power purchases, but it seems to have used 8000 h.p. up to 1906 when it raised its consumption to 9000 hydraulic horsepower. By that time it was probably also purchasing electricity from the Shawinigan company.

In spite of the expansion in its hydraulic business, the time had come when the Shawinigan company was in a position to discourage such sales. In 1908 the company had contracts for the sale of 30,000 h.p. of each type of power, hydraulic and electrical, but the hydraulic contracts yielded only 20 per cent of the total revenues from power sales. Moreover, the demand for electricity was growing steadily. The shareholders were thus informed that:

> . . . the position of the Company is now so fully assured, its field of operations so extensive that your Directors feel that the best interests of the Company will be served by a conservative policy of husbanding the resources of the Company's plant and disposing of the balance of its available power to the greatest possible advantage. . . While these water power contracts were, at the outset, desirable for the purpose of establishing the Company locally, the return from this form of contract is comparatively small. . . It is not the policy of your Directors to make further contracts for water power, but to sell the remainder of the Company's power in the form of electricity exclusively.[23]

This policy appears to have been followed quite strictly, although from the few figures available, hydraulic sales seem to have crept up to a high of 65,000 h.p. in 1927. Since that time, and especially in recent years, with demand pressing on capacity, the Shawinigan company has found it advisable to buy back the water power which it had originally sold to the aluminum company. Today, only 15,000 hydraulic h.p. is sold to the pulp and paper plant, now controlled by the Consolidated Paper Corporation, Ltd., and it is likely that this too will be repurchased before long.

The two large markets for electrical power that were already being served in 1905, Montreal and the carbide company, were expanded, and new markets were opened. Montreal was the company's largest single market.[24] The original contract with the Montreal Light, Heat and Power Company had made provision for eventual delivery of up to 20,000 h.p., of which about 9000 h.p. was being purchased in 1905. At first the market grew in a gratifying fashion. In 1907, under the terms of a new long-term contract signed with the Montreal company, Shawinigan was allowed to make contracts directly with large power customers in the Montreal area, and two important contracts were immediately signed with the "Montreal Street Railway, and . . . [with] the Vulcan Portland Cement Company now building at Longue Pointe one of the most complete plants in America for the manufacture of Portland cement."[25] The capacity of the Shawinigan company's equipment in Montreal was increased in order to take delivery of 20,000 h.p. from Shawinigan Falls, and with the stimulus of the new contract, sales to the Montreal area jumped to 16,000 h.p. in 1907, and 18,000 h.p. in 1910.

In spite of the increase in sales, however, it had already become apparent that full entry to the Montreal market was not going to be easily gained, for here the Shawinigan Company had to reckon with Holt's Montreal Light, Heat and Power Company, which by then virtually monopolized the distribution of electricity in the Montreal area. The annual reports of the Shawinigan company—those of the Montreal company are more reticent—afford occasional glimpses of the struggle which was waged. In 1908 the Montreal company's Soulanges plant on the St. Lawrence River came into operation and Shawinigan's sales were confined to the contract amount, whereas formerly the Montreal company had always made additional purchases during the months of peak demand.[26] With competition from the water power of the St. Lawrence, the Montreal market was obviously not going to provide an automatically increasing outlet for Shawinigan power: the Shawinigan company would have to take energetic measures to safeguard its position in Montreal. By 1910 the struggle had been resolved—inevitably, an accommodation between the two contestants had been arranged—and the market situation was clarified. In that year, the Shawinigan company owned 10,000 shares of Montreal Light, Heat and Power Company stock, which it had acquired only recently, and J. E. Aldred was appointed to the board of directors of the Montreal company. On the other hand, the Shawinigan company had disposed of a million dollars' worth of its stock "at a premium by private sale, with the resultant increase of stock holding in Montreal, where your Company does a substantial part of its business,"[27] and the Montreal company was to be represented on Shawinigan's board of directors. Following this display of corporate friendship, the two companies signed a new contract providing for the eventual delivery by Shawinigan to Montreal of an additional 40,000 h.p. beyond the existing contracts, which then covered sales of 23,000 h.p. For the benefit of its shareholders, the Shawinigan directors noted that "it is hardly necessary to comment on the strength of the position of the Shawinigan Company and its ally the Montreal Light, Heat and Power Company, as bearing upon the general situation in Montreal and vicinity."[28]

With the assurances contained in the 1910 agreement, the Shawinigan company immediately started to build a second powerhouse at Shawinigan Falls, and by the end of 1911 the initial installation of 37,000 h.p. was completed.[29] A new transmission system to Montreal, with duplicate lines strung from steel towers, was put into service in October 1911. Sales in the Montreal market jumped to approximately 45,000 h.p. in 1913 and 48,000 h.p. in 1914. Montreal was supplied from the new powerhouse, and the output of the older generating station was thus released to provide for the growing power demands at Three Rivers and Shawinigan Falls itself.

Preoccupation with the Montreal situation did not imply lack of attention to other markets for Shawinigan power. The growth of industry at Shawinigan Falls was energetically promoted, although without outstanding results until World War I led to the foundation of the Shawinigan chemical industries. The carbide plant was the important consumer of electricity at Shawinigan Falls. Calcium carbide, a relatively new product, was a creation of the electrical age since it could be manufactured economically only in an electric furnace.[30] Carbide was much in demand because, when acted upon by water, it gave off acetylene, an excellent gas for domestic illumination.[31] From Shawinigan's point of view, the carbide plant was an excellent market for off-peak power. It was probably mainly for this reason that the Shawinigan company increased its holdings of stock in the carbide company; by 1908 it controlled the enterprise and in 1909 the Shawinigan Carbide Company became a wholly owned subsidiary of the power company. Carbide became a by-product of power, the policy being that "the Power Company should be in a position to utilize such a Company with regard to its interests alone, in other words to utilize the subsidiary company so as to meet the requirements of the Shawinigan Company as they exist from time to time."[32] As a market for off-peak power, the carbide plant complemented the firm power market in Montreal, and the Shawinigan company's annual load factor increased from 30 per cent in 1907 to 55 per cent in 1910 and nearly 70 per cent in 1912. Equally important, probably, was the fact that the carbide works, "as an auxiliary consumer of power," mitigated the pressure of overhead costs on the power company and reduced the temptation to force sales on the open market. In 1908 the directors noted that there was no effort to press the sale of power, "believing it wiser to sacrifice somewhat the showing for the present year in favour of the future . . . While at the outset it was a question if your Company could utilize the large amount of power at its disposal, this is no longer a consideration, but the present question is where power can be sold to the best advantage."[33]

Apart from the three large power-consuming industries in the town (aluminum, pulp and paper, and carbide), industrial development at Shawinigan Falls was discouragingly slow.[34] The only other plant of any importance to locate there before the first world war was the Shawinigan Cotton Company, a subsidiary of the Wabasso Cotton Company of Three Rivers. This company, in which the Shawinigan company bought a large block of stock, built a mill in the town in 1909. It produced thread that was sent to the parent plant at Three Rivers to be woven into cloth. The mill was particularly welcome in the town because it provided employment for female labor, of which there had been an excess supply ever since the construction period.[35]

Manufacturing at Three Rivers was somewhat further advanced,[36] and the Shawinigan company had two transmission lines serving the town. The Canadian Iron Foundries had been established there since 1910, the modern successors of a long series of iron forges which reached back to the early eighteenth century.[37] In 1907 a group of Scottish capitalists led by Mr. C. R. Whitehead had established the Wabasso Cotton Company, and three years later the same group founded the Wayagamack Pulp Company. Some of the Kraft paper produced by this firm was used to make bags for cement by another Three Rivers firm, the Union Bag and Paper Company. There were two other pulp and paper concerns in the area, The Grès Falls Company, and a pulp mill which had been built at Cap de la Madeleine (across the river from Three Rivers) in 1912. In addition to these recently established plants, there were various small industries in the town which were also Shawinigan customers. By 1912, only five years after Shawinigan had entered the market, the load at Three Rivers was some 12,000 h.p. and was growing so rapidly that a third transmission line to the city was being planned.

Another market for power was found south of the St. Lawrence River. Thetford Mines, Black Lake, Danville and the other centers of the asbestos mining and manufacturing business in Megantic and Richmond counties formed a market for power which attracted Shawinigan's attention from an early date.[38] Power was transmitted across the St. Lawrence by submarine cable from Three Rivers. Completed in 1906, the trunk line went to Victoriaville, with branches from that point eastward to Thetford Mines and, three years later, southward to Windsor Mills. Contracts for over 5000 h.p. in the asbestos district were signed in 1906, and power was distributed in Victoriaville and other towns along the route. By 1910 a company pamphlet reported that 7000 h.p. was being sent to Thetford Mines and Black Lake, 2000 h.p.

to Danville, and 1000 h.p. to the Canada Paper Company at Windsor Mills.[39] The asbestos market did not grow rapidly and thus became relatively less important to Shawinigan in later periods, but it was an important outlet for power before World War I.

In its search for markets the Shawinigan company had not overlooked the retail market for lighting services. To serve this market Shawinigan followed a policy of setting up new companies for distribution purposes and purchasing existing companies which generated and sold electricity on a local basis. Shawinigan's first delivery of electricity had been made in Shawinigan Falls on December 1, 1902, and a subsidiary company, the Shawinigan Electric Light Company, had been formed to distribute the power in the town.[40] This became the St. Maurice Light and Power Company in 1904, and the Electric Service Corporation in 1920. The latter company became the main corporate vehicle for retailing Shawinigan power and later absorbed many other small distribution systems. In 1904 the policy of acquiring local systems was extended. The Laval Electric Company, covering the area north and east of the Island of Montreal, became a subsidiary concern, and in the same year the Sorel Electric Company was acquired. To deliver current to Sorel, the Shawinigan company built the first transmission system across the St. Lawrence, a submarine cable between Joliette and Sorel. Shortly thereafter, the charter of the Continental Heat and Light Company was acquired. This company enjoyed wide powers for electrical distribution under a Dominion charter and was the corporate instrument which the Shawinigan company used for the distribution of its electricity in the asbestos district. In 1907 the North Shore Power Company was purchased. This company which had built the generating plant at St. Narcisse in the 1890's, owned the distributing network in Three Rivers, and was thus "a most desirable acquisition from a strategical standpoint."[41] By means of these companies, and by the local business which it picked up along the route of its main transmission line to Montreal and Victoriaville,[42] the Shawinigan company was delivering power to some twenty-two communities by 1907. The policy of distributing power through subsidiary companies had been firmly established; it was reported that:

> It has been found that the employment of subsidiary companies is the most desirable method of developing business in particular sections and in each case the securities representing the companies more than meet the charges involved in financing the same, and their future operation will enhance the value of these securities.[43]

Shawinigan's retail business grew, and forty towns and villages were using the company's power by 1914. In terms of kilowatt-hours, this market was very small, probably less than 5 per cent of total sales. But because the revenue per kilowatt-hour was relatively high, the retail market's contribution to gross revenues was much greater than its addition to physical sales, and it became even more important as a source of revenue in later years.

III. *The Entrepreneurial Performance*

By the outbreak of World War I, then, the Shawinigan company had firmly consolidated its position. Electrical generating capacity had increased from two 5000 h.p. generators in the first powerhouse in 1903, to nearly 150,000 h.p. in two powerhouses in 1914. (In addition, 45,000 hydraulic h.p. was being sold to the Northern Aluminum Co. and the Belgo-Canadian Pulp and Paper Company.) Over 600 miles of transmission lines carried the company's power to Montreal and the various intervening points on the north shore of the St. Lawrence as well as to Sorel on the south shore, and to Victoriaville and the asbestos district deep in the Eastern Townships. Only a local distribution line extended eastward, and the Quebec City market did not, as yet, look sufficiently encouraging to justify a power line to that city, but we may be sure that the situation there was being watched carefully. The company had been profitable from the beginning; dividends had been inaugurated at a rate of 4 per cent in 1907 and were 6 per cent in 1914, while common stock in the hands of the shareholders had increased from $6.5 million to $12.4 million in the same period. Sales of electricity had increased steadily, except for the depression year of 1907, and, as we have seen, the policy of the company, at least after the first four or five years of operations, was to build up a firm load for existing capacity rather than to develop capacity far in advance of sales. Peak load (including off-peak sales) was pressing on capacity in 1906, 1908, and 1909 before construction of the second powerhouse was undertaken. (See Chart 3.) A chart in the annual report for 1914 indicates that capitalization [44] per horsepower output dropped from approximately $200 in 1907 to $150 in 1912 and $105 in 1914.

This record bears witness to an entrepreneurial performance of high caliber. The prerequisites of successful enterprise in the early hydroelectric industry were at least two in number. A high degree of technical ability and initiative was necessary to maintain a firm's position in a new and technologically progressive industry. And in an industry which required a fixed investment of such large proportions, financial acumen and access to capital supplies were minimum conditions of survival. Mr. Aldred, alive to the technological requirement, was quick to gather round him a group of able young engineers at the very beginning of his venture. That he was fortunate in his choice, and that the quality of the original group was maintained as the engineering force expanded, are revealed by the technological history of the enterprise. It has always maintained its position in the forefront of technical practice and has built up over the years an impressive list of "firsts."

The publications of the Shawinigan company give a fairly full account of the technological history of the enterprise, but, not unnaturally, given the financial mores of the business world, little is said of its financial history. But it is clear that Aldred, once a Boston banker and with important financial contacts in London, was thoroughly at home in the rarefied atmosphere of large-scale dealings in credit and securities. Scattered references to financial policy appear in the annual reports of the company,[45] but they are not sufficient to piece together a coherent account of the financial history of the enterprise. A layman's impression, for what it is worth, is that the company in its formative period was financed with great ability and that the securities of the company were representative of a fine physical plant. Its dividend record and security prices attest as much.[46]

Success must also have been in part due to the broad horizon adopted by the company's leaders. While long-distance transmission was still in its infancy, the company immediately branched out to markets within a hundred-mile radius of its plant. Long-range plans for the home territory included purchase of land as sites for industries that the company hoped to attract to Shawinigan Falls and encouragement of railway facilities for the town. Nor did the company hesitate to plunge into the competitive carbide industry as an outlet for surplus power and as a start on industrial development. Its purchase of controlling interests in small power companies and its heavy investments in the stock of nonaffiliated companies had been brought about "first, as a necessary means of making a market for power, and second, as a means of creating a wide diversity factor in the use of power."[47]

One other characteristic of Shawinigan policy should be noted. From the first, the major part of the power was sold on the basis of long-term contracts to large customers. Shawinigan has always been, and still is, primarily a wholesaler of power to municipalities or subsidiary companies, and to large industrial consumers. The retail business has always been negligible in terms of kilowatt-hours sold. Its ability to sell power by contract has helped to insulate the company from fluctuating power demands over the business cycle and has facilitated a stable dividend policy. Moreover, the Shawinigan company, not enjoying a monopoly position in the large retail market at Montreal, found it necessary as well as profitable to build up an industrial market in its own area, and power sales under long-term contracts were probably offered at prices that would attract industries. A stock circular of 1900 claimed that the Pittsburgh Reduction Works (Northern Aluminum Company), by locating at Shawinigan Falls rather than increasing their plant at Niagara Falls, would save $60,000 per annum on their power bill, and that the Belgo-Canadian Pulp Company could deliver pulp in Belgium at $10 per ton as compared with a production cost in Belgium of $20 per ton.[48] The policy of encouraging industries to locate in the area and to buy power on long-term contracts has been followed consistently; on its fiftieth anniversary the company could write with some justice that:

> The greatest proportion of the power is distributed in large amounts at high voltage under long-term contracts to large industrial customers [and also, surely, distributing companies], who consume more than 90 per cent of the power sold. These include sections of Quebec's aluminum, pulp and paper, chemical, textile and mining industries, and many forms of manufacturing and other enterprises. Many of these industrial consumers established themselves in the territory only after electricity was made available at low cost by the Company, which has thus played an integral part in the rapid industrial development and increased employment opportunities in the Province of Quebec.[49]

Perhaps we can best summarize the early stage of Shawinigan's development by quoting from a document in Baker Library, a (presumably verbatim) report of a speech given by Aldred in Boston on December 6, 1917. (The year is inferred from internal evidence.) The report was mimeographed at the office of Lee, Higginson and Company, a Boston investment house, and, again from internal evidence, it can be assumed that Aldred's audience was a small group of financiers. At least some members of the audience were creditors of the Shawinigan company. In 1916, when the financial markets were still deranged by the Great War, Shawinigan had borrowed money on two-year notes to provide capital funds for the construction of La Loutre (now Gouin) Dam and to set up a wholly owned subsidiary, the Canadian Electrode Company, Ltd., for the manufacture of carbon electrodes. During the course of his remarks, Aldred said that $2.5 million of these notes would be paid off next October, and the others "that you gentlemen are talking about at this time" when they fell due.[50] Whatever the occasion of this address — perhaps some of the remarks should not be taken at face value — its relatively candid character admirably reveals the status of the Shawinigan company at the time.

Shawinigan, said Mr. Aldred, was "more or less a baby of mine." He had been brought up in Lawrence, Massachusetts, and had been familiar with the power developments on the Merrimac.

> What we have done in Canada is but an imitation of what the Lowells and Lawrences did years ago when they went to the Merrimac and there developed power, took up town sites, created industries to use the power, and finally made the Essex Company and similar concerns known among the most valuable companies in New England.

Having heard of the St. Maurice, he and one or two associates had gone to look it over and had been delighted with what they found. There was no shortage of summer water, as there was in New England, because of the heavy snowfall on the northern watershed. Costs of development were very low and, at a guess, would not be much more than half the cost of developments of equal size anywhere else on the continent. From the first the company had tried to attract industries to the area, and Aldred took the credit for bringing the Aluminum Company to Shawinigan Falls.

"A paper mill was built (having offered this site to the International Paper Co. of this country and being turned down we had to go as far as Belgium to find anybody who would build a paper mill, which is now an extremely profitable enterprise)." The manufacture of calcium carbide was started; but here, apparently, all was not plain sailing. The carbide company had to compete with Norwegian production and with the Union Carbide Company in the United States. Shawinigan had competed for seven or eight years in the carbide market, with little result, but the concern was now on a profitable basis.[51]

> These initial industries put us on our feet locally. We went to Montreal and after something of a scrap there persuaded some of the leading industrialists that they ought to do business with us and made a contract resulting in our being the principal source of supply to the city of Montreal. We went to Three Rivers and acquired a company there.

The company enjoyed a wide diversity factor for its power and had perhaps the best load factor in America, around 90 per cent. None of the Shawinigan companies had a load factor of less than 80 per cent, and one had a basic load factor of 97 per cent.[52] A few years before, hydroelectric power had sold at a discount from steam electricity, but prices had been raised "and after this [we] propose to get a fair price for the output of these plants." [53]

The Shawinigan company, Aldred said, could make money by selling electricity at half the price of steam electricity—but had no intention of doing so. Nevertheless it was maintained that Shawinigan rates were the lowest in the country, and that "the maximum rate per kw[h] is five cents."

The meeting proceeded by way of question and answer:

Q. Are there any other [water] powers in the vicinity which could be bought by other companies which would compete with this [rate]?
A. Yes, there are quite a number of smaller powers, but I can only say to you that over a period of fifteen years or more there has not been anybody who could successfully carry out a big project in this territory. We have all the large customers and can make the rates so low that any new company would have considerable difficulty.
Q. How does your cost per horsepower compare with similar development in other parts of the country?
A. It is extremely difficult to answer that question owing to the diversity of properties included in the Shawinigan Company, but I can tell you that the primary power at Shawinigan as such would not represent a cost of over $30 a horse power and there is no other development on as low a basis as that. It is about $200 a horse power at the Mississippi River Power Co., and about the same at Niagara Falls.

There was "not a dollar of water in the stock. Whatever water there was has been squeezed out and the company has a surplus of about $5 million . . . Mr. Whitney of Stone and Webster then stated to the meeting that the $2.5 million Shawinigan notes offered last year sold very quickly on a 5⅛ per cent basis."

Q. Where is the stock held?
A. There are comparatively few stockholders in the United States. Considerable portions of stock are held in Canada by investors of the best class. There are thousands of shareholders in England, who have stuck to this company because they have made money out of the very large number of securities which I have placed there, both for this company and others in which I am interested. I have placed in England $40 million of securities which at the beginning of the war were worth double what I had sold them for.[54]

CHAPTER 4

The Shawinigan Water and Power Company, 1915-1940

1. *General Trends, 1915–1930*

The period between the start of the Great War and the onslaught of the Great Depression witnessed a tremendous growth of the hydroelectric industry in Quebec, a growth in which the Shawinigan company fully shared. Shawinigan's expansion, however, did not proceed at an even rate throughout the period. With an additional installation of 40,000 h.p. in the second powerhouse in 1914, the company for the first time had excess generating capacity on a significant scale. In 1913 there had been an "unprecedented increase in demands for power," but the beginning of the down-swing of the business cycle in that year checked the increase. Peak power sales remained roughly at the 1913 level through the first three years of the war, and then rose rapidly in 1917 to a new but irregular plateau. Excess capacity reappeared temporarily in 1918, 1919, and again in the slump of 1921. By this time capacity was about 225,000 h.p., representing an increase of some 80,000 h.p. since 1914 as a result of purchases of power from the Laurentide Power Company at Grand'Mère. From the middle of 1921 on, demand grew very rapidly and by the end of 1922 had caught up to capacity. From then until 1930 increases in peak load followed hard on the heels of increases in capacity, which now took 100,000-h.p. jumps rather than the 10,000-h.p. and 15,000-h.p. additions of the prewar period. By the beginning of 1930, capacity, only slightly over 100,000 h.p. at the beginning of 1914, was over 700,000 h.p. (See Chart 3.)

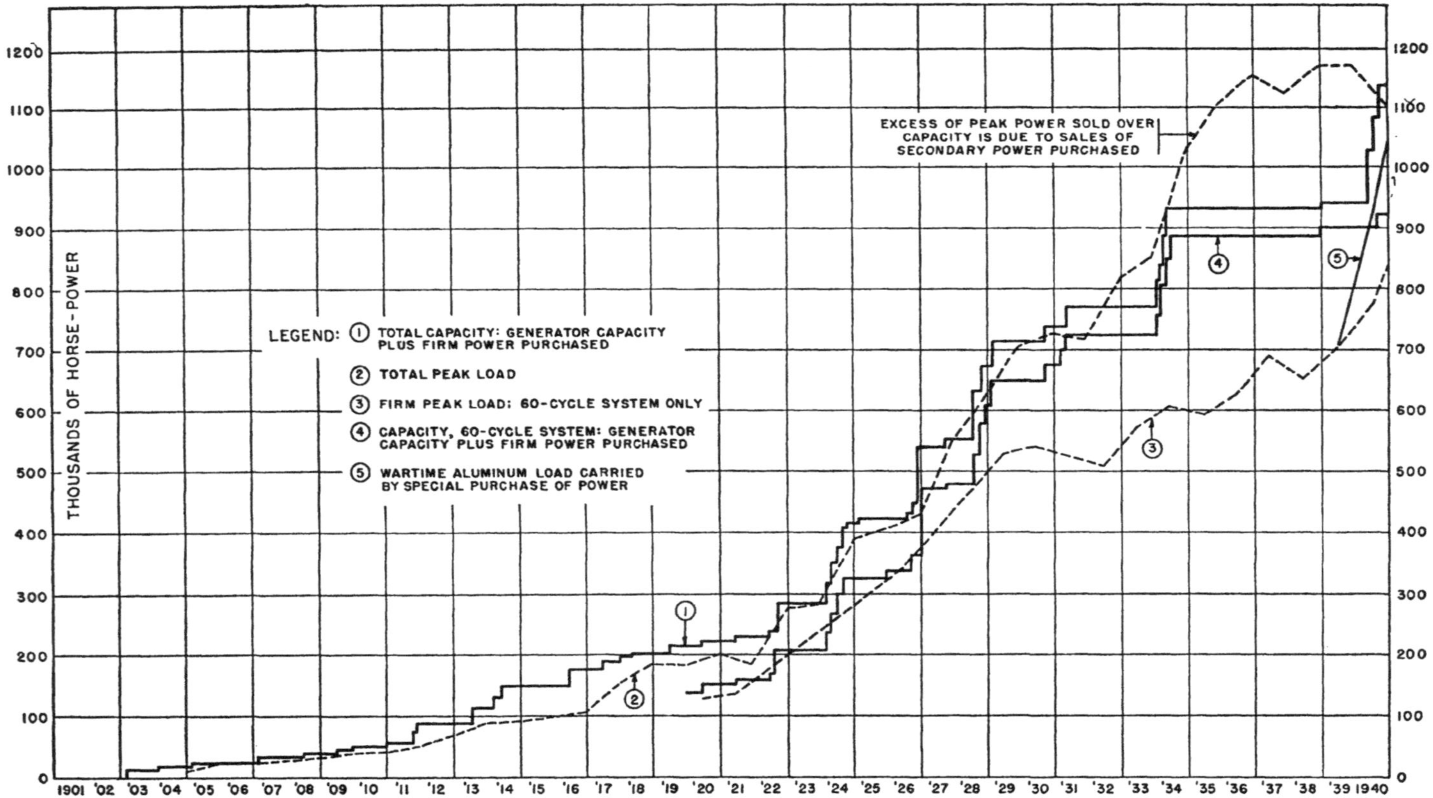

Chart 3. The Shawinigan Water and Power Company. Growth of Capacity and Load, 1901–1940

II. *Wartime Expansion*

Resource Expansion, 1911–1922

Increased capacity was made possible by an expansion of waterpower resources available to the company that resulted in part from the construction of water-storage projects, and in part from the purchase of new power sites.[1] As early as 1908, the company had built a small control dam above Shawinigan Falls to help regulate the flow at the powerhouse, but the first significant storage project was constructed three years later at the headwaters of the Manouan River, a tributary of the St. Maurice. Three storage dams were built, with a total capacity of 17 billion cubic feet of water (see Figure 2), and these were of great importance in demonstrating the feasibility of river control in Quebec.

> Uncertainty as to the quantity of water which would reach the plant (at Shawinigan Falls) under winter conditions, when let out of reservoirs located more than two hundred miles from the plant, was dissipated by the experience with the Manouan reservoirs. It was found that the water let out from these dams reached the plant with no appreciable loss. This experiment was followed by attempts to regulate the flow on a much larger scale.[2]

The Quebec Streams Commission was set up in 1912 as a result of "the efforts of the various power and lumbering interests on the St. Maurice River in bringing to the attention of the Provincial Government the necessity for making provision for the proper conservation and storage of water at the head waters of the St. Maurice."[3] The Shawinigan company had taken the initiative in storage developments, and in 1915 the St. Maurice Construction Company Ltd., a new subsidiary of the power company, was awarded the contract to construct La Loutre (later Gouin) Dam on behalf of the Quebec government. This huge dam, at the headwaters of the St. Maurice itself, was completed late in 1917 (see Figure 2). It provided a reservoir of 220 billion cubic feet and greatly benefited the Shawinigan company. The following year it was reported that "the flow of the river has been largely increased as a result of La Loutre Dam and has been maintained at substantially 50 per cent greater quantity than was possible before the operation of the storage dam"; and that with experience in operating the dam even better results could be expected.[4] The project provided the water for an increased installation at Shawinigan Falls, which, however, because of the trend of demand, was not needed until 1922. The third major storage project in the watershed, the Taureau Dam on the Mattawin River, was completed in 1930; it created a reservoir with a capacity of 33 billion cubic feet. Like Gouin Dam, Taureau

Dam was built for the Quebec Streams Commission by the Shawinigan company. As a result of all these storage works, the power capacity of the St. Maurice was tripled.

Perhaps in anticipation of heavy wartime demands, and perhaps because other interests were moving to develop power on the St. Maurice, the Shawinigan company began to extend its control over undeveloped power sites in 1915. In that year, the company bought in fee simple the Grès Falls power site, below Shawinigan Falls, from the Union Bag and Paper Company. The original plan was to develop this site in isolation, but at the end of the war the picture changed. In 1919 the International Paper Company began to move into the region. It set up a subsidiary, the St. Maurice Lumber Company, at Three Rivers, and through this company bought the La Gabelle and Forges power sites just below Grès Falls. The threat to Shawinigan led to negotiations with the paper company, with the result that a new concern, the St. Maurice Power Company, controlled by Shawinigan, was set up in 1922. The new plan was to consolidate all three power sites into one head and develop all power at one station, the La Gabelle power plant.[5]

To the north of Shawinigan Falls, an accommodation had to be made with another potential competitor at Grand'Mère. The Falls at this point had already been harnessed

> many years ago to supply power to a small pulp mill, which later, owned by the Laurentide Company, expanded into the manufacture of paper and gradually grew to be an industry of very large proportions. In 1913 this Company, owning the Falls, decided to develop them to their fullest extent, and completed in 1915 a power development and dam whereby the falls were raised to a height of 85 feet, which makes it possible to obtain at this point about 60 per cent of the power that can be developed at Shawinigan Falls.[6]

The Laurentide company had developed the water power to provide electricity for its own operations and to sell the surplus power. "The Shawinigan Company in 1916 entered into a contract with the Laurentide Power Company whereby the former purchases all the power output of this development in excess of 37,500 h.p. reserved for the purposes of the Laurentide Company for the manufacture of pulp and paper."[7] The agreement was outlined in greater detail in the annual report for 1916. After extended negotiations between the two companies, a new concern, the Laurentide Power Company, Ltd., was set up to take over all the power properties of the Laurentide company. Shawinigan acquired control of this new company, Aldred became its president, and the Shawinigan company was to operate the Grand'Mère plant in conjunction with its own stations. The report added that the arrangement was "an equitable one, furnishing a happy solution of the problem confronting the Laurentide Company and realizing for your Company the control of this additional large power supply."[8]

Business Expansion, 1915–1919

The year 1915 was one year of exceptional activity for the Shawinigan company. In addition to beginning construction of the Gouin Dam and acquiring two new power sites, the company took active measures to increase the demand for its power. In the first place, the time apparently having become ripe, the company finally gained an entree to Quebec City. Quebec City seems to have been a battleground on which rival groups of financiers warred and intrigued amid a tangle of corporate structures — a situation that will require some further comment presently. Here, it is sufficient to note that the Dorchester Electric Company, a distributing company in Quebec which had been incorporated in 1912, was taken over by a new organization, the Public Service Corporation of Quebec, in which the Shawinigan company owned a controlling interest.[9] The following account of the reorganization suggests that the Dorchester company had been in financial straits:

> The plan of reorganization conserved the interests of the former owners of the property and involved your Company financing through the purchase of bonds, the payments of the debts of the Dorchester Electric Company and also made provision for the cash requirements of the new company.
> The arrangement also vested in the Shawinigan Water and Power Company controlling interest in the stock of the Public Service Corporation of Quebec, and a contract for its requirements of power has been made.[10]

There were many skirmishes yet to be won before Shawinigan became master in Quebec City, but at least the door to a new market of potential importance had been eased open. A transmission line was built, and power was delivered to Quebec City in March of the following year. The North Shore Power Company took care of the requirements of the towns between Three Rivers and Quebec.[11]

Secondly, the war led to a great expansion and diversification of Shawinigan's chemical enterprise; in this period Shawinigan Falls became an important Canadian chemical center. The chemical development grew out of the carbide industry: the acetylene gas obtained from carbide was used at first to manufacture acetic acid and later as the basic raw material for a great many other products. In his speech at Boston (see Chapter 3), Aldred reported that

A little over two years ago [i.e., in 1915] a representative of the British Government came to us and asked if there was any way in which the Shawinigan power could be utilized to help the Government in connection with certain work that it required to be carried on. We made calcium carbide in a plant owned by the Shawinigan Company. They had found out that in Germany acetic acid was being made starting with acetylene gas as a raw material. Nobody on this continent knew how it was done. We formed a small company and got together some chemists, clever fellows,[12] that went to work and finally we sent to London a few bottles of liquid that looked like spring water. The British Government reported back that this was the best acetic acid that they had been able to buy anywhere in the world.

A new company, the Canadian Electro Products Company, was set up in 1916, and a new two-million-dollar plant for the manufacture of the acid, financed by the Imperial Government, was erected.[13]

The Imperial Munitions Board was also responsible for another research project that laid the basis for an electrometallurgical industry at Shawinigan Falls. Magnesium was required for use in flares and signals, and the war had cut off the main source of the world's supply of this material, which had been produced as a by-product of the German potash industry. Shawinigan was asked to develop a process for its production, and after intensive experimentation a small plant was set up and the Shawinigan Electro-Metals Company organized. "It is believed that this company was the first to produce metallic magnesium in commercial quantities on the continent of North America."[14] The market for magnesium disappeared at the end of the war and shortly thereafter the enterprise was sold to the Aluminum Company of Canada.

The electrometals company had also been asked to experiment in the production of ferrosilicon. "The lack of transformer capacity and a growing demand for calcium carbide prevented the Shawinigan company from actively pursuing this work at Shawinigan Falls during the war,"[15] but the experimental work had not been in vain. In 1916 a new enterprise, the Shawinigan Electro Products company, built a plant at Baltimore to use the process developed,[16] and the same process was used by the Canadian Ferro-Alloys Company which, with the encouragement of the Shawinigan company, was established at Shawinigan Falls in 1918.

By 1915 the Canada Carbide Company had doubled its capacity to 40,000 tons per year (another furnace, specifically for war production, was added in 1916) and was using 23,000 h.p. of electricity — an expansion which was "substantially increasing the profits of the Company. . . . In connection with the carbide business and other electric furnace operations, it has been found necessary to fortify our position by entering into the manufacture of carbon electrodes." [17] For this purpose another wholly owned subsidiary was set up, the Canadian Electrode Company, Ltd., which became part of the carbide company in 1923.

General demand for power began to rise rapidly in the later years of the war. In 1916 it was noted that Three Rivers and Shawinigan Falls were experiencing a remarkable growth. The latter now had a population of over 11,000 and a power demand of nearly 100,000 h.p. In 1917 the Canadian Aloxite Company Ltd., a subsidiary of the Carborundum Company of America, constructed a plant at Shawinigan Falls and signed a contract for 12,000 h.p. In the same year came the Prest-O-Lite Company, using acetylene gas, and Fraser, Brace and Company, which built a small electric furnace for the processing of low-phosphorus pig iron; in 1918 the Canadian Ferro Alloys Ltd. signed a contract with the Shawinigan company for 6000 h.p. Another outlet developed in 1917 when the company signed a contract to sell power to the Southern Canada Power Company. This load required a new transmission line from Windsor Mills to Sherbrooke which was put into operation in January 1917.

Because of the additions to capacity which had been made in 1914 and the availability of power from Grand'Mère after 1916, Shawinigan had no difficulty in taking care of the peak demands for power during the war years.[18] (Wartime demands did lead to power shortages in other parts of Canada in 1917.) The Laurentide power supply also enabled Shawinigan to postpone major construction projects during the inflation of the postwar years. The Annual Report for 1918 stated that costs were rising rapidly, "insulators, copper coils for generators and many similar items having trebled or quadrupled in price." In this situation, only minor extensions to the transmission system and small additions to substations were made, and construction at Grès Falls was set forward until prices fell. Most of the investment in plant for the electroprocess and chemical developments had been made by the government; it was stated in the Annual Report for 1918 that the plants for the manufacture of acetone, acetic acid, and magnesium had been built for the government by the engineering department of the Shawinigan company. Similarly, the plant of the American Electro Products Company, Ltd., a subsidiary company, that was being built at Shawinigan Falls to manufacture acetic acid for the United States government, did not involve the company in much loss. Construction was stopped by the armistice, but the American government paid most of the cost incurred.[19]

III. *The Postwar Pause*

The end of the war, of course, brought its shocks, but Shawinigan recovered rapidly. The Canadian Electro Products Company which had supplied acetic acid to the Imperial Munitions Board, its sole customer, was closed in January 1919. It was hoped, however, that the shutdown would be only temporary, and Shawinigan, with its acetylene process, expected to be able to compete with other methods of producing acetic acid. A sales force was established to create new markets, and since "the use of acetic acid and other chemicals produced by the plant has largely increased as the result of the war . . . it is confidently expected that this plant will continue as a permanent addition to the industries of Shawinigan Falls."[20] But recovery was not immediate: in 1921 the war chemical plants were still not being used to capacity and their capital value was written down by $300,000 taken from reserves. The carbide market also slumped badly at the end of the war, and despite a partial recovery in 1919, the industry was still in difficulties in 1921. The industry depended on exports for a large part of its sales and was apparently being subjected to price cutting in foreign markets. By 1922, however, markets were reported to be firmer, improved manufacturing processes had been introduced, and the development of new products was leading to a diversification of output and markets. It was planned to expand production in anticipation of a large growth in demand for carbide products.

Other markets were also temporarily deranged after the armistice. "The cessation of the war has not affected appreciably the demand for power outside the City of Montreal though it has temporarily stopped any new enterprises, and it will doubtless be several months before any new plants will demand power."[21] During 1919 the manufacturing demand in Shawinigan Falls fell off, but by 1920 all plants were again running at full capacity. The year 1920 brought a boom, and peak loads, running at about 200,000 horsepower, were again pressing on capacity. Moreover, contracts for new power deliveries in the course of the next two years were expected to increase the gross revenue of the company by more than a million dollars a year. This necessitated an expansion of plant: a new generating unit of 40,000 h.p. was ordered for the Shawinigan Falls station, and additional transmission lines were built to Montreal, Quebec, and Thetford Mines. The sharp deflation of the following year put a damper on the expansion program, but the setback was only temporary. By the end of 1921, the stage was set for a period of rapid growth. Business conditions throughout the Shawinigan area were recovering (with the exception of the asbestos district which remained in the doldrums until the late twenties), and building costs had been reduced so that large construction projects could again be profitably undertaken.

IV. *Peacetime Expansion, 1921–1930*

Growth in Capacity

During 1922 the Shawinigan company took delivery of the remaining power under its contract with the Laurentide Power Company at Grand'Mère. This brought the total power which Shawinigan had available for sale to about 240,000 h.p. At the end of 1931, the corresponding figure was over 750,000 h.p. Thus in nine years the company added over half a million horsepower to its capacity, more than double the amount that it had built up in the first twenty years of its operations. The power came from four sources: (a) additions to existing plants; (b) development of new power sites; (c) purchases of power; and (d) purchase of independent companies.

In the Number Two powerhouse at Shawinigan Falls, a sixth turbine of 40,000-h.p. capacity was installed in 1924, and turbines Number Seven and Eight, of equal capacities, were added in 1928 and 1929. In 1928, the Laurentide Power Company was merged with the Shawinigan company. At that time, the installed capacity of this development was 165,000 h.p.; a further unit of 25,000 h.p. was added in 1930. (The total, 190,000 h.p., was not all additional power from Shawinigan's point of view, of course, since that company had been making "purchases" from the Laurentide company since 1916.)

Under the heading of new construction, the most important development of the period was the building of the La Gabelle plant, between 1922 and 1924, with an installation of 120,000 h.p. As we have already noted, the La Gabelle site was developed by the St. Maurice Power Company, Ltd., which was controlled through stock ownership by the Shawinigan company. A fifth unit was added to the La Gabelle station in 1931, bringing its capacity up to 150,000 horsepower. In 1926 a new development of 25,000 h.p. was built at St. Narcisse on the Batiscan River to replace the old plant at that point. A third small plant of 4000 h.p. for local distribution was built at St. Alban on the Ste. Anne de la Pérade River in 1927.

Two long-term contracts were made for the purchase of power. In 1925 a contract was made for the purchase of 10,000 h.p. from the Southern Canada Power Company, the power to be supplied from that company's new station on the St. Francis River at Hemmings Falls, three miles from Drummondville. To take delivery of the power, the Shawinigan Company built a line from Windsor Mills to Drummondville. In 1926 negotiations with the Duke-Price power interests resulted in Shawinigan's acquiring a stock interest in the Duke-Price Power Company and a contract to purchase 100,000 h.p. from the Duke-Price plant on the Saguenay River. A 135-mile transmission line was immediately built from Île Maligne to Quebec City, and from there the power was distributed through the Shawinigan system.

Besides these additions to its power supply, the Shawinigan company acquired control of various other small hydro developments. With the purchase of the Quebec Power Company in 1923 came control over five small generating stations; and in 1925 the Quebec Power Company bought a controlling interest in the Laurentian Power Company, which owned a 24,000-h.p. plant on the Ste. Anne de Beaupré River. Through the purchase of the St. Francis Water Power Company in the middle twenties, the Shawinigan company became the owner of another small development of 3000 h.p. on the St. Francis River near Disraeli. Finally, the company acquired control of two picayune plants on the Shawinigan River totaling 1300 h.p. in capacity. By 1931, therefore, the power capacity controlled by Shawinigan was approximately that shown by Table 5. The steps in the growth of that capacity since 1920 appear in Chart 3.

Growth of Demand [22]

Pulp and Paper. Of the several contributors to Shawinigan's rapid development during the 1920's, the phenomenal growth of the pulp and paper industry was the most important. Since the rise of this industry has been dealt with by numerous authors, it is necessary here to give only a brief description of its development in Shawinigan territory.

The St. Maurice valley was an old lumbering area, the scene of large sawmilling operations after 1850. By 1880, however, the best of the forest resources had been exhausted and lumbering in the valley began to decline.[23] A financial crisis in 1883 resulted in many bankruptcies and the industry never recovered. Three Rivers lost three hundred inhabitants between 1881 and 1891, and although a few small industries came in the following decade, it was not until the rejuvenation of the area after 1900 — a renaissance in which the Shawinigan company played an important part — that the town

TABLE 5

POWER AVAILABLE TO THE SHAWINIGAN WATER AND POWER COMPANY, 1931 [a]

(Figures in 1000's of h.p.)

	Station	Horsepower
Directly (Total, 650.0)		
St. Maurice River	Shawinigan Falls #1	58.5
	Shawinigan Falls #2	220.0
	Grand'Mère	190.0
	La Gabelle	150.0
Ste. Anne de la Pérade River	St. Alban	4.0
St. Francis River	Disraeli	3.0
Shawinigan River		1.3
Batiscan River	St. Narcisse	24.0
Through the Quebec Power Company (Total, 36.0)		
Ste. Anne de Beaupré River	Seven Falls	20.0
Montmorency River	Montmorency	4.0
	Natural Steps	2.0
Chaudière River	Chaudière	3.5
Jacques Cartier River	St. Gabriel	2.0
Rivière du Sud	St. Raphael	4.5
Purchased Power (Total, 110.0)		
Southern Canada Power Co.		10.0
Duke-Price Power Co.		100.0
Miscellaneous (Total, 58.3)		
Shawinigan Falls Hydraulic Power		55.0
Steam Station (Quebec Power Co.)		3.3
General Total		855.1

[a] The figures in this table have been compiled from a variety of sources. Figures for horsepower capacity of a given plant customarily differ slightly at different times or in different publications. These discrepancies appear to result from one of the following factors, or a combination of them: (a) capacity may be measured in a different way; (b) the capacity of the generators may be reëvaluated; or (c) old generators may be rewound and their capacities increased. The figures in the table relate to 1931. The total rating for these same stations in 1950 had been increased by 38,150 h.p. over the 1931 rating. Most of this difference arises from an increase in the ratings of the Grand'Mère and La Gabelle plants, whose present capacities are given as 201,000 h.p. and 172,000 h.p., respectively.

again became prosperous.[24] A fire in 1908 razed the old town, and the modern city was born: "plus moderne mais moins sereine et moins gracieuse, surtout avec l'addition des quartier ouvriers rendus nécessaires par le développement de la grande industrie," laments its historian.[25] By that time all the sawmills had disappeared except one on Cap de la Madeleine which supplied cordwood to a paper factory.

Fortunately, the spruce, despised by the lumbermen, had attracted the attention of paper manufacturers as early as 1882. In that year John

Forman, the Montreal merchant involved in Shawinigan's early history, chose Grand'Mère as the site for the first pulp mill in the St. Maurice valley. Grand'Mère was but two miles from a railway to Les Piles which had been opened in 1878, and the falls at Grand'Mère were small enough to be developed with the techniques that were then available. Forman obtained authorization for his project in 1882, but because of the ensuing depression he was unable to collect enough capital to found the Laurentide Pulp Company until 1887. By 1890, the pulp mill, together with a 5000-h.p. water-power development, was ready to begin operations. In 1897 the plant was enlarged and transformed into a mill which made not only groundwood pulp, but also chemical pulp and paper.[26]

Forman was the pioneer by a decade in the new industrialism in the St. Maurice valley. The Shawinigan company was next; it was followed by the Aluminum and Belgo-American companies, and the town of Shawinigan Falls was incorporated in 1902. The third important group of newcomers was the Brown family, paper manufacturers in Berlin, New Hampshire. They bought water-power rights and forest limits at La Tuque in 1904 and began to build a chemical pulp mill in 1908. By 1910, the new economy was taking form.

Meanwhile, since the pulpwood resources of the United States were showing signs of depletion, American newsprint manufacturers had begun to have designs on Canadian forests. Although they would probably have liked to buy only the pulpwood from Canada, a combination of economic and political factors eventually induced them to transfer their mills to Quebec and Ontario. Economically, the spruce forests and the hydroelectric power of the Canadian shield were a powerful attraction to the industry. Political considerations added further incentive to move to an area that was already attractive from an economic viewpoint. Quebec put an embargo on the export of logs cut on Crown lands in 1910, and American newspaper publishers, fearful of high prices for newsprint, succeeded in having the American tariff on that commodity removed in 1913.[27] With these beckonings and proddings, the industry made plans to migrate northward, and the movement began in full force at the end of World War I.

We have already mentioned in Chapter 3 the mills that were located in the Three Rivers area in 1911. In 1912 a pulp mill was built at Cap de la Madeleine, which in 1925 became the St. Maurice Pulp and Paper Company. The International Paper Company, which had been building in New Brunswick during the latter years of the war, decided to move to Three Rivers, and in 1920 the huge, modern plant of the Canadian International

Paper Company was built on the site of a former sawmill. In 1922 the St. Lawrence Pulp and Paper Company built its mills in the western part of the city. The impetus given to the region by these new concerns was further enhanced by an expansion of capacity in the older mills at Three Rivers, Shawinigan Falls, Grand'Mère, and La Tuque.

The pulp and paper industry was also expanding in other areas served by Shawinigan. Along the St. Francis River in the Eastern Townships, another old lumbering area and the site of some of the earliest pulp and paper mills in Canada,[28] the industry was prospering. The two important customers of the Shawinigan company in this area were the Canada Paper Company at Windsor Mills, producing specialty papers, and the Kraft mill at East Angus which had been reorganized as the Brompton Pulp and Paper Company in 1907.

Along the north shore of the St. Lawrence, too, between Three Rivers and Quebec City, the industry was developing. The small plant of the News Pulp and Paper Company had been established on the Ste. Anne de la Pérade River in 1902; it was served after 1927 by Shawinigan's St. Alban development. At Portneuf there were three small specialty paper mills which had been established early in the century, and a newsprint mill was located at Pont Rouge on the Jacques Cartier River. The most important enterprise in this area was the Donnacona Pulp and Paper Mills, established by English capitalists in 1912 at the mouth of the Jacques Cartier River. At Quebec City, the large Anglo-Canadian Pulp and Paper Mills, founded in 1926 by a group of English capitalists headed by Lord Rothermere, began production in 1928. The Ste. Anne Paper Company at Ste. Anne de Beaupré, below Quebec, became a Shawinigan customer in 1926, and in the same year, a transmission line was built from Quebec to Murray Bay to serve the new Murray Bay Pulp and Paper Company.

By 1930, the pulp and paper industry accounted for a large part of Shawinigan's business. Sales figures before 1925 are very scarce, but some idea of the order of importance of the industry as a market can be gained from the following comparisons. In 1925 the pulp and paper load was 125,000 h.p., larger than Shawinigan's Montreal load and almost as large as that of the electroprocess industries at Shawinigan Falls. In 1920 the pulp and paper industry provided 16.4 per cent of the Shawinigan company's revenue; the following year, with the Canadian International Paper Company's load and better conditions throughout the industry, the figure jumped to 25 per cent. A comparison of the figures for 1925 and 1929, the peak year for the industry before the depression, appears below.

Shawinigan Sales to the Pulp and Paper Industry

	Millions of kwhs.		Thousands of dollars	
	1925	1929	1925	1929
Firm power	500	1,403	1,552	4,389
Secondary power	444	682	403	605
Hydraulic power	107	82	64	59
Percentage of total power sales	45	63	38	44

The largest increase took place between 1926 and 1927. In his annual report for the former year, Aldred commented that he expected sales to the booming industry to reach a peak within a couple of years, but he did not deplore the prospect: "The general industrial conditions in this Province will be better stabilized if the power demand becomes more diversified in the future."[29] With over forty cents of every dollar of income from power sales coming from one industry, Shawinigan had reason to be apprehensive.

An important qualitative aspect of the pulp and paper market was the industry's demand for off-peak power to be used in electric boilers. These boilers were designed by Shawinigan engineers, led by Mr. F. T. Kaelin, as a means of utilizing the excess power capacity which appeared immediately following World War I.[30] They seem to have been developed to the point of practical usefulness by 1920, and in the following year the first installation, a boiler of 25,000-kw. capacity was made in the mill of the Belgo-Canadian Paper Company.[31] The boilers, installed mainly in pulp and paper mills, had low capital, installation, and maintenance charges, and could be cut in or out of the power lines by an automatic switching system. By 1924 electric boilers in the pulp and paper industry had been installed to the extent of 150,000 h.p. in Canada, mostly in Quebec; a considerable number were also in use in the United States.[32]

The pulp and paper industry uses a tremendous amount of process steam, especially for cooking purposes in the manufacture of chemical pulp and for drying purposes in paper manufacture.[33] To use electricity for steam-raising is physically wasteful of energy, and except when surplus power is available, uneconomic, so that it is unlikely that electricity will ever displace coal as the prime source of heat in the industry.[34] Nevertheless, as an outlet for surplus power, the electric boiler proved to be of great importance to the hydroelectric industry in Quebec. The amount of electricity available to pulp and paper mills for steam-raising varies greatly, of course, and depends on the state of the market for firm power. In the 1930's, when a great deal of surplus power was available, the Quebec newsprint industry often generated more steam from electricity than from coal. "In 1935, for example, 72 per cent of the total fuel bill in Quebec mills was for the purchase of secondary power." [35]

For the power industry, the electric boiler market was profitable in spite of the fact that rates on boiler electricity were very low. In the case of Shawinigan the average revenue from such sales was less than one-tenth of a cent per kwh. throughout the twenties, and went as low as seven-hundredths of a cent per kwh. during the depression of the thirties. "While this provided a market for the surplus power of the [Company], the net gain to the Shawinigan Company was small as the price paid for such power is regulated by the price of coal." [36] The marginal cost of such sales was virtually zero, however, and the market provided about a half million dollars annually for the company throughout the late twenties. This figure climbed to almost a million dollars in 1933, and averaged more than one and a half million dollars annually from 1935 to 1939. With sales of boiler power, Shawinigan's plant utilization factor jumped from 50–55 per cent during the later war years to 70–75 per cent during the period 1922 to 1929. The electric boiler market had, in fact, taken the place of the carbide industry as an outlet for Shawinigan's surplus power.

It is convenient at this point to complete our sketch of the role that secondary power has played in Shawinigan's development, even at the expense of running ahead of the main narrative. In the early years of the depression, it was not possible to sell enough boiler power to take up the increases in capacity made in the preceding boom, and surplus capacity developed for about two years, from the middle of 1930 to the fall of 1932. After that date, secondary power sales grew tremendously, and from 1933 on Shawinigan began to purchase large amounts of secondary power, mainly from the Montreal company, to carry the load.[37] As a result, the peak loads on the Shawinigan system greatly exceeded the Shawinigan company's generating capacity from 1935 to 1940. (See Chart 3).

With the outbreak of war in 1939, Shawinigan's firm load grew rapidly, and secondary sales fell to a very small figure. During the war years, indeed, as a result of facilities providing for an interchange of power between the larger Quebec companies, Shawinigan made special purchases of firm power to carry the heavy aluminum load at Shawinigan Falls.[38] Since the war, the trend of demand has continued strongly upward, and the peak load for firm power has been pressing on the company's capacity. Thus, from 1940 on, secondary power has been of little importance as far as the Shawinigan company is concerned. It now generates secondary power only under two circumstances: for a month or so during the spring run-off, when the reservoirs are full and the water would otherwise run to waste; and after heavy summer rains, to utilize the run-off of the drainage basin below the storage dams. Seasonal declines in demand are not now, as they were during the thirties, compensated for by sales of secondary power; instead, the water is stored for use during the months when the natural flow of the river drops below the amount necessary to satisfy the demand for firm power.

Chemicals. During the 1920's the carbide industry came of age. No longer was it a dumping ground for surplus power; on the contrary, it soon was the basis of an electrochemical industry at Shawinigan Falls which became a good market for firm power. The energetic measures directed to the rehabilitation of the Shawinigan chemical enterprises, after the disappearance of the wartime market on which they had been built, had been successful.[39] The Canadian Electro Products Company, which had been closed down in 1919, was operating profitably, and there was a steadily increasing demand both for its products and for the output of the carbide plant. In 1919 the company had built a small laboratory for research in the chemistry of acetic acid (produced from carbide), and the group of scientists working on this project had developed new products and improved manufacturing processes. The new Shawinigan Black, for instance, proved to be well adapted for use in the manufacture of dry cell batteries and, especially after 1928, found a rapidly growing market in that industry. Most important was the work on the derivatives of acetic acid. Towards the end of the decade, the resulting products found markets in the artificial silk industry, as solvents in paint and lacquer manufacturing, as an interlayer substance in the manufacture of shatterproof glass, and in the production of various materials for electrical insulation.[40]

It was fortunate that the acetic acid industry provided a new market for the output of the carbide plant, because traditional markets for calcium carbide had been hard hit at the end of World War I by a decline in the demand for acetylene gas for lighting purposes. The carbide market in the twenties was also disrupted by the intense competition in the industry which had resulted from the expansion of production facilities during the war, and by marketing difficulties, especially the imposition of an American tariff of $20 per ton in 1922. Sales effort was increased, notably by the opening in 1920 of sales offices in London (Shawinigan Ltd. of London) and New York (Shawinigan Products Corporation),[41] but it was the chemical industry at Shawinigan Falls itself which saved the day and reduced carbide's former dependence on export markets. Acetylene gas, produced from the carbide, was delivered to the Canadian Electro Products Company, and there was used as the basic raw material in the manufacture of heavy chemicals, principally acetoldehyde and acetic acid.[42] In 1926 the company could boast that "These plants now form one of the greatest chemical groups of the kind in the world." [43]

The Shawinigan chemical industries, organized as one concern, Shawinigan Chemicals Ltd., in 1927, supplied the parent power concern with large profits in the late twenties; as new products were developed and sold, the chemical industries also served as a buffer for the parent company against the depression of the thirties. But the industry did *not* provide a growing market for power after its initial expansion during the war. Scattered figures in the annual reports indicate that all industries at Shawinigan Falls (which would include the aluminum company, textile mills, and, perhaps, the Belgo-Canadian pulp and paper mill) took slightly less than 100,000 h.p. in 1916, over 130,000 h.p. in 1919, and about 130,000 h.p. in 1925. From 1925 to 1929 the electrochemical and electrometallurgical sales of the Shawinigan company (which would include sales to the aluminum industry) fell from 813 million kwhs. to 626 million kwhs., no doubt reflecting improved technology in this group of industries. Revenue figures, however, show that in the later twenties the electroprocess market was able to pay a higher average price for the power that it did buy, and that the total revenue to the power company from such sales increased by $100,000 between 1925 and 1929, despite the smaller volume of sales in the latter year.

Other Utility Companies and Retail Sales. While the pulp and paper industry was mainly responsible for the growth of Shawinigan's physical plant in the 1920's — the whole increase of over 1 billion kwhs. in power sales between 1925 and 1929 could be accounted for by increased sales to that industry alone — the revenue picture was quite different. In 1925 the pulp and paper industry provided 38.4 per cent of gross revenue from all power sales; in 1929 this figure had grown only to 44.3 per cent in spite of the industry's huge increase in physical purchases. Moreover, the contribution of the electroprocess industries to gross power revenue had fallen from 19.4 per cent to 9.9 per cent between the same two years. It is clear, then, that revenue from utility companies and retail sales contributed a disproportionately large share to Shawinigan's income in the late twenties. Figures for physical sales in these markets are not available for this period.

TABLE 6

ELECTRIC POWER SALES OF THE SHAWINIGAN WATER AND POWER COMPANY, 1925–1940[a]

(Millions of kilowatt-hours; thousands of dollars)

Year	Total power		Secondary power		Firm power					
					Total		Pulp and paper		Electroprocess	
	Total — net of losses (kwhs.)	Total revenue (dollars)	Secondary[b] power sales (kwhs.)	Rev. from sec. power (dollars)	Sales (kwhs.)	Revenue (dollars)	Sales (kwhs.)	Revenue (dollars)	Sales (kwhs.)	Revenue (dollars)
1925	2003	4950	474	445	1529	4505	500	1552	560	738
1926	2130	5504	343	325	1787	5180	635	1986	560	742
1927	2508	8388	598	637	1910	7751	1008	3133	405	533
1928	2763	9952	583	515	2180	9437	1168	3929	442	875
1929	3110	11100	721	653	2389	10447	1403	4389	362	840
1930	2964	11252	643	563	2321	10689	1321	4519	365	708
1931	3000	11205	667	564	2333	10641	1283	4438	275	618
1932	2916	10891	936	732	1980	10158	1089	4093	234	655
1933	3495	10613	1344	979	2151	9634	1209	3853	239	738
1934	4152	10771	1654	1138	2498	9634	1399	3652	295	784
1935	4805	11546	2220	1562	2565	9983	1451	4002	332	801
1936	5057	12407	2252	1786	2805	10621	1542	4243	371	813
1937	4993	13213	1899	1608	3094	11606	1713	4790	438	921
1938	4574	12979	1778	1470	2796	11508	1474	4509	358	737
1939	5065	13727	2038	1720	3027	12007	1562	4569	429	852
1940	4895	15468	1167	1126	3728	14342	1800	5163	789	1915

TABLE 6, *continued*

Year	Firm Power								Losses
	Other utility companies		Retail [c]				General industry [d]		
	Sales (kwhs.)	Revenue (dollars)	Sales (kwhs.)	Revenue (dollars)	Kwhs.[e]	Revenue [e]	Sales (kwhs.)	Revenue (dollars)	Amount (kwhs.)
1925	469	2215			Included in utilities.				—[f]
1926	592	2452			Included in utilities.				—[f]
1927	342	1564			154	2,520			173
1928	387	1736			173	2,898			187
1929	427	1984			198	3,234			259
1930	442	2097			193	3,364			241
1931	589	2234			185	3,352			248
1932	492	2144			165	3,264			255
1933	537	2102	46	1718			119	1,223	333
1934	613	2137	48	1725			143	1,325	383
1935	597	2074	52	1683			154	1,422	448
1936	656	2207	57	1745			182	1,614	474
1937	668	2198	62	1903			214	1,794	420
1938	687	2308	69	2100			208	1,853	389
1939	732	2369	75	2288			229	1,934	401
1940	799	2585	80	2466			259	2,213	376

[a] Source: The Company.

[b] These sales are made mainly to the pulp and paper industry. However, some secondary sales were made to other markets. Over 100 million kws. annually were taken by the electroprocess industries from 1933 to 1941, and by the textile group from 1935 to 1939, while negligible quantities of secondary power were also delivered to the utilities and miscellaneous categories in various years.

[c] Includes domestic, farm, commercial and street lighting sales.

[d] Includes sales to the textile and asbestos industries, small power sales, and miscellaneous sales.

[e] Retail plus general industry.

[f] Not recorded.

But there can be no doubt that although such sales increased considerably in absolute terms, their proportion of total sales, always small, declined sharply in the face of the great expansion of the pulp and paper market. Their contribution to Shawinigan's gross revenue, however, which was 40 per cent in 1925, dropped only to 37.3 per cent of a greatly increased total in 1929.[44] The company was therefore vitally concerned with the health of its utility and retail business.

Shawinigan improved its position in the Quebec City market in 1923 after a corporate struggle which resulted in the formation of the Quebec Power Company, a Shawinigan subsidiary that in effect represented a consolidation of all the gas, power, light, and traction utilities in Quebec City and the surrounding region.[45] In the years following the formation of the new company the utilities in Quebec were rationalized; the old duplicate systems were coordinated into one service, and the physical plant was improved in various ways.[46] With vigorous new management[47] and the advantage of starting operations during the upswing of the business cycle, the company was profitable. Sales increased from 76 million kwhs. in 1924 to 165 million kwhs. in 1929; the number of customers served increased from 30,000 to 41,000 during the same period. By 1929, as the result of the purchase of various small local distribution companies, power was being delivered to 69 towns and municipalities. Some of this business was handled by the generating plants owned and operated by the Quebec Power Company, but since these had been operating close to their capacity at the time of their consolidation, most of the increase in sales represented purchases from the parent Shawinigan company.

The Montreal and Southern Canada companies were Shawinigan's other main utility customers. The Montreal market was an expanding one. A new contract for increased power deliveries was made with the Montreal Light, Heat and Power Consolidated in 1925, and the Shawinigan company built a new terminal station at Montreal to handle the heavier load.[48] Under the new contract, sales to the Montreal market rose from 273 million kwhs. in 1925 to 453 million kwhs. in 1929 (see Table 7). On the other hand, the Southern Canada Power Company completed a 33,600-h.p. development of its own on the St. Francis River in 1925, and considerably reduced its purchases of Shawinigan power. (Indeed, Southern Canada after 1925 became on balance a seller of power to Shawinigan, for as we have seen the Shawinigan company purchased 10,000 h.p. from the St. Francis development and built a transmission line from Windsor Mills to Drummondville to take delivery of the power.) Retail sales,[49] although small in volume, offered high dollar returns, and the Shawinigan company therefore devoted much attention to this sector of its business after 1922. In that year some 125 communities were using Shawinigan power, of which 70 were served directly by the Shawinigan company or its subsidiaries, 10 by municipal systems which purchased Shawinigan power, and 45 by small private companies (in 20 of which power that originated at Shawinigan Falls was distributed by the Montreal Light, Heat and Power Company). By 1930, Shawinigan power was being used in 406 communities: "The company's distribution business has increased by over 100 per cent within the last five years and . . . the service is being developed to its fullest extent, not only to increase the use of power for industrial purposes but also for lighting and electrical appliances of all kinds." [50] This expansion, of course, involved a considerable investment in transmission lines and substation facilities. In some cases new facilities were built; in others, the investment took the form of purchasing existing local systems. "The initial costs of serving [the retail load] have in some cases been heavy but the Company finds a moderate and steady growth in its income from this source." [51] The gross revenue from retail sales increased from $1.7 million in 1927 (the first year for which they are separated from utility sales) to $2.4 million in 1930.

Some of the highlights of this expansion may be briefly noted. In 1924, through a holding company arrangement with the Montreal Light, Heat and Power Company, Shawinigan gained a half interest in a 22,500-h.p. generating plant at St. Timothée on the St. Lawrence River.[52] Two years later the Shawinigan Company purchased four small companies in this area and thus became concerned with the distribution of electricity in the triangle of territory west of Montreal and between the St. Lawrence River and the American border. This distribution system drew its power from the St. Timothée station and was not tied in with the main Shawinigan network. In 1924 also the company bought the St. Francis Water Power Company, which owned a small hydro station at Disraeli on the St. Francis River. Two or three local systems in this area were purchased, carrying the Shawinigan network eastward from the asbestos district to the Maine border. To provide for the increased demands of the asbestos industry and of the distributing business in this area, a high-tension transmission line from Quebec City to Thetford Mines was built in 1929. More generally, whereas at the end of World War I Shawinigan's retail business was mainly confined to towns along the route of its main transmission lines, by 1930 numerous Shawinigan distribution lines stretched out to towns on both sides of the transmission skeleton. By the end of the decade Shawinigan had become not only the largest generating company in Canada, but also the second largest retail distributor of electricity in Canada.[53] Including the transmission lines of the Quebec Power Company, the Shawinigan network stretched along the north shore of the St. Lawrence from the Ottawa River to Murray Bay, 75 miles east of Quebec City, and along the south shore from the western extremity of the province to a point about 80 miles east of Quebec City. South of the river the company's lines served a large territory bounded on the south by the American border, on the east by a line drawn southeastward from Quebec City to the border, and on the west by a line from Three Rivers to Sherbrooke (see Figure 1).

Sales to small manufacturing establishments throughout Shawinigan's territory formed one of the most important sectors of the retail market, and the company was energetic in promoting this part of its business. From the first it had been active in attracting manufacturers to its area, and this work was put on a formal basis by the organization of an industrial development department in the 1920's.[54] New channels for the attraction of foreign firms were offered by the opening of the company's offices in New York and London. Shawinigan treats the industrial development aspect of its business as confidential — regrettably, from our point of view — and very little specific information on the industrial development department is given in the company's annual reports. In 1930, however, it was reported that during the preceding 18 months, some 21 industries, employing 1685 people and using electricity to the extent of 6500 h.p., had been established in the area served by the company.[55] As compared with the massive loads of the pulp and paper companies, such business may appear insignificant, but over a period of years the aggregate load thus gained by the company was appreciable. And for Quebec the yearly additions to manufacturing plant were important steps along the road to an industrial economy.

v. *Stagnation, 1930–1940*

Capacity

The curve of peak firm power load on the Shawinigan system rose steadily and rapidly from late in 1921 to about the middle of 1929. It then flattened out and increased only slightly during the next year. Then, beginning in the middle of 1930, the curve fell continuously for two years (see Chart 3). This reversal in the trend of demand came at a most inopportune time, for the construction boom of the late twenties had developed a momentum which resulted in further additions to Shawinigan's capacity in both 1930 and 1931. The conjuncture of falling demand and increasing generating potential resulted in a serious problem of excess capacity which plagued the Shawinigan company throughout the decade.

As we have seen, the purchase of the Laurentide Power Company in 1928 had added directly to Shawinigan's generating capacity. Furthermore, the dam at Grand'Mère created a lake some twenty miles long and, by using this as a storage reservoir, "the plants at Grand'Mère, Shawinigan Falls, and La Gabelle can be operated at much greater efficiencies and substantially larger amounts of power made available." [56] The Taureau Dam on the Mattawin River (see Figure 2), the last of the large storage projects on the St. Maurice, was completed in the fall of 1929 and increased still more the power potential of the lower river. On the basis of the greater flow of water thus made available, extensions were made to the Shawinigan Falls plant in 1928 and 1929, an additional generator of 25,000 h.p. was installed at Grand'Mère in 1930, and another unit of 30,000 h.p. was put into operation at La Gabelle in 1931.

Even more disturbing than these increases in capacity, however, were certain arrangements which Shawinigan had made to develop still more power on the St. Maurice. As we have seen, the company had gained control over all the power sites on the lower river by its arrangements with the St. Maurice Power Company at La Gabelle Falls and the Laurentide Power Company at Grand'Mère. In 1928 Shawinigan consolidated its position on the lower river by merging these two companies.[57] Above Grand'Mère, there were seven power sites, and of these only the one at La Tuque, owned by the Brown Corporation, had been alienated from the Crown. With the rapidly increasing demand of the twenties, the Shawinigan company moved to gain control of the power resources of the upper St. Maurice. In 1928 the company acquired a 75-year emphyteutic lease from the provincial government on all the unalienated rapids of the upper river. These undeveloped powers were located along a 70-mile stretch of river above La Tuque, and all of them were within a 150-mile radius of Montreal. In 1931 Shawinigan bought half ownership of the La Tuque Falls for $2.5 million, and in partnership with the Brown Corporation set up the St. Maurice Power Corporation, Ltd., to develop the site.[58] Shawinigan was now master of the river (see Figure 2).[59]

There was no need to proceed immediately with the La Tuque development. But the leases which had been obtained from the government to the falls above La Tuque contained a definite schedule for the progressive development of the upper river. The company was bound to start construction in 1930, to complete one development of at least 100,000 h.p. by 1933, and to begin work on a second site not later than 1938.

Those commitments became very embarrassing once the depression struck, but the company succeeded in having them modified in 1932 under the terms of a revised agreement with the government. The date for completion of the first project was set forward until 1935, and the obligation with respect to further developments now provided only "that the beginning of construction work on any one of the other water powers need only be commenced after 75 per cent of the capacity of the preceding development has been sold as firm power."[60]

The company now had a free hand, but in the meantime it had taken steps to honor the first item in the original agreement by initiating construction work at Rapide Blanc. Although a relatively expensive project, since it involved moving a section of Canadian National Railways track in order to provide for the storage pond which stretched for almost 30 miles above the dam, the absolute cost of the developed power was small. "The capital cost of this plant, owing to economies effected since the work was first planned, is to be considerably lower than the original estimate, so that it is now considered that the capital cost per installed horsepower on the completion of the first installation of 160,000 h.p. will be under $100. This will still further be reduced on the completion of the ultimate installed machine capacity of 240,000 h.p."[61] The initial installation at Rapide Blanc was completed in 1934, but none of its capacity was required to supply Shawinigan's firm power load until after the outbreak of war in 1939 (see Chart 3). Needless to say, it was the last addition to Shawinigan's capacity during the decade. Not until the La Tuque project was rushed to completion in 1940 to serve wartime needs, was Shawinigan's power capacity again increased.

Demand

General Trends. We have noted that the Shawinigan company experienced a decline in the demand for firm power from 1930 to the middle of 1932. From then on there was a slow and irregular increase in peak sales, with declines registered again in 1935 and 1938. Sustained growth in demand on the pattern of the previous decade became evident only when the beginning of war brought new loads onto the company's lines. Measured with reference to firm peak power sales, Shawinigan had a large amount of excess capacity in every year, from 1929 through 1939. With reference to total peak power sales, however, excess capacity was in evidence only from mid-1930 to mid-1932. After 1932, sales of secondary power on a very large scale took up all the slack. From 1935 to 1940, owing to very heavy purchases of secondary power for resale, the combined peak-load power delivered by Shawinigan greatly exceeded the company's generating capacity (see Chart 3).

How are we to measure the impact of the depression on the Shawinigan company? In terms of kilowatt-hours, firm power sales dropped from 2389 million in 1929 to 1980 million in 1932 and did not reach the former level again until 1934. Firm plus secondary power sales dropped from 3110 million in 1929 to 2916 million in 1932, but jumped to a record figure of 3495 million in 1933 and rose to 5057 million in 1936. Gross revenue from all power sales fell from $11.3 million in 1930 to $10.6 million in 1933, and it was 1935 before the former figure was surpassed: revenue from firm power sales dropped from $10.7 million in 1930 to $9.6 million in 1934, and regained the former figure only in 1937 (see Table 6). Perhaps the best indication of the depression's effect is seen in the record of profits. From $4.8 million in 1928, Shawinigan's profits before depreciation and taxes rose to $6.57 million in 1930, fell to $2.9 million in 1933, rose fairly steadily (although with a moderate drop in 1938) to $4.5 million in 1939,[62] and then rose very rapidly during the war years. Dividends were reduced by stages from an annual rate of $2.50 per share for the first half of 1931 to 50¢ in 1932, and only began to rise in the last quarter of 1935. They reached 90¢ per common share in 1940, where they held steady until 1944.

On the whole, Shawinigan's experience during the depression conformed to the typical experience of new and rising industries. The effect of the depression was to check expansion — even to turn rapid growth into a small decline for a few years — rather than to reduce production by half and turn profits into losses as was the case in many older industries. Shawinigan was never in danger of suffering losses. Nevertheless, the figures quoted above for net profits indicate that for a whole decade the company lacked buoyancy. It was a long depression.

Pulp and Paper. The decline in power sales in the early thirties was most severe in the pulp and paper, electroprocess, and asbestos[63] markets. Sales at retail declined only slightly, while the textile load rose slowly and deliveries to utility companies generally increased, although with erratic fluctuations, throughout the period. Quantitatively, of course, the pulp and paper load was by far the most important part of Shawinigan's business. The only large new customer in this industry during the depression years was the Brown Corporation at La Tuque. This concern was a large manufacturer of specialty pulps and papers, newsprint being but a minor part of its production. Until 1931 it used mainly steam power, having only a very small hydraulic development of about 2000 h.p. on the St. Maurice. In that year, when the St. Maurice Power Corporation was set up, and pending the development of the power site at La Tuque, contracts were entered into "providing for the supply of all power required by the Brown Corporation (through the intermediary [*sic*] of the new company), and when the development of the water power is ultimately completed, the new company will then supply power directly to the Brown Corporation and to this company."[64] For the rest, the pulp and paper market presented a picture of unrelieved gloom in the early thirties. The history of the overexpansion of this industry in the twenties, its collapse in 1929, and its chronic depression throughout the thirties, is well-known and need not be repeated here.[65]

Shawinigan followed two main policies in an attempt to protect itself against the loss of sales resulting from the crash of its largest customer. In the first place, sales of secondary power to the pulp and paper industry were rapidly expanded from 575 million kwhs. in 1930 to 1967 million kwhs. in 1935. This neccessitated the installation of electric boilers on an enlarged scale. In 1931 the company installed a 35,000-kw. boiler for the Brown Corporation at La Tuque, and a 30,000-kw. boiler at the mill of the Donnacona Paper Company; in the following year, 90,000 kws. of boiler capacity were installed in plants at Three Rivers and Quebec. Secondly, contracts were modified. Primary-power contracts provided that none of the power bought under them could be used for secondary purposes. By 1932, however, the Shawinigan company was allowing some of its customers to break their contracts in this respect. Contracts must have been modified in another respect too; while firm power sales to the pulp and paper industry were virtually the same in 1934 as they had been in 1929, the revenue derived from these sales was some $720,000 less in the latter year than in the former (see Table 6).

Gradually the industry recovered, and by 1934 Shawinigan could report that, "as applying to the business of the Shawinigan Company, the past year has shown increased consumption by the newsprint companies of electric current, both primary and secondary, and the quantity of electricity so taken by these companies is now approaching the high figure of 1929 and 1930."[66] The consumption of the industry kept above the 1929 rate for the remainder of the thirties, although annual purchases fluctuated considerably.

Chemicals. The depression in the electrochemical industries was sharp, but relatively short. Here too the twenties had left a legacy of excess capacity for the thirties, for extensions to the plant of the Shawinigan Chemicals Company which had been started in 1929 were completed in 1930. At that time, though it was working at less than capacity, the plant was still making a substantial profit. By 1932, however, no interest or dividends were being received from the chemicals company. Total sales of firm power by the Shawinigan company to all electroprocess industries fell by 130 million kwhs. between 1930 and 1932, but from then on sales to these industries followed an upward trend. By the end of 1933 the Shawinigan Chemicals Company was able to make part payment on the bond interest it owed to the parent company, and in 1935 it began to pay a dividend on its preferred stock. The chemical industry had suffered largely because the rayon industry, a heavy consumer of acetic acid and acetone, slumped badly from 1930 to 1932 and again in 1938, and at both times the results showed up in reduced power consumption by the chemicals plant. On the other hand, markets for other products of the Shawinigan chemical group were growing: acetylene was increasingly used for welding purposes, and the market for vinyl resins, another important Shawinigan product, held up well. By the end of the decade the chemical company was also producing the bulk of Canadian requirements of certain industrial solvents, notably ethyl acetate. It was research that had been the salvation of Shawinigan's chemical enterprises. The research laboratory established after World War I was complemented by a center for applied research in 1929. From these facilities came new products and new uses for old products which led to a diversification of output and markets and kept the Shawinigan enterprise in the forefront of the rapidly changing chemical industry.[67]

Utilities. Sales of electricity to other utility companies followed an upward trend during the depression years, increasing irregularly from 442 million kwhs. in 1930 to 613 million in 1934 and 761 million in 1939. An increase in sales from 1930 to 1931 followed the signing of a revised contract with Montreal Light, Heat and Power Consolidated. This contract, "which would have been due for renewal, under ordinary circumstances, in January, 1936, was renewed in January, 1931, for a period of 36 years on mutually satisfactory terms."[68] Sales to the Southern Canada Power Company were also increased after 1931 as the result of "a further firm contract for 15,000 h.p. to be taken gradually over a term of years."[69] The Quebec City market was less prosperous, and in 1932 the Quebec Power Company reduced its dividends from $2.37 to $1.00 per share per annum. In Quebec, too, the only large urban market in which Shawinigan retailed power directly through a controlled subsidiary, the Shawinigan company engaged in an unseemly quarrel with civic authorities. However, by what seem to have been very high-handed methods, the company finally got the city to sign a street-lighting contract for another 10 years in 1935, and retained its franchise for electrical distribution in the city.[70]

Retail Markets. Shawinigan's retail sales slumped slightly in 1932 and 1933, and then rose rapidly during the remainder of the decade from 87 million kwhs. in 1933 to 140 million kwhs. in 1939. A drop in average revenue per kwh. on such sales, from 2.65 cents per kwh. in 1933 to 2.19 cents per kwh. in 1935, suggests that this expansion of sales was touched off by rate reductions. If so, demand proved to be elastic (the result indicated by almost every study of the demand for electricity), for total revenue from retail sales advanced steadily from $2.3 million in 1933 to slightly more than $3 million in 1939. Retail sales were small in physical terms; indeed, until World War II Shawinigan never sold more than 4 per cent of its kilowatt-hour output at retail. The revenue from these sales, however, had risen from slightly more than 6 per cent of total revenue from power sales in 1921 to 17 per cent in 1925, and 20 per cent in 1927. Throughout the thirties, the retail markets continued to account for almost one-fifth of all revenue from power sales (see Chart 4).

Shawinigan had devoted much attention to its retail business during the later twenties, and this policy was continued during the thirties. In 1937, it was reported that "during the past few years, the distribution system of the Company has been extended so that now practically all towns and villages within the territory served have the benefit of electric service. There still remain scattered villages and farm ranges, which call for service and require consideration. In eight years the company has increased its distribution system from 2000 miles to 3385 miles of lines and the number of towns and communities served from 298 to 427."[71] The number of customers served directly by the Shawinigan company (i.e., excluding all those served indirectly through the Quebec Power Company or other public-utility companies) rose from 57.6 thousand in 1933 to 74.6 thousand in 1938, and consumption per domestic customer, excluding the power used in water heaters, increased from 405 to 459 kwhs. per annum during the same period. The company encouraged the use of electric water heaters and opened stores to promote the sale of electrical appliances, since at the beginning of the depression it had been noted that "the growing demand for current for commercial and domestic refrigeration and radio is contributing noticeably to the Company's income."[72] By the outbreak of war Shawinigan was

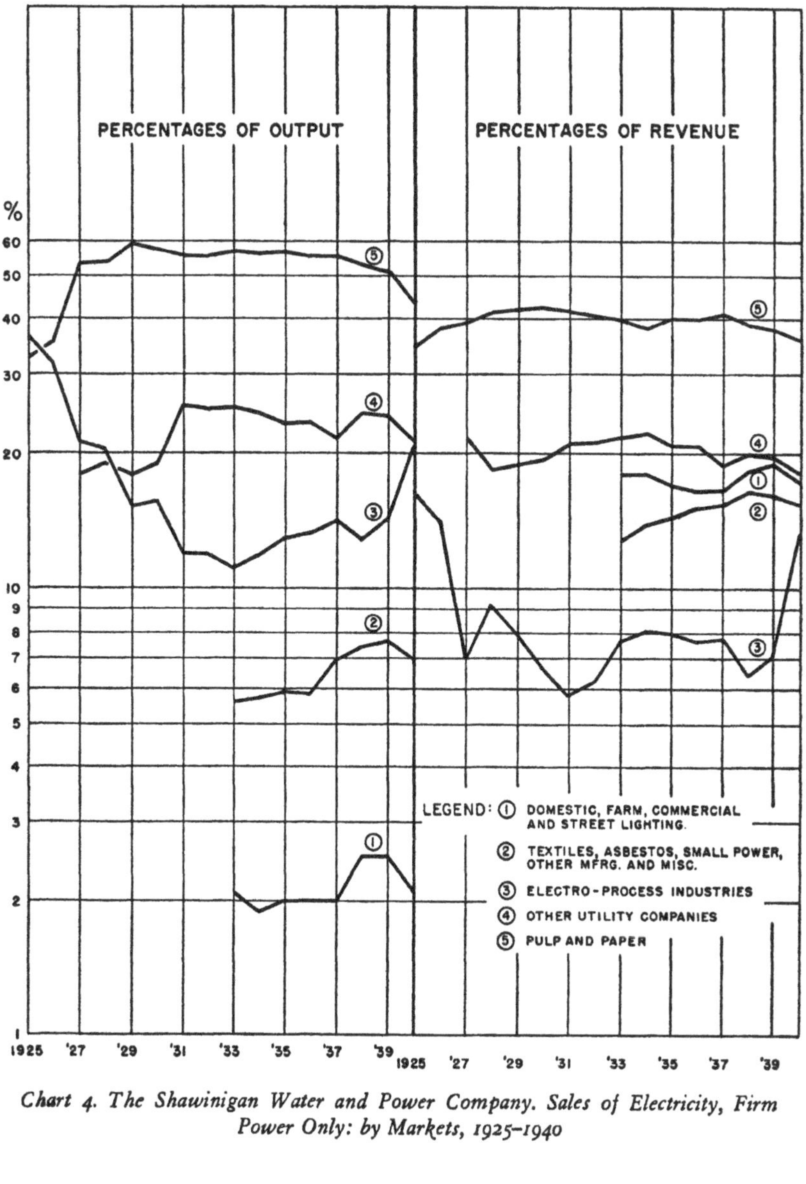

Chart 4. The Shawinigan Water and Power Company. Sales of Electricity, Firm Power Only: by Markets, 1925–1940

serving nearly 500 communities through a network of almost 4000 miles of distribution lines. Retail sales in 1939 amounted to over 139 million kwhs. distributed approximately as follows: 65 million kwhs. to some 500 small industrial consumers; 40 million kwhs. to domestic customers; 26 million kwhs. to commercial customers; and over 4 million kwhs. to each of the municipal street-lighting and farm markets.

Part of the increase in retail sales, and a large part of the increase in distribution-line mileage after 1925, reflected the program of rural electrification which the company had inaugurated in the middle twenties. The percentage of farms served in the Shawinigan area rose from 15 per cent in 1931 to over 33 per cent in 1942, or some 15,790 farms.[73] The cost to the company of serving this market was relatively high. Dr. Massue, the Shawinigan statistician, estimates that in 1939 the company's average investment per farm served was about $280 and that the total cost to the company of providing such service amounted to about $40 per year per farm; on the other hand, average consumption per farm was low and in 1942 the average farm bill was $19.50.[74] The Shawinigan company has thus subsidized the farmer heavily; Dr. Massue calculates that in 1941 the company lost about $350,000 on this business. Shawinigan has performed a notable service to farmers in its area through its rural electrification activities, and it may be uncharitable to inquire why a business concern should choose to be philanthropic to the extent of hundreds of thousands of dollars per year. But the rural vote in Quebec is of primary importance in provincial elections, and it is politic for large power companies to remain on good terms with both the electorate and the elected.

From the beginning of its history, as we have seen, the Shawinigan company took an active part in attracting industries to its area in order to build up its power load, and the industrial development department of the company was active throughout the depression years. By far the largest power consumer persuaded to locate in Shawinigan territory in the thirties was the cellophane plant of Canadian Industries Ltd., which was built at Shawinigan Falls in 1931. This was the beginning of another important chemical development at Shawinigan Falls, for C.I.L. added a hydrogen peroxide plant in 1934, a solvents plant in 1936, and a caustic soda plant in 1939. As well as providing important new customers for the power company, this building program greatly helped to relieve unemployment in the area. Shawinigan gained another important customer in 1938, when International Foils, Ltd., manufacturing aluminum foil for use in the tobacco industry, established itself at Cap de La Madeleine and contracted for

3000 h.p. from the Shawinigan company. Besides these large establishments, many other small factories were located in the area through the efforts of the industrial development department. Over 60 such firms, largely in the textile and shoe-manufacturing industries, became new customers for Shawinigan during the years 1930 to 1939. By the end of the decade, with the approach of war, industry began to boom. The Shawinigan company was again increasing its power capacity, with construction underway at La Tuque, and was building a high-tension line across the St. Lawrence to Sorel, where the rising Sorel Steel Industries were already foreshadowing the wartime activity in that center.

VI. *Summary*

The Shawinigan company was founded at the very beginning of the hydroelectric industry, only two years after the completion of the pioneer Niagara Falls installation. It was a daring promotion. Shawinigan Falls itself, a 145-foot drop in the lower St. Maurice River, presented a major engineering challenge to those who would harness it; its location in rugged, relatively inaccessible country some 25 miles north of the St. Lawrence posed difficult construction problems; and the economically undeveloped state of Quebec offered few ready markets for electricity even if the engineering problems were solved and the construction difficulties overcome. But these problems were boldly faced by a group of Boston capitalists and Quebec men of affairs led by J. E. Aldred, who in his youth in Lawrence, Massachusetts, had known at first hand the potentialities of water power. Money was somehow raised, and construction was started in 1898. An attack was made on the marketing problem by attracting the Northern Aluminum Company and the Belgo-Canadian Pulp and Paper Company to Shawinigan Falls, and hydraulic power was sold to these companies as a means of earning some immediate revenue. A contract was made to sell electricity to the Montreal Light, Heat and Power Company, and with the completion of a 90-mile transmission line to Montreal in 1903, the longest line then in existence, the Shawinigan company established a firm hold on life. The success of the line gave investors confidence in the company, and finance became less of a problem. Company engineers were emboldened to lay the first submarine cable across the St. Lawrence. A carbide company was set up in Shawinigan Falls to provide a market for off-peak power. Retail sales were energetically promoted.

Progress was gradual but steady in the next dozen years, and then the company began to grow rapidly as the first world war brought an acceleration in the general demand for electricity. The war years also saw the foundation of the Shawinigan chemical industries when, on the invitation of the British Government, the Shawinigan company devised a means of manufacturing acetic acid from acetylene gas, itself a product of calcium carbide. A brief recession at the end of the war was replaced by a peacetime boom in the twenties. Shawinigan's growth during the decade was in large part based on an enormous expansion of the pulp and paper industry in Quebec, but it also reflected a strong upward trend in the general demand for electricity for lighting and power purposes. The chemical industry was the part of the Shawinigan enterprises that had suffered most from the disappearance of wartime markets, but an expanded research program into the derivatives of acetylene gas proved fruitful, and by the end of the twenties a wide variety of chemical products for peacetime uses was being manufactured at Shawinigan Falls.

By 1930, after fifteen years of rapid expansion, the Shawinigan company, with a generating plant of nearly 700,000-h.p. capacity, had become firmly established as the leading power company in Quebec and one of the largest hydroelectric companies in the world. The depression was, of course, a severe blow to the company, but except for a couple of years at the beginning of the thirties it had the effect of slowing down Shawinigan's growth rather than reversing it. The company's main problem was one of excess capacity, resulting on the one hand from the large additions to plant that had been brought into operation in the late twenties and on the other from the prostration of its largest customer, the pulp and paper industry. This problem was met by selling enormous amounts of secondary power for use in electric boilers which were installed mainly in pulp and paper plants. The electric boiler had been invented at the end of the first world war to help solve the surplus power problem that resulted from the disappearance of wartime demands and the depression of the early twenties, but its large-scale use was deferred until the next decade when it provided the major means of dealing with the much larger excess capacity problem of the thirties. The thirties were a long, sluggish decade, but Shawinigan was shielded from the devastation that overcame many other industries in the depression by a continued trend to electrification in the home and in the factory, and by the company's vigorous chemical affiliate, which by the middle thirties was participating in the growing plastics industry. By the end of the decade, with the partial recovery of the pulp and paper industry, Shawinigan was again thinking in terms of increasing its generating capacity.

Then came World War II and growth on a scale that the company had never before experienced.

In 1939, the Shawinigan company stood on the threshold of the greatest expansion in its history. The new war led to an expansion of the chemical industry at Shawinigan Falls comparable to its expansion in World War I, and after 1939 the aluminum industry's demands for power grew to unprecedented proportions. Nor has the postwar period brought any cessation in the growth of Shawinigan's business, if we except the reduction of part of the abnormal wartime aluminum load. Chemicals, pulp and paper, and especially the retail business of the company, are all booming,[75] and the inauguration of the new Quebec Iron and Titanium company brought a huge new load onto the company's lines in 1953.

Two of the main architects of the Shawinigan company did not live to witness this chapter of Shawinigan's history. Julian C. Smith, who had come to the company in 1910 on the invitation of Wallace C. Johnson, with whom he had worked at Niagara Falls, and who had been president of the company since 1933, died in 1939. And Mr. Aldred, who had guided the enterprise, first as treasurer and then as president, until 1933, at which time he became Chairman of the Board, died in 1941. He had lost a large part of his fortune in the stock market crash of 1929. For all his financial experience he thought in terms of industrial rather than pecuniary values; as a former colleague of his expresses it, he knew that Shawinigan was "good" and therefore refused to sell his holdings in the company in the firm belief that the crash of 1929 was but a temporary financial aberration. Characteristically, he built the Aldred Building in Montreal as a gesture of defiance in the very teeth of the depression.[76] Initiative, stubborn persistence, and integrity are traits admirably suited to the task of building up an industry, but they become liabilities in a fickle stock market. The Shawinigan Water and Power Company, rather than the Aldred Building, is the living reminder of Aldred's contribution to the economic development of Quebec.

In a later chapter we shall attempt to appraise the contribution of the electric power industry as a whole to the economic development of Quebec. The last two chapters have shown what a prominent role The Shawinigan Water and Power Company has played in Quebec's electrical history. From the point of view of the industry itself, the Shawinigan enterprise has been an exemplary technological leader, an imaginative and aggressive business concern, and the main source of electrical supply for the province. From the point of view of Quebec, Shawinigan's impact has been felt in various ways. Indirectly, by supplying power to the Montreal Light, Heat and

Power Company, Shawinigan has supported the growth of the metropolis and main manufacturing center of Quebec. More directly, it has organized the power supply of a large part of the province and provided electricity for general purposes, either by retail sales to final consumers or through wholesale deliveries to distributing companies. Finally, the most striking aspect of the Shawinigan enterprise has been its direct promotion of manufacturing development in the province. It brought the aluminum reduction and carbide industries to Shawinigan Falls, built up a large chemical industry, encouraged the pulp and paper, textile, chemical, and other industries to locate in the St. Maurice Valley, and has been instrumental in bringing many smaller factories to its territory along the banks of the St. Lawrence.

CHAPTER 5

The Montreal Light, Heat and Power Company

1. *Introduction*

The Montreal Light, Heat and Power Company[1] is the only power company in Quebec that has been built up on the basis of an exclusively urban market. Such a development has been uncommon in hydroelectric affairs, for major water-power sites commonly are found in relatively inaccessible areas remote from large cities and therefore usually supply electricity to at least that part of the countryside between the power site and the main load centers. Montreal, however, is situated at the confluence of the Ottawa and St. Lawrence Rivers and is within a few miles of enormous water resources. The Montreal company has therefore been able to confine its energies to a very small geographical area. Until the construction of the Beauharnois plant on the St. Lawrence River in the early 1930's, only a minute fraction of the power resources in the Montreal area had been developed, but this fraction was sufficient to supply a large part of the city's demand. For the rest, Montreal purchased its requirements from the Shawinigan company, and since this power was delivered at Montreal, the Montreal company again did not need to extend its operations beyond the city.

The Montreal concern thus forms the strongest possible contrast with the Shawinigan company in the geographical extent of its operations. In other respects, too, the two companies are quite different. Whereas Shawinigan was founded as a production enterprise, the Montreal company was promoted by Mr. (later Sir) Herbert Holt as a consolidation of the existing electric and gas utilities in the city. Aldred of Shawinigan, though by profession a financier, was in essence a builder and a producer. Holt, who was the dominant personality in the Montreal Company — he was its president until 1932, and then chairman of the board until his death in 1941 — was an engineer by training, but his chief qualities seem to have been those of the astute businessman and clever financier. Shawinigan was technologically precocious and built up its own physical plant. The Montreal company was technologically undistinguished and bought most of its power stations. The Shawinigan company has been mainly a wholesaler of power; the Montreal company has been primarily concerned with the retail markets for domestic and commercial lighting and industrial power. Shawinigan had to develop much of the market for its power; the Montreal company in order to prosper had only to defend its monopoly position in Montreal. The Shawinigan company was quite profitable, the Montreal company enormously so.

II. *Early Electrical Installations in Montreal*

The history of electricity in Montreal goes back to the early days of electric lighting and the time when each inventor was promoting his own electrical "system."[2] Street lighting was regularized in 1889 when the city signed a contract for this purpose with the Royal Electric Company, which already had arc-lighting installations on a few of the main streets.[3] A second contract ran for ten years from 1893, at a price of $124 per arc per year for the first five years, $120 for the next three years, and $117 (later reduced to $90) for the final two years. In 1903 a new five-year contract was signed with the Royal Electric Company, by then part of the Montreal Light, Heat and Power Company, at a rate of $60 per arc. At that time, there were 1280 arc lights in the city and 600 gas lamps, the latter operated by the Montreal Gas Company at a charge of only $17 per lamp per year.[4]

Other markets for electricity were beginning to appear in Montreal in the 1890's. Arc lights were increasingly used in commercial establishments and domestic sales for incandescent lighting began to mount rapidly, but the growth of a market for electric power was the development of major interest. The Montreal Street Railway Company, which had been operating with horse-cars since 1861, introduced its first electric car in 1892. "The progress under the electric regime was immediate . . . and the business of the Company grew in such manner as to enforce frequent increases in its capital, while dividends at the rate of 8 per cent per annum were paid."[5]

At first the tramway company produced its own electricity; in 1894 it operated two steam plants in Montreal with an aggregate capacity of between 3500 and 4000 h.p. As its business expanded, the company found it necessary to rely increasingly on purchased power to supplement its own generating facilities. In 1901, it had more than doubled its own capacity and in addition was purchasing 5000 h.p. from the Montreal Light, Heat and Power Company. The company contracted for 2000 h.p. from Shawinigan in 1905 and made additional purchases in the following years. By 1910 the tramway system had a steam capacity of some 15,000 h.p. and was purchasing 12,800 h.p. from other companies.[6]

Manufacturing industry was also experimenting with electric drive. In 1898 the Dominion Cotton Mills had to replace their old steam equipment; after carefully considering the probable reliability of electrical power and its cost relative to steam power, they decided to switch to electricity. A contract for 3000 h.p. was signed with the Royal Electric Company

> which, on account of limited service, made the price attractive to the Cotton Company, and the agreement was so drawn as to provide every possible safeguard and penalty against interruption of service. The limited service provided that power should not be used by the Cotton Company during the six winter months between the hours of 4 and 7 p.m. so as not to lap onto the Electric Company's lighting load. . .[7]

The experiment was fully satisfactory. The initial investment was smaller than what would have been required to build a new steam plant, and

> Considering the interest and depreciation on a steam plant, the cost of the rental electric power was no more than steam would have cost. . . [Moreover] all that could reasonably be expected in the way of flexibility, centralization of control, reduction of attendance, and minimization of stoppages together with ability to make up for delays by running any desired section overtime was accomplished. . .[8]

By 1904, the works of the Locomotive and Machine Company of Montreal were electrified. Two generators, one operated by a steam engine, and the other by power purchased from Shawinigan Falls, provided current for the lighting system (both arc and incandescent) and for the operation of some 140 electric motors of from 3- to 60-h.p. capacity. The Angus Shops of the Canadian Pacific Railway, which were built in 1902, used 200 motors, most of them alternating-current machines. The power for these motors, and for the lighting system, was produced on the premises by steam engines connected to Canadian General Electric Company generators.[9] These plants were the important forerunners of the electrical age in Montreal industry.

III. *Formation and Early Development, 1901–1910*

It was in this experimental stage of a new industry that the various electrical enterprises in Montreal were brought together to form the Montreal Light, Heat and Power Company in 1901. Promoted by Herbert S. Holt, formerly an engineer with the Canadian Pacific Railroad, and R. Forget, a financier, the new consolidation soon became the sole supplier of all gas and electricity used in the Montreal area. The initial amalgamation brought one gas and three electric companies under unified control.[10]

The major electrical component of the new concern was the Royal Electric Company in which the Forget brothers were interested, and its merger with the Montreal Gas Company in 1895 was the forerunner of the main consolidation in 1901. The Royal Electric Company, formed in 1884, had become the most important electrical company in Montreal. A very profitable firm, it had paid 8 per cent dividends on its stock since its inception. The company's physical assets included arc- and incandescent-lighting systems and a steam-generating plant.[11] The other two electrical companies acquired were the Montreal and St. Lawrence Light and Power Company and the Imperial Electric Light Company. The former was the successor to the Chambly Manufacturing Company which had been incorporated in 1888 to harness the rapids on the Richelieu River. It was a pioneer enterprise, having built a 20,000-h.p. station at Chambly on the Richelieu River in 1898.[12] Power from this station was first transmitted to Montreal, 16 miles distant, over a 25,000-volt line in August 1899. The Imperial Electric Light Company, formed in 1896 as successor to La Compagnie Electrique St. Jean Baptiste which had been incorporated three years earlier, operated a distribution system in Montreal that was supplied from a steam station in the north end of the city.[13]

The new Montreal concern had no sooner been formed than it came into violent competition with the Lachine Rapids Hydraulics and Land Company Ltd. This company, backed by a strong group of industrial and financial interests in Montreal, had recently absorbed three small electrical companies[14] which operated steam stations in the city. The Lachine company had built the first hydroelectric plant on the St. Lawrence River, its 8000-h.p. plant at Lachine having been brought into operation in 1897. With its acquisitions in Montreal, the Lachine concern was in a position to challenge the Montreal Light, Heat and Power Company, and for a couple of years these two groups engaged in a spirited struggle for city franchises and lighting contracts. The Lachine group greatly strengthened its position toward the end of 1902 when it signed a contract to purchase a large block of power from the Shawinigan company.[15] This increase in its power resources made it a potentially formidable competitor and the Montreal Light, Heat and Power Company accordingly found it the better part of wisdom to coöperate rather than to compete. It therefore bought both the stock and the assets of the Lachine company in 1903 for the exorbitant sum of over $5 million in cash,[16] raised mainly by an issue of 5 per cent bonds. With this purchase, the Montreal Light, Heat and Power Company was for the moment in complete control of the Montreal market.

In terms of physical plant (ignoring the gas properties), the Montreal company now owned hydroelectric stations at Chambly and Lachine, with their transmission lines of 16 and 5 miles respectively; various steam plants, three of which, with an aggregate capacity of between 7000 and 8000 h.p., were being operated; four transformer stations; and a number of separate distribution systems within the city itself, some of which, reflecting the competition of the previous few years, had duplicate poles and lines. The first chore of the new company was to integrate and unify these properties.

The generating plant was in particularly poor condition. The Lachine station produced 60-cycle, 3-phase current; the Chambly plant generated 66-cycle, 2-phase current. Ludicrous measures were taken to overcome the discrepancy. The company first decided to reduce both stations to the common denominator of 63-cycle current, and actually attempted, by speeding up one set of generators, and slowing down the other, to operate them in parallel. Then, since Shawinigan power was 60-cycle, it was decided to standardize at this figure and to reduce the frequency of the Lachine and Chambly stations by one-quarter of a cycle a year until the basis figure of 60 was reached. What in fact was done is not known, but this tampering with frequencies involved the company in a great deal of technical difficulty. Eventually some of the motor equipment in the city had to be rebuilt, and until the frequency was settled, it is not hard to guess that alternating-current motors operated by purchased power in Montreal gave something less than satisfactory performance.[17] The operation of the Chambly plant was giving much difficulty because of the formation of frazil ice in the Ste. Thérèse Rapids above the power dam. The company decided, therefore, to rebuild the station and to raise the dam in order to drown out the rapids; a pool of still water that would reduce the menace of frazil ice would thereby be created at the headrace. Work was started on this project in 1901 and was to be completed in 1903, but in the latter year the dam broke, causing serious damage to the property, and it was not until 1907 that the company could announce the completion of the reconstructed station. Even afterwards, ice troubles plagued the Chambly station, and it never gave full satisfaction.

From the first, the company had determined to use its steam station for reserve capacity only; even at that time hydroelectric power probably enjoyed a clear cost advantage over steam electricity, and the rapid progress in hydraulic and hydroelectric technique gave promise that the enormous power resources of the St. Lawrence could soon be successfully harnessed. After 1909, when the company brought into operation a new hydroelectric plant at the Soulanges rapids, the steam stations were operated only to a limited extent. Nevertheless, in the early years the company attempted to keep a rough ratio between its steam reserve and its total capacity. A 2000-h.p. addition was thus made to its Queen Street stream station in 1907, and plans were being made to build a large new steam station in 1913.[18]

Integration of the competing distribution systems in the city was effected over a period of years. A new modern substation was built in 1902, and this and the other four substations in the city were interconnected. The company's various stores and repair shops, scattered throughout the city, were brought together into one building, thus providing for more efficient servicing facilities.

Relations with the city authorities were bad from the beginning. In certain sections of the city, the civic authorities insisted on distribution by underground cable, and the company complained that this was so much more expensive than overhead lines that rates would have to be raised in the underground distribution areas.[19] A long dispute with the City Council about charges for street lighting during the period when there had been no contract, and about taxation of the company's property along the city streets, was not settled until 1911. The company complained of heavy depreciation because of the city's demands: "To conform with [the] contract secured from the City of Montreal during the year and to meet the advancement in the art, the city street-lighting system has undergone a complete change, involving the replacement of the entire equipment of lamps and station apparatus at a cost of upwards of $225,000.00, and consequent discarding of the old equipment."[20] This statement may refer to the changeover from arc to incandescent lamps for street-lighting purposes.[21]

As well as rationalizing its existing plant, the Montreal company had to increase its supply of power in order to meet the growing demands on its system. Domestic customers had nearly doubled from 10.4 thousand in 1903 to 19.4 thousand in 1910; a similar growth had taken place in the number of industrial customers; and sales had risen from 79.5 million kwhs. in

1903 to 176.5 million kwhs. in 1910. This increase was met partly by increased production in the company's plants and partly by increased purchases from Shawinigan under the 1903 contract, about 70 million kwhs. coming from this source in 1910. Demand was pressing on capacity, however, and provision for further supplies had to be made. The first step in this direction was made in 1907 when the company started construction on its Soulanges station — the only station which the company ever planned and built entirely by itself.

The initial expansion of capacity followed a financial consolidation by which, in 1904, the Montreal company had acquired the Provincial Light, Heat and Power Company. This company, incorporated in 1901, had been promoted chiefly by one M. P. Davis, who had secured for the concern the right to the use of all the surplus water of the Soulanges Canal.[22] Davis was paid handsomely for his efforts and used the money to acquire most of the Provincial company's stock, which he then transferred to the Montreal company.[23] Herbert Holt became president of the Provincial company in 1904, and two years later an agreement was signed under which the Montreal company was to develop the site and transmit the power to Montreal. Construction began in 1907, but there was a delay in the proceedings, caused by the failure of a contractor to fulfil his agreement, and it was not until 1909 that the Soulanges station, of approximately 5350 h.p., came into operation.

In the same year, the capacity of the Lachine plant was raised from 10,000 h.p. to 15,800 h.p. By 1910, then, the company was operating three stations, one of 20,000 h.p. at Chambly on the Richelieu River, and two on the St. Lawrence River at Lachine and the Soulanges Canal — in all, a combined capacity of some 41,000 h.p. About 11,000 h.p. of this total came into operation in 1909 and the Montreal company probably used the increase to good effect in negotiating a new contract with Shawinigan in 1910. The contract provided for an immediate increase in power deliveries from Shawinigan Falls and for annual increments in such deliveries up to a level of 63,000 h.p. Under these arrangements, the annual purchases of the Montreal company more than doubled in the next few years. Such purchases not only helped to provide for future growth in the Montreal load, but also provided a reserve on which the company could draw in years when production in its own plants was seriously reduced by ice problems.

By 1910 the Montreal Light, Heat and Power Company had become well established. It dominated the Montreal market, its sales were growing every year, and it had made provision for power supplies which were adequate for the immediate future. Moreover, it was a very profitable concern. In spite of the large inflation of both bonded indebtedness and share capital involved in the formation of the company in 1901 and its purchase of the Lachine company in 1903, bond interest was paid regularly, dividends rose from $587,000 in 1902 to $1,190,000 in 1910, and during the same period undistributed profits and reserves other than depreciation accumulated to the extent of $2,543,000.[24] The promoters, even the most avaricious among them, must surely have been satisfied.

The early history of the Montreal company set the tone for its subsequent development. Founded by financiers, the company's obvious purpose was to achieve control of the lucrative urban market. Defense of its monopoly position and exploitation of its market — with all the overtones of that word — were, first and last, to be the guiding principles of its operations.

Thus dedicated to pecuniary success, the company was uninterested in technological matters. It displayed an appalling engineering weakness, as shown in the early manipulations of frequency, in the bungling of the reconstruction at Chambly, and in the delays involved in the construction of the Soulanges plant. More generally, none of the three plants owned by the company was ever completely satisfactory in operation. For this, of course, the company was not wholly to blame — it had inherited the first two plants, and the technology of the time had not yet proved very successful in dealing with the ice problems that bedevilled all three plants — but it is fair to point out that the company displayed no great initiative in improving the situation.

Primarily, indeed, it was a distribution company, and its technological record in that branch of operations was somewhat better. Although it had had to be goaded by the civic authorities into improving its street-lighting system in 1910, it later seems to have invested sufficient funds to keep its general service in Montreal at a satisfactory level of efficiency. In the course of time, the company constructed a ring of high-tension wires around the city, which was fed by various power stations in the area and by Shawinigan power, and which fed in turn the thirty-six substations owned by the company at the time of its expropriation in 1944.

Technological unconcern and acute concern for profits made for passivity. Although it was situated within a few miles of the largest power resources in the province, the Montreal company never made a move entirely on its own initiative to develop them or to extend its influence outside of Montreal. It was satisfied to act as lord of its own domain, a policy which required only defense of that domain. Curiously, as a by-product of defense, the Montreal company became the second largest power producer in Quebec.

IV. *Defense of Monopoly and Expansion of Capacity*

The Problem

Although the Montreal Light, Heat and Power Company held an apparently enviable position by 1910, in reality its situation was by no means secure from the long-run point of view. Its very profitability was a standing invitation to competitors, which did not fail to materialize. It was also insecure for another reason. As a monopolist, the company had no desire to see its market deluged by large supplies of power, but it was bounded on three sides by large water powers, any one of which if developed by a competitor might seriously threaten to take control of the Montreal market. To the east, the large powers of the St. Maurice River were already being developed. To the north lay the immense undeveloped powers of the Ottawa River, and to the west the still larger undeveloped resources of the St. Lawrence. The Montreal company had no desire to utilize these resources itself, since it did not want to flood its own market, and it could not afford to have others do so. Yet the company had to increase its own generating capacity sufficiently to provide for its growing market — or at least sufficiently to avoid falling into the arms of Shawinigan through too much dependence on that company for its power supplies. A delicate balance would have to be maintained: development of resources would have to be geared to the market's requirements; more rapid development would be ruinous. The best strategy seemed to be to proceed cautiously, to build up financial strength, and to deal with each challenge as it arose.

Rivalry and Partnership with Shawinigan

The first thrust came from the east, and we have already described how it was met. Shawinigan's determination to transmit power from the St. Maurice River to Montreal and to deliver it to the Montreal company's chief rival, the Lachine company, was met by the purchase of that rival at a generous price. The struggle, however, went on. By the terms of a 1907 agreement, Shawinigan was allowed to deliver power directly to large customers in the Montreal area, and Shawinigan immediately signed contracts with the Montreal Street Railway and with a large cement company. Obviously the Montreal company was becoming embarrassed by a shortage of power, and the tide of battle was running in favor of Shawinigan. The Montreal group then expanded its capacity at Lachine and built a new plant at Soulanges. Purchases from Shawinigan in 1910 fell slightly below the level of the previous year, and this break in the trend seems to have frightened the Shawinigan company. An honorable peace was arranged in 1910 whereby the Shawinigan company was assured of a growing market for its power in Montreal, and the Montreal company gained much needed power supplies and assurance of retaining its independence. On the whole, the Montreal company had made a good bargain.[25] It profited still more when its recent rival became an ally for the purpose of developing a large power site at Cedars Rapids on the St. Lawrence River, some thirty miles west of Montreal.

The Cedars Rapids project was ideally suited to the Montreal company's purposes. It would protect its western flank from potential competitors, and there was little danger that the Shawinigan company, with its main interests on the St. Maurice would become the dominant partner in a St. Lawrence project. Moreover, the Cedars Rapids development would not embarrass the Montreal market, since the Aluminum Company of America at Massena, New York, was anxious to buy the bulk of the station's output; on the contrary, by means of future extensions the Cedars Rapids development could provide for the needs of the Montreal market for some years to come. Finally, one might add, with Shawinigan engineers supervising the construction, there would be no question of the technical performance of the Cedars Rapids plant. Thus, in equal partnership, the Shawinigan and Montreal companies in 1912 undertook the first sizable hydroelectric development on the St. Lawrence River.[26]

Construction was begun in 1912 under the direction of Shawinigan's engineering staff, and the installation was completed to the extent of 100,000 h.p. by 1914.[27] The station was operated by the Montreal company, although the Cedars Rapids company's top executives were Shawinigan people: J. E. Aldred was its president and Howard Murray its vice-president. In 1916, however, control of the company passed to the Civic Investment and Industrial Company, Holt's newly organized holding company.

The station had been built to supply power to the Massena plant of the Aluminum Company of America, and also to service the Montreal market. In 1913 the Montreal company built a transmission line from Cedars Rapids to Montreal and contracted for 60,000 h.p. from the new development, 20,000 h.p. of which was to be taken immediately on completion of the project. Another 60,000 h.p. was exported to Massena under an 80-year contract with the Aluminum company. In addition, "a certain amount of local business has been satisfactorily taken care of through the operation of the Vaudreuil Electric Company, Ltd., a subsidiary . . . which has installed lines as far as the plant of Curtis's and Harvey, near Rigaud, providing also for the intervening Towns of Hudson and Como."[28] With its purchases from

Cedars Rapids, and with the additional power that could be obtained there simply by installing more generators, the Montreal company was assured of ample power supplies for some time to come.[29]

Competition in Montreal

Meanwhile, a threat to the company had developed in Montreal itself with the formation in 1912 of the Montreal Public Service Corporation. This concern was the end product of a consolidation engineered by J. W. McConnell, a Montreal financier who in 1912 brought together an independent hydroelectric company, the Montreal Street Railway Company, and three small steam electric companies which had grown up in the Montreal area.

We must go back to 1904 to begin the story:

Sometime during the years 1903 or 1904, a French-Canadian by the name of E. A. Robert acquired certain water power sites on the St. Lawrence which were transferred to Canadian Light and Power Company (incorporated 1904) and financed by J. W. McConnell. Originally this company was financed by selling bonds with bonus common stock. It appears $4 million of bonds was sold to make the initial 20,000 h.p. development and $6 million of stock was issued. The stock in 1910 was selling around 62.[30]

The power site referred to was near St. Timothée on the south shore of the St. Lawrence (opposite the Cedars Rapids site), and water for the power development was to be drawn from the old Beauharnois Canal. The site was developed to the extent of 22,500 h.p. in 1910, and as the project neared completion the Canadian Light and Power Company began to look around for a market for its power.

In the Fall of 1910 it was evident that the McConnell interests were buying up the stock of the Montreal Street Railway Company (paying 10%) and the price rose to $251 a share. The Directors of the Montreal Light, Heat and Power Company, from whom the railway purchased its power, met with the idea of forming a consolidation which would ward off the McConnell interests. They outlined a plan of forming a holding company into which the stocks of the lighting and railway companies would be turned . . . it soon appeared that this move was hopelessly too late and the matter was dropped.[31] . . . On November 2, 1910, the McConnell interests appeared at the annual meeting of the Montreal Street Railway Company with the controlling vote, and ejected the entire old management.[32]

Plans were immediately made by the victors to amalgamate the Canadian Light and Power Company with the tramway company. A new corporation, the Montreal Tramways and Power Company, was incorporated in London in December 1910, and having obtained permission to do business in Canada, proceeded to exchange its shares for the common stock of the power and tramways companies. By 1912, then, Messrs. McConnell and Robert, who controlled the new company, were in charge of the street railway system in Montreal and had thus found one outlet for the power from their generating station at St. Timothée.

Preparations had also been made to sell electricity at retail in Montreal, for the Canadian Light and Power Company had acquired the Central Heat, Light and Power Company, which owned a small distribution system in the city. This latter company, however, soon became part of a larger corporate structure; again we must go back a few years to begin the story. In 1908 an amalgamation of three small electrical companies in the Montreal area had been effected by the Saraguay Electric and Water Company,[33] which in 1912 changed its name to the Public Service Corporation of Montreal. In the same year, the Central Heat, Light and Power Company was sold by the Canadian Light and Power Company to the Public Service Corporation,[34] which then became the distributing organization for the St. Timothée power plant. Who the promoters of these earlier companies were is not known, but the McConnell interests were almost certainly in charge by 1912. In any event, by the end of World War I the Public Service Corporation was an integral part of McConnell's holding company, the Montreal Tramways and Power Company, Ltd.

A circular issued by the Public Service Corporation in 1919 stated that it delivered 10,000 h.p. under a 50-year contract to the Montreal Tramways Company, furnished street lighting in part of the city and suburbs, and served nearly 14,000 domestic customers throughout a large section of Montreal. Besides obtaining power from the hydroelectric plant at St. Timothée, the corporation had a small steam reserve capacity in Montreal. The circular ended with the following, probably overly optimistic, statement of its position:

> The system of the Montreal Public Service Corporation has been well maintained and operated. The Company is the only real competitor of the Montreal Light, Heat, and Power Company, and as such has been largely instrumental in securing and maintaining the present low rates for electrical light and power, and as the distribution system now well covers the city of Montreal, the Company is in a position to materially increase its business. . . . and we believe that the future of the Company is assured and most promising.[35]

Thus by a series of moves, the McConnell-Robert group seems to have built up a small but integrated system that could compete effectively with the Montreal company. Its strongest feature was its control of the tramways market; its fatal weaknesses proved to be the lack of power resources for expansion and a deficiency of financial strength. Its only developed power site was at St. Timothée, and its only undeveloped resources consisted of a power site on the south shore of the St. Lawrence at Lachine, which had a potential of about 50,000 h.p.[36]

The structure began to break up in the early twenties. In its decade of existence, the tramways company had encountered unsettled financial markets and a business recession upon the outbreak of war, followed by supply difficulties and inflation after 1917; perhaps the sharp depression of 1921 was the final blow. At any rate the Montreal Tramways and Power Company had never been financially successful. By 1923 it had lost control of the Montreal Public Service Corporation,[37] and the following year the holding company itself succumbed.[38]

In 1924 the Shawinigan and Montreal companies combined to form United Securities Ltd., which took over the Montreal Public Service Corporation (now known as the Quebec–New England Hydro-Electric Corporation) and the Montreal Tramways and Power Company, Ltd. Shawinigan executives took over the direction of the Canadian Light and Power Company (which owned the St. Timothée power station) and the Montreal Tramways Company.[39] In 1926 the shares of the Quebec–New England Hydro-Electric Corporation were all sold to the Montreal Light, Heat and Power Consolidated,[40] which had already written the obituary of its former competitor:

> [During 1924 the Company] acquired the business of the Quebec–New England Hydro-Electric Corporation, operating in the same territory as your Company with parallel lines and substations — a duplication unnecessary and unwarranted. This absorption, like past consolidations, will ultimately accrue to the benefit of the public by the elimination of waste and duplication; incidentally it will clear the streets of a lot of unnecessary poles and wires.[41]

"Ultimately" may mean a very long time. The immediate result of the purchase was that the Montreal company celebrated the recovery of its monopoly position by raising its dividend rate from 6 per cent in 1923 to 8 per cent in the last quarter of 1925. Between the same two years electric rates were reduced from 4 cents per kwh. to 3.5 cents per kwh.

The Montreal Island Power Company

Another enterprise which was building a generating station on the north shore of Montreal Island was bought out before its development was completed. This was the Montreal Island Power Company, incorporated in 1923. Owned by the Harold Walker paper interests, the plant was built to supply power for a paper mill nearby. In 1927 the Montreal company contracted with this company "for the output of its pending development on Rivière des Prairies, commonly known as Back River. The power from this source is estimated at 65,000 h.p. and with other unsold resources of the kind will keep Montreal supplied with electric power for many years to come. Incidentally, your Company has a substantial interest in the Montreal Island Power Company."[42] Ownership of this company was at first shared with a holding company, the Power Corporation of Canada, but the Montreal group later became the owner of over 90 per cent of the shares of the Montreal Island Power Company.

The purchase of this company seems to have been largely a defensive move on the part of the Montreal company to protect its recently restored monopoly position in the area. It had no urgent need for increased generating capacity at the time, especially in view of the fact that additions made at Cedars Rapids in 1924 had brought that plant to its full capacity of 197,400 h.p.

Beauharnois Power Company

After 1930, the Montreal company was engaged in gently parrying another potential threat of enormous proportions on its western flank. At last an entrepreneur had undertaken to harness the St. Lawrence on a scale appropriate to its resources: one R. O. Sweezey had plans under way to build a hydroelectric plant with an initial capacity of 650,000 h.p. near Beauharnois, on the south side of the river.[43] Most of the power from this initial development was to be exported to Ontario, but the magnitude of the undertaking was a clear and present danger to control of the Montreal market.

The Montreal company took the challenge in its stride. It established contact with the new concern in 1929 by contracting for the purchase of 150,000 h.p. of Beauharnois power, delivery to be taken in stipulated quantities over a period of years commencing in 1932.[44] To this end, the company in the following year built a high-tension transmission line interconnecting its Cedars Rapids plant, the Beauharnois plant, and its Atwater substation in Montreal. The next step came in 1933 when the Montreal company underwrote nearly nine million dollars' worth of Beuharnois bonds in order to allow the company to complete its development.[45] Finally, the Beauharnois company's position having been undermined by Ontario's unilateral repudiation of its power contracts in 1935 and 1936, the financial strength of the

Montreal company was called into play and in 1937 the Beauharnois Power Company became a subsidiary of Montreal Light, Heat and Power Consolidated.[46] For thirty-five years, then, the Montreal company had successfully protected its position in Montreal.[47] In the process it had acquired all the hydroelectric capacity in the area — the huge installation at Beauharnois, the large Cedars Rapids plant, and the two smaller stations of the Montreal Island Power Company and the former Canadian Light and Power Company.[48] With its final purchase of the Beauharnois property in 1937, the Montreal company became something more than an urban electrical enterprise. By its very size it was now forced into the arena of politics and exposed to the full glare of the public gaze.[49] Its financial strength was insufficient protection in its new position — became, in fact, political weakness — and in 1944 the company went down under the *force majeure* of the state. In a sense its greatest triumph led directly to its downfall.

v. *The Company's Business, 1902–1940*

The Montreal company grew up with its city — whose population increased from about one-third of a million in 1901 to over a million in 1941 — and with the electrical age. Throughout these forty years the population of Montreal grew at an average rate of almost 3 per cent per annum, while the company's sales grew at an average rate of nearly 10 per cent per annum. The Montreal company had no need to search for markets: it proved very profitable simply to service the customers clamoring at its door. The locational attractions of the city itself were sufficient to ensure industrial growth, and the company's industrial development activities were confined to arranging for a secondary-power market during the depression of the thirties. The growth of the company's business therefore poses no particular problem,[50] and in its quantitative aspect is adequately described by Table 7. Here it remains only to comment briefly on qualitative aspects and on the company's financial results.

In 1902, when it was making application to be listed on the New York Stock Exchange, the company described its business as follows:

> The Company controls all the gas business in the City of Montreal and its suburbs, does all the municipal lighting of the City and several of the suburbs, furnishes 133,299 incandescent lights, 1,536 arc lights, 6,315 electrical horsepower to the city and public and 5,000 electrical horse power to the Montreal Street Railway Company under contract running until 1923.[51]

By 1908 the incandescent lighting load had increased to about 339,000 lamps, and the installation of arc lamps for street-lighting and commercial purposes

TABLE 7

THE MONTREAL LIGHT, HEAT AND POWER CONSOLIDATED et al., 1913–1940 [a]

(Millions of kwhs.)

Year	Supply									Sales							
	Chambly [b]	Lachine [c]	Soulanges [d]	St. Timothée [e]	Cedars	Montreal Island Power Co.	Beauharnois	Shawinigan (purchases from) [f]	Total available	Export to Aluminum Co. of America	To Hydro-Electric Power Comm. of Ontario	Total sales in Montreal area [g]	Secondary sales	Domestic and commercial [h]	Other [i]	Total sales	Total available minus total sales [j]
1913	52	50	48					158	309			324				324	—15
1914	48	45	39					208	341			352				352	—11
1915	59	38	39		340			163	640	303		350				653	—13
1916	79	43	43		539			183	887	449		459				908	—21
1917	77	41	45		567			200	930	394		539				934	— 3
1918	79	40	47		594			208	968	390		575				965	— 3
1919	64	23	28		536			187	840	321		523				844	— 5
1920	65	37	35		543			215	895	329		571				900	— 5
1921	43	11	28		600			211	893	336		563				898	— 5
1922	48	6	16		628			232	930	342		593				935	— 5
1923	49	13	29		730			253	1074	405		678				1084	—10
1924	59	6	25	28	753			269	1141	426		709				1135	6
1925	61	2	34	78	711			273	1159	374		786	10	126	650	1160	— 1
1926	55	4	21	74	773			314	1242	400		851	10	139	702	1251	— 9
1927	48	4	18	80	849			339	1338	449		895	10	158	727	1345	— 7

1928	38	9	22	64	919			378	1430	440		979	15	176	788	1419	11
1929	33	14	23	55	953	17		453	1548	498		1061	15	201	845	1558	−10
1930	33	5	11	79	957	106		440	1632	547		1089	20	220	849	1637	− 4
1931	19	3		79	723	144		572	1539	424		1088	20	239	829	1512	27
1932	8			81	469	172	61	478	1270	241	26	1000	29	250	721	1267	3
1933	1			84	617	136	422	518	1768	310	201	1101	181	240	680	1612	156
1934	7			87	631	168	746	576	2215	403	346	1387	391	244	753	2137	78
1935	23			86	789	194	822	568	2482	406	348	1551	527	252	771	2304	177
1936	25			82	768	214	717	602	2408	433	—	1651	579	272	801	2084	324
1937	24			91	942	245	846	607	2755	666	28	1852	690	291	871	2546	208
1938	18			90	826	227	1106	597	2865	658	602	1420	285	304	831	2680	185
1939	28			85	905	238	1477	628	3362	696	729	1703	490	323	890	3128	233
1940	30			85	1087	257	1888	647	3994	774	738	2227	777	345	1105	3738	256

[a] Source: Hydro Quebec. Some of the figures relate to companies which were at first independent but which later were absorbed by Montreal Light, Heat and Power Consolidated — e.g., Cedars Rapids Power and Manufacturing Company until 1917, Beauharnois Power Company until 1937, etc.

[b] Installed 1896, to be shut down and dismantled 1952.

[c] Installed 1898, shut down and dismantled 1932.

[d] Installed 1906, shut down and dismantled 1931.

[e] Installed 1910, acquired by the Montreal Light, Heat and Power Cons. in 1924.

[f] Figures for purchases from Shawinigan are available from 1907 on. In millions of kilowatt hours, from 1907 to 1912 inclusive, they are as follows: 45.4; 62.8; 70.4; 67.6; 74.5; 120.3.

[g] These figures are available from 1903 on, and are as follows from 1903 to 1912 inclusive: 79.5; 85.6; 93.5; 116.7; 130.9; 135.4; 164.4; 176.5; 211.4; 269.3.

[h] Not available until 1925.

[i] These figures are arrived at by subtracting secondary sales and domestic and commercial sales from total sales in the Montreal area. They are presumably comprised mainly of industrial sales. Sales to other utility companies on the island of Montreal, and miscellaneous items would account for the remainder.

[j] Apart from items unaccounted for, these differences probably result from two factors. Output from the Company's steam station is not included in the table, and this probably explains the surplus of sales over power available. Sales to industries and domestic consumers in the neighbourhood of the Cedars Rapids and Beauharnois stations, not included in the table, probably account for the surplus of power available over sales.

had risen to over 2900 units. Sales to the tramway system increased when a 25-year contract for 7000 h.p. was signed with the Montreal Street Railway Company in 1905, and, in spite of the frequency difficulties of the early years, the industrial load grew as additional motors to an aggregate capacity of over 32,000 h.p. began to draw power from the company's lines during the period 1902 to 1908.[52]

By 1910 the company was well established and thereafter its progress was one of natural growth. Arc lights gave way to incandescent lighting on the streets, the domestic lighting market grew, industrial sales grew rapidly, and after the war the household appliance market began to expand.

The outbreak of war led to a temporary retardation of growth in physical sales, but gross income and profits grew continuously throughout the war years. A large number of disconnections were made in 1915, but in the following year it was noted that satisfactory progress was again being made despite "the fact that there are at present upwards of eight thousand vacant stores and houses in the city and suburbs, incident to the war and recruiting amongst householders. As a matter of fact our increased earnings are in large measure due to electrical power and gas sales for munitions purposes and are, consequently, of a more or less temporary nature." [53] In spite of labor troubles and rising costs during the war, and small reductions in electric-lighting rates in 1916 and 1919, the net earnings of the company after bond interest grew from $2.6 million in 1915 to $3.6 million in 1919. Part of the increased business came from the domestic appliance load which began to grow rapidly during the war, and to promote this business the company opened an electrical-appliance store in the city in 1918. The electrification of the home became possible as the exorbitant rates in existence at the beginning of the century were reduced. Domestic rates in Montreal before the formation of the company were 12.75 cents per kwh., and they were kept at that level until 1908; thereafter they were gradually reduced until they stood at 5 cents per kwh. in 1916.[54]

Throughout the twenties the company's business grew steadily as gas and electric services were extended to the new suburbs of the growing city and as electric appliances in the home became commonplace. Domestic rates were reduced by stages from 4.8 cents per kwh. in 1920 to 3.5 cents in 1925; in 1928 the company belatedly adopted a sliding scale of rates starting at 3.25 cents, and in 1930 the basic rate was lowered to 3¢ per kwh. A special "inducement" tariff was introduced in 1935 and the readjustment of the schedule resulted in a further slight reduction of rates, but no other reductions were made during the depression years.

The opening years of the depression brought a drop in firm power sales from a record 1069 million kwhs. in 1930 to 920 million kwhs. in 1933, but thereafter recovery was rapid and the 1930 peak was exceeded in 1936. Between 1928 and 1933 the company bought out some 15 small electrical companies in the suburban areas around Montreal. Most of these companies were owned by the municipalities concerned, and most of them were simply distributing concerns which purchased their power from the Montreal company. Some, though, like the Lachine and Verdun companies, had generated their own electricity in small steam stations, and the purchase of these systems resulted in a net increase in sales for the Montreal concern. One purpose of these purchases was no doubt to obviate the almost continuous friction which had characterized the company's relations with the municipally owned systems. As one means of establishing more harmonious relations and increasing sales, the company extended its Montreal rates for domestic service to all the municipalities under its control. These numbered 48 in 1934, at which time there were only 2 independent distributing companies left operating in the area. During the depression, domestic sales held up much better than industrial sales of firm power.[55] To take up the slack, secondary-power sales were made in increasing volume after 1932, rising from 181 million kwhs. in that year to nearly 700 million kwhs. in 1937. As in the case of the other electrical companies in the province, the depression for the Montreal company was a decade of retarded growth rather than a business catastrophe.

From the first, the financial policy of Montreal Light, Heat and Power was characterized by a textbook simplicity. The policy was to maximize monopoly profits, and its simplicity was modified only by various corporate reorganizations designed to disguise the real rate of return on invested capital. It was implicitly assumed that the demand for electricity (at least the domestic demand) was inelastic, so that rates were reduced only charily. Even after the gradual reductions of the twenties, Montreal electrical rates were high relative to costs of production and relative to the rates in force in neighboring Ontario.[56] All the economies from the amalgamation of competitive systems into a monopoly organization must have gone directly to bondholders[57] and shareholders. On capital which was liberally watered at the time of amalgamation, the company raised its dividend rate from 4 per cent in 1902 to 5 per cent in 1907, 6 per cent in 1908, 7.5 per cent in 1911 and so on up to almost 10 per cent from 1914 to 1916. In all, from 1902 to 1916 inclusive, the company distributed $16,950,000 in dividends, and at the latter date had $5,742,000 in profits retained in the business.[58]

The management of the company seems to have recognized some "danger point" above which dividends could not in all conscience be allowed to go. Dividend rates of more than 10 per cent were avoided whenever possible, and from 1920 to 1930 the attempt seems to have been to keep the rate under 8 per cent—perhaps because that was quite generally considered to be a "fair" return on capital invested in utilities in the United States. By 1916 the company had been paying nearly 10 per cent dividends for three years, and to remedy this situation a financial reorganization was engineered. In that year, Holt and his colleagues set up the Civic Investment and Industrial Company to acquire control of the Montreal Light, Heat and Power Company and the Cedars Rapids Manufacturing and Power Company. In 1918 the new company changed its name to the Montreal Light, Heat and Power Consolidated, the style which was retained thereafter. The reorganization seems to have had two main purposes. In the first place it was designed to gain control of the Cedars Rapids company for the Montreal group: this was achieved by an offer to exchange one share of stock in the new company for one share of Cedars Rapids stock. (In effect, the Shawinigan company exchanged its half-ownership of the Cedars Rapids development for an increased holding in the Montreal company.) Secondly, and probably of major importance, the reorganization served as a camouflage under cover of which the shareholders of the old Montreal company were enabled to draw increased dividends from their holdings. For each of their old $100 shares the shareholders in the Montreal Light, Heat and Power Company received three $100 shares in the new company, a move by which the book value of the stock in the new company was increased by some $40 million over its previous figure. This inflation of capital allowed the shareholders to assume the appearance of humility and to begin once more at the bottom of the dividend ladder with a shabby, but respectable, 4 per cent payment on the new capital—which was, however, nearly 14 per cent on the old.

During the postwar decade the company again became embarrassingly profitable. Net earnings after bond interest increased from $4.3 million in 1920 to $10.2 million in 1931. During these eleven years $51.6 million were paid out in dividends and interest on debentures, while retained profits increased from $3.5 million to $25.8 million.[59] The dividend rate had been raised from 4 per cent to 5 per cent in 1920, 6 per cent in 1923, 7 per cent in 1924, and 8 per cent in 1925. The danger point had again been reached and another financial reorganization became prudent. The following year, therefore, the owners of the company decided to turn in their old shares and for each such share to give themselves three new, no-par-value common shares and a bonus of one $50 preference share. The bonus preference shares were then promptly redeemed by the company in cash.[60] This capital bonus reduced the book value of the capital invested, and accordingly aggregate divided payments were reduced in an attempt to keep the rate under 8 per cent.

The policy of curtailing dividends, however, involved such enormous yearly additions to profits retained in the company that it soon proved impossible to hold the line and the dividend rate began to creep up beyond 8 per cent. Profits grew so rapidly in the last years of the decade that by 1929, when dividends paid out were over 10 per cent on the book value of capital (or about 35 per cent on the invested capital),[61] a further financial reorganization was clearly necessary. Thus in the following year, the company's stock once more demonstrated its fissiparous qualities when one four-year-old share became two brand new shares. As in 1926, the diluted stock was then given a transfusion of hard cash through the sale of a block of the new shares to the company's employees, customers, and admirers.[62] This new investment of over $20 million raised the book value of capital sufficiently to allow dividend payments to be raised from $4.9 million in 1929 to $5.8 million in 1930 and $6.5 million in 1931 without raising the dividend rate above 10 per cent. Dividends were kept at a constant rate of $1.50 per share throughout the thirties, this figure representing a rate of about 9.8 per cent on the book value of capital. The company had abandoned the unequal struggle to keep dividends down to 8 per cent. Apparently it no longer thought this necessary because, although the depression led to a reduction of profits in 1932 and 1933, the $1.50 dividend rate established in 1930 was maintained simply by setting aside smaller annual amounts to the retained profits account. With recovery in the later thirties and prosperity after 1939 the dividend rate was still maintained, but only at the expense of having the retained profits account grow from $25.8 million in 1931 to $35.6 million by the time of the company's expropriation in 1944.

Such was the fabulous financial record of the Montreal company. Of the $58.5 million which was listed as the book value of its capital in 1944, Ellis found that $42.5 million represented no assets at all, and that only $25.3 million had been paid into the company in cash. All but $1200 of this amount, moreover, had been received from the sale of stock and debentures to customers and employees,[63] a device which power companies used in an attempt to influence the public in favor of private ownership of electrical utilities. Thus, on the promoters' cash investment of virtually zero, the company succeeded in distributing to its shareholders, by way of dividends, interest on debentures, and a cash bonus, about $200 million during its forty-odd years of operations — and still retained in its treasury over $35 million of undistributed profits at the end of the period.

VI. *Summary*

It is difficult to assess the part played by the Montreal Light, Heat and Power enterprise in the economic development of Quebec. It can be said that the company has provided the power necessary for Montreal's industrial growth, and throughout our period Montreal has accounted for about half of all industry in the province. On the other hand, the company appears to have done nothing to stimulate that growth, and therefore deserves no direct credit for it. Nor have the company's large plants at Cedars Rapids and Beauharnois resulted in any significant industrial development along the river above Montreal. Except for a few large power consumers located near Beauharnois, the power from these stations has either been sent to Montreal or exported, Cedars Rapids selling large quantities of its power to the Aluminum Company of America plant at Massena, New York, and Beauharnois selling most of its power to Ontario.

We have suggested that the Montreal company, a monopolist interested primarily in the Montreal market, was a vested interest whose protection involved a retarding of the development of the huge water powers of the St. Lawrence and lower Ottawa Rivers. In turn, this retardation has perhaps acted as a restraining force on the industrial development not only of the western fringe of the province but also of the industrial areas lying to the east of Montreal. Protected from an avalanche of power from the west by the passive, not to say restrictive, policies of the Montreal company, the Shawinigan company and the Southern Canada Power Company have been free to pursue monopolistic policies in their own regions, although the restrictive policies of these companies have been much more apparent in the retail than in the industrial sectors of their businesses.

To place entire responsibility for the slow development of the St. Lawrence powers and for the lack of development of the Ottawa sites on the Montreal company would be unreasonable. Until after World War I, hydraulic technology was perhaps unequal to the task of harnessing these huge powers. Moreover, the difficulty of getting control of the sites as a result of the divided political jurisdiction over these rivers has been a barrier to their development, although how serious this political obstacle has been in fact cannot be determined. Again, if the slowness of development has in part been the result of conscious policy, responsibility for that policy should probably be borne partly by other power companies in the province as well as by the Montreal enterprise. St. Lawrence power was an obvious threat to monopoly in the Montreal market, but it was also, to a lesser extent, a threat to the power industry in the whole province as far east as Quebec City. Finally, of course, it can easily be argued that the Quebec market for power was not large enough to absorb large additions to supply from the St. Lawrence River, and that therefore the rate of development of these resources has not been too small from an economic point of view. This argument, however, does not carry full conviction because of the interdependence between the demand and supply sides of the market for hydroelectric power: with large supplies of power on their hands power companies will display quite amazing enterprise and ingenuity in disposing of it. On the whole, one cannot help wondering what the effect on Quebec's industrial development would have been had the Montreal company been an aggressive enterprise eager to develop the large water powers in its immediate vicinity.

CHAPTER 6

The Southern Canada Power Company

1. *Introduction: The Eastern Townships*

The Southern Canada Power Company, Ltd., is much the smallest of the power companies dealt with in this study, with a total generating capacity of slightly less than 60,000 h.p., or about the size of one large turbine at Beauharnois or Shawinigan Falls. For our purposes, however, its interest is disproportionate to its size because of the part the company has played in the industrial growth of the Eastern Townships, the part of Quebec lying southeast of Montreal on the south side of the St. Lawrence River. Most of this region is served by the Southern Canada company, whose territory is the roughly triangular area formed by the United States border on the south, the Richelieu River on the west, and the St. Francis River on the east (see Figure 1). It is to this Southern Canada territory that we refer when we speak in this chapter of the Eastern Townships, or the Townships, although in general usage the Eastern Townships are considered to include, besides this area, certain counties to the east of the St. Francis River (including the asbestos mining area of Quebec) and a section of the south shore of the St. Lawrence, both of which areas are served by The Shawinigan Water and Power Company.

Except for a belt of mountainous country along the American border, the Townships form part of the St. Lawrence lowlands, and thus include some of the most fertile lands in the province. In spite of this, the Townships have always been something of an economic backwater in the main stream of Canadian development. Only after the American Revolution did they begin to acquire settlers, first a few Loyalists and then Americans moving northward from New Hampshire, Vermont, and New York. In the 1820's immigrants came from the United Kingdom and by mid-century the area was fairly well populated. Then began a demographic revolution. Young English-speaking people began to move westward to new American frontiers, the area was by-passed by immigrants, and the English-speaking population entered a long period of decline. It was replaced by a French-Canadian population which began to move down into the Townships from the St. Lawrence in the 1830's and increased in volume as railways made the area more accessible after 1850. By the end of the century, almost three-quarters of the population was French-Canadian, and the English-speaking group was decreasing absolutely as well as relatively.[1]

When railroads opened the region,[2] a diversification began in the economy of the Townships, which until then had been a typical backwoods agricultural area. From the mixed forests now came raw materials for sawmills, furniture factories, and later for a number of small pulp and paper plants. The mineral resources of the area were made accessible to prospectors, leading to a series of minor "rushes" to gold and copper deposits, some of which supported small mines. (A major mineral discovery occurred in 1876 when asbestos was found around Thetford, to the east of the area in which we are interested.) Finally, the coming of the railroad led to a growth of manufacturing industry in the Townships. In the towns along the railway lines, old village industries were expanded and new enterprises — woodworking plants, metal-working shops, flour mills, and textile plants — were established. In particular, the last quarter of the century saw the opening of a number of textile and garment factories which marked the beginning of what is today the most important industry in the region. Small woolen mills were established at Sherbrooke in 1867 and Coaticook in 1875. The most important newcomer was the Dominion Textile Company, which harnessed a waterfall on the Magog River and established a cotton factory at Magog, southwest of Sherbrooke, in 1882. The silk industry remained unimportant, although a small lace manufactory was set up at Coaticook in 1886, and this enterprise later became part of the Belding-Corticelli firm.

Unlike the industry growing up at the same time in southern Ontario, these new manufacturing establishments in the Townships lacked easy access to coal supplies, and therefore relied mainly on water power.[3] The water-power resources of the Townships were not impressive when judged by the standards of the Laurentian areas of the province. There were, however, many small waterfalls distributed throughout the region, and in the contemporary state of hydraulic technology their smallness was a distinct asset because it meant that they could be harnessed without difficulty. Based on water power, then, this growing manufacturing industry was a type of development similar to that in New England half a century earlier, and indeed the Townships became known as the "New England of Canada." "On pourrait dire familièrement," writes Blanchard, "que le chemin de fer est le père de l'industrie dans les Cantons de L'Est, mais que les forces hydrauliques en sont la mère." [4]

Manufacturing, however, was but a small part of the total economy. Agriculture still was the predominant occupation. The Townships were rural in nature, and by 1910, when the rest of Canada was booming, they had become a drowsy countryside of placid farms. The coming of the French-Canadians had resulted in a decline in commercial farming, for the French-Canadian countryside was made up of family farms operated primarily for sustenance rather than profit, and agricultural technique left much to de desired.[5] By the turn of the twentieth century, the Townships were rapidly assuming the aspect of old Quebec. The scattered manufacturing activity that had grown up since 1850 had made only a feeble impression on the region, for in an industrial sense, too, the growth of the fifties and sixties had been replaced by stagnation. In the latter part of the nineteenth century the vigorous industrial areas were those that could command large supplies of cheap coal; as the comparative industrial history of New England and Pennsylvania demonstrates, hydraulic power had lost its hegemony to steam. Thus by 1900 it had become clear that southern Ontario, with its proximity to the coal areas of the United States, was to be the manufacturing center of Canada. The small waterfalls of the Townships provided at best only a narrow power base for manufacturing development. In spite of its growth during the previous few decades industry in the area had apparently made a false start. Establishments already located there were trapped: sunk costs made it uneconomic to move, power limitations restricted future expansion. Industry in the Townships seemed doomed to slow decay.[6]

II. *Early Electrical Developments*

How would the electrical age affect this somnolent area? Prospects of economic revitalization through the new power were not promising because of the scarcity of large power sites. The St. Francis is the only significant power river in the area, and in spite of the fact that it is fed by half a dozen lakes, the largest of which are Memphremagog, Aylmer, and St. Francis, the river's flow is very irregular. Small storage dams built in 1917 by the Quebec Streams Commission at the outlets of lakes Aylmer and St. Francis ameliorated conditions to some extent, but even today the river is subject to heavy flows in the early spring and very low water in the later summer. The best power sites are located at East Angus, Sherbrooke, Bromptonville, and Drummondville. Today the river is developed by the Southern Canada Power Company and various other interests to the extent of slightly more than 100,000 h.p., and the Southern Canada company controls undeveloped sites along the St. Francis, and also two sites on the Yamaska River, with a potential capacity of between 125,000 and 150,000 h.p. The total power resources of the area are thus roughly equivalent to the power developed at one individual site on the St. Maurice. Power, of course, could have been imported from the St. Lawrence regions — the whole area lies within a 125-mile radius of both Shawinigan Falls and the power developments on the St. Lawrence — but in 1900 the prospective market for electric power in the Townships was anything but attractive. The few sizable manufacturing plants in the area developed their own power, and the scattered small towns and the farming areas hardly provided a market of any scope. Thus in the electrical age too, the Townships promised to become a forgotten enclave, neglected by the two power centers to the north and west. In spite of its intensive search for markets, the Shawinigan company did not invade the area, although in 1905 it reached out to the neighboring asbestos district east of the St. Francis River.[7] The Montreal company, preoccupied with the Montreal market, was uninterested in the area[8] and even denied the Townships the benefit of the one good power site on the Richelieu River by tying the Chambly site into its own system.

Hence for the first fifteen years of the twentieth century, electrical developments in the Townships were insignificant. In 1902 the Canada Paper Company began to transform some of the hydraulic power from its development at Windsor Mills into electricity, and some years later, between 1905 and 1911, the Brompton Pulp and Paper Company developed two sites, each having an installed capacity of between 10,000 and 11,000 electrical h.p., to power their mills at East Angus and Bromptonville. (The Dominion Textile Company, which operated the other large manufacturing enterprise in the region, did not switch to electricity until 1921, when it installed generators to develop 3000 h.p. at its site on the Magog River.) Electricity was already being used for lighting purposes in some of the towns of the area, especially in Sherbrooke, whose electrical history had started in 1887 when the Royal Electric Company of Montreal demonstrated street lighting there. Electricity was supplied by a private company until 1908 when the city bought it out and began the development of three small sites on the Magog River near its confluence with the St. Francis.[9] By 1917 the aggregate capacity of these plants was almost 7000 h.p., and Sherbrooke began a fourth development of 5500 h.p. on the St. Francis River some 30 miles above the town. In 1929 the municipality of Sherbrooke completed its generating capacity up to the present figure of over 18,000 h.p. by building a 5800-h.p. station on the same river about 10 miles above the city. Many other smaller towns throughout the area, such as Coaticook, on a tributary of the St. Francis, and Farnham, near the headwaters of the Yamaska, provided themselves with electric light early in the century by installing turbines and generators at the small waterfalls which had formerly powered gristmills and sawmills.

The Townships, therefore, could not boast of much in the way of electrification before World War I. The situation was about to change, however, for already the Southern Canada Power Company had been formed and was making plans to extend a modern system of electrical transmission and distribution throughout the area.

III. *Growth of the Southern Canada Power Company*

The beginnings of the Southern Canada Power Company date from 1910 when a small company, the Sherbrooke Railway and Power Company, was incorporated by C. J. McCuaig, a Montreal stock broker. The company owned a waterfall in Sherbrooke at the mouth of the Magog River, and in 1911 a 4000-h.p. generating station was completed at this site. Power was used to operate the street-railway system in the city and to provide general electrical service to a number of small distribution systems which the company acquired by purchase during its first two or three years of operations. When the enterprise became part of the Southern Canada Power Company in 1916, its business could be described as follows: "[It] supplies the populous manufacturing district between Sherbrooke and the International Boundary Line with electric power and light and the City of Sherbrooke with part of its power requirements, and owns and operates the street railway system in that city."[10] In 1913 McCuaig extended his holdings in the area by acquiring control of the South Shore Power and Paper Company, which owned valuable water rights on the St. Francis River at Hemmings Falls and Drummondville,[11] and the electrical companies operating in St.

Jean and St. Hyacinthe, located respectively on the Richelieu and Yamaska Rivers. These three acquisitions were then amalgamated into a newly created concern, the Southern Canada Power Company. McCuaig was president of the company until 1916, when he sold his interests to A. J. Nesbitt, another Montreal financier.

From its outset, however, the company developed under the guidance of J. B. Woodyatt. Woodyatt, a recent graduate of McGill University in electrical engineering, was hired by McCuaig in 1910 to develop the Sherbrooke Railway and Power Company's power site at Sherbrooke. In 1913 McCauig commissioned Woodyatt to make a power survey of the Townships, and during the course of his investigations he became impressed with the power possibilities of the St. Francis near Drummondville. On the basis of this survey and an issue of three million dollars' worth of common stock, the Southern Canada Power Company was incorporated with Woodyatt as general manager. In 1921 he was appointed vice-president and in 1926 he became president.

The Southern Canada company started operations with 1600 customers in 6 communities, the largest of these being St. Hyacinthe and St. Jean. St. Hyacinthe generated its power in an 800-h.p. hydroelectric plant and a small steam station; St. Jean had a steam station and also purchased power from the Montreal Light, Heat and Power Company's station at Chambly. In the early part of 1914 the company acquired the municipal electric system in Drummondville, and at the end of its first full year of operations was able to report a modest profit of nearly $8000 on a gross revenue of over $165,000. By 1916 operations had been extended by the purchase of electrical systems in another half-dozen towns; the generating equipment at St. Jean, St. Hyacinthe, and Drummondville had been improved; and a 48-kv. transmission line had been built from Chambly to St. Hyacinthe to provide a more dependable power supply for that part of the company's territory. In the same year the Sherbrooke Railway and Power Company's network was added to the company's system, and arrangements were made with the Shawinigan company to increase the power supply available in the area south of Sherbrooke. For this purpose Shawinigan had extended its transmission lines from Windsor Mills to Sherbrooke. An organized system was beginning to emerge, but the company's operations were still scattered and fragmentary: the Annual Report for 1916 stated, "the Company is at present operating its system with power obtained from its hydroelectric developments at St. Hyacinthe, Drummondville, Sherbrooke, Richmond, Foster and Cowansville, and its steam plants at St. Hyacinthe, St. Johns, Iberville, supplemented by temporary power purchased from the Montreal Light, Heat and Power Company and Shawinigan Water and Power Company."

Larger plans had been evolved, however. In a twenty-five-mile strip along the St. Francis River below Hemmings Falls, the company owned the rights to six undeveloped power sites. A complete survey of this stretch of the river had been made, lands necessary to the exploitation of the sites had been purchased, and arrangements were being completed for the development of the first two projects at Hemmings Falls and Drummondville. After a number of capitalists had declined to become interested in the project, financial backing for the development was arranged by A. J. Nesbitt, of Nesbitt Thompson Company, Ltd., a financial house in Montreal. Nesbitt bought out McCuaig's interest in the Southern Canada Power Company and appointed W. C. Hawkins, then managing director of the Dominion Power and Transmission Company of Hamilton, Ontario, as president of the company, a post he held until his death in 1926.

The power from the prospective stations would be much in excess of what the area could then absorb so that special marketing arrangements had to be made. The problem was solved when the Shawinigan company offered to buy a block of power from the new station and retail it in its own area east of the St. Francis River. "Very important contracts have been made with the Shawinigan Water and Power Company for the sale to it of two blocks of power out of our first and second developments . . . These two contracts alone will practically cover the interest on the cost of these two developments. This Company is indebted to Shawinigan Water and Power Company for its friendly cooperation and assistance in taking care of the very pressing demands for power in the City of Sherbrooke and vicinity and at other points." Upon these arrangements, the company was ready to start construction "as soon as the prices of labour, material and machinery recede to normal."[12]

It was some years, however, before prices did return to normal, and in the meantime the company consolidated its position by acquiring more local systems and forming them into an integrated network through the construction of connecting transmission lines.[13] In 1917 the main transmission line of the company ran from Sherbrooke to the Vermont border: this was the line formerly operated by the Sherbrooke Railway and Power Company. The company now made plans to interconnect all of its properties by building a ring of 48–kv. transmission lines running from Drummondville up the St. Francis River to Sherbrooke, thence westerly to St. Jean, down the Richelieu to Beloeil, and then northeasterly through St. Hyacinthe back to

Drummondville (see Figure 1). The southern part of this line, from Sherbrooke to Granby, and a section down the St. Francis from Sherbrooke to Bromptonville, were completed in 1918. The ring was built up gradually over a number of years; sections were added as demand grew in a particular area or when another distribution system was purchased and had to be connected to the company's lines. By 1925 the only gap in the ring was along the southern perimeter for a distance of about 25 miles east of St. Jean; and the acquisition of the Farnham municipal system [14] in that year paved the way for the construction of the final section of the line. By that time, too, the company had built two lines across the area enclosed by the transmission belt, one north and south from Drummondville to Granby, and one east and west from Richmond, on the St. Francis, to St. Hyacinthe (see Figure 1). Branch lines were built out from this main system at various points. The main outlines of the company's present transmission system had been constructed by 1925; it had taken twelve years for the company to stake out its small territory. Progress had been steady, but slow; as might have been expected, the Townships were not to be hurried.

In the meantime, Southern Canada had brought its first large generating plant into operation. The company had apparently tired of waiting for prices to recede to normal and had begun construction on the Drummondville project in the spring of 1918. Two units of 3500 h.p. each were installed in 1919, but the station was not completed up to its designed capacity of 18,400 h.p. until 1926. Demand grew quite rapidly after the War and by 1923 the company had decided to begin work on its second development at Hemmings Falls, three miles upstream from the Drummondville station. The new plant was completed to its ultimate capacity of 33,600 h.p. in 1926. Ten thousand horsepower from this development were purchased by the Shawinigan company on a long-term contract. (The delay in construction of the company's generating stations had resulted in a revision of the arrangements made with Shawinigan in 1916, and instead of purchasing a block of power from each of the two stations, as had been originally intended, it took power only from the Hemmings Falls plant.[15])

The company has built no large power development since the Hemmings Falls station was completed; the only addition to its generating facilities since 1926 has been a small 2000–h.p. station built at Burroughs Falls in 1929. This station, located on a tributary of the St. Francis some fifteen miles north of the Vermont border, was originally intended to serve as a reserve station for the southeastern part of the company's distribution system, but with the growth of demand in the area it was soon used to carry part of the basic load on the Sherbrooke-Vermont line.[16] Since 1930 the company has apparently found it more economical to provide for additions to its available supplies by purchases from Shawinigan rather than by increasing its own generating plant.[17] Power purchases fluctuated from year to year depending on water conditions in the St. Francis watershed (see Table 8), but they increased in relative importance after 1930 and by 1951 Shawinigan power accounted for about half of the electricity sold by the Southern Canada Power Company.

The Annual Report for 1930 gives a good picture of Southern Canada's business at that date. Its five hydroelectric plants, plus power purchased from Shawinigan Falls and small amounts from the Chambly plant of the Montreal Light, Heat and Power Company, fed a transmission system of some 463 miles. This system, composed of 307 miles of 50-kv. lines, 42 miles of 25-kv. lines, and 115 miles of 13-kv. lines, in turn fed 578 miles of low-voltage distribution lines. The network, along with numerous large and small transforming stations, delivered power to 26,594 customers (including both domestic and industrial service) in 116 municipalities throughout the area. The company's industrial business was growing and in 1930 the rated capacity of motors using Southern Canada power was nearly 47,000 h.p. Electricity sales in that year were approximately 170 million kwhs. and the peak load on the system was about 33,000 kws. Domestic sales were stimulated by the company's policy of operating retail stores for the sale of electrical appliances: in 1930, 24 such stores in its territory had gross sales amounting to $423,551.[18] The enterprise had been moderately profitable: earnings had risen to approximately 5 per cent on the book value of the company's assets in 1929, and dividends had been paid on the common stock since 1924 at a rate of 4.5 per cent in 1930.[19]

The above sketch of Southern Canada's business relates specifically to 1930, but with appropriate modifications for growth it might well serve for any other year in the company's history. Its business has not changed significantly in kind since its inception, and quantitatively its development has been characterized by a slow, reasonably steady rate of growth (see Table 8). About half of the company's revenue comes from sales of electricity to householders and municipalities.[20] Municipal sales, mostly for street-lighting purposes, are, of course, mainly a function of the population in the centers served by the company, so that this load has increased as lines have been extended to new communities and as the population of the area has grown. The rise in the household load has reflected the same factors and the increasing use of domestic electrical appliances. To promote this business, the

TABLE 8

SOUTHERN CANADA POWER COMPANY, 1914–1946[a]
(Millions of kwhs.)

	Supply			Sales		
Year	Generated	Purchased from S.W. & P. Co.[b]	Total available	Firm power sales	Sold to S.W. & P. Co.[b]	Secondary power sales
1914			5			
1915			5			
1916	2	5	6			
1917	15	10	25			
1918	14	12	26			
1919	15	14	29			
1920	24	11	35			
1921	20	13	32			
1922	27	14	41			
1923	29	18	46			
1924	30	18	49	49		
1925	71	13	84	55	29	
1926	121	1	122	63	59	
1927	122	1	123	66	58	
1928	134	4	138	75	64	
1929	149	6	155	87	68	
1930	161	9	171	99	72	
1931	134	21	155	105	50	
1932	163	9	171	100	71	
1933	163	12	175	101	61	12
1934	156	29	185	121	54	10
1935	173	30	203	127	58	18
1936	181	25	206	136	54	16
1937	235	22	257	148	82	26
1938	196	34	230	151	63	16
1939	206	36	242	155	67	19
1940	187	57	244	176	53	16
1941	176	68	244	194	39	11
1942	201	77	278	210	57	11
1943	244	43	288	206	78	3
1944	201	63	265	192	53	20
1945	216	57	273	232	19	22
1946	221	71	292	258	15	19

[a] Source: The Company.

[b] The Shawinigan Water and Power Co.

company increased the number of its retail appliance stores from 2 in 1913 to 24 by 1930. Sales were discouragingly slow at first because of the generally low standard of living which prevailed in the area, but they increased greatly after the end of the first world war and the retail stores soon became a very important part of the company's business. In 1921 it was noted that, "the decreased revenue from industrial power users was fortunately more than offset by the revenue derived from the rapidly increasing use of electricity for domestic purposes, which has been promoted through the sale of labor-saving appliances from the retail stores of the Company. . . ."[21] Appliance sales continued to rise throughout the twenties, but slumped badly during the thirties.[22]

In common with other power concerns, of course, the Southern Canada Power Company experienced a dull period during the thirties. Growth in its physical plant almost ceased; from 1930 to 1938 only 43 miles of transmission line and 19 miles of distribution line were added to its network, and service was extended to only four new towns. In 1933 a 15,000–h.p. electric boiler was installed by the Dominion Silk Dyeing and Finishing Company of Drummondville, and thereafter the company augmented its revenue by the sale of small amounts of secondary power. In contrast to the experience of the Shawinigan and Montreal companies, Southern Canada's industrial sales held up better than its domestic sales during the depression years. We shall note the reason for this presently. Gross revenues were reduced by a decline in sales of appliances from the peak of $423,551 in 1930 to a low of $187,567 in 1933, by reduced income from investments, and by losses on American exchange required to pay bond interest.[23] Quarterly dividend payments were reduced from 25 cents to 20 cents a share in the middle of 1933 and remained at that level until the end of 1946. During the depression years the surplus account was reduced to write down the value of investments held by the company, and also, from 1932 to 1936, to maintain dividend payments.

IV. *The Southern Canada Power Company and Industrial Development*

The most interesting part of the Southern Canada Power Company's history is concerned with the part it has played in the industrial renaissance of the Townships during the last thirty years. Today the industrial power sales of the company account for about half of its gross revenue and more than half of its physical sales. Through its industrial development department, the company has devoted sustained effort to the building up of this load, and in so doing can justly claim to have contributed largely to the industrial growth of its territory. As early as 1918, it was noted that many new industries were being attracted to the Eastern Townships, and the company was carrying on

an energetic campaign to secure the location for its district of new industries, of which a large number with which it is in communication have signified their intention of locating plants in this country. In this work the Company is working in close co-operation with the Municipal authorities and Boards of Trade in the various municipalities, to whom the Company is indebted by reason of the frank recognition given to the efforts of the Company in the upbuilding of the district, resulting in the most cordial relations between the public and the Company.[24]

Great emphasis was placed on this phase of the company's work, and from 1920 on a list of the new plants in the towns served by the company was included in its Annual Reports. Not all these plants were located through the efforts of the company, but in 1938 it did claim that, "directly attributable to Company activity, more than 60 manufacturers, representing a capital investment of over $70,000,000 have been placed throughout the district served, giving employment to over 10,000 people . . ."[25] The towns for their part promoted the growth of manufacturing by offering tax concessions to firms locating within their boundaries; to quote a circular sent to interested firms by the power company, the municipalities

are willing to do everything permitted by Provincial laws to keep municipal and school taxes on factory properties as low as possible. They assess industrial properties on a very reasonable basis, and will apply to the Provincial Government for a Special Act to permit fixed assessment and partial commutation of municipal taxes for a sound and reputable industry bringing substantial employment to the municipality.

Sometimes, too, the town would erect a building which could be used on favorable terms by a manufacturing enterprise. Thus in 1933 it was reported that "the industrial building erected by the Town [of Waterloo] has been taken over by Mack Molding, Limited, a subsidiary of the Mack Molding Company of Wayne, N.J.," and again in 1938 the Duchess Shoe Company, Ltd., had started manufacturing operations "in a new building provided by enterprising citizens of Richmond."[26]

The Southern Canada Power Company's interest in promoting the growth of manufacturing in its area is not primarily, as might be thought, in building up a large industrial market for power. Rather, it sees industrial development as a means of supporting and extending the domestic market for electricity. The company's own power resources are inadequate to support industries that are large consumers of electricity, such as pulp and paper or electroprocess plants. As it has become more dependent on purchased power, the company has become even less interested in heavy power consumers, since the profit margin between purchased power and industrial sales is very small. On the other hand, industries which use a high proportion of labor relative to power indirectly increase the more profitable retail markets for electricity. Manufacturing industry helps to raise the standard of living in the region and attracts people from the rural areas to the towns; this in turn increases the demand for commercial and domestic lighting services, for electrical appliances, and, as towns grow, for street-lighting and other municipal purposes. The power company's marketing strategy hence is directed toward raising the retail demand for electricity through developing the area industrially, and in this endeavor its industrial development department has been of signal service.

The interest of the power company in attracting firms that are relatively large employers of labor has coincided with the basic capabilities of the region, because the main attraction of the Townships for industry has been the large and ready supply of prospective employees. The main virtue of this available labor force is no doubt its cheapness, but the boosters of the region never fail to vouch for its dexterity and adaptability to factory conditions and, cynically, to stress its "docility" and "tractability." In economic terms the labor supply is stable (i.e., its rate of turnover is low) as well as cheap. The industry of the Townships is thus to a large extent labor-oriented. The various branches of the textile industry, from spinning to the manufacture of clothing, are predominant in the industrial pattern; metal-working establishments make a good showing; rubber-working establishments and the boot and shoe industry provide employment for many people; a large number of woodworking establishments are based on the forest as well as the labor resources of the area; and for the rest the industrial scene is made up of a large number of light manufacturing plants producing everything from paper boxes and lead pencils to hairpins and coffee-makers.[27] Employment figures given by Blanchard relating to the late thirties show that 14,000 were employed in the textile industries (1300 in woolen goods; 3400 in cotton goods, 7900 in silk and artificial silk, and 1400 in ready-made clothing); 4750 in forest industries, excluding sawmills and woods operations (with 2000 in pulp and paper, 1200 in furniture, and 1550 in miscellaneous forest work); 2800 in metal-working establishments; 1400 in rubber-working enterprises; 1350 in the boot and shoe industry; 550 in tobacco manufacturing; and 250 in miscellaneous employment — a total of just over 25,000.[28]

Some of the highlights of this picture should be briefly noted. The cotton industry is dominated by the Dominion Textile Company with large factories at Magog, Sherbrooke, and Drummondville. The artificial silk division of the textile industry includes the largest manufacturing firm in the Townships, namely, the Canadian Celanese Company, established at Drummondville in 1926, which was employing some 2800 workers in 1936. The Belding-Corticelli plant at Coaticook, and hosiery mills at Richmond, Granby, Cowansville, Sherbrooke and Drummondville are other sizable units in the silk goods industry. Nearly all the pulp and paper establishments and most of the furniture industry, which centers around Victoriaville, are located in Shawinigan's part of the territory. The metal-working industry is organized mainly in medium and small-scale establishments, the largest plant being that of the Canadian Ingersoll Rand Company at Sherbrooke. The rubber-working factories are located in Granby, Sherbrooke, and Actonvale. Some of the largest boot and shoe factories are located in Shawinigan territory, but there are also plants at Richmond and Actonvale in the Southern Canada area. Employment in the tobacco industry in 1936 was accounted for entirely by the plant of the Empire Tobacco Company at Granby. Blanchard's figure for miscellaneous establishments was undoubtedly low, even for 1936, including as it did only some of the larger enterprises, employing from 15 to 100 people each, in a half-dozen towns.

In brief, by the outbreak of World War II, there had been an appreciable development of industry in the Townships, and the towns of the area had become centers of a prosperous and diversified manufacturing activity. Most of this economic growth dated from the first world war, and it is reasonable to view this miniature industrial revolution as evidence of what a quarter-century of reliable electricity supply can do for an area.[29]

Some of the outstanding examples of the direct role which the Southern Canada Power Company has played in the growth of industry in its area are contained in the submission which the company made to the provincial Electricity Commission in 1934.[30] St. Jean had grown from a population of 5900 in 1911 to over 11,000 by 1934. In the former year the town had 15 industries which gave work to less than 800 employees, while in the latter year 40 factories provided employment for over 2400 people. The company claimed credit for at least 10 of the new industries in this town. Farnham came into the company's system in 1925, and since that time "the town has obtained a number of industries including such substantial firms as The American Wringer Company of Woonsocket, R.I., the Collins and Aikman Co. of Philadelphia, and the Barry and Staines Linoleum Co. of Kircaldy,

Scotland. The local municipal plant could not have taken care of even 50 percent of the linoleum Company's load alone."

Granby, which had 15 industries and 1450 employees in 1911, boasted 31 plants employing 2900 workers in 1934. Cowansville had been merely a rural hamlet in 1911 "and its local power resources were so limited that, to conserve water, electricity could not be used in daytime nor after midnight. There are 10 industries there today, employing over 600 people with a payroll of nearly $600,000." Of the towns in the power company's territory, Drummondville had shown the greatest growth between 1911 and 1934: population had increased from 1725 to nearly 15,000, the number of industries from 12 to 21, and factory employment from 128 to 3800. St. Hyacinthe was the largest town originally included in the company's territory. In 1911, it had a population of nearly 10,000, 25 industries, and 1670 factory employees: "In recent years, the direct result of industrial work by this Company has added such plants as those of Consolidated Silk Company, the Canadian U.S. Knitting Company, Donahue Corporation, Hump Hair Pin Manufacturing Company, Gotham Hosiery Company, and . . . . Goodyear Cotton Company. The Goodyear Cotton Company, one of St. Hyacinthe's largest factories never would have considered locating in St. Hyacinthe, had it been dependent upon a local plant for its power supply." By 1934 the city had a population of over 15,000, and was the site of 55 industries with 2800 employees.

While it is clear that promotional efforts of the power company and the town authorities have played a direct and important role in the modern industrial development of the Townships, more general forces tending to the same result have also been at work. To a large extent the growth of manufacturing in the Townships has proceeded through establishment of branch plants of American, Canadian, and occasionally, British parent firms. The setting up of branch *manufacturing* plants, as distinct from sales offices or the maintenance of "factors" abroad, which is a very old form of business organization, is distinctly a twentieth-century type of enterprise and, appropriately, the Americans have been its chief exponent. In an early study of the movement of the American branch plants to Canada, W. H. Carter, Jr. notes that the "tendency towards a decentralization of industry and towards the establishment of branches rather than the concentration of the production of a company in one large plant, is one which characterises all of our recent industrial expansion, domestic and foreign." [31] The branch plant movement is a form of industrial decentralization. A more general discussion of this trend in modern industry, of which both Ontario and Quebec have been beneficiaries, is deferred to a later chapter, but some of the factors specifically involved in the Eastern Townships may be mentioned here.

The location of factories in the small cities and towns of the Eastern Townships has been made feasible by at least two permissive conditions — a reliable supply of electric power, and the construction of a highway network that has enabled the plants to use truck transport. The incentives for industry to take advantage of these conditions may be found in such circumstances [32] as low land values, special concessions offered to industry by the towns, low wages, and perhaps most important, a labor supply with a low turnover. Finally, the Eastern Townships have offered American branch plants the general advantage of proximity to the main Canadian market and the particular tariff advantages of a Canadian location, namely, avoidance of the Canadian tariff for sales in Canada and preferential treatment in other Commonwealth countries for exports from Canada.

The yearly summaries of industrial development in the towns served by the Southern Canada Power Company, published in that concern's annual reports since 1920, show some of the factors at work in the area. A count [33] of the new firms listed in these reports from 1920 to 1939 inclusive indicates that some 137 located in the company's territory during that period. Although precise dating is impossible, since varying lengths of time intervene between the decision to build a new factory and the actual beginning of production, some approximate statement of the time-distribution of these new arrivals is possible. Sixty-two firms are listed in the 1920's (although some of the 10 included in the 1920 report had already been established for a few years), while in spite of the depression of the thirties 75 new firms located in the area during that decade. From an average of 3 or 4 new firms a year up to 1927, the number rose to a combined figure of 29 for 1928 and 1929, and held up well the next decade, with 17 new firms locating in the area from 1930 to 1932 inclusive. Arrivals rose to 25 for the period 1933 to 1935, numbered 23 from 1936 to 1938, and were 10 in 1939.

There is obviously no correlation between these figures and the course of the business cycle during the period, although the large number of new firms and the numerous extensions to old firms in 1928 and 1929 may perhaps reflect the buoyant business conditions of the late twenties. The relatively high figure for 1930 and 1931 (seven new firms in each year) may in part represent enterprises projected in the preceding boom; in part, they may have resulted from the increased Canadian tariff of 1930. Although it may only have been a gesture of approval for the new tariff, the company stated in its Annual Report for 1930 that "during the last few weeks a very marked increase in activity has been manifested by American and European manufacturers who now find it necessary to establish branch plants in Canada to retain their Canadian business. Your district should benefit materially from this activity." It is in the next few years, however, that the effect of tariff policy shows up clearly in the series. The full-blown Imperial Preference arrangement made at Ottawa in 1932 served to attract many American branch plants to Canada.[34] The bulk of these new enterprises were located in Ontario, but Quebec shared in the business, and undoubtedly this factor led to the high number of new establishments in the Townships from 1933 to 1935. In 1934 the company noted that industrial activity in its territory was good and attributed it to the effect of Imperial Preference in drawing American branch plants to the country. After 1935 however, this stimulus seems to have petered out.[35] In 1938 it was noted that the disturbed European situation was resulting in fewer requests for information concerning the establishment of new plants from the United States, and in the following year it was stated that the majority of the new industries in the area were branches of Canadian firms.

v. *Summary*

For the past thirty years, the Townships have been one of the most rapidly growing industrial areas in Canada, and today the busy manufacturing towns south of the St. Lawrence contrast strongly with the farmlands and dormant villages which characterized the area around the turn of the century. From the evidence, it is not unreasonable to conclude that hydroelectricity has played a major role in this development, especially in two ways. In the first place, the Southern Canada Power Company has gradually provided the whole area with a reliable power supply, which is a prerequisite of industrial growth. Lacking that, a region will not be able to attract manufacturing industry, regardless of its other advantages. Secondly, the power company, in the interests of building up its load, has actively canvassed industrialists and urged them to take advantage of the opportunities which the region offered once power had been made available. Growth was slow at first, but advance on one sector aided advance on others. The power company promoted industrial development, and industrial growth built up the power company's load directly, and also indirectly through its effect on the municipal, commercial, and domestic demands for electricity. The advent of factories led to the growth of cities and towns, which provided markets for the countryside and outlets for the surplus population of the farms; these new opportunities made the countryside more prosperous, and this in turn promoted the trade and commerce of the towns. The area began to pull itself up by its own bootstraps. All-round expansion and the rising standard of living that accompanied it redounded to the benefit of the power company through increased sales of electricity and of electrical appliances, and to the benefit of general business by increasing the demand for other goods and services. From little spirals such as these, economic development results; it is doubtful if the spirals would have started in the Eastern Townships had it not been for the introduction into the area of an organized network of electrical transmission lines.

CHAPTER 7

The Ottawa Valley and the Saguenay River

The Gatineau Power Company and the Maclaren-Quebec Power Company in the Ottawa Valley, and the Saguenay Power Company and the Aluminum Company of Canada on the Saguenay River, have much in common. Situated in the shield areas of the province, they have been closely associated with the specialized, large power-consuming industries that flourish there—pulp and paper mills in the Ottawa region, aluminum plants and pulp and paper mills in the Saguenay region. All are primarily power wholesalers; throughout their histories, their sales almost exclusively have been large blocks of power delivered under a few long-term contracts. In addition to contracts with the industries mentioned above, the Saguenay company sells power to the Shawinigan company, and the Ottawa valley companies sell large proportions of their outputs to the Hydro-Electric Power Commission of Ontario. These power companies have therefore exercised only an indirect influence on the development of general manufacturing industry in Quebec. The Saguenay company has passively supported general industry in Quebec through its power sales to Shawinigan, and the Ottawa Valley companies have performed a similar function for the industrial development of southern Ontario. It may also be argued that these companies, through their support of the pulp and paper and aluminum reduction industries, have contributed to the growth of that part of Quebec manufacturing which is technologically or economically "linked" to these industries. But these relationships are tenuous. The companies here reviewed are specialized concerns, and their histories, compared to those of the organizations discussed previously are both short and simple.

1. *Early Developments in the Ottawa Valley*

Before World War I, the only significant development of power on the Ottawa River had taken place in the immediate vicinity of Ottawa and Hull. On the Ontario side of the river, the J. R. Booth pulp and paper enterprise had developed a site of nearly 29,000 h.p., and the Ottawa Light, Heat, and Power Company (formerly the Ottawa Electric Company)[1] had three plants[2] with an aggregate capacity of 11,500 h.p. at Chaudière Falls. On the Quebec side of the river, there were the E. B. Eddy development of slightly over 14,000 h.p. at Chaudière Falls, the 14,100–h.p. plant of the Ottawa and Hull Manufacturing Company Ltd., at the same site, and the 3200–h.p. station of the Hull Electric Company at the Deschênes Rapids about 6 miles above Hull.[3]

In the 1920's another 75,000 h.p. of capacity was added in the Ottawa-Hull area, which will be described presently. The first large-scale development on the river, however, came only in 1931 and 1932 when a 224,000–h.p. station, jointly owned by the Hydro-Electric Power Commission of Ontario and the Ottawa Valley Power Company, was built at Chats Falls, about 25 miles up-river from Ottawa.

These developments, altogether about 370,000 h.p., represented the only use made of the enormous water powers of the Ottawa River before the end of World War II. The development of the Ottawa had been held back mainly, it seems, by the legal problems of divided ownership of the river. In 1943, however, Ontario and Quebec finally agreed on terms for a division of the river's power resources, and at last the water powers of the Ottawa have been made available for hydroelectric development.[4]

The tributaries of the Ottawa did not suffer from the jurisdictional disabilities that hamstrung the development of the main river, but the power developments on these rivers were nevertheless small and haphazard before 1925. In the early years of the century a number of small stations, ranging from a few hundred to a few thousand horsepower each, were located along the small rivers which enter the Ottawa between Hull and Montreal.[5] The majority of these stations became the property of the Gatineau Power Company through its acquisition, between 1926 and 1930, of some twenty-five local electric companies operating in the lower Ottawa valley. Many of the plants, including the Deschênes plant of the Hull Electric Company, which had been installed in 1896, were subsequently closed down, but today the

Gatineau company still operates eight small stations in the area — the Bell Falls plant of 7200 h.p. on the Rouge River; two stations totaling 915 h.p. on the Blanche River; one of 564 h.p. at Ripon on the Petite Nation River; three developments totaling 3500 h.p. on the North River, at Wilson Chute, St. Jerome and St. Adèle; and one of 2300 h.p. built by the company itself in 1928 at Rawdon on the Ouareau River. These plants, supplemented by power from the company's main developments on the Gatineau River, supply electricity for the Laurentian towns to the north and west of Montreal, and for the communities along the north shore of the Ottawa River between Montreal and Hull.

By the beginning of the twenties the fragmented development of the power industry in the Ottawa valley was obviously anachronistic, and the situation invited consolidation and further development by some enterprising corporation that could command the requisite funds. There were two contenders in the field who had ideas for power development on a somewhat larger scale than had yet been attempted.[6] In the first place, the old Hull Electric Company, founded in 1896, owned the electrical distribution system and street railway in Hull and small distribution systems in Aylmer and Deschênes. The electricity to service these properties was supplied by a small generating station at Deschênes and by the purchase of bulk power from the Ottawa and Hull Power and Manufacturing Company. Towards the end of the first world war, the Canadian Pacific Railway, which controlled the Hull Electric Company through stock ownership, commissioned G. G. Gale, vice-president of the power company, to investigate the practicability of the railway company's electrifying its lines in the Ottawa-Hawkesbury area. Since the results of the investigation were promising, plans were made to exploit a large undeveloped power site at Paugan Falls[7] as a first step toward the implementation of the project. This was the largest development yet to be projected in western Quebec, and had the plans matured normally, the electricity supply of the Ottawa valley might have been organized under the auspices of the Canadian Pacific Railway.

Another group that had designs on the power resources of the area was led by A. J. Nesbitt of Montreal and was largely composed of the same men who were then engaged in building up the property of the Southern Canada Power Company. This group was interested in the resources of both the tributaries of the lower Ottawa and the main river itself above Hull. In 1923 the Nesbitt interests moved into the latter region by purchasing the old Ottawa and Hull Power and Manufacturing Company and rechristening it the Ottawa and Hull Power Company, Ltd. This concern owned two power plants at Chaudière Falls, an old one of 14,100 h.p. which had been installed in 1902, and a new one of 22,500 h.p. which had been constructed between 1919 and 1921.[8] It sold power to a number of industrial customers in Hull and Deschênes and made bulk deliveries to the Hydro-Electric Power Commission of Ontario for distribution in Ottawa and to the Hull Electric Company for distribution in Hull.[9] In 1923 also, Nesbitt set up the Ottawa River Power Company, Ltd. as a subsidiary of his new acquisition and made plans to exploit a power site which the company owned in fee simple near Bryson at Calumet Falls on the Ottawa River, 50 miles above Ottawa.[10] This development, declared to be for the purpose of providing additional power for the Ottawa-Hull area, was installed to the extent of 27,000 h.p. in 1925,[11] and a line was built from Bryson to the parent company's generating stations at Chaudière Falls.

Having gained entry to the industry in the upper river, the Montreal group began to acquire properties in the lower Ottawa area. Thus the Ottawa-Montreal Power Company, Ltd. was incorporated in 1924 for the purpose of acquiring the Hawkesbury Electric Light and Power Company and the Western Quebec Power Company, Ltd., small concerns with plants on the Rouge and North Rivers.[12] The new company bought other businesses and began to consolidate the electric business in the area northwest of Montreal, between the St. Lawrence and the Ottawa Rivers. By 1926, the company had a generating capacity of about 11,000 h.p. in five small plants and was building a transmission network to interconnect them and to distribute its electricity. It sold power to the Riordon Pulp and Paper Corporation and to a few other industries at Hawkesbury on the Ontario side of the river; retail sales were made to some 3900 customers in 40 communities scattered over an area of approximately 900 square miles; and the company was also promoting the sale of electrical appliances through a retail store which it operated.[13]

In brief, the Nesbitt group was starting to organize the electrical business in the Ottawa valley along the same lines that were proving successful in the Eastern Townships. But these plans too, like those of the Hull Electric Company, were rudely terminated by the advent of the International Paper Company to the region and the formation of its power subsidiary, the Gatineau Power Company, Ltd., in 1926.

II. *The Gatineau Power Company*

The Gatineau company was one manifestation of the enormous expansion undertaken by the International Paper Company from 1924 to

1929 under the presidency of A. R. Graustein, an expansion which carried the operations of that company not only to the Ottawa valley, but also to New Brunswick, Newfoundland, and the southern United States. The immediate event leading to International's entry to the Ottawa valley in 1925 was the bankruptcy of the Riordon pulp and paper interests in the early twenties,[14] after which the properties of this concern, including the rights to large undeveloped power sites on the Gatineau River, were purchased by the Canadian International Paper Company in 1925. International immediately launched an enormous pulp and paper and hydroelectric construction program, and within a few years over 500,000 h.p. had been added to the developed power resources of the Ottawa valley, an increase which amounted to roughly four times the power that had been developed in the area in the previous thirty years.

Incorporated under a Quebec charter in March 1926, the Gatineau Power Company was set up as a subsidiary of the International Paper Company to administer the power properties of the parent concern. It then began to merge other power companies; the chief properties acquired were those of the Hull Electric Company in 1926 and the various Nesbitt companies in 1927 and 1928. With these purchases, the Gatineau company controlled all the power developments in the lower Ottawa valley except the Eddy plant at Hull and the developments on the Lièvre River.[15]

The Gatineau Power Company has had a checkered corporate history. The Canadian Hydro-Electric Corporation was organized in 1928 to hold the stock of the Gatineau Power Company and of the St. John River Power Company, the New Brunswick power property of the Canadian International Paper Company. The stock of this holding company, in turn, was held by the International Hydro-Electric System, which controlled all the power properties of the International Paper Company, both in Canada and the United States. This impressive pyramid of companies was brought to the ground by the holding company acts of 1933–1935 in the United States; in 1937 the Gatineau Power Company merged and then dissolved its parent, the Canadian Hydro-Electric Corporation, and by 1938 the International Paper Company had put into effect a plan to divest itself of its power subsidiary, the International Hydro-Electric System. As a final result, the Gatineau Power Company since 1939 has not been controlled by the International Paper Company,[16] but although the ownership of the company has thus changed at various times, the operational direction has been continuous. Its management has largely been the responsibility of G. G. Gale, who became vice-president and general manager of the concern at its inception in 1926, and who has been president of the company since 1934.

The physical plant of the Gatineau company was built up very rapidly between 1926 and 1931 and has changed very little since that time. The purchase of other companies between 1926 and 1928 brought to the company a variety of generating plants with an aggregate capacity of about 75,000 h.p., the only sizable installations being those at Chaudière Falls and Bryson formerly owned by the Nesbitt companies. By 1931 the company's capacity was about 600,000 h.p. The increase in capacity was accounted for by the construction of the Paugan Falls plant (238,000 h.p.), the plant at Chelsea (136,000 h.p.), and the plant at Farmers (98,000 h.p.), all on the Gatineau River; the Kipawa plant (24,000 h.p.), on the Ottawa River about 200 miles above Ottawa; the small plant at Rawdon (2300 h.p.); and by an addition of 27,000 h.p. to the Bryson plant. The only extensions to this generating capacity since 1931 have been additions at Chelsea (34,000 h.p.) in 1938; Farmers (24,000 h.p.) in 1947; and Bryson (27,000 h.p.) in 1949. On January 1, 1950, the installed capacity of the company's hydroelectric properties in the Ottawa valley stood at slightly less than 690,000 h.p. The Gatineau River on which most of this capacity is located, is regulated by two storage reservoirs, one of 95 billion cubic feet capacity at Lake Baskatong and the other of 45 billion cubic feet capacity at Lake Cabonga. The dams which impound the water in these two reservoirs were built in 1928 and 1929 by the Gatineau company at its own expense, under an agreement with the Quebec Streams Commission. On completion the properties were vested in the Quebec Streams Commission and are operated by that organization.

The company's distribution system, too, was organized very rapidly in the first few years of its operations, and has grown hardly at all since that time. By 1930 it was reported: "The consolidation of transmission and distribution systems . . . has so far progressed that over 97 per cent of the energy supplied by this Company can now be freely interchanged between the geographical divisions. Many operating economies have been effected, while the service has been greatly improved as a result of this interconnection."[17] The map of the company's transmission system published in its Annual Report for 1929 shows its main line extending down the north shore of the Ottawa River from Bryson to the St. Lawrence River, with branches up the Gatineau, Blanche, Nation, and Rouge tributaries, a long branch curving up the North River to St. Agathe and St. Jovite in the Laurentians, and a cluster of lines in the Rawdon district about 50 miles north of Montreal (see Figure 1). In addition there were a few lines in Ontario, mainly around Hawkesbury; a system serving the corner of Quebec south of the Ottawa River; and a small line running south from Montreal to the American border at Rouse's Point. This latter line, which was acquired through the purchase of the Napierville Electric Company in 1927,[18] is not connected to the other lines of the company and purchases its power from the Montreal company.[19] Comparison of this 1928 system with a map issued by the company in 1950 indicates very little difference for the two years. Lines have been extended for short distances here and there and new substations have been added, but fundamentally the area served has not changed since 1928.

III. *Markets*

The Gatineau Power Company, then, emerged practically full-blown in the five years between 1926 and 1931. On what basis was this huge enterprise projected? The following quotation from the Canadian Hydro-Electric Corporation's Annual Report for 1934 is a succinct answer to this question, an answer which makes a clear distinction between primary motives and secondary results:

> The power and storage developments made on the Gatineau River were initially undertaken for the purpose of supplying power to the Gatineau mill of the Canadian International Paper Company and to the Hydro-Electric Power Commission of Ontario. The benefits of service from these large modern hydro-electric plants have been extended by Gatineau Power Company to the territory previously served by seventeen separate companies or organizations, most of which depended upon small isolated plants for their supply of power.

Table 9 shows that the combined power sales to Ontario and to the Canadian International Paper Company (including its New Brunswick properties) account for between 70 and 80 per cent of the company's gross revenue and for over 90 per cent of its physical sales. The Gatineau company is very sparing in its publication of statistics, but the increase in its domestic business between 1928 and 1940 was not great. In the former year it was stated in the company's Annual Report that it served 17,000 customers in 111 municipalities; in *Moody's Public Utilities* for 1940 the company (along with its subsidiary operating in Ontario) is listed as serving about 22,300 customers in approximately 145 communities. Since the last war, however, the growth of the company's retail business has been very much more rapid, and by 1950 the company sold electricity to over 60,000 customers in 171 communities, of which 5 were in Ontario.

The main pulp and paper customer of the company is the large mill of

TABLE 9

GATINEAU POWER COMPANY: POWER SALES, 1928–1945 [a]

(Millions of kwhs.; thousands of dollars)

	Total sales		Hydro-Electric Power Commission of Ontario		Canadian International Paper Co.			Other power consumers		Other electric utilities		Domestic, commercial, and other	
Year	Kwhs.	Revenue	Kwhs.	Revenue	Sec'y kwhs.	Firm kwhs.	Total revenue	Kwhs.	Revenue	Kwhs.	Revenue	Kwhs.	Revenue
1928	1,130												
1929	1,750												
1930	2,200												
1931	2,100												
1932	2,200												
1933	2,340												
1934	2,368	7,985	1,406	4,656	441	366	1,812	48	431	73	436	35	649
1935	2,463	7,990	1,361	4,555	555	390	1,917	45	414	74	447	37	658
1936	2,357	6,849	873	3,055	866	434	2,194	54	429	90	484	39	687
1937	2,541	7,158	897	3,095	998	464	2,388	72	424	90	524	20	728
1938	2,278	7,298	1,020	3,438	731	332	2,084	66	419	108	581	21	776
1939	2,595	7,863	1,300	3,912	740	354	2,074	67	415	112	635	23	827
1940	2,684	8,211	1,542	4,225	438	454	1,905	88	516	136	692	25	873
1941	2,594	8,313	1,547	4,255	303	470	1,829	95	537	152	758	27	934
1942	2,812	8,777	1,562	4,315	477	485	2,079	106	631	153	781	28	971
1943	2,697	8,675	1,512	4,262	451	440	1,971	94	646	169	838	30	959
1944	2,329	8,337	1,480	4,098	95	456	1,640	87	655	177	896	34	1,047
1945	2,467	8,655	1,460	4,017	162	491	1,824	113	770	199	952	41	1,093

[a] Sources: Two submissions of the Gatineau Power Company to the Securities and Exchange Commission of the United States: (1) Registration Statement under Securities Act of 1933 (First Mortgage Bonds 3¼ per cent due April 1, 1969) and (2) a prospectus filed with the S.E.C. dated June 15, 1946 (Sinking Fund Debentures 2¼ per cent due 1961). Figures for the total kwh. sales from 1928 to 1933 inclusive are taken from Moody's and adjusted as explained in the Appendix, Section 2. The figures for Total Sales include small amounts (2 to 3 million kwhs. per year) of purchased power.

the Canadian International Paper Company which was built in 1928 at Gatineau, some five miles below Hull on the Ottawa River. Power is also sold to the Hawkesbury sulphite mill of the same company, and to the E. B. Eddy mill at Hull. The Kipawa power plant on the upper Ottawa was built exclusively to supply a sulphite mill which, like the Hawkesbury plant, had been acquired as part of the Riordon properties. In addition to supplying a large part of the company's primary load, the three pulp and paper customers in the Ottawa area used large amounts of secondary power in electric boilers during the 1930's.[20] Secondary power sales also served to bridge the gap between the installation of the generating capacity and the delivery to Ontario of the full amount of power for which it had contracted. In 1931 it was reported that "although the major portion of the power sold . . . on long-term primary power contracts has now been delivered, there still remains an amount of 77,472 h.p. sold for future delivery and now being sold at comparatively low rates for the production of steam."[21] The price of secondary power was "calculated in accordance with a stated formula and the total cost depends upon the amount of steam taken and the cost of coal."[22]

Besides the pulp and paper plants, the Gatineau company has had one other large industrial customer since it first began operations, namely, the Canada Cement Company at Hull. It also supplies power to a few other industrial customers, including textile mills, in Hull, Ottawa and Hawkesbury. This business, however, has been a very small part of Gatineau's total load. Power is also sold at wholesale to the Ottawa Light, Heat, and Power Company, this business representing a continuation of the contract which the Ottawa and Hull Power Company had signed with the Ottawa concern. In 1930, when the Ottawa company was purchasing approximately 21,500 h.p., a new contract calling for an ultimate delivery of 45,000 h.p. was negotiated, and in the following year an arrangement was made whereby the Ottawa company would close down its stand-by steam station and buy its temporary requirements from the Gatineau company. In 1946 the Ottawa company purchased 200 million kwhs. of electricity and was Gatineau's third largest customer.[23]

The Hydro-Electric Power Commission of Ontario has always been the company's largest customer. In 1934, before the repudiation of the Ontario power contracts, sales to the "Hydro" accounted for over 50 per cent of gross revenues, and although this proportion was reduced after the revision of the contracts, such sales still accounted for over 40 per cent of the company's gross revenue in 1939. Indeed, nearly 300,000 h.p. of the company's generating plant, including the entire Paugan plant and individual generating units at Chelsea and Farmers, were installed specifically to supply 25-cycle power to the Niagara System of the Ontario Hydro-Electric Power Commission. This power was delivered to the border by the Gatineau company and then transmitted over 200 miles to Leaside, a suburb of Toronto, at a 220-kv. voltage. This was the longest line then constructed in Canada and the first to use 220-kv. transmission. In addition, the company sells 60,000 h.p. of 60-cycle current to the Hydro for its eastern Ontario system.

IV. *Power Contracts with Ontario*

During the 1920's the demand for electricity in Ontario grew so rapidly that the Hydro-Electric Power Commission was forced to take steps to provide adequate power supplies for both the immediate future and for the expected long-run increase in its load. The large power sites in the southern portion of the province had already been developed, and further development at Niagara Falls was impossible since all the water that Canada could claim under the then existing treaty with the United States was already being used. Sir Adam Beck of the Hydro constantly pointed out that an impending power shortage could be avoided only by one of three alternatives: the building of steam plants, development of the power resources of the St. Lawrence or Ottawa Rivers, or purchase of power from Quebec.[24] The province was loath to build steam stations while a million hydroelectric horsepower were still available on the St. Lawrence,[25] but it proved impossible to get agreement with the United States to develop St. Lawrence power. Similarly, it was impossible to get agreement with Quebec to develop the Ottawa River's resources. There remained the purchase of power from Quebec, and as early as 1923 Sir Adam Beck was negotiating to this end with private interests in Quebec.[26] Finally, towards the end of the decade the matter could no longer be delayed, and between 1926 and 1930 long-term contracts for the purchase of large amounts of power were established between the Hydro and four Quebec companies. The largest of these contracts was with the Gatineau company, providing for delivery of power to be increased by stated amounts until by 1936 total deliveries would amount to 260,000 h.p. of 25-cycle current and 60,000 h.p. of 60-cycle current. Similar contracts were signed with the Beauharnois Light, Heat, and Power Company for 250,000 h.p.; with the Ottawa Valley Power Company for 96,000 h.p.; and with the Maclaren-Quebec Power Company [27] for 125,000 h.p. All these amounts were to be 25-cycle power for use in the Hydro's Niagara system.

By the time the last contract had been signed, the depression had started, and Ontario's power problem, at least in the short run, was one of surplus rather than shortage. What followed reflected this economic pressure. One author put the matter at once realistically and delicately: "Throughout the Canadian economy rigid contractual obligations have made the process of readjustment to the fall in the national income since 1929 a slow and painful process. The cancellation in Ontario of the Hydro-Electric Power Commission's contracts with four Quebec companies has been one incident in this process. . ."[28] The cancellation was made by an act proclaimed by the provincial legislature on December 6, 1935. The final increments of power which were to have been delivered the following year were refused. On December 20, 1935, new contracts were arranged between the Hydro and the Gatineau and Maclaren companies. The other two companies went to court and won their cases both in the lower court and the Supreme Court of Ontario. The Ontario government then passed legislation preventing the plaintiffs from recovering the damages which they had been awarded. Both sides prepared to carry the case to the Privy Council in 1937, but litigation was dropped when new contracts were signed with the Ottawa Valley Power Company in February 1937 and with the Beauharnois company in December 1937. Both sides had by then become more willing to negotiate: the economic revival of 1937 and the slow growth in load since the end of 1935 made it clear that Ontario, while not able to absorb the amounts of power stipulated in the original contracts, was nevertheless in no position to cut herself off entirely from Quebec. On the other hand, the Beauharnois company (now owned by the Montreal Light, Heat and Power Consolidated) was anxious to patch up the quarrel and begin to utilize its plant once more.[29] The whole "power contracts" issue was settled in December 1937 when the new contracts with all four companies were put on a stable basis, and the Ontario government affirmed the contracts by special legislation in the following year. Under the new contracts three companies were to provide the same amount of power as before, while the Maclaren-Quebec company was to provide 20,000 h.p. less than in the original contract. Acceptance of the maximum amount of power was to be delayed in each case until 1944; the price was reduced from $15.00 to $12.50 per horsepower; and sundry irritating clauses included in the original contracts, such as payment in American dollars and acceptance by the Hydro of the risk of any future increase in Quebec taxation, were removed. Thus ended one of the more acrimonious disputes in Canada arising from the depression, a dispute which was reflected in a Cabinet crisis in Ontario, a change of Commissioners in the

Hydro-Electric Power Commission, and, as we have noted, probably in the absorption of the Beauharnois Light, Heat, and Power Company by the Montreal Light, Heat and Power Consolidated.[30]

v. *The Saguenay River*

The Saguenay Power Company was incorporated in Quebec in 1924 as the Duke-Price Power Company Ltd.; the present style was adopted in 1935. The original company "was organized by James B. Duke and Sir William Price to take over the large hydro-electric project which they had for several years been developing at Isle Maligne in Quebec. Following Mr. Duke's death in 1925, Aluminum Company of America interests acquired 53 1/3% of stock and Shawinigan Water and Power Company 20%, the remaining 26 2/3% being retained by the Duke-Price interests."[31]

The two original promoters of the company came from widely different backgrounds. The name of Price is one of the oldest in the annals of the Canadian forest industries; the first member of the family to come to Canada was sent out from England by the Admiralty to search for timber during the Napoleonic Wars. In 1817 he set up a lumber business in the Ottawa and St. Maurice regions and in the 1840's entered the Saguenay country. Since then the forest industries of the Saguenay valley have been dominated by Price enterprises. It was a grandson of the original William Price who started the first paper mill in the valley in 1904, and who was the original promoter of the Duke-Price Power Company.[32]

James Duke, from the tobacco industry, had long been interested in power ventures and had been concerned with hydroelectric developments in South Carolina. Nor was he a stranger to the Saguenay. He had inspected the river in 1912 along with J. B. Willson, of carbide fame,[33] and had first thought of the falls in terms of nitrogen fixation. Later he became interested in the aluminum industry and with this in mind joined Price in the project of harnessing the river.[34]

The relatively late date of the development and the financial power represented by the promoters both indicate that the engineering problems were formidable. The country was wild, and a railway line had to be built to the site to assemble the construction materials for the dams and powerhouses. The main fall in the river comes in the short stretch below Lake St. John, which has two outlets, the Petit Décharge and the Grand Décharge. Both of these had to be dammed in order to bring the river under control. The dam on the Grand Décharge serves as a storage and regulating dam,[35] holding the waters back in Lake St. John, as well as a power dam. It was here that the Isle Maligne power plant with an initial capacity of 360,000 h.p. (later raised to 540,000 h.p.) was completed in 1926.

This represented only the first stage of the construction program, however. A second development was planned at a site about 25 miles downstream at the junction of the Saguenay and the Shipshaw, but in fact this project was undertaken by the Aluminum Company of Canada to provide power for its aluminum reduction works at Arvida. A plant, known then as Chute à Caron but now as Shipshaw No. 1, was started in 1928 and finished at its present capacity of 280,000 h.p. in 1931.[36] As a result of the depression, further construction was postponed, and not until World War II was the harnessing of the river finally completed by the construction, during 1942 and 1943, of the huge 1,200,000 h.p. Shipshaw No. 2 plant. At that time this was the largest hydroelectric station in Canada.

The Isle Maligne plant was projected on the basis of the aluminum and pulp and paper markets; the power from subsequent developments has been devoted almost entirely to the aluminum industry. In 1926, Moody's listed the main contracts held by the Duke-Price Power Company: 100,000 h.p. each to the Aluminum Company of Canada, Price Brothers, and The Shawinigan Water and Power Company; and 30,000 h.p. to the Port Arthur Pulp and Paper Company. Except for some changes in the pulp and paper industry, the market was virtually the same in 1940, with the following contracts listed in Moody's: the Aluminum company and the Shawinigan company, 100,000 h.p. each; Price Brothers, 60,000 h.p.; Consolidated Paper Corporation, 42,000 h.p.; Lake St. John Power and Paper Company, 20,000 h.p.; and the Saguenay Electric Company, 10,000 h.p. The Saguenay company has also supplied electricity for local consumption, a business which has increased as industry in the area, mainly aluminum, has expanded. Following the pattern of development in other areas of the province, the Saguenay company merged a number of local electrical enterprises in 1927 and as a result now owns a number of small powerhouses, the only one of any account being a 3500-h.p. station on the Chicoutimi River.

VI. *Summary*

The companies discussed in this chapter exploited immense power resources located in the Precambrian shield area of the province, where agricultural resources were very poor, population sparse, and opportunities for the growth of general manufacturing activity very limited. The water powers of both the Gatineau and the Saguenay Rivers were within easy transmission distance of the populous St. Lawrence lowlands, but the markets for electricity in this area had already been supplied from the more easily developed and more centrally located water powers of the St. Maurice. For this reason, and also because the character of the power sites on the Gatineau and the Saguenay required development in large blocks if they were to be developed at all, utilization of these rivers for power had to await the appearance of extraordinary markets. Such markets materialized in the late 1920's: the growth of the pulp and paper industry and the emergence of a large demand for power in Ontario made the Gatineau development feasible, and expansion of the pulp and paper industry and the advent of an aluminum reduction industry provided the basis for harnessing the Saguenay. The Gatineau and Saguenay companies thus matured as specialized concerns dependent on a few large customers. Their domestic and general industrial business, confined to supplying the needs of the small populations in their immediate areas, has been insignificant, and whatever effect they have had on the general economic development of Quebec must be traced through the impact of their two chief customers, the pulp and paper industry and the aluminum reduction industry.

CHAPTER 8

Hydroelectricity and Industrial Development

1. *Introduction*

The preceding historical narratives testify to the diverse patterns of growth of individual firms in the hydroelectric industry. Except for the Gatineau and Saguenay companies, whose histories share several important features, each power enterprise in Quebec has grown in a pattern peculiar to itself and has affected the economy of the province in different ways. Insofar as generalizations can be formulated from these histories, an inverse rule seems to hold. Where hydroelectric enterprises have been built up in response to "guaranteed" markets, their significance for the growth of a diversified manufacturing economy in Quebec has been either indirect, as in the cases of the Gatineau and Saguenay enterprises, which can claim to have furthered such growth only insofar as the pulp and paper and aluminum industries have done so themselves; or passive, as in the case of the Montreal Light, Heat and Power Company, which has indeed provided the leading city in the province with a satisfactory electricity supply, but which has not promoted in any active way the development of industry in its territory. Conversely, where power enterprises have been built in advance of markets, or have had to scramble to find markets in order to provide for their own growth — situations illustrated by the histories of The Shawinigan Water and Power Company and the Southern Canada Power Company — the hydroelectric firms themselves have directly and actively encouraged the development of a wide range of manufacturing activities in their areas. It is through this latter process, the cultivation of markets, that the hydroelectric industry has made its most obvious contribution to the growth of manufacturing in Quebec.

But even so, is there not much more to be said? True, in an attempt to build up their markets, hydroelectric firms, like railways, may strive to attract industries to their territories. But is there not some less obvious, more pervasive way in which hydroelectricity, by its very presence, fosters industrial development? Is there not some wisdom in the popular notion that the "vast water powers" of Ontario and Quebec somehow "explain" the growth of industry in central Canada? [1] These questions lead away from hydroelectric firms to hydroelectricity, away from historical narrative to a more analytical discussion of the relations between hydroelectricity and industrial development.

Let us first review summarily what has already been written about this general problem. Students who have thought at all about the relationship between electricity and industrial growth [2] incline to the moderate view that electricity is essentially a supplementary form of energy, improving and modifying the old steam-powered industrialism but which by itself scarcely constitutes an adequate energy basis for industrial development.[3] Two general modifications of industrial structures based on coal have been noted by many writers.

In the first place, certain inherent characteristics of electricity give it a clear advantage over steam power in many uses. The divisibility, controllability, and transportability of electricity contrast strongly with the inflexible character of steam power generated by the steam engine and delivered by a complicated system of shafts and belts. Electricity has therefore all but eliminated steam as a form of motive power in modern industry. To a small extent, electricity has also invaded the market for industrial heating. The control over temperature and quantity of heat that electric heating makes possible often results in finer products than can be made with the use of fuel-generated heat, for example, alloy steels made in electric furnaces. Again, the properties of electricity make it technologically indispensable in the electroprocess industries. In still other cases, electricity may solve refractory production problems that resist steam processes. Thus, although base metals can ordinarily be reduced by the use of coal, many of the complex base metal ores of Canada yield only to electrolytic treatment. In these and other ways, electricity has certainly strengthened and improved coal industrialism.

Secondly, it has frequently been suggested on theoretical grounds that electricity should have a decentralizing influence on industrial structures. It seems obvious on the face of the matter that a highly divisible form of power which can be easily transported for distances of two or three hundred miles should give manufacturing industry a significantly greater range of choice, both as to size and location of plant, than was available in the age of coal. On the other hand, no empirical evidence has yet been marshalled to show either any striking decrease in size of plant or any large-scale geographical relocation of industry away from coal beds. We shall suspend comment on this apparent inconsistency of fact and theory for the moment, since the whole question of the locational effects of electricity is discussed in Section III below.

II. *Heat, Power, and the Composition of Industry* [4]

Before considering how Quebec's water-power resources have conditioned the composition of industry, we must be clear about certain technical and economic relationships between different energy sources. We need not dwell on the relations between the fuels — coal, petroleum, and natural gas — because for most industrial purposes they are technical substitutes, and the choice between them depends mainly on their relative prices. It is quite otherwise in the matter of fuels versus water power. Here it is essential to make a sharp distinction between heat and motive power.

In the literature of industrial development, this distinction, when noticed at all, has usually been slurred over, except in the important writings of Professors Nef and Usher. The reason for this lack of discrimination is probably historical; academic discussions of industrialism have centered around the classical industrial structures that have developed in a coal setting. In such a setting, coal has been the source of *both* heat and power, and for that reason it has probably seemed unnecessary to distinguish between them. But in regions like Quebec, where hydraulic resources are plentiful and fuel resources deficient, the distinction is of major importance because the difference in type of demand is paralleled by a difference in source of supply; heat is associated with fuels and power with water power.

Stated briefly, the reason is as follows. Because of the technical efficiency and convenience of the electric motor as compared with the cumbrous apparatus of belts and shafting necessary to operate machinery when a steam engine or waterwheel is used, electricity is, as we have already noted, the predominant form of energy used for motive power in modern industry. On the other hand, electric heat is more expensive than fuel-generated heat on a B.T.U. basis, so that it is not normally used for industrial heating.[5] Electricity itself, of course, will be generated either from fuels or from water power, depending on which is the cheaper source. Thus in a region rich in fuels but poor in water power, industry will use fuels burned directly for heat and fuels in the form of electricity for power. Regions rich in water power and poor in fuels will generate hydroelectricity: the industrial demand for heat is then in effect a demand for fuels, and the demand for industrial motive power is a demand for water power.[6]

The main exceptions to this rule are provided by three instances where electricity *is* used for heating purposes, two of which have already been noted briefly in Section I. First, electricity is technically indispensable in many electroprocess industries where its action may be electrolytic (as in some chemical industries) or heat-producing (as in electric steel furnaces) or both (as in aluminum reduction). Secondly, electric heat is used in an increasing range of industrial processes where it is not a technical necessity, but where its inherent properties of controllability, cleanliness, and convenience give it an advantage over fuel-produced heat.[7] In Quebec, as we have seen, the use of "secondary" electricity for steam-raising purposes, mainly in pulp and paper mills, provides a third exception to the rule. Secondary electricity is sold only when surplus generating capacity is available. It is specially priced so as just to undersell fuels in the market for steam, and while the average revenue from such sales more than covers the marginal costs of production (which are sensibly zero in hydroelectric plants), it is well below total average costs of production.[8] These three exceptions, however, are unimportant except in a few industries.

The significance of the division of function between fuels and water power in hydroelectric economies becomes evident when we realize that virtually every product of modern industry requires heat as a factor of production at one or more stages in its manufacture. It then becomes clear that fuels (which can supply both heat and electricity) provide an energy base adequate to the whole range of modern production, while water power alone (which can supply only electricity) will be able to support only a very narrow range of industry centering around a few electroprocess industries.[9] A region where water power is in great supply, but fuels are not, will be able to attract the electroprocess industries and those industries requiring only small amounts of heat in their production processes.

The distinction between heat and power takes on added significance when it is realized that, for technological reasons, little substitution between heat and power in manufacturing processes can take place. Fuels and electricity must be used in fixed proportions in any one industry, or more accurately, in any one process.[10] This means that in regions where industry would not have developed if hydroelectric power had not been available, water power and fuels are strictly complementary factors of production.[11] Other things being equal, therefore, industrial adjustment to energy patterns that consist of different proportions of fuel and water power will take place according to the "Walrasian" mechanism whereby particular industries will appear in different proportions from one region to another. The adjustment will not take place according to the "Marshallian" mechanism, whereby the factor proportions used in each industry will vary among regions but the industrial pattern of one region will be, or may be, roughly similar to that of another.[12]

Here then is a theoretical base for the empirical study of industry in Quebec. A statistical study has allowed us to calculate the relative quantities of heat and power used by manufacturing industry in Quebec, Ontario, and the United States, and the results (Chart 5), show clearly that manufacturing activity in Ontario and Quebec has been selectively influenced by the energy situation in each province. The chart indicates that from 1944 to 1946 manufacturing industry as a whole in the United States used the heating equivalent of about 4.8 lbs. of bituminous coal to 1 kwh. of electric power. The corresponding ratio for Ontario from 1932 to 1946 averaged about 2 to 1. The Quebec figures are distorted by the relative importance of the aluminum reduction industry (a heavy consumer of electricity), and particularly by the wartime expansion of that industry. The heat-power ratio for Quebec over the period 1932 to 1946 averaged about .9 to 1 for all industry in the province, and about 1.4 to 1 for all industry except the nonferrous metals group.

These results, interpreted in the light of the analytical discussion, reveal a good example of the "Walrasian" path to industrial equilibrium. Speaking generally, if we rank the three areas in descending order of availability of fuel, United States leads by a wide margin, and Ontario and Quebec follow, separated by a narrower margin.[13] On the basis of availability of electricity, the reverse order emerges, with Quebec having a slight but definite lead over Ontario,[14] and Ontario enjoying a large advantage over the United States. These patterns are reflected in the patterns of industrial development in the three areas. Chart 5 shows that, compared with American industry, manufacturing in central Canada is heavily weighted toward those industries using much power and little heat; Quebec shows the same inclination, but to a lesser degree, compared with Ontario.[15]

The fuel-power resource pattern is, of course, only one among many

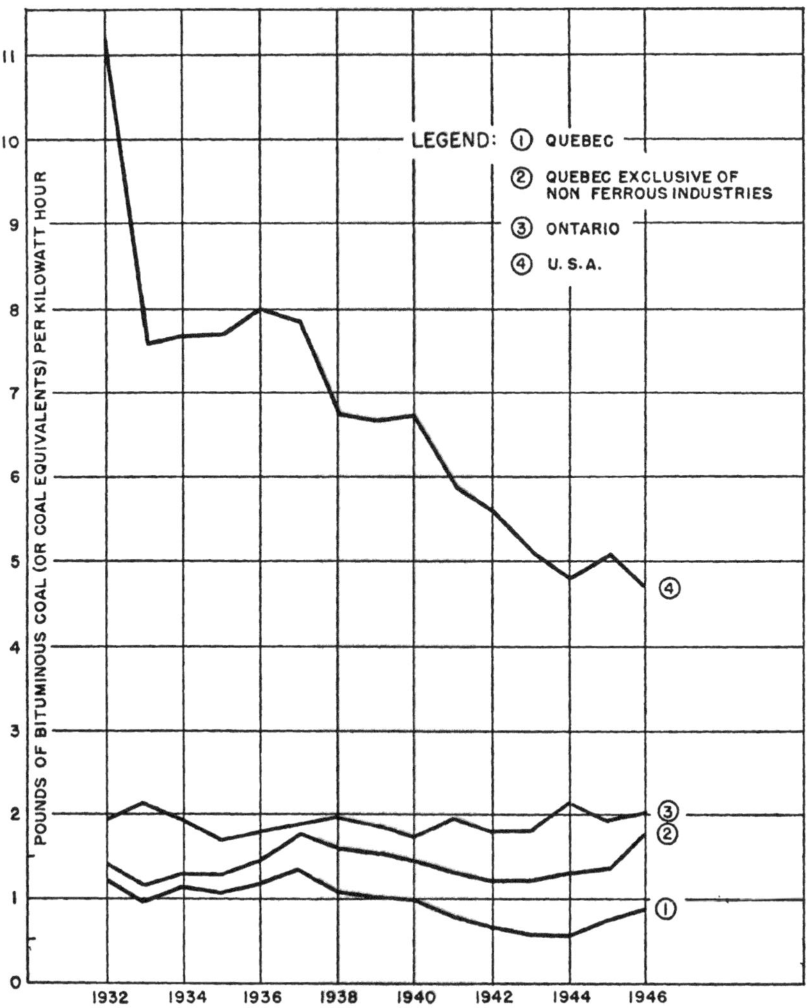

Chart 5. Ratios of Heat to Power used by Manufacturing Industry in Quebec, Ontario, and the United States, 1932–1946

parameters which govern the industrial development of an area, and it would be single-minded to try to account for Quebec's industrial pattern on this basis alone. In a general way, though, we can see how it has made its influence felt. Plentiful power in Quebec has played the major role in locating the aluminum reduction industry in the province; has been an important part of the growth of the pulp and paper industry and the carbide industry, with its derivative products, in the St. Maurice Valley; and has favored the development of such industries as cement, silk and artificial silk, general chemicals, and textiles, all relatively heavy consumers of electrical energy. Some of these industries, notably pulp and paper, carbide, and cement, are also heavy fuel consumers — as are other important Quebec industries such as boots and shoes, glass products, petroleum products, clay products, breweries, and butter and cheese plants.[16] These latter industries serve to remind us that Quebec has large fuel supplies available and does not provide an extreme case of an area which has to rely almost entirely on water-power resources. But the bias imparted by the resource pattern nevertheless shows up clearly in the deficiencies in Quebec's industrial structure, especially in the relative unimportance of heavy fuel-using industries in the province.

The gaps in Quebec's industry may be indicated by a brief comparison of manufacturing industry in Quebec and Ontario.[17] A chart published in the 1945 *Canada Year Book* (facing page 434) compares, for 1939, the net value of production of the thirty leading industries of Quebec with the thirty leading industries of Ontario, and this chart, suggesting the point in industrial development that each province had reached just before World War II, will be sufficient for our purposes.[18] In the main, industries which use large amounts of heat ranked much higher in Ontario than they did in Quebec. Thus the primary iron and steel industry ranked sixth among Ontario industries, with a net value product of $26 million; in Quebec it ranked twenty-ninth with a net value product of $5 million. General machinery-producing industries ranked eighth in Ontario ($21 million) and twenty-first in Quebec ($7 million). Agricultural machinery, twenty-ninth in Ontario with a net value product of $9 million, did not rank among the thirty leading industries of Quebec. Electrical apparatus and supplies ranked second in Ontario ($37 million) and eighth in Quebec ($11 million). Other industries significantly higher in Ontario than in Quebec were rubber goods, food products (biscuits, confectionery, fruit and vegetable preparations, butter and cheese factories), slaughtering and meat packing, and sheet-metal products — all these using relatively large amounts of process heat. The automobile industry, castings and forgings, and hardware and tools, all heavy fuel consumers, ranked among the thirty leading industries in Ontario but not in Quebec. Railway rolling stock and petroleum products,[19] however, provide examples of industries with large fuel requirements that ranked in Quebec but not in Ontario.[20]

More generally, it would not be far wrong, I think, to correlate heavy fuel-using industries with the early stages in the manufacturing process, where much heat is required to reduce, mold, and force natural resources into forms used in later stages of manufacturing. In this latter stage — that is, in the light, or consumer-goods industries — semi-processed materials are fashioned into specific forms and combinations to produce a finished product. As compared to the massive amounts of heat demanded by the early stages of production, this work requires very modest applications of heat, perhaps at only a few points in the production process; on the other hand, a premium is put on controlled power, which is needed to operate those complicated machines that turn out the standardized end-products of our industrial economy.

Thus we see that an area with plentiful supplies of coal will have as its industrial base the primary iron and steel industry and its affiliated metal-working establishments, and that these industries will provide an adequate foundation to support all the other layers of manufacturing from machine industries to gadgets. A water-power area with seriously deficient fuel supplies, on the other hand, will have as its industrial show-pieces a number of electroprocess industries. Such an industrial base can provide a collection of light metals and chemicals on which to build a few other manufacturing industries, but most of the area's output of base metals and electrochemicals will probably have to be exported in a relatively "raw" state to feed the factories of coal-based areas. If the water-power area has a moderate supply of fuels available, however, it will probably be able to compete with coal areas over a fairly wide range of light manufacturing industry. But for its iron and steel goods — for machinery, girders, automobiles, locomotives — such an area will have to rely heavily on imports, and thus on exports, of its staple products. Water-power areas with reasonable access to fuel supplies, such as Quebec, can hope for a respectable degree of industrial development but, at least until atomic heat becomes available to industry, they will continue to have strong ties of dependence to the coal centers of the world.

III. *Electricity and the Location of Manufacturing Industry*

We have noted that many writers have suggested that, on theoretical grounds, electricity should be a force tending to replace the large-scale urban factory of the nineteenth century with a new industrial pattern of small-scale, geographically decentralized, manufacturing plants.

Stated more carefully and in greater detail, the first part of the argument seems to run as follows. One of the main economies of the large-scale plant in the age of steam resulted from the size of its power installation, since large steam engines were physically more efficient than smaller ones. The central electric station, by replacing individual power plants, has removed this important control on the economical size of a manufacturing establishment. Since electric motors can be used to provide individual drive for each machine, the typical production lay-out, formerly unified by the belting that ran from the steam plant to the machines, can now be broken up into a number of separate installations.[21] This "segmentation" of production evidently puts small and large plants on a common footing as far as power supply is concerned, and on purely technological considerations of power supply the optimum size of plant has perhaps become indeterminate. There is one important respect, however, in which the economic implications of electricity have been favorable to the small establishment. By making small-scale production technologically feasible, and by obviating the necessity of a separate power plant for each individual factory, electric power has reduced the investment required to initiate a manufacturing enterprise and has thus made the field more accessible to small entrepreneurs.

Just as electricity has loosened the grip in which the steam engine formerly held the factory and has tended to promote small-scale plants, so, it is contended, the ease with which electricity can be transmitted has loosened the grip of the city on manufacturing activity and tended to promote a geographic decentralization of industry. The assumption underlying this latter contention seems to be that whereas steam power was available mainly to the city, electric power is available almost equally to the city and to the country town.

This argument needs to be carefully stated and should not be pushed too far, because, as we have seen in the preceding section, coal is still a necessity in nearly every manufacturing process, and because coal as well as electricity can be transported with relative ease and economy. If we think in terms of long distances, say one hundred miles or more, it is by no means clear whether it is cheaper to transport coal or electricity. The argument that electricity tends to decentralize industry is strongest when we think of an area within easy trucking distance of established industrial centers. Within such an area the flexibility of electrical-power transmission, in combination with the flexibility of truck transportation for coal, raw materials, and finished products, permits the entrepreneur great freedom of location. Manufacturing industry, particularly industry that does not have heavy fuel requirements, is no longer bound to those "nodal centers" of harbors and railway termini which in the pre-trucking period had definite advantages over other towns in the price and availability of coal. The large city as a coal market has thus lost much of its hold on industry, both because the demand for coal as a source of power has been replaced by a demand for electricity, and because the remaining demand for coal as a fuel can now, as a result of the truck, be satisfied almost as easily in the country town as in the metropolis. This being so, one would expect more and more entrepreneurs to respond to the attractions offered by smaller towns — cheaper and more stable labor supplies, lower land values, and, perhaps, proximity to local raw materials or local markets.

Students who argue along these lines think that they discern a break in historical trend. Coal was centralizing: in terms of steamships, it built up large harbors and destroyed the outports; in terms of railways, it built up large cities and neglected the flag stops; in terms of steam engines, it built up the large factory and weakened the small plant. On the other hand, electricity and oil, once their full implications are worked out, will prove to be decentralizing: in terms of industry, the small-scale plant has been offered new hope by the electric motor; in terms of transportation, the electric-transmission line and the internal-combustion engine promise to revivify the hinterland towns. With this argument and its conclusions, both interpreted as statements of tendency, the author can find little that is wrong — and this in spite of the fact that not very much empirical support for the conclusions appeared during the first three or four decades of this century.[22]

It is necessary to distinguish three different contexts in which the location of industry may be discussed. In the first place, we may take the urban center as a geographical unit and discuss the industrial configuration of cities and towns. Second, we may take the industrial area as our unit of study and discuss the geographical patterning of industry within that area, i.e., the division of industry among different towns and cities. Third, we may take a still larger field of reference and discuss the division of industry among different regions (see Section IV below).

How has electricity affected the city? Its initial impact, in the form of the tramway, exerted an immediate effect on the residential and commercial contours of major cities; as it became feasible to travel greater distances to and from work, suburbs grew and the city began to assume its present sprawling aspect.[23] This decentralization of population and of retail trade was not accompanied by a decentralization of urban industry to anything like the same extent. Nevertheless there were good reasons for expecting industry to share in the movement. On the one hand, with electric power available in the suburbs, and with the truck available as a flexible means of transport for raw materials and finished products, industry was no longer so strongly tied to waterfront or railway-line locations. On the other hand, as compared with central locations, the suburbs offered strong locational advantages to industry, such as lower land values, lower taxes, and more room for expansion. Why, then, was there no large-scale outflow of industry from the centers of cities during the first third of the twentieth century?

There are, of course, good reasons why traditional industrial centers still remain very attractive to many firms: agglomerative forces are strong since a concentration of industries often provides important external economies to the individual firm; and some industries will probably always find it more economical to use water or rail transportation in preference to the truck. Such cases apart, however, it is suggested that the theoretical expectations with respect to decentralization were justified and are now, after a lag of 20 or 30 years, being fulfilled. Neither the electric motor nor the internal-combustion engine was well developed until the 1920's, and the thirties were no time for investment in new suburban plants. The result was that the locational influence of the new technology did not take effect until the prosperous years of the war and postwar period. Personal observation of developments in Toronto and Montreal during the last few years suggests that industrial decentralization is now proceeding rapidly in these two cities at least. Both to the east and west of Toronto, the many new one- or two-story factories along the highways suggest at once low taxes, electric power, and motor transport. In Montreal, electricity and the truck have at last "forced new industry away from the water front to the heretofore empty reaches of the island north of Mount Royal. A vast plain of modern factories has grown up there in the last few years."[24] After a lag of a quarter-century, the centrifugal forces of oil and electricity may have started to break up the hard core of urban industry.

Shifting our attention from the city to the industrial area, should we expect the centrifugal force of the new technology to be operative there too? The same a priori argument seems to apply equally well to both problems. In both cases electricity and the internal-combustion engine have removed some of the restrictions imposed by steam on the location of industry, and just as the attractions of the suburbs seem to be creating a movement of industry away from the center of the city, so we might expect the attractions of the hinterland towns to lead to a still further decentralization of manufacturing. In part, however, the two movements are competitive, and it may be that the attractions of the small town are weaker than those of the suburb. A suburban location offers many of the advantages of the town or village (for instance, lower land values and lower taxation than in the city), and in addition offers the many noneconomic attractions of the large city to both labor force and management. On the other hand, the small town will usually be able to supply cheaper labor than is available in the metropolitan area, a factor important to many industries. Moreover, labor turnover may be significantly less in the hinterland than in the metropolis. Nevertheless, without some special factor that favors a particular town, the advantages of hinterland locations do not seem to be impressive. It is doubtful if the permissive factors of electrical-transmission networks and highway complexes will by themselves lead to any significant revival of the country town.

Canadian statistics on the numbers of employees in manufacturing by province and by major cities allow us to attempt a rough measure of the trend in industrial location between metropolitan centers and the hinterland in Quebec and Ontario. The percentage of Quebec workers employed in Montreal and the percentage of Ontario workers employed in Toronto were calculated for the years 1917 to 1946. Average percentages were then computed for each city for the three decades 1917–1926, 1927–1936, and 1937–1946. Montreal averages for these three periods were respectively 53.9, 49.6, and 46.3; the Toronto averages were 31.4, 31.7, and 28.9. The analysis is crude, and nothing is claimed for its results except that they are consistent with, and lend some measure of support to, the following qualitative comments on the industrial development of Quebec and Ontario.

In Ontario there were many manufacturing towns of importance outside Toronto at the beginning of the electrical age. Indeed, the reluctance of these towns to see Toronto monopolize the electrical power of Niagara was an important force leading to public ownership of electricity in Ontario. From 1917 to 1946, according to our figures, there was no significant change in the industrial balance between metropolitan center and hinterland. All one could say in favor of the hypothesis that electricity strengthens the outlying centers industrially is that the towns founded on coal have maintained their position vis-à-vis Toronto in the age of gasoline and electricity. It is significant though, that in the great industrial expansion of the second world war — an expansion much greater than that of the previous two decades combined — the towns have also maintained their position and perhaps even improved it slightly.

In Quebec the situation has been different, and special circumstances have resulted in a discernible trend to decentralization in the last thirty years. As compared with Ontario, the industrial life of Quebec has always been highly concentrated. At the beginning of electrical development in the province, Quebec City and Sherbrooke were the only centers outside of Montreal that could boast any significant amount of manufacturing industry. This situation was changed both directly and indirectly by the growth of the power industry. Hydroelectric firms, especially the Shawinigan and Southern Canada companies, have actively promoted the industrial development of their areas as a means of building up power sales. Indirectly, the provision of a reliable supply of electricity throughout the province, and especially in the Eastern Townships, has in a sense valorized the other attractions of the hinterland and thus further stimulated its manufacturing development. Thus today, as contrasted with thirty years ago, there are a number of flourishing manufacturing towns to be found outside of Montreal, notably in the St. Maurice valley and in the Eastern Townships. By these routes, then, electricity has certainly promoted a decentralization of industry in Quebec. The relative decline of Montreal has not been great, and the metropolis still accounts for almost half the industry in the province. From the point of view of the rest of the province, however, the new manufacturing towns have been of capital importance. As markets for both labor and produce they have introduced industrialism and an exchange economy into rural Quebec.

IV. *Water Power and the Quantity of Industry*

We now turn to the more difficult problem of the relation between hydroelectricity and the quantity of industry in a region. Here it will be convenient to consider Ontario and Quebec as a single region, and to direct our analysis to "central Canada" rather than to Quebec alone. To what extent can the growth of industry in central Canada be attributed to the region's water-power resources? How is it that central Canada, with no fuel resources of its own, can still compete in industrial development with the northeastern United States, a region with unexcelled fuel resources? Are the water-power resources of Quebec and Ontario sufficiently attractive that modern industry can afford to move to central Canada, even though it must then import all its fuel requirements? Once phrased in these terms of "attraction" and "movement," the problem is revealed as one in the theory of industrial location.

Before we proceed to apply that theory, however, we must be careful to adapt received doctrine to the particular requirements of our problem. Ever since Alfred Weber wrote on the subject, the main stream of locational theory has been devoted to a study of the location of an individual industry (or firm) between different sites *within* a region. Our problem is macroscopic: what determines the location of "industrial structures" *between* regions?

Let us state the assumptions and principles of our analysis and note in passing the modifications which we must make in conventional location theory. The locational problem in general terms consists of explaining the spatial adjustment of mobile things to geographically fixed things. The conventional microscopic problem is to explain the location of an industry according to the location of raw materials, energy resources, labor supply, and the market—all these geographically fixed from the point of view of the individual industry.

Here the macroscopic approach must modify conventional theory. The market is *not* fixed from the point of view of industry as a whole, nor is the labor supply. Indeed a moment's thought makes it clear that today the major markets for manufactured goods and industrial labor supplies are both provided by the populations which grow up around—we may even say are created by—industrial structures themselves.[25] We assume, then, that the locations of the market and of the labor supply are themselves determined by the industrial structure. Not being geographically fixed, they accordingly disappear from our analysis. There remain the geographical fixities, which can be grouped into (1) agricultural resources for food production;[26] (2) resources for industrial raw materials—agricultural products other than food, forest products, and mineral products other than energy materials; and (3) energy resources. This classification embraces most of those materials requirements of an industrialized area that are likely to be regionally localized. It omits, however, such things as climate and water supply, which are regionally localized, and which may have an important bearing on the location of industrial structures[27] as well as on the location of particular industries. It also omits "quarry" products, such as sand, gravel, stone, clay, etc., on the assumption that these construction materials, or substitutes for them, are regionally ubiquitous, although this assumption would be difficult to defend in the case of prairie areas such as western Canada or Argentina.

The principle by which the location of production is determined is the same in our problem as in the conventional one: production will be located at the site or in the region where transport costs are minimized. In what follows, we give only the analysis for a two-region model, and ask simply whether the industrial structure will be located in one region or the other. This procedure greatly simplifies matters since in dealing with only two regions we do not have to speak of the relative distances of the regions from each other, as we should have to do if we used a multiregional model. No sacrifice of principle is involved, however, since our analysis can easily be extended to three or more regions by taking account of the distance factor. Moreover, we do not seem to sacrifice much realism by using a two-region model, since one region's struggle for industrialization often takes the form of competition with its nearest rival.

By applying the general locational principle to our particular model, we arrive at a simple criterion by which to measure the adequacy of a region's natural resources for industrial development. Consider two regions, Region A which has more than 50 per cent by weight of the materials requirements of an industrial structure, and Region B which has less than 50 per cent of the requirements. Assume that different materials have equal geographical mobility. In this situation, the real costs of transport will obviously be smaller if Region A imports its remaining industrial requirements from Region B, than if Region A's materials are exported to Region B. In brief, assuming that different materials have the same geographical mobility, a region will or will not be able to support an industrial development depending on whether it has more than or less than 50 per cent by weight of the materials requirements of an industrial structure.[28]

In locational analysis it is convenient to speak of the "attraction" of each of the various parameters of the problem under discussion. Here it is necessary to clarify rather than modify conventional analysis. In general, the *locational attraction* of x is the weight of x involved (either as a factor or a product) in production, divided by a figure representing the geographical mobility of x. The locational attraction of any material thus varies directly with the amount of that material used in production, and inversely with its mobility.[29] In terms of our problem, the locational attraction of, say, coal, is thus the aggregate weight of coal required by industry in central Canada, weighted (in the statistical sense) by its mobility. In practice, mobility can be adequately measured by the freight rate applicable to the commodity in question over the particular route in question. Basically, the transportability or mobility of a commodity is determined by those things which determine its freight rate — such things as its perishability, the type of carrier employed, and its value in relation to its bulk or weight. In the analysis which follows, we make the simplifying assumption that the mobilities of our various materials groups are equal, but in discussing the results of the analysis we drop this assumption and make allowance for the main differences in the mobilities of the different groups.

Finally, we take explicit notice of the fact that our analysis in general, and the above measure of locational attraction in particular, implicitly assumes fixed coefficients of production. We have no hesitation in making this assumption. It is implicit in most locational analyses; it is an increasingly popular assumption, as witness input-output analysis; and, although the point will not be argued here, I believe that for the analysis of most problems of economic development it is realistic to assume fixed proportions of inputs, at least for the materials requirements of manufacturing industry.[30]

Let us now relate this analysis, which will center around the figures in Tables 10 and 11, to central Canada. Both tables involve (a) "conceptual" decisions as to what magnitudes are desired, i.e., what figures we want, and (b) "statistical" decisions in estimating these magnitudes. The purely statistical problems posed by incomplete data and the (often crude) methods we have used to arrive at our estimates cannot, unfortunately, be dealt with here (see Appendix, Section 4). The conceptual schemes, however, must be clearly set forth.

In our first approach to the study of industry in central Canada, we attempt to state all the materials requirements of the economy which are attributable, directly or indirectly, to manufacturing industry in the area. The figures, therefore, should represent not only the direct materials consumption of manufacturing industry but also the materials requirements of the trade, commerce, finance, construction, and service industries associated with it. This of course includes nearly the whole economy. The only deductions which should be made from the total materials requirements of the economy[31] in order to get the magnitude we want are the materials requirements of those economic activities that would remain in the area if it contained no manufacturing industry; i.e., the materials requirements of the primary industries and the tertiary activities associated with them. Most of these deductions, if we could make them, would almost certainly be small in relation to total materials requirements, because the primary industries constitute a small (and declining) proportion of total economic life, because they probably consume an even smaller proportion of the forest products, mineral products, and energy materials used in the economy, and because only a small fraction of the tertiary activities in the economy are devoted to servicing them. Perhaps the largest deductions that should be made are the food requirements of the population engaged in primary activities and the fuel requirements of that part of the transportation industry used to service the primary industries. As a matter of practical statistics, however, it is not feasible to make all these corrections.

The figures in Table 10, therefore, except for Item A, "Food and drink," are estimates of the materials requirements of the whole central Canadian economy. Item A is obtained by taking the figure for the *per capita* consumption of food and drink in central Canada and multiplying it by the urban population; it thus excludes the food requirements of the agricultural population and of the nonagricultural population living outside urban areas. No adjustments have been made in the other figures, but we must note that the deduction which should be made from Item F (coal) is probably fairly large: its absolute size would depend mainly on what proportion of the total coal consumption of railways one thinks should be charged to the primary production sector of the economy.

The treatment of industrial raw materials involves the special difficulty of deciding at what stage of processing a "natural resource" becomes a "raw material." The figures give the weights of natural products *after* they have been initially processed and are in a relatively "pure" state. This seems to be the relevant stage for measurement for two reasons. In the first place, most raw materials are received at the factory door in a semi-processed condition. Secondly, in many cases the difference between the weights of natural resources and the raw materials derived from them is so great that the initial stage of processing is most efficiently located at or near the site of the natural resource itself. Thus, as a general rule, manufacturing industry draws from the mine and the forest not mineral ores and logs, but metals and lumber. The figures for raw materials therefore refer to paper and sawn lumber

TABLE 10

ANNUAL MATERIALS REQUIREMENTS OF THE CENTRAL CANADIAN ECONOMY, 1949 [a]

Item	Materials	Thousands of tons
A	Food and drink	4,620
B	Raw materials: agricultural	798
C	Raw materials: chemical	908
D	Raw materials: forest products	7,037
E	Raw materials: mineral products	5,766
F	Coal	23,612
G	Petroleum	7,551
H	Hydroelectricity (coal equivalent)	21,359
	Total	71,651

[a] Source: See Appendix, Section 4.

rather than to pulpwood or saw logs, rolled and drawn steel rather than iron ore, and base metal concentrates rather than base metal ores.

The figures of Table 10 highlight two things. They emphasize once again the importance of energy resources to an industrial economy. Of the nearly 72 million tons of materials listed in the table, over 52 million tons represent energy materials. Any region without easy access to large supplies of energy would obviously fall far short of an adequate resource base for industrial development. The table also indicates the large tonnage of food consumed annually by an industrial population and thus suggests the importance of agriculture to industrial development.

The total weight of materials in Table 10 is 71.6 million tons. The main imports included in these figures are coal, petroleum, and an estimated 3 million tons of processed iron and steel (or the iron-ore equivalent thereof), amounting in all to 34.2 million tons. Let us take total imports to be 36 million tons, a figure which provides a generous allowance for other imports of food and raw materials. This leaves a domestic production of 35.6 million tons of materials, or just under 50 per cent of the total requirements. The "50 per cent criterion" of the model is therefore not quite met. If, however, as discussed above, we could make the appropriate deduction from Item F for the coal requirements that should be charged to the primary production sector of the economy, the adequacy criterion would no doubt be satisfied.

The tentative suggestion of this analysis is that central Canada has only just managed to become industrialized, a suggestion supported by the consideration that central Canadians have not reaped the full benefits of industrialization, in the sense that their standard of living is still somewhat lower than that of their American neighbors. However that may be, the analysis brings out two important points. First, when we look at the figure for coal in Table 10 we immediately realize that one of the main reasons why industrialization has been possible at all in central Canada is that the region has had easy access, by lake transportation, to the immense coal resources of the United States. Second, if central Canada had had to import an additional quantity of coal sufficient to generate the electricity which was in fact generated from domestic water-power resources, the region's chances of industrialization on its present scale would have been slim indeed.

Table 11 provides a basis for further analysis.

The conception of industrial requirements in Table 11 is narrower and more arbitrary than that in Table 10. Here the figures are based on two principles. First, we try to visualize the materials requirements of a hypothetical "central Canada" whose industrial structure is made up solely of "light" industry, or more explicitly, of all industry save those "basic" or "primary" manufacturing industries devoted to the first stages of transforming natural resources into industrial raw materials. To approximate this conception the figures of Table 10 are adjusted to exclude the primary iron and steel industry and the staple export industries of pulp and paper and non-ferrous metal reduction. The main effect of this operation is to reduce the energy figures of Table 10 by subtracting from them estimates of the fuel and electricity consumption of these three industries.

Secondly, we assume that every region can command, at reasonable prices, fuel resources sufficient to supply the lighting, space heating, and transportation requirements of an industrialized economy, so that the only energy magnitudes relevant to industrial development are the amounts of fuel and electricity used directly in "light" or "general" manufacturing industries. This is a severe and arbitrary assumption, drastically discounting the significance of fuel resources to industrial development; it thereby increases the locational significance assigned to food and raw materials, since, as explained above, figures for these items are based on the direct *and* indirect requirements of industry. In defense of this procedure, we are content to point once more to the energy figures of Table 10, and to suggest that regions which cannot readily supply at least their domestic and transport energy requirements have little, if any, chance of industrialization. For the rest of our analysis, we simply ignore such regions and confine attention to the more likely candidates for industrial development.[32]

In Table 11, the data are classified into six main groups and the percentage which each group forms of the total materials requirements of the hypothetical economy is given in the last column of the table. The percentages represent the locational attraction of the various materials groups under the assumption of equal mobilities. The problem is to show to what extent the quantity of "light" industry in central Canada may be attributed to the region's water-power resources. We are dealing here with a region which for all practical purposes is devoid of fuels[33] and in which, from 1924 to 1939, no iron ore was mined. Ontario produced about a half million tons of ore annually from 1939 to 1944; thereafter output increased rapidly to over 2.5 million tons by 1951, but most of this was exported to the United States.[34] For the purposes of our analysis, let us assume that central Canada is entirely dependent on imports for its iron and steel needs. In terms of Table 11, therefore, we are dealing with an economy that must import the materials of Groups I and IV.

TABLE 11

MATERIALS REQUIREMENTS OF "LIGHT" INDUSTRY
IN A HYPOTHETICAL "CENTRAL CANADA," 1949[a]

Group	Description	Millions of tons		Per cent
I	Fuel resources		5.6	21.4
	Coal	4.2		
	Petroleum	1.4		
II	Power resources		6.1	23.4
	Hydroelectricity	6.1		
III	Food resources		4.6	17.6
IV	Iron and steel requirements		3.8	14.6
V	Forest resources		3.8	14.6
	Wood	2.4		
	Paper	1.4		
VI	Other raw materials		2.2	8.4
	Mineral	.5		
	Agricultural	.8		
	Chemical	.9		
	Total		26.1	100.0

[a] *Source*: See Appendix, Section 4.

With hydroelectricity, good food resources, excellent forest resources, and much of its own requirements of "other raw materials," central Canada probably has about 60 per cent of the materials requirements of "light" industry, and thus easily meets the criterion of adequacy for industrial development.

The arrangement of the data in Table 11 highlights the importance of food supplies to industrial development; the figure for food is of the same order of magnitude as that for mineral requirements, and considerably larger than that for forest products. With hydroelectricity and with all her raw-material needs (except iron and steel), but without food, the region would have only 46.4 per cent of its materials requirements. Without hydroelectricity, central Canada would have only some 40 per cent of the materials requirements for an industrial structure, and would have had virtually no chance of industrialization. Water power has been a *sine qua non* of industrial growth in central Canada, and the same could be said of the region's agricultural resources. Central Canada's large mining and forest resources, on the other hand, would have been unavailing for the region's industrial development if they had not been coupled with good hydroelectric and agricultural resources.

When the assumption that all the commodity groups have equal geographic mobility is dropped, the conclusion as to the importance of hydroelectricity to industrial development in central Canada is strengthened. In general, the mobility of coal is less than that of petroleum and raw materials (in a semi-processed state), so that the figure for coal probably understates its locational attraction relative to these items. The mobility of coal relative to food or electricity in the general case is less evident. But in our specific case one very important institutional factor has restricted the mobility of central Canada's hydroelectricity and rendered it even less mobile, interregionally, than coal: both the Dominion and provincial governments have put restraints on the export of electricity from Ontario and Quebec to the United States, and these restraints have been effective in keeping exports to a low level.[35] Consequently, when industry has wanted to take advantage of central Canada's excellent water power, it has had to move to Ontario or Quebec to do so.

It must be remembered that these conclusions are at once analytical and specific. They derive from a very simplified model and a study of one particular region. Both the model and the conclusions should, we think, have significance for other areas. But they cannot be transferred to the study of other regions without great care: in the study of economic development in any given region the particular facts of the case are of crucial importance. Having given these warnings, let us note two more general ideas that our analysis helps to make clear—ideas which, though not novel, are useful guides to thought in the field of economic development.

Table 11 suggests that certain parameters of industrial location have become less powerful as a result of twentieth-century technological trends,[36] and especially because of the development of hydroelectric technology. In the nineteenth century, energy meant coal, and a region without coal, even if it was endowed with all the other resource requirements for industry, could entertain little hope of industrial development. The figures in Table 11 suggest that hydroelectricity has changed that. Moreover, such things as fuel economies, which may have been of the order of 50 per cent reduction in fuel consumption per unit of output over the past thirty years,[37] and the rise of light metals and plastics (which reduce dependence on iron and steel and therefore on coal), are probably reducing still further industry's bondage to coal. Some of those regions which had no hope of industrialization as recently as fifty years ago may now have a reasonable chance of developing at least a "light" manufacturing economy.

As the locational attraction of coal diminishes, that of food certainly becomes much more important.[38] The analysis here serves to underline the emphasis that Dr. W. H. Dean, in *The Theory of the Geographical Loca-*

tion of Economic Activities, placed on the importance of food resources to industrial development. Just as a concentration of interest on classical industrial areas has blurred the distinction between fuel and power because of the importance of coal in such areas, so it has disguised this important relationship between agriculture and industry because the major industrial areas have also had a better than average agricultural endowment. A shifting of attention to "new" areas throws into sharp relief problems that have escaped detection in older areas. Our figures suggest the considerable locational importance of food relative to other materials requirements of industry; when relative mobilities are considered, its locational attraction becomes still greater. Food resources are of much greater significance to industrial development in a region than raw materials, which, in a semi-processed form, are highly mobile. Food, on the other hand, is bulky and not susceptible to initial processing by which its weight is reduced to nearly the same extent that raw materials are; most of its weight is "lost" only on consumption. The food requirements of an industrial civilization introduce a certain biological fixity into the locational problem. Energy and raw-material requirements depend to a large extent on the technological setting in which industry operates, and their locational attractions tend to pivot about the more constant attraction of food resources. Dr. Dean has shown how the Industrial Revolution changed a medieval food-oriented industry into a nineteenth-century coal-oriented industry.[39] Present technological trends suggest that the future geographical pattern of industry may more nearly resemble that of medieval times than that of the nineteenth century.

v. *Consumption, Electricity, and Economic Expansion*

So far the theme of electricity and industrial development has been discussed in terms of technology and location theory, that is to say, from the standpoint of production. We have thus displayed the economist's usual bias in favor of arguments from production rather than arguments from consumption. In the past the study of consumption patterns has been much neglected in economics, partly, perhaps, because consumption has been viewed as the end of economic activity, and therefore not a proper concern of a science of means; and partly because any discussion of tastes soon becomes involved in sociology, a subject in which the economist would rather not become involved. Times have changed, happily, and it is now respectable to think of consumption not only as the end of economic life but also, as the Mercantilists thought of it, as a means to such things as full employment and economic development.[40] But there still is no accepted framework for the analysis of consumption's role in economic development, and here we seek merely to suggest one possible linkage between electricity, consumption, and economic growth.

Electricity is a strategic commodity from the viewpoint of consumption.[41] In the first place, its complementarity in consumption to a wide variety of other goods and services is striking. The electrified home is a new kind of dwelling-place. Secondly, during the past thirty years, electrical appliances have perhaps rivalled the automobile as objects of conspicuous and emulative consumption. Finally, by reducing household labor, electricity has been largely responsible for loosing the female of the species on the department store and the neighborhood shopping center. The cartoonist's picture of the poor male surveying the month's harvest of bills is purely a twentieth-century conception.

For these reasons electricity may fairly be viewed as a product with tremendous consumption leverage. Purchases of electrical appliances represent the direct effects of electricity on consumption, but the indirect effects may be even more important. Electricity has perhaps played a not unimportant part in raising the economic position of women in North America. Though doubtless it is true in a sense, as Professor Schumpeter used to say, that one good household servant is worth a couple of tons of household gadgets, the economic repercussions of the two systems are quite different. The disappearance of maids implies that they have become purchasers on their own account, capable of wielding a larger effective demand in the economy. Although less effective than birth control as a means of increasing women's leisure, electricity has been a factor in that development.

The purchase of electrical appliances on a large scale is a necessary first step in the development of an "electrical civilization," and because of the complementarity between electricity and electrical appliances, the rates charged for electricity occupy a position of central importance in the whole process. The demand for electric vacuum cleaners and washing machines depends to an important extent on the price of electricity.

The relationship of costs to consumption of electricity is a circular one of interdependence, and discussions of the problem become involved in the same circularity. To the charge that consumption is small because rates are high, the power companies reply that rates are high because consumption is low. Thus in a tendentious document entitled "Study of the Conditions Affecting the Consumption of Electrical Energy in the Provinces of Ontario and Quebec," prepared by the Shawinigan company[42] and presented as a brief to the Quebec Royal Commission on Electricity by the Montreal Light,

Heat and Power Consolidated, a multitude of statistical series, ranging from numbers of telephone subscribers to postal revenues, is presented to demonstrate that the standard of living is higher in Ontario than in Quebec. All this "proves" that consumption of electricity per capita is low in Quebec and that rates must therefore be high. Argument along this line is sound as far as it goes (for there can be no doubt that there are powerful social and cultural barriers to economic development in Quebec), but its futility becomes obvious when it is confronted with the opposite half-truth, that if rates were lower consumption would be higher. To break this deadlock, long-run forces must be introduced into the argument. The discussion in this section has been designed to suggest that, owing to the special features of electricity viewed as a consumption good, power companies themselves seem to be in a strategic position to break through the parameter of a low standard of living and set in motion both the economic and social forces that make for economic growth.

In this respect, the power companies in Quebec may fairly be said to have restricted, though no doubt unwittingly, the economic development of the province. That retail electricity rates in Quebec have been unreasonably high is suggested by a comparison with Ontario rates, or, if that comparison is rejected, by the rate reductions in Quebec during the early depression years — when one would have expected per capita consumption to be reduced and thus, on the power companies' argument, rates increased.[43] As we have seen, the power companies in Quebec have developed mainly around large industrial markets for electricity and have been less interested in the small retail markets for electricity. The power companies have been active in *extending* the residential market for light and power, but not in *deepening* it: in the main they have either treated it passively as a welcome source of high-value business, or actively exploited it on well-known monopolistic principles. The power companies may point with pride to their contribution to the pulp and paper, aluminum, and chemical industries in the province. On the other hand, it should be realized that monopolistic policies have been in evidence in the retail markets for electricity, with the usual constricting effects of monopoly.

By keeping retail electric rates high, the industry has failed to tap the dynamic possibilities of the consumer side of the market. A policy of low rates to large industries and high rates to small industries and consumers is perhaps partly responsible for the development in Quebec of a lopsided industrial structure — a few big industries at one end of the scale, a host of small furniture, boot and shoe, and cheese factories at the other, and relatively little in between. High domestic rates have worked to keep the standard of living low. A low standard of living provides cheap labor for the large industries, but keeps purchasing power low and inhibits the growth of industries producing consumer durables and other semi-luxury products. Through their rate structures, the power companies have favored the imposition of twentieth-century big business on a *habitant* culture — with all that that implies in terms of social and cultural friction.

VI. *Summary*

In this chapter an attempt has been made to suggest some of the wider economic and social implications of the electrical revolution, and also to relate the general discussion to the particular case of Quebec. Discussion of the industrial limitations of hydroelectricity from a technological point of view has suggested that water-power areas can support a selective industrial structure composed predominantly of "secondary" or "consumer goods" industries that require relatively small amounts of heat in their production processes. Evidence has been presented to indicate that manufacturing industry in Quebec has been selectively influenced in this way.

The argument underlying the proposition that electricity, together with other technological innovations of the last half-century, should lead to a decentralization of industry has been reëxamined. That the new technology permits decentralization seems to be a sound conclusion; that it actively demands decentralization is pushing the proposition too far. Other factors, however, should be expected to induce entrepreneurs to take advantage of the new possibilities. In Quebec there is some evidence of decentralization but not as much as one would have expected; Montreal is still a powerful magnet for Quebec manufacturers. It seems, however, that a decade of depression and six years of war have tended to "freeze" industry and that the decentralizing effects of electricity will be more obvious in the immediate future.

Thirdly, we have presented an analysis designed to answer the question, "What part has water power played in bringing industry to Quebec and Ontario?" The analysis is experimental and not conclusive. It suggests, however, that hydroelectricity has been a prerequisite to central Canada's industrial growth; and it also, in passing, draws attention to the importance of food resources in industrial development. Finally, the consumption side of the problem has been considered — the significance of consumption to industrial development, and the significance of electricity to consumption. The argument is not tractable from a statistical point of view, but is not for that reason unimportant. Indeed, over the long haul, the "consumption effect" of electricity may be more important than its "production effect" in the promotion of economic development. In Quebec the hydroelectric industry, as a result of its rate structure, has neglected to explore this particular avenue, but with lower rates, and with government-sponsored extension of rural electrification, the next decade in Quebec may serve to suggest the importance to industrial growth of cheap electricity for the domestic consumer.

CHAPTER 9

Summary

The hydroelectric industry constitutes a Great Divide in the economic development of Quebec, and, by implication, of Canada. On the one hand it belongs to a young, pioneer, economy: it is one of that succession of "staple industries" on which Canada's economic development has been based, and its growth nicely illustrates that "application of mature techniques to virgin natural resources" which thus far has been the predominant pattern of Canadian economic history. On the other hand, certain special features of the hydroelectric industry become apparent when we look at its marketing problems, and in seeking solutions to these problems the industry has pointed the way to a more mature, more diversified economy. Historically, Canadian staple industries have been characterized by dependence on export markets, and in part the Quebec hydroelectric industry fits this pattern: small amounts of electricity are exported directly to the United States, and a large portion of the output is exported indirectly in the form of newsprint or aluminum. But export outlets have not been a complete solution to the marketing problems of the industry, and it is in situations where power enterprises have had to develop their own local markets that the distinctive quality of the industry emerges. In such situations, hydroelectric development has been a powerful agent in the promotion of a twentieth-century industrial revolution in Canada — an agent, that is to say, in the transition from an economy based on the exploitation and exportation of a few natural resources to an economy which is more diversified, which depends to a larger extent on manufacturing industry, and which is more self-reliant in that a larger proportion of its people make their living by taking in each other's washing.[1] To understand the rise of the hydroelectric industry in Quebec, we must look at it from the traditional point of view; to understand its implications, we must look down the other side of the Divide and see it as a revolutionary force leading the province into a new type of economic development.

1. *Rise of the Industry in Quebec*

The rise of the electrical industry in Canada may be divided into two phases. The first phase, following almost exactly the American development, was experimental in nature and of purely local significance. As European contributions were worked into electrical "systems" by American inventors and businessmen, the latter brought the new techniques to Canada. From 1880 on, first arc- and then incandescent-lighting systems, usually installed by the subsidiaries of American firms or by Canadian firms operating under license from the patentee, began to appear in Canadian cities. As the new technology became more familiar electric lighting systems were set up in smaller towns and villages; a local mill owner, for example, might install a generator at his dam, string a couple of lines through the town, and enter the electrical business. The investment required was moderate and the technique involved was quite elementary, with the result that the number of such installations grew rapidly.

These pioneer electrical works were rendered obsolete by the advent of the large hydroelectric station around the turn of the century, but they did not immediately disappear — in fact, they displayed that tenacity of life characteristic of small-scale enterprise in most industries. Eventually their common fate was to succumb to the superior financial and engineering resources of a large regional power system, but the timing of the process varied from area to area and from firm to firm. As we have seen, the pioneer enterprises in Montreal were amalgamated into the Montreal Light, Heat and Power Company in the early years of the century; and by the first world war The Shawinigan Water and Power Company had absorbed a number of local enterprises operating in the towns along the St. Lawrence River. In the twenties and thirties, the absorption of small firms was speeded up throughout the province as new regional systems were formed and the two older ones extended. Today, the process is still not quite complete. Some local enterprises have escaped amalgamation in form, if not in fact, by continuing to operate as retailers of power they buy from a regional generating company; a few, with larger water-power resources, such as those at Sherbrooke and Magog, have so far managed to maintain their identity, but their resistance is bound to weaken as demand grows and they are forced to purchase part of their power requirements from the larger systems; finally, in the less developed districts of the province, a few villages still obtain their electricity from local plants. Even in the aggregate, though, these local enterprises are of negligible importance to the province's electricity supply. Indeed, even during their heyday around the turn of the century, they were experimental lighting systems, catering to those with newfangled notions, rather than public utilities in the full sense of the term. The local establishments were financially and technologically weak affairs — even in the cities breakdowns were frequent, and in the towns and villages much of the engineering was definitely amateurish — but they did perform two functions. They introduced a generation of Canadians to the electric light, and they served as a training ground for a corps of Canadian electricians, many of whom took active parts in the subsequent growth of the industry.

The second phase of Canadian electrical development was inaugurated by the construction of large hydroelectric stations at Shawinigan Falls in Quebec and at Niagara Falls in Ontario. Both these projects followed hard on the heels of the successful installation at Niagara Falls, New York, and this latter enterprise in fact was responsible for more of a break in the trend of Canadian power development than of American. In the United States, where most of the electricity is produced from coal, the significant development which led to the growth of giant urban power stations was the changeover from the steam engine to the steam turbine. In Canada, where water power is the source of electricity, the Niagara Falls plant indicated the value of Canada's large waterfalls and thus the direction which future electrical development would take. Once the possibility of giant hydroelectric stations had been demonstrated, the days of the urban steam station and the small local (steam or hydro) station were numbered.

When the large power site rather than the small waterfall became the center of interest in Canadian electrical circles, the whole character of the industry changed abruptly. From an enterprise of local significance, the central station became a developmental project which provided the social capital for the power requirements of a whole region, and, in contrast to the relatively modest requirements of money and skill involved in local stations, the promotion and construction of a major hydroelectric plant became an essay in finance and engineering. Although on a somewhat smaller scale, the hydroelectric industry resembled the railway in many respects. The power station succeeded the railway as the main developmental agency in the country, as a major field for investment, and as an outlet for engineering energies.[2]

Because of the industry's large capital requirements, large both absolutely and relative to annual revenue, the problem of finance has been of major importance to hydroelectric development. In Quebec, the industry has been financed completely by private enterprise — we ignore a number of municipally owned systems, of which the Sherbrooke enterprise is the largest — except for the construction of storage dams, some of which have been built by the Quebec Streams Commission and then amortized by charges to the benefiting companies. Canadian capital resources were inadequate, and the great majority of the funds invested in the Quebec industry has come from abroad, mostly from the United States.[3]

Although there is no detailed information available on the financing of the Quebec companies, we can see in a general way how the capital problem was met in each instance. Shawinigan, as a pioneer enterprise, faced severe difficulties in fund-raising in the early years. Risk capital came in the first instance from the Boston capitalist, John Joyce. Additional requirements were raised by J. E. Aldred's energetic canvassing in Quebec, and probably through his financial connections in Boston. Even so, it was necessary to make arrangements for the construction contractor to accept his payment in Shawinigan stock. Once the company had proved its technical competence and indicated its business prospects by delivering current to Montreal, the problem of raising funds was greatly reduced. Partly owing to his success with Shawinigan, Mr. Aldred became well-known in financial circles and later set up his own investment company with offices in New York, London and Montreal. With a good operating record, and with these connections, Shawinigan securities soon gained a secure position in the financial world.

The Montreal Light, Heat and Power Company, as such, has never faced a severe financial problem for two reasons. In the first place, investment risks have been reduced to a minimum since the company itself has done little building. Risks were borne by original investors in companies that were later taken over by the Montreal company as going concerns, or, in the case of the large Beauharnois plant, after capital costs had been reduced by bankruptcy. Other risks were shifted to Shawinigan investors insofar as the Montreal company's supply of electricity was purchased from that company, and investment risks were shared with Shawinigan in the construction of the Cedars Rapids plant. Secondly, and of at least equal importance, the company's position in the Montreal market gave it tremendous earning power and assured its bonds of a high financial rating. Sir Herbert Holt solved his capital problems indirectly through his capabilities as a business strategist.

In three other instances, capital for the power industry has come from, or has been raised on the credit of, other industries. The Maclaren-Quebec Power Company grew out of the lumbering enterprises of the Maclaren family; the Gatineau Power Company was backed by the International Paper Company; and the Saguenay projects have drawn on the resources and credit of the Price forest industries, the Duke tobacco interests, and the Aluminum Company of America. Only such formidable backing as this could have permitted the construction of the large power plants on the Gatineau and Saguenay Rivers within the short period of a few years in the late 1920's.

The Southern Canada Power Company is on a much smaller scale than any of the other major power companies in the province, and its historical development has been quite different. Because it was the exceptional case of a power company which was built up gradually, it has been able to avoid the more severe capital problems of other companies. It has been able to purchase power from Shawinigan as its requirements increased, and when it did have a surplus of its own power, after the completion of its one large development at Hemmings Falls in 1925, Shawinigan again helped out by purchasing a portion of that station's output. Southern Canada's financial path has been smoothed by close association with a Montreal financial house, and its capital requirements have been so modest that security sales to its customers have been an important source of capital for the enterprise.

In the rise of the hydroelectric industry, not only in Quebec but throughout Canada, the Shawinigan company has played a role of considerable importance. It was the Canadian counterpart of the Niagara Falls Power Company, and from that pioneer American enterprise it drew its first Chief Engineer, and in 1910, a young engineer, Julian C. Smith, who later became president of the company. One of the builders of its chemical subsidiary had previously been employed by one of the electroprocess concerns at Niagara Falls. Like its prototype, the Shawinigan company was technologically enterprising. Its transmission line to Montreal, put into operation in 1903, was the longest commercial line which had been constructed up to that time, and the success of this line may be said to have established the credit not only of the Shawinigan company but also of the whole Canadian hydroelectric industry. Shawinigan took the initiative in experimenting with storage dams and river control, a technique which has more than doubled power production on the major Quebec rivers. Its engineers designed the electric steam boiler which provided a market for much of the industry's surplus power during the 1930's, not only in Quebec but also in other parts of Canada and in the United States. These are only the highlights of the Shawinigan company's technical history. They were based on a continuous concern for technological excellence which produced many less spectacular improvements in its physical plant. The quality of its engineering work was widely recognized, and its subsidiary, the Shawinigan Engineering Company, Ltd., formed in 1919 as an outgrowth of the parent concern's engineering department, has done custom work for other hydroelectric enterprises both in Canada and abroad.

II. *Marketing and Industrial Development*

When viewed from a marketing standpoint, high investment requirements become heavy overhead costs, and techniques of "spreading the overhead" have dominated the selling side of the power, and more especially the hydroelectric power, industry. Of these, price discrimination — a technical term which has no evaluative significance — is an obvious example. Price discrimination in the electrical industry has been a business stratagem designed to increase the volume of business and to spread overhead costs by increasing the utilization of fixed investment. Insull took credit for bringing the two-part lighting tariff to Chicago from England, and was precocious in developing the industrial market for electricity in Chicago by means of wholesale rates and various forms of incentive pricing. In the early history of the industry, much ingenuity was expended in the search for a "scientific" electrical tariff — meaning thereby a schedule of rates that would accurately reflect costs — but in the final analysis it was realized that overhead costs are indivisible and rates were set on the basis of what the traffic would bear, modified by considerations of economic and political expediency. Given the cost structure of the industry, discriminatory pricing was inevitable. That it has served the businessman's purposes of expansion and profits there can be no reasonable doubt. Whether the forms and degrees of price discrimination that have been used have been optimal from a social point of view is a question that cannot be answered confidently. Economic theory provides a criterion for social efficiency on the basis of a number of simplifying assumptions, but it cannot easily be applied to the complexities of the power industry. Nor is it likely that a theoretical criterion would be a sufficient guide in this instance. Electrical power is now a parameter of our economic life, and economic theory is notoriously insufficient when it comes to the analysis of parameters.

The active development of demand is a second major means whereby hydroelectric firms can provide for expansion and for fuller utilization of capacity. In simple commodity markets, supply schedules and demand schedules may be considered independent entities whose interaction determines price, and in the long run the amount supplied will vary according to changes in the demand schedule. In the hydroelectric industry, the demand and supply sides of the market are by no means independent, and though capacity may indeed change as a result of changes in demand, it is also clear that demand may be increased as a result of increases in capacity. Because supply and demand are not independent, the price of electricity cannot be explained as a simple result of them: indeed, in the market for electricity, price becomes an independent variable which can be used to regulate demand — a consideration which provides an analytical rationale for discriminatory and developmental pricing in the industry. The fact that in the long run the demand for hydroelectricity may be responsive to capacity, in contrast to simple commodity markets where the reverse is the usual case, arises from the indivisibility of water-power resources and the consequent difficulty in many cases of adjusting hydroelectric capacity to demand. In such cases an attempt must be made to adjust demand to supply.

The difficulty of providing the adjustment between demand and capacity varies from company to company depending on the nature of their water-power resources and the markets that are available or can be developed. When markets are available to absorb power in large blocks corresponding roughly to the large blocks of capacity that are to be developed, the problem may be solved simultaneously. Thus, in Quebec, the Saguenay River was developed when it became possible to pair off the capacity of the power site with the demand from the pulp and paper and aluminum industries. The pulp and paper industry in the area (which had been using hydraulic power) was unable itself to absorb all the power, and thus the exploitation of the site was delayed until another large consumer, the aluminum industry, appeared on the scene. Similarly, the power sites on the Gatineau and Lièvre Rivers were developed on the basis of block demands from the pulp and paper industry and from the Ontario Hydro-Electric system; and the Beauharnois enterprise, the first large-scale development of St. Lawrence power, was promoted primarily on the basis of selling large blocks of power to Ontario and to the Montreal Light, Heat and Power Consolidated. In these cases, a rough equilibrium has been achieved, so to speak, in one step.

The development of the St. Maurice River illustrates a different type of adjustment. Particularly during the first twenty years of the Shawinigan company's operations, capacity had to be built in advance of demand because the market for electricity was still in its infancy and the harnessing of Shawinigan Falls involved developing large amounts of power at one time. The first station at Shawinigan Falls had a designed capacity of nearly 60,000 h.p.; between 1901 and 1910 this power was put on the market in blocks of about 5000 h.p. as additional generating units were installed in the station. After 1910 the pace quickened, a second development was built, and another 90,000 h.p. were put on the market by the end of 1914. Such increments of power are modest by present standards, but relative to the market for electricity before World War I were very large. During the 1920's, power was put on the market in increments of 100,000 h.p. and more, but the buoyancy of the pulp and paper market during that decade made the problem of marketing relatively simple, and there was a close correlation between increases in capacity and increases in the peak load for firm power. With the slackening of the rate of growth of demand in the 1930's, and with two large additions to capacity in 1929 and 1934, a large gap appeared between capacity and the demand for firm power. The increased capacity of 1929 was not fully utilized until 1936, and the 1934 capacity was not required for firm power deliveries until 1940. Throughout its history, the Shawinigan company has had to increase its capacity by large increments as a result of the size of the St. Maurice's waterfalls, and has been under pressure to develop new power sites not only because of the increasing demand for power but also in order to forestall the development of the river by other interests. Consequently, in order to foster full utilization of its plant and thus to reduce the pressure of overhead costs, the company has been forced to carry on an energetic campaign to expand its market. A large part of Quebec's industrial development has been the result.

In building up its industrial market, the Shawinigan company first of all attempted to attract large power-using industries to the St. Maurice area. At the outset, it obtained an aluminum plant as a customer, built up a carbide company, and sold power to a pulp mill. The aluminum industry provided for its expansion by retreating to more remote areas where there was less competition for power, but the two latter industries grew to large proportions in the St. Maurice valley. In the promotion of the pulp and paper industry, the Shawinigan company played no direct part, but in the expansion and diversification of the chemical industry in Shawinigan Falls it has been the prime mover. From the initial carbide plant grew the company's subsidiary, Shawinigan Chemicals Ltd. It expanded greatly during the first world war; managed to survive on a much reduced scale after the lapse of war contracts; and as the result of much research was able to enter a new period of expansion based on plastic products in the late 1920's. In 1931 the Shawinigan company helped to persuade Canadian Industries Ltd. to build a cellophane plant in Shawinigan Falls, and this company has been responsible for the growth in the town of another chemical complex including hydrogen peroxide, solvents, and caustic soda. Finally, after World War II, Shawinigan participated in the research that has led to the development of a titanium and iron industry at Sorel. In the search for markets, other industries were not neglected. Textile firms were encouraged to locate at Shawinigan Falls to take advantage of the labor supply offered by the wives of men who were attracted to the industries already mentioned. A variety of other firms were attracted to Shawinigan Falls and Three Rivers. The power company set up an industrial development department, with offices in New York and London, and constantly sought to bring new enterprises, large or small, to its area.

The Southern Canada Power Company has also, throughout its history, been very active in industrial development. Its purpose in attracting industries, however, has been somewhat different from that of the Shawinigan company. Its power resources are small, and it has been able to minimize the problem of relating supply to demand through the coöperation of the Shawinigan company in the exchange of power between the two systems. The Southern Canada company has not been faced with any serious problem of disposing of large increments of power, and the problem of overhead costs has been posed mainly in terms of making as full use as possible of its own generating plants and the power which it purchases under long-term contracts. It has, therefore, not sought to attract large power-consuming industries to its area: such loads would only require it to increase its purchases from Shawinigan, and the profit margin on the resale of the power would be small. The company has, however, devoted much energy to attracting small industries, preferably large labor-users, to its area — and that for two reasons. In the first place, the factories provide a daytime load which dovetails with the lighting market and thus improves the company's load factor. Secondly, and more important, such industries increase the population of the towns and thus lead to the growth of the company's high-value domestic, commercial and street-lighting markets. The industrial development in the Eastern Townships is thus of a different nature from that of the St. Maurice valley, the Saguenay area, and the banks of the St. Lawrence. In contrast to the heavy, power-consuming industries of the latter areas — pulp and paper, aluminum, heavy chemicals, cement, and titanium — the Townships[4] have attracted a considerable number of "light" industries — all sorts of textiles, rubber products, specialty metal-working plants, and a wide variety of consumer small-wares. The economic revival of the Townships during the last forty years owes much to the hydroelectric power industry.

III. *Hydroelectricity and Industrialization*

The close connection between hydroelectricity and industrial growth in Quebec, illustrated in our historical work, raises the general analytical problem of the relationship between water-power resources and industrial development. In attacking this problem we have asked three specific questions. To what extent may water power be said to "attract" industries to a region? What sort of industry develops on the basis of water-power resources? And what effect does hydroelectricity have on the locational pattern of industry within a region?

Economists are frequently of two minds when it comes to a discussion of the relationship between power resources and industrial development. On the one hand, the conventional history of the Industrial Revolution is told largely in terms of the steam engine and the application of power to industry, while even today the strong geographical correlation between power resources and industry is unquestioned. On the other hand, locational theorists have emphasized that power costs are but a small fraction of total costs in modern industry, and have led us to believe that therefore power resources are unimportant in determining the location of manufacturing activities, except in a few well-known cases of large power-consuming industries. The apparent contradiction arises partly from the fact that the first statements, with their implicit emphasis on the importance of power resources to industrial development, refer to the location of industrial structures *between* regions, while the second proposition relates to the location of a firm or an industry between different sites *within* an industrial region. In part, too, the contradiction arises because the second argument is based on a measure of locational attraction — the ratio of the cost of a factor of production to total costs — which is theoretically indefensible and which may be seriously misleading in practice. The locational attraction of a factor of production, it is clear, is an inverse function of the difficulty of moving that factor. Thus the locational attraction of a factor is properly measured by the weight of that factor required in production divided by some index of its geographic mobility, such as the freight rate it takes. When we reflect that most industries require large tonnages of coal, and that coal, being bulky and heavy in relation to its value, is not a highly mobile commodity (in spite of the preferential treatment it usually receives in freight rate structures), it is not surprising that industry has gone to the coal beds.

We have approached the question of the locational attraction of water power to industry by two quite different lines of argument. First, we have attempted to adapt received locational theory, which deals predominantly with the location of firms or industries within a region, to the problem of the location of industrial structures between regions. By so doing, we were able to arrive at a judgment of the locational attraction to industry of the water-power resources of central Canada; namely that the attraction of hydroelectric resources, relative to that of other factors of production, was large, both because of the large amounts of electricity used by modern industry and because of the limitations imposed on the interregional mobility of electricity by the governments of Ontario and Quebec. Water power was shown to have a much greater attraction for industry than any other group of industrial requirements with the single exception of coal. Our conclusion was that the water powers of central Canada have been a necessary condition of the region's industrial development. The common Canadian impression that the industrial growth of Ontario and Quebec has in large part been a result of the water-power resources of those provinces seems to be well founded.

Our second line of argument, developed with respect to Quebec alone rather than to central Canada, suggests, however, that the hydroelectric industry in Quebec has failed to take full advantage of the potential for economic development inherent in the province's water powers. Industrial development is a matter of the economics of demand as well as of the economics of production. Electricity, we have suggested, is a commodity which is almost unique in its impact on demand curves; because of its complementarity with a wide range of other goods and services, and because of its influence on a community's whole pattern of life, electricity may under favorable conditions induce that desire for a higher material standard of living so characteristic of an economically progressive society. In Quebec, the hydroelectric industry's policy of charging high rates for electricity in retail markets, and particularly in the domestic market, has dampened down and restrained these forces making for economic progress. The industrialist's reluctance to test the elasticity of his demand curve for downward price movements is notorious, but the electric entrepreneur's timidity[5] in this respect has perhaps been more costly to society than that of any of his fellows. In Quebec, no doubt, the power companies have been faced with stubborn cultural barriers to an expansion of the per-household consumption of electricity; but it is also clear that they have made but grudging attempts to overcome those barriers by offering their commodity at attractive rates.

To help answer our second question concerning the type of industry that develops in a water-power region we have argued from technology. Water power, an excellent source of electricity, provides a much more limited energy base for manufacturing industry than does coal, for electricity, though the preferred form of energy for industrial motive power, has severe limitations as a source of heat. Coal, on the other hand, is a good source of both electricity and heat. Since individual industries require heat and power in approximately fixed proportions, the industrial adjustment to an energy resource pattern characterized by plentiful water power and a scarcity of fuels, will be worked out, not by individual industries adjusting their production coefficients to the energy situation, but by a selective process whereby the industries locating in the region will for the most part be those which, technologically, require small amounts of heat in their production processes. Statistical evidence strongly suggests that the industry of Quebec has been selectively influenced in this manner. In descriptive terms, this bias seems to mean that the manufacturing sector of Quebec's economy is comprised mainly of light, consumers'-goods industries.

And what of the geographical pattern of this industry? Does it provide evidence of that "decentralizing" influence which is supposed to result from electrical development? Our results here parallel those of other investigators. The evidence for any significant dispersal of industry away from nineteenth-century manufacturing centers is surprisingly small, and what change there has been seems to have taken the form mainly of a movement of industry to the suburbs of large cities rather than to hinterland towns. (Only the most confirmed devotees of the decentralization thesis ever expected industry to be diffused at all evenly throughout the countryside.) A rough calculation for Quebec suggests that whereas thirty-five years ago Montreal accounted for slightly more than half of the industry of Quebec, it now accounts for slightly less than half of the province's manufacturing. But this calculation is apt to disguise the significance of the industry which the hinterland towns *have* gained. What has been a small relative loss to Montreal has been a large gain, both absolutely and relatively, for the outlying towns. In Quebec, the passive decentralizing tendencies of electricity itself which allows manufacturing industry greater freedom of location, have been reinforced by the active policies of the Shawinigan and Southern Canada power companies in building up the industrial demand for electricity in their respective areas. The result has been a pronounced quickening of economic life in the towns along the St. Lawrence and in the Eastern Townships.

In terms of trend, or historical time, the hydroelectric power industry is still very young, and its implications for economic development have not yet been fully worked out by any means. Advances in the utilization of electricity for heating purposes may allow hydroelectric areas in the future to compete with coal areas over a wider range of industry. Continuation of those technological improvements in the use of fuel which during this century have already greatly reduced the fuel requirements of industry may further weaken the locational attraction of coal, and thus enhance the attraction of food resources and water-power resources. In Quebec, political pressure points in the direction of lower electrical rates for domestic consumers, and the rate of industrial growth in the province may thus be stimulated from the side of demand to a much greater extent than it has been in the past. Finally, the implications of electricity for the geographical pattern of industry within a region may be more apparent in the future than they have been in the past. Industry first became electrified on a significant scale during the 1920's; but the locational adjustments implicit in this new form of power were prevented from taking effect for some twenty years by the "freezing" of industry first by depression and then by the exigencies of war. At the end of the present investment boom, we may very well find that the geographical pattern of industry has been substantially altered. Our study of the electrical revolution in Quebec closes at the outbreak of the second world war. It has been a study only of beginnings, not of full achievements.

APPENDIX

Appendix: Statistical Materials and Notes

The output and sales statistics used in this book come mainly from two sources: (1) the Dominion Bureau of Statistics' annual publication *Central Electric Stations in Canada*, and (2) certain compilations made by Dr. Huet Massue, statistician for The Shawinigan Water and Power Company, who kindly made his data available to me. Dr. Massue's figures, apart from estimates which he himself has made in a few cases, are also D.B.S. figures, some of which are published and some unpublished, the latter having been obtained directly from the D.B.S. by Dr. Massue. Dr. Massue's figures in many cases provide a finer breakdown of the data than do those published by the D.B.S., and I have therefore used them extensively.

The Dominion Bureau of Statistics started to collect data on central electric stations in 1917 and began to publish statistics of "kilowatt hours generated" in 1919, but only since 1932 has a breakdown of electrical consumption been appended to the table entitled "Electric Energy Generated" in the annual publication mentioned above. This breakdown is adequate for the retail markets, but otherwise simply divides consumption into "exports" and the vague category of "large power." Secondary power production by provinces was reported from 1933 to 1941; since then only the monthly production in Canada has been published, while provincial consumption of power has been reported under the headings of electricity used for "Power and Light" and for "Other Purposes." The latter heading apparently includes at least the two qualitatively different categories of secondary power and power used for electroprocessing. Such statistics as are available refer to "central electric stations," that is, to all electrical generating plants except those installed by industries purely for their own use. Throughout Canada, according to the *Canadian Statistical Review* (September 1948, p. 1), plants not classed as central electric station "represent considerably less than 10 per cent of the total output [of electricity]." Furthermore, "about 98 per cent of the electrical output of central stations in Canada is generated from water power."

The following notes should warn the reader that the statistics here presented are perhaps even less capable than most figures of bearing too fine an interpretation. They are meant primarily to indicate trends and orders of magnitude, and for such purposes they are thought to be reliable. Percentages and average revenue figures have been calculated on a slide rule.

Section 1

Note to Table 1

The figures for the period 1900 to 1920 overstate the size of hydroelectric development because they include hydraulic power used directly in pulp and paper and other industries. The discrepancy for 1920 can be read from the table. The figures for 1920 to 1940 include small amounts of steam capacity, but its proportion to the total is insignificant. The more important bias is in the opposite direction, in that the figures refer only to central electric stations and thus exclude hydroelectric capacity installed by industries, especially pulp and paper, purely for their own use; however, this capacity is also small relative to the total.

Notes to Chart 1 and Exhibit A

The attempt here has been to show the output of electricity from stations owned by, or which came to be owned by, the various power companies discussed in the study. The Montreal Light, Heat and Power Company and The Shawinigan Water and Power Company, in their own statistical records, have of course listed as "purchased power" electricity purchased from concerns which at the time were subsidiaries, or which later became subsidiaries. Such purchases have been included here in the power output of the two major concerns: thus, for example, the output of the plants at Cedars Rapids and Beauharnois has been included in the Montreal figure, and the output of the Laurentide Power Company has been included in the Shawinigan figure.

No direct figures for Shawinigan purchases from the Saguenay Power Company were obtained. It is known, however, that the 100,000 h.p. involved has been taken at very nearly 100 per cent load factor, so that an estimated deduction has been made from the "total electricity generated and purchased" figures provided by the Shawinigan company, yielding the figures listed in Exhibit A. A deduction of 500 million kwhs. was made for 1927, the year in which deliveries began to be made under the contract, and 653 million kwhs. for the following years; the latter figure represents (very nearly) the kilowatt-hour production of 100,000 h.p. at 100 per cent load factor.

No correction has been made for the small excess of Shawinigan purchases from the Southern Canada Power Company over sales to that company, and to this extent the Shawinigan figures are overstated. On the other hand, figures for the power generated by a number of small stations owned by the Quebec Power Company, a subsidiary of the Shawinigan company, are not available, and such production therefore is not included in the output attributed to Shawinigan.

Output figures for the Gatineau Power Company since the beginning of operations in 1928 are available in *Moody's Public Utilities*, and from 1934 on are also given in two documents filed with the Securities and Exchange Commission, a *Registration Statement* under the Securities Act of 1933, and a *Prospectus* dated June 15, 1946, for 2¼ per cent Sinking Fund Debentures due 1961. Moody's figures include small amounts of purchased power, and for the overlapping years are slightly higher (approximately 60–65 million kwhs. per year) than those given in the S.E.C. documents. This difference is small, however, and in order to get a more continuous series, we have used Moody's figures throughout as a basis for the computations. The figures as given in Moody's include electricity sales in New Brunswick.

Net figures for Quebec are obtained as follows. From 1934 on, the sum of power sales to the New Brunswick International Paper Company and to the Fraser companies,

EXHIBIT A

OUTPUT STATISTICS

(Millions of kwhs.)

Year	Montreal Light, Heat & Power [a]	Shawinigan Water & Power Co.[a]	Southern Canada Power Co.[a]	Gatineau Power Co.[b]	Saguenay Company [b]	Total Quebec [c]
1904		26				
1905		38				
1906		47				
1907	86	60				
1908	74	105				
1909	94	151				
1910	109	149				
1911	137	210				
1912	149	272				
1913	151	361				
1914	133	432				
1915	477	401				
1916	704	479	2			
1917	730	629	15			
1918	760	741	14			
1919	652	730	15			1,924
1920	680	833	24			1,915
1921	683	700	20			1,791
1922	698	1,145	27			2,540
1923	821	1,314	29			2,816
1924	872	1,668	31			3,715
1925	886	2,003	71		161	4,045
1926	928	2,130	122		842	4,916
1927	999	2,181	122		1,720	6,524
1928	1,053	2,296	134	1,130[d]	2,097	7,682
1929	1,095	2,766	149	1,750[d]	2,094	8,664
1930	1,193	2,573	161	2,200[d]	2,014	8,823
1931	968	2,594	134	2,100[d]	1,520	8,066
1932	792	2,517	163	2,200[d]	1,647	8,491
1933	1,250	3,190	163	2,340[d]	1,703	9,611
1934	1,639	3,883	156	2,431	1,937	11,336
1935	1,914	4,600	173	2,528	2,212	12,629
1936	1,806	4,879	181	2,419	2,375	13,020
1937	2,148	4,760	235	2,620	2,369	14,341
1938	2,268	4,310	196	2,339	2,327	13,707
1939	2,734	4,813	206	2,656	2,367	15,234
1940	3,347	4,617	187	2,748	2,451	16,011

[a] Figures supplied by the company concerned.
[b] Figures taken from *Moody's Public Utilities*, various years.
[c] Figures taken from *Central Electric Stations in Canada*, various years.
[d] Estimated.

as given in the S.E.C. documents, is subtracted from Moody's figures. For 1928 to 1933 inclusive, where only Moody's total sales figures are available, 87 per cent of these figures are taken as estimates for the output of the Quebec properties of the Gatineau Power Company. This is done on the basis that the New Brunswick plant accounts for about 13 per cent of the company's total capacity; the procedure assumes that the capacity factor was the same in the New Brunswick plant as in the Quebec plants. This correction seems reasonably accurate, since when it is applied to post-1934 figures, it gives about the same result as that given by subtracting sales in New Brunswick from total sales.

Unfortunately, as has been mentioned in the text, there are no output figures available for the Maclaren-Quebec Power Company, or for the Chute à Caron plant of the Aluminum Company of Canada.

Section 2

Notes to Chart 2, Tables 2–4, and Exhibit B

The treatment of line losses poses difficult problems for any statistical analysis of the electric power industry, particularly since the D.B.S. figures for "losses" are so unstable as to suggest that they are merely residual quantities. In Table 2, the losses figures are pure estimates, made after consulting the figures quoted by D.B.S. and those quoted for "losses and other" in Dr. Massue's compilations. In Quebec the estimates for losses work out to 10 per cent of total production for 1931 and 1932 and to 6 or 7 per cent thereafter. In Ontario (Exhibit B) they come to 10 or 11 per cent of total production. Since losses are proportionately much higher in retail business than on bulk sales (where power can be delivered at high voltage, or where the consumer is located near the power station) and since retail sales are much larger in Ontario than in Quebec, it is logical that the percentage of losses in the former should be higher than that in the latter province. These estimates are very crude, and unfortunately affect directly the consumption percentages for "all other" power given in Chart 2 and Table 3, because these percentages are based on residual figures that remain after all the other divisions, including losses, have been subtracted from the total output.

The estimates for losses, however, do not affect the average revenue series given for "General Manufactures" in Table 4: in these calculations the figure for kilowatt hours is obtained by subtracting from "total power used in manufacturing" the power used by the pulp and paper and nonferrous smelting industries, and all these magnitudes, taken from Dr. Massue's figures, are net of losses. (The revenue figure involved in the calculations is derived in an identical fashion from the analogous revenue magnitudes.) Thus the only series in Table 4 that include losses are those for "Total Sales" in Quebec and in Ontario.

Columns 8 and 9 in Table 2, and also in Exhibit B, were derived by subtracting from Dr. Massue's figures for the *total* power used in the wood and paper industries, the figures for *secondary* power given in Columns 5 and 6. This treatment of the wood and paper industries was adopted on grounds of simplicity and expediency; the assumption that all secondary power was used by the pulp and paper industry seemed to be the only way in which secondary power could be disentangled from primary power in the absence of an adequate breakdown of secondary sales. The procedure is not grossly unrealistic, since the great majority of secondary power sales were made to pulp and paper mills for the purpose of raising steam. Nevertheless, it does understate the primary power consumption of the wood and paper products industries, and thus overstates the primary consumption of other groupings which did, in fact, buy some secondary power. This overstatement would probably be most important in the case of the nonferrous industry group.

Section 3

Notes to Chart 5

The tables underlying this rather simple chart are themselves so complex and bulky that they are not published here. They are available as Exhibit K in my doctoral dissertation, *The Hydro Electric Industry in Quebec, 1898–1940*, deposited in Widener Library at Harvard University.

Roughly, the procedure in developing the tables was to collect figures on the industrial consumption of gas, oil, coal, and (in Quebec and Ontario) secondary electricity, and then express these magnitudes in coal equivalents. This figure provided the numerator of the desired ratio: the denominator was simply the industrial consumption of electricity. The raw data for the tables were collected from such a variety of sources that there are probably minor incompatibilities between them. I am satisfied, however, that the resulting ratios give correct impressions of orders of magnitude and are sufficiently accurate for the use I make of them.

In Line 2 on the chart an attempt has been made to exclude the influence of the aluminum reduction industry in Quebec, since this industry obviously depresses the fuel-power ratios because of its inordinate consumption of electricity. No similar calculation is presented for Ontario, because the relative importance of the "nonferrous" group of industries to total manufacturing in Ontario is small.

It might be thought that the "wood and paper products" group of industries, like the "nonferrous" group would be a seriously disturbing influence on the Quebec ratios, because of the large pulp and paper industry in the province. Such is not the case, however, because the pulp and paper industry, although a large power consumer, is also a large fuel consumer. Calculations of the fuel-power ratios for the "wood and paper products" group indicated that they were only slightly less than the ratios for all manufacturing industry exclusive of the "nonferrous" group.

The pronounced downward trend of the United States ratios from 1932 to 1944 calls for brief comment. It reflects, on the one hand, a large and continuous increase in the use of electricity by American industry, and, on the other, low fuel consumption during the thirties followed by only moderate increases during the forties. The trend toward electric drive in the United States continued during the 1930's, although at a less rapid rate than during the preceding three decades. The large, publicly sponsored hydroelectric developments which came into operation during the thirties, and the rapid expansion of the electroprocess industries during the period, also led to heavy increases in the use of electricity. Fuel economies, and severe depression in the heavy industries (the large fuel consumers), kept the industrial market for fuels in the doldrums during the thirties. In contrast to the trend of industrial fuel consumption in the United States, there was an upward trend in such consumption in Ontario and Quebec throughout the depression years, which matched the upward trend in the consumption of electricity — a clear example, as we noted in the text, of the complementarity between (firm) hydroelectricity and fuels in "water-power" economies. When all this has been said, however, the sharp contrast between the trend of the fuel-power ratios in the United States on the one hand and that of the Canadian provinces on the other remains somewhat surprising.

It should be noted that the ratios for the United States have a consistent upward

EXHIBIT B

PRODUCTION AND SALES OF POWER IN ONTARIO, 1931–1940 [a]

(Millions of kwhs., thousands of dollars)

Year	Produced and Purchased		Exports		Secondary		Firm power used in province (1) – (3) – (5)	Firm power used in wood & paper industry	
	Kwhs. [b] (1)	Revenue (2)	Kwhs. (3)	Revenue [c] (4)	Kwhs. (5)	Revenue [c] (6)	Kwhs. (7)	Kwhs. [d] (8)	Revenue [d] (9)
1931	6,162	46,543	824	2,500	67	50	5,271	863	4,404
1932	5,556	49,953	467	3,000	128	100	4,961	920	3,362
1933	6,146	48,877	637	1,000	646	500	4,863	929	3,335
1934	8,268	52,786	912	2,000	1,155	800	6,201	1,034	3,334
1935	8,494	53,535	920	2,200	1,385	1,100	6,189	1,104	3,340
1936	9,324	56,209	1,080	2,900	1,130	900	7,114	1,195	3,702
1937	10,104	58,934	1,253	3,200	1,001	850	7,850	1,257	3,972
1938	9,776	58,176	1,302	3,370	966	1,000	7,508	1,079	3,587
1939	11,066	61,589	1,401	3,611	1,297	1,100	8,368	1,246	3,577
1940	12,303	67,968	1,614	4,143	833	800	9,856	1,259	3,927

Year	Nonferrous industries		Ordinary consumption (7) − (8) − (10)	Retail [f]		Small power		Losses	All other	
	Kwhs. (10)	Revenue (11)	Kwhs. (12)	Kwhs. (13)	Revenue (14)	Kwhs. (15)	Revenue (16)	Kwhs. [e] (17)	Kwhs. [g] (18)	Revenue [g] (19)
1931	136	1,110	4,272	1,336	25,061	170 [c]	3,200 [e]	750	2,016	10,218
1932	188	1,058	3,853	1,364	25,758	175 [c]	3,300 [e]	650	1,664	13,375
1933	241	1,046	3,693	1,355	25,593	186	3,507	700	1,452	13,896
1934	347	1,248	4,820	1,437	26,373	210	3,278	900	2,273	15,753
1935	417	1,392	4,668	1,507	26,999	218	3,515	900	2,043	14,989
1936	505	1,399	5,414	1,613	27,868	229	3,795	1,000	2,572	15,645
1937	658	2,351	5,935	1,735	27,738	242	3,960	1,000	2,958	16,863
1938	609	2,171	5,820	1,893	28,842	235	3,856	1,000	2,692	15,350
1939	692	2,815	6,430	2,023	30,564	252	4,152	1,200	2,955	15,770
1940	853	3,076	7,744	2,167	32,487	293	4,366	1,350	3,934	19,169

[a] Sources: *Central Electric Stations in Canada*, various years. Statistics compiled by Dr. H. Massue.

[b] Generated plus purchased from Quebec.

[c] Estimated by Dr. H. Massue.

[d] These figures are based on the assumption that all secondary power was sold to the wood and paper products industries. They have been derived by subtracting from the figures of total consumption (and revenue) for these industries the figures for secondary power consumption (and revenues therefrom) for the province. The component figures are all Dr. Massue's.

[e] My estimate.

[f] Domestic, farm, commercial and street lighting.

[g] This is a residual category. It is made up primarily of general manufacturing industries, but also includes mines, electric railways, and items unaccounted for.

EXHIBIT C

MATERIALS REQUIREMENTS IN CENTRAL CANADA, 1949
(in tons)

		All industry	Hypothetical "light" industry
A. Food and Drink		4,620,000	4,620,000
B. Principal Raw Materials			
Agricultural			
1. Cotton	108,000		
2. Wool	42,800		
3. Flax	84,800		
4. Other natural fibres	23,400		
5. Artificial fibres	18,800		
6. Imports of rags and waste	18,200		
7. Hides	55,500		
8. Other nonedible animal products	81,800		
9. Vegetable oils	220,000		
10. Tobacco	56,200		
11. Rubber	88,000	797,500	797,500
Chemicals			
12. Sulphuric acid	690,400		
13. Chlorine	106,900		
14. Caustic soda	111,000	908,300	908,300
Minerals			
15. Materials charged to steel furnaces, plus sales of semi-finished forms, plus imports of finished steel	4,852,000		
16. Finished iron and steel	3,800,000		
17. Nonferrous bullion, matte, pig, and ingot	460,000		
18. Refined base metals	275,000		
19. Asbestos	21,400		
20. Sulphur	433,000		
21. Sulphur (excluding pulp and paper industry)	246,000		
Total: Items 15, 17, 19, 20		5,766,400	
Total: Items 16, 18, 19, 21			4,342,400
Forest			
22. Wood pulp	4,686,800		
23. Paper	1,420,000		
24. Lumber	2,350,000		
Total: Items 22 and 24		7,036,800	
Total: Items 23 and 24			3,777,000
C. Energy Materials			
Coal		23,612,000	
1. Consumption			
2. Retail sales	7,182,000		
3. Coke and gas	3,192,000		
4. Wood and paper and nonferrous	2,860,000		
5. Railways	6,200,000		
6. Residual: mainly general industry	4,178,000		4,178,000

Hydroelectricity (Coal equivalents)			
7. Consumption		21,359,000	
8. Domestic sales	2,445,000		
9. Mining and nonferrous	5,845,000		
10. Pulp and paper	4,375,000		
11. Primary iron and steel	895,000		
12. Residual: general industry, commercial, losses	7,799,000		
13. General industry and commercial			6,088,000
Petroleum			
14. Fuel oil deliveries (excluding bunkering)	4,127,100		
15. Gasoline sales	3,423,700		
16. Fuel oil: industrial uses	1,925,700		
17. Fuel oil: three excluded industries	571,000		
18. Fuel oil: general industry			1,354,700
Total: Items 14 and 15		7,550,800	

bias because of the importance in that country of thermal electricity generated by manufacturing industries themselves. The fuel for such generation is included in the numerator of our ratios as heat, whereas ideally it should be excluded. Supplies of electricity generated from coal by manufacturing plants in Quebec and Ontario are insignificant. However, this bias is less damaging to our figures than at first appears, since much of the plant-produced electricity in the United States is generated as a by-product of steam used primarily for heating purposes. On this point, see National Resources Planning Board, *Industrial Location and National Resources*, pp. 170–174.

Section 4

Notes to Tables 10 and 11 and Exhibit C

The raw data for Exhibit C have been collected from a great number of individual sources (in many cases from Census of Industry publications of the D.B.S.) Moreover, in order to get the magnitudes required, I had to resort to very rough estimates in a number of cases. While the individual figures thus command no strong confidence, the table as a whole, I believe, gives a substantially correct impression of the relative magnitudes involved and is sufficiently reliable for the uses to which it has been put in the text.

It has not been thought worth while to publish a detailed explanation of how each individual item in Exhibit C was derived. An earlier version of the table together with explanatory notes is to be found in Exhibit L of my dissertation. The present exhibit represents a substantial revision of the earlier work. A brief account of sources used and methods employed in deriving each individual item in Exhibit C has been filed at Widener: it will be found in the pocket on the inside back cover of the thesis. I would also welcome direct queries or comments on the compilation. Compilations of this sort have not often been made, but an estimate of the annual per capita materials consumption in the United States is to be found in the *Report of the President's Materials Policy Commission* (Washington, 1952), Vol. I, p. 4. Insofar as my figures can be compared with the figures in that Report, the two estimates seem reasonably consistent.

In the text, brief mention is made of the problem of measuring the raw-materials requirements of the economy, but it may be useful to comment further on this matter. In general, as has been stated, the attempt is to measure the raw materials after they have been subjected to an initial processing, and when they are in a form suitable for use in manufacturing plants. The situation is not always this simple, however. In many cases imports of such things as textile yarns must be added to the materials used in the domestic spinning industries in order to get the total "raw materials" used by the domestic textile (spinning, weaving, and finished garments) industries. In the iron and steel industry, we have measured the materials requirements at the steel furnace stage for our first estimate and at the rolling and drawing-mill stage for our second estimate. In both cases, however, we have had to add the net imports of finished steel shapes and the sales of "earlier stage" products such as iron castings, ferro-alloys, and steel castings, in order to get the total iron and steel consumption of the economy. It has been impossible, therefore, to adopt a uniform procedure in making our raw-material estimates: different materials have had to be measured at different stages of processing, and, as just illustrated, the estimate for one item may include weights of the same material at different stages of processing. In the end, each case has had to be treated on its merits. With only a lay knowledge of the technological and business practices of the different industries, it is likely that some of my estimates are too high (as a result of double counting where transactions between firms at different stages in the same industry are involved) and others too low (through omissions). It is also possible that there are important omissions in the list of materials itself. (In this connection, though, it should be noted that the consumption of such commodities as sugar and cocoa are included in the estimate for food; and that the consumption of salt is largely allowed for in the estimate for food and for caustic soda.)

Finally, it may help the reader to understand the difference between Tables 10 and 11 in the text if we explain our rationale in one particular case, say, minerals. Table 10 purports to give the materials requirements of industry in central Canada as it actually existed *circa* 1949, neglecting those "first-stage" industries which subject natural resources to their first processing. In Table 10, then, we must count the materials used in central Canadian steel furnaces, *plus* the pig iron, steel ingots and castings and semi-finished steel forms used in other industries, *plus* imports of finished steel forms, again used by other industries. For base metals, we record the weight of the concentrate which is to be processed in the refineries. These figures, plus the consumption of asbestos and sulphur (Items B19 and B20, Exhibit C) give us the "mineral products" total of Table 10.

In the hypothetical economy of Table 11, we exclude the materials requirements of the heavy iron and steel industry, the pulp and paper industry, and the base metals refining industry. Putting it another way, we are attempting to study the materials requirements of an economy which might have to import the products of these industries. Accordingly we count only the consumption of *finished* iron and steel in central Canada (Item B16), the weight of refined base metals (Item B18), and the sulphur used in industries other than the pulp and paper industry (Item B21). We also add asbestos (B19). The resulting magnitudes give us the "iron and steel requirements" and the "other raw materials: minerals" in Table 11. (Of course ideally we ought to subtract also the asbestos, base metals, iron and steel, and so on that are used in the "basic" industries which we want to exclude from consideration — heavy iron and steel, base metals reduction, and pulp and paper — but as a matter of statistical practicability this cannot be done.) A similar rationale explains the differences in the two estimates for the forest section, and for the three sections of energy materials.

Bibliography

I. Secondary Materials

General Literature

Ashton, T. S. *The Industrial Revolution 1760–1830*, Oxford, 1948.
Bowden, W., M. Karpovich, and A. P. Usher. *An Economic History of Europe Since 1750*, New York, 1937.
Coase, R. H. "Price and Output Policy of State Enterprise: A Comment," *Economic Journal*, LV (1945), 112–113.
Falardeau, J.-C., ed. *Essais sur Le Québec contemporain*, Quebec, 1953.
Florence, P. S. *Investment, Location and Size of Plant*, Cambridge, 1948.
——— *The Statistical Method in Economics and Political Science*, New York, 1929.
Friedrich, C. J., (tr.). *Alfred Weber's Theory of the Location of Industries*, Chicago, 1929.
Gilboy, E. W. "Demand as a Factor in the Industrial Revolution," in *Facts and Factors in Economic History*, Cambridge, 1932, pp. 620–639.
——— *Wages in Eighteenth Century England*, Cambridge, 1934.
Hansen, M. L. *The Mingling of the Canadian and American Peoples*, New Haven, 1940.
Hicks, J. R. "Annual Survey of Economic Theory: The Theory of Monopoly," *Econometrica*, III (1935), 1–20.
——— *Value and Capital*, Oxford, 1939.
Hoover, E. M. *The Location of Economic Activity*, New York, 1948.
Houtthaker, H. S. "Electricity Tariffs in Theory and Practice," *Economic Journal* (March 1951), pp. 1–25.
Innis, H. A. "Economic Nationalism," *Proceedings, Canadian Political Science Association*, 1934, pp. 17–31.
——— *Settlement and the Mining Frontier*, in W. A. Mackintosh and W. L. G. Joerg, eds., *Canadian Frontiers of Settlement*, Vol. IX, Toronto, 1936.
Innis, H. A. and A. F. W. Plumptre, eds. *The Canadian Economy and Its Problems*, Toronto, 1934.

Innis, M. Q. *An Economic History of Canada*, 2nd ed., Toronto, 1948.
Isard, W. and V. Whitney, *Atomic Power*, New York, 1952.
Lewis, W. A. *Overhead Costs*, London, 1949.
Lower, A. R. M. *Colony to Nation*, New York, 1947.
Marshall, H., F. A. Southard, and K. W. Taylor. *Canadian-American Industry*, New Haven, 1936.
Meade, J. E. and J. M. Fleming. "Price and Output Policy of State Enterprise," *Economic Journal*, LIV (1944), 321–339.
Mitchell, W. C. *The Backward Art of Spending Money*, New York, 1950.
National Resources Planning Board. *Industrial Location and National Resources*, Washington, 1943.
Political and Economic Planning. *Report on Supply of Electricity in Great Britain*, London, 1936.
Quigley, H. *Electric Power and National Progress*, London, 1925.
Report of the President's Materials Policy Commission, 5 vols. Washington, 1952.
Robbins, L. *An Essay on the Nature and Significance of Economic Science*, 2nd ed., London, 1949.
Stigler, G. J. "Production and Distribution in the Short Run," American Economic Association, *Readings in the Theory of Income Distribution*, Philadelphia, 1946.
Sutton, G. D. "Productivity in Canada," *Canadian Journal of Economics and Political Science* (May 1953), pp. 185–201.
Usher, A. P. "Resource Requirements," *The Journal of Economic History*, Supplement, VII (1947), 35–46.
Zimmerman, E. W. *World Resources and Industries*, 1st ed., New York, 1933.

Technological History of Electric Power

Adams, E. D. *Niagara Power*, 2 vols., New York, 1927.
American Society of Civil Engineers. "Economic Aspects of Energy Generation: A Symposium," *Proceedings*, Vol. 63, No. 10 (Dec., 1937), pp. 1883–1949.
Annals of the American Academy of Political and Social Science, *Giant Power*, March 1925.
Bauer, J. and N. Gold. *The Electric Power Industry*, New York, 1939.
Bessesen, B. B. "Governor Sensitivity and Frequency Control," *Transactions Third World Power Conference*, I. (Washington, 1938), 249–250.
Bright, A. A., Jr. *The Electric-Lamp Industry*, New York, 1949.
Bush, V. "Technical Trends," *Transactions Third World Power Conference*, II (Washington, 1938), 655–672.
Cassier's Magazine, 1895 and 1904.
Danielian, N. R. "Certain Developments in the Electric Light and Power Industry," unpublished doctoral dissertation, Harvard University, 1932.
Dannatt, C. and J. W. Dalgleish. *Electric Power Transmission and Interconnection*, New York, 1930.
Dawes, C. L. *A Course in Electrical Engineering*, 2 vols., 2nd ed., New York, 1928.
Dow, A. *Some Public Service Papers*, Detroit, 1927.
Edison Illuminating Company of Detroit. *The Development of Scientific Rates for Electricity Supply*, Detroit, 1915. Reprints of "selected original rate papers."
Electrical World, December 1885; February 1891; September 1892.
Encyclopaedia Britannica, 1946 ed. Articles on "Electrical Power Generation"; "Electrical Power Transmission"; "Electricity"; and "Motor, Electric."
Fleming, J. A. *Fifty Years of Electricity*, London, 1921.

Gruening, E. *The Public Pays*, New York, 1931.

Howell, J. W. and H. Schroeder. *History of the Incandescent Lamp*, Schenectady, 1927.

Insull, S. *Central Station Electric Service*, Chicago, 1915.

——— *Public Utilities in Modern Life*, Chicago, 1924.

Jones, Payson (comp.). *A Power History of the Consolidated Edison System 1878–1900*, mimeographed, 1940, by the Consolidated Edison Company of New York.

Leupp, F. E. *George Westinghouse*, Boston, 1918.

Lewis, B. W. "Public Policy and the Growth of the Power Industry," *The Journal of Economic History*, Supplement, VII (1947), 47–55.

Maclaren, M. *The Rise of the Electrical Industry During the Nineteenth Century*, Princeton, 1943.

Martin, T. C. and S. L. Coles, eds. *The Story of Electricity*, New York, 1919.

Mendenhall, T. C. *A Century of Electricity*, London, 1887.

Mumford, L., "Power and Culture," *Transactions Third World Power Conference*, I (Washington, 1938), 287–302.

National Resources Committee. *Energy Resources and National Policy*, Washington, 1939.

——— *Technological Trends and National Policy*, Washington, 1937. Part III, Sections V and VII.

O'Neill, J. J. *Prodigal Genius: The Life of Nikola Tesla*, New York, 1944.

Parsons, R. H. *The Early Days of the Power Station Industry*, Cambridge, 1940.

Passer, H. C. "The Electric Light and the Gas Light," *Explorations in Entrepreneurial History*, Vol. 1, No. 3 (March 1949), pp. 1–9.

——— *The Electrical Manufacturers 1875–1900*, Cambridge, Mass., 1953.

Person, H. S. "Economic and Social Significance," *Transactions Third World Power Conference*, II (Washington, 1938), 672–685.

Pring, J. N. *Some Electro-Chemical Centres*, Manchester, 1908.

Ramsay, M. L. *Pyramids of Power*, New York, 1937.

Richards, J. W. "Niagara as an Electrochemical Centre," *Electrochemical Industry*, I (1902), 11–49.

Rushmore, D. B. and E. A. Lof. *Hydro-Electric Power Stations*, New York, 1917.

Sporn, P. and A. C. Monteith. "Transmission of Electric Power at Extra-High Voltages," *Transactions of the American Institute of Electrical Engineers*, 66 (1947), 1571–1577.

Taylor, H. B. *The Golden Age of the Francis Hydraulic Turbine*, Address to the Newcomen Society, New York, 1945.

Taylor, L. W. *Physics*, Cambridge, 1941.

The Niagara Falls Electrical Handbook. Issued under the auspices of the American Institute of Electrical Engineers in connection with the International Electrical Congress at St. Louis, Mo., September 1904.

The Twentieth Century Fund. *Electric Power and Government Policy*, New York, 1948.

Transactions Third World Power Conference. Papers on "Electrical Equipment," I (Washington, 1938), 287–302.

United States Department of Commerce. Trade Information Bulletin No. 469, *Central Light and Power Plants in the Western Hemisphere*, Washington, 1927.

Usher, A. P. *A History of Mechanical Inventions*, New York, 1929.

Walmsley, R. M. *Electricity in the Service of Man*, 2 vols., 2nd ed., London, 1911.

Whipple, F. H. *Municipal Lighting*, Detroit, 1888.

Materials on the Canadian Industry

Note: A bibliography of Canadian hydroelectric development is included in the *Bibliography of Canadian Economics* published in *Contributions to Canadian Economics* (University of Toronto Press, 7 vols., 1927–1934), and in *The Canadian Journal of Economics and Political Science* (University of Toronto Press, vols. 1–18, 1935 et seq.).

Books and Articles

Atherton, W. H. *Montreal 1535–1914*, 2 vols., Montreal, 1914.

Baldwin, G. B. "The Invention of the Modern Safety Razor," *Explorations in Entrepreneurial History*, IV (1951), 88–93.

Biggar, E. B. *Hydro-Electric Development in Ontario*, Toronto, 1920.

Biss, I. Articles on "Water Powers" and "Hydro-Electric Power," in W. S. Wallace, ed., *The Encyclopedia of Canada*, VI, Toronto, 1937.

——— "Recent Power Legislation in Ontario," *The Canadian Journal of Economics and Political Science*, II (1936), 212–214.

——— "Recent Power Legislation in Quebec," *The Canadian Journal of Economics and Political Science*, III (1937), 550–558.

Bladen, V. W. *An Introduction to Political Economy*, Toronto, 1951.

Blanchard, R. *Le Centre du Canada Français*, Montreal, Librairie Beuchemin, 1947.

——— *L'Est du Canada Français*, 2 vols., Paris, 1935.

——— *La Mauricie*, Les Trois-Rivières, Editions du Bien Public, 1950.

Brady, A. "The Ontario Hydro-Electric Power Commission," *The Canadian Journal of Economics and Political Science*, II (1936), 331–353.

Brouillette, B. *Le Développement Industriel de la Vallée du Saint-Maurice*, Three Rivers, 1932.

Canada, Department of the Interior. *Canada, Natural Resources and Commerce*, prepared by the Dominion Water Power Bureau, Ottawa, 1923.

——— *Report of the Commission Appointed to Investigate the Different Electro-Thermic Processes for the Smelting of Iron Ores and the Making of Steel in Operation in Europe*, Ottawa, 1904.

——— Dominion Water Power Branch, *Water Resources Paper No. 33*, Ottawa, 1923; *Water Resources Paper No. 16*, Ottawa, 1916; *Water Resources Paper No. 17*, Ottawa, 1916; *Water Resources Paper No. 60*, Ottawa, 1927.

Canada, Dominion Water Power Bureau. *Annual Reports*, 1913 et seq. Earlier reports on water power are included in the Annual Reports of the Department of the Interior.

Canada, Dominion Coal Board. *Annual Reports*, 1948–49 et seq.

Canada. *House of Commons Debates*, IV (1925), 3339–3390.

Canadian Electrical Association. *Proceedings*, Annual Volumes, 1911–1940.

Carr, C. C. *Alcoa, An American Enterprise*, New York, 1952.

Carruthers, G. *Paper in the Making*, Toronto, 1947.

Carter, W. H., Jr. "American Branch Plants in Canada," doctoral dissertation, Harvard University, 1932.

Christie, C. V. "The Cost of Hydro-Electric Power," *Engineering Journal* (April 1924), pp. 177–180.

Commission of Conservation. *First Annual Report*, 1910.

Creamer, D. B. *Is Industry Decentralizing?* Philadelphia, 1935.

Davies, P. T. "Cost of Electric Power," *Engineering Journal* (August 1925), pp. 337–343.

Dean, W. H., Jr. *The Theory of the Geographical Location of Economic Activities*, doctoral dissertation, Harvard University, 1938.

Denis, L. G. *Electric Generation and Distribution in Canada*, Publication of the Commission of Conservation, Ottawa, 1918.

Denis, L. G. and A. V. White. *Water Powers of Canada*, Ottawa, 1911.

Desilets, A. *La Grand'Mère*, Three Rivers, 1933.

Engineering Journal. July 1924; papers on Canadian power matters presented at the First World Power Conference. July 1930, Canadian papers presented at Second World Power Conference.

Fairchild, B. C. "The C. E. A.: A History . . . During the First Fifty Years," *Proceedings of the Canadian Electrical Association*, 1940.

Fay, C. R. *Youth and Power*, London, 1931.

Field, F. W. *Capital Investments in Canada*, Montreal, 1914.

Filteau, G. *L'Epopée de Shawinigan*, Shawinigan Falls, 1944.

Green, G. "Some Pioneers of Light and Power," *British Columbia Historical Quarterly* (July 1938), pp. 145–162.

Guthrie, J. A. *The Newsprint Paper Industry*, Harvard Economic Studies, LXVIII, Cambridge, 1941.

Hogg, T. H. and O. O. LeFebvre. "Ottawa River Power Sites Agreement," *Engineering Journal* (June 1943), pp. 334–336.

Hopkins, J. Castell, ed. *Canadian Annual Review*, 1928–29, 1930–31, 1932, 1933, 1934, 1935 and 1936, 1937–38.

Hughes, E. C. *French Canada in Transition*, Chicago, 1943.

——— "Industry and the Rural System in Quebec," *The Canadian Journal of Economics and Political Science*, IV (1938), 341–349.

Hunter, J. I. "The French Invasion of the Eastern Townships," unpublished M.A. thesis, McGill University, 1951.

Hydro-Electric Power Commission of Ontario. *The Bulletin*, February 1922; December 1923; January 1924; July 1924; September 1924; February 1925; January 1935; February 1935.

Keith, F. S. "Fifty Years of Industrial and Manufacturing Development," *Engineering Journal* (June 1937), pp. 365–383.

Lamothe, J. C. *Histoire de la Corporation de la Cité de Montréal*, Montreal, 1903.

Lawson, A. J. "Generation, Distribution and Measurement of Electricity for Light and Power," *Transactions of the Canadian Society of Civil Engineers*, 1890, pp. 179–237.

Lefebvre, O. "Nos Forces Hydrauliques, Leur Valeur Economique," *Revue Trimestrielle Canadienne* (March 1939).

——— "Les Forces Hydrauliques de la Province de Quebec," *Revue Trimestrielle Canadienne* (June 1926).

List of Water Powers in the Province of Quebec, coöperatively prepared by the Dominion Water Power and Reclamation Service, Department of the Interior, Ottawa; The Quebec Streams Commission; and The Hydraulic Service, Department of Lands and Forests, Quebec, n. d.

Machlachan, W. "The Electrical Utility in Canada," *Proceedings of the Royal Canadian Institute*, Series III A, Vol. VI (1940–41, pp. 17–28.

Maclennan, H. "City of Two Souls," *Holiday Magazine*, August 1951.

Moody's Public Utilities. Annual.

National Electric Light Association and the Metropolitan Life Insurance Company. *Industrial Development in the United States and Canada, 1926 and 1927*, n. d.

Normandin, A. B. "La Législation et l'Administration des Eaux," *Revue Trimestrielle Canadienne*, June 1929.
——— *Undeveloped Water-Powers in the Province of Quebec*, mimeographed reprint of a paper delivered at the Sixty-Seventh Annual General and Professional Meeting of the Engineering Institute of Canada at Quebec, May 12, 1949.
Patton, M. J. "The Water Power Resources of Canada," *Economic Geography*, II (1926), 168–196.
Prentice, J. S. "Canada's Objection to the Exportation of Hydro-Electric Power," *Journal of Political Economy* (1928), pp. 592–624.
Provincial Electricity Board. *First Report*, 1937–38; *Second Report*, 1939.
Quebec. *Tableau des Forces Hydrauliques concédées par la Province de Québec du 1er juillet 1867 au 30 juin 1923*. Deuxième Edition revue et augmentée. Pub. 10 of the Service Hydraulique, Quebec, 1923. Also Pub. 11 of the same service, covering the period October 31, 1923 to August 14, 1934; Quebec, 1934.
Quebec Electricity Commission. *First Report*, 1935–36; *Second Report*, 1936–37.
Quebec Streams Commission. Annual Reports, in *Quebec Sessional Papers*, 1912 et seq.
Rapport Annuel De L'Office De L'Electrification Rurale, 1947, 1948, 1949. Mimeographed.
Report of the Electricity Commission of the Province of Quebec, January 21, 1935.
Report of the Public Service Board. August 1, 1940 to March 31, 1941. Quebec, 1942.
Report of the Royal Commission on Coal 1946. Ottawa, 1947.
Report of the Royal Commission on Transportation, 1951. Ottawa, 1951.
Rioux, A. *L'Electrification Rurale du Québec*, Sherbrooke, 1942.
Robbins, J. E. *Hydro-Electric Development in the British Empire*, Toronto, 1931.
Ross, A. D. "The Cultural Effects of Population Changes in the Eastern Townships," *The Canadian Journal of Economics and Political Science*, IX (1943), 447–462.
Surveyer, A. "The White Coal of Quebec," *Industrial Canada*, April 1948, pp. 54–56.
Tessier, Abbé A. *Trois-Rivières 1535–1935*, Three Rivers, 1935.
The Montreal Electrical Handbook, issued under the auspices of the American Institute of Electrical Engineers in connection with the International Electrical Congress at St. Louis, Mo., September, 1904.
Wallace, D. H. *Market Control in the Aluminum Industry*, Harvard Economic Studies, LVIII, Cambridge, 1937.
Wilson, J., "Hydro Development in Province of Quebec," *Electrical News and Engineering* (February 15, 1949), pp. 70–71, 79.
Wright, C. P. *The St. Lawrence Deep Waterway: A Canadian Appraisal*, Toronto, 1935.

Pamphlets

Beck, Sir A. *A Statement by Sir Adam Beck protesting against the Exportation of Electric Power with special reference to the Proposed Lease of the "Carillon" Power Site*, Toronto, 1925.
Bouchard, T. D. *La Domination des Trusts Electriques*, St. Hyacinthe, 1934.
——— *La Régie Publique et l'Exploitation des Forces Hydro-Electriques*, St. Hyacinthe, 1928.
——— *La Municipalisation de l'Electricité à Saint-Hyacinthe*, St. Hyacinthe, 1933.
——— *La Vote de St. Hyacinthe sur la Municipalisation et ses raisons d'être*, St. Hyacinthe, 1934.
——— *La Metropole commerciale et l'Electricité*, St. Hyacinthe, 1934.

——— *Les Reformes qui s'imposent dans la Régie de nos Ressources Hydro-Electriques,* St. Hyacinthe, 1935.
——— *L'Electricité dans la Province de Québec,* submission for the Union of Municipalities to the Electricity Commission, October 22, 1934.
Crépeau, A. *Municipalization of Electricity in Sherbrooke,* address before Union of Municipalities of the Province of Quebec at Sherbrooke, November 1929.
Industrial Shawinigan 1941. Published by the Shawinigan Falls *Standard.*
Le Saguenay Industriel. Published by Aubin et Grenou, 1929.
McGregor, J. R. *Report on Development of Public Utilities in Sherbrooke from 1880 to date,* City of Sherbrooke, Gas and Electricity Department, February 28, 1928.
Nicholls, F. *Niagara Power,* reprint of Address to Empire Club, Toronto, January 19, 1905.
Sweezey, R. O. *Les Forces Hydrauliques et les Ressources Naturelles du Québec,* n. d.
Troisième Centenaire Trifluvien 1634–1934, third number of the *Almanach Trifluvien.* Three Rivers, 1934.
White, A. V. *Power Possibilities on the St. Lawrence River,* Ottawa, 1918. Reprinted from the Ninth Annual Report of the Commission of Conservation.
White, J. *Conservation in 1918,* Reprinted from Tenth Annual Report of the Canadian Commission of Conservation.

Statistical Compilations

Canada

Canada, Department of Mines and Resources. *Petroleum Fuels in Canada 1927–1940* and *Petroleum Fuels in Canada 1940–1944,* Bureau of Mines Publications Nos. 808 and 814, prepared by John M. Casey.
Canada, Department of Trade and Commerce, Dominion Bureau of Statistics. *The Canada Year Book.* Annual, 1906 et seq.
——— *Manufacturing Industries of Quebec.* Annual, 1919 et seq.
——— *Manufacturing Industries of Ontario.* Annual, 1919 et seq.
——— *Geographic Distribution of Manufactures.* Annual, 1932 et seq.
——— *Central Electric Stations in Canada.* Annual, 1918 et seq.
——— *Use of Electric Power in Manufacturing and Mining Industries.* Annual, 1928 et seq.
——— *Report on Index Numbers of Electric Light Rates . . . .* Annual, 1913 et seq.
Canadian Statistical Review, September 1948.
Quebec, *Statistical Year Book.* Annual, 1915 et seq.

United States

Bituminous Coal Institute. *1950 Bituminous Coal Annual.* Washington, 1950.
Federal Power Commission. *Industrial Electric Power Requirements, 1939–1945.*
Historical Statistics of the United States 1789–1945. Prepared by the Bureau of the Census with the coöperation of the Social Science Research Council, Washington, 1949.
National Coal Association. *Bituminous Coal Data 1935–1948,* Washington, 1949.
Statistical Abstract of the United States.
United States, Department of the Interior, Bureau of Mines. *Minerals Yearbook, 1937.*

II. Primary Materials

Annual Reports

The Annual Reports of the following companies for the years indicated are available in the Corporation Records Collection of the Baker Library, Harvard Business School.

Canadian Hydro-Electric Corporation. 1928–1936.
Canadian Light and Power Company. 1926–1940.
Cedars Rapids Manufacturing and Power Company. 1915.
Civic Investment and Industrial Company. 1917.
Gatineau Power Company. 1937–1947.
International Hydro-Electric Company. 1929–1943.
Laurentide Power Company. 1916–1927.
Montreal Light, Heat & Power Company. 1902–1916.
Montreal Light, Heat & Power Consolidated. 1918–1943.
Montreal Street Railway Company, The. 1897–1911.
Montreal Tramways Company, The. 1912–1947.
Ottawa Electric Company. 1906–1912.
Ottawa Light, Heat and Power Company. 1909–1937.
Ottawa-Montreal Power Company. 1925–1926.
Quebec Power Company, The. 1923–1943.
Quebec Railway Light and Power Company, The. 1908–1909.
Quebec Railway, Light, Heat and Power Company. 1911–1926.
Shawinigan Water & Power Company, The. 1906–1947.
Southern Canada Power Company. 1917–1947.
United Securities Ltd. 1925, 1926, 1930, 1936–1940.

Power Company Publications

Canadian Hydro-Electric Corporation Limited. Brochure issued by the corporation, Ottawa, 1928.
Cedar Rapids Manufacturing and Power Co. Brochure issued by the company, n. d.
Gatineau Power Company. Brochure issued by the company, Ottawa, 1927.
Gatineau Power Company. *A Quarter Century of Progress and Service*, n. d.
International Hydro-Electric System. A brochure issued by the concern, March, 1929.
Laurentide Power Company. Brochure issued by the company, 1917.
Montreal Light, Heat & Power Consolidated. *Record of Expansion and Progress 1925–1943.* Brochure issued by the company, n. d.
The Shawinigan Water & Power Company. *Fifty Years of Achievement*, 1948.
——— *Twenty-Five Years of Progress*, n. d.
——— *A Record of Services Rendered to Canada's War Effort by The Shawinigan Water & Power Company 1939–1945*, Montreal, 1946.
The Shawinigan Water & Power Company. Issued by the company, probably around 1905. Brochures of the same title issued in 1910, 1913, and 1919.
——— *Study of the Conditions affecting the Consumption of Electrical Energy in the Provinces of Ontario and Quebec*, n. d. In Commerce Library, McGill University.
Southern Canada Power News, 25th Anniversary Number, 1938.

Miscellaneous Documents

Relating to the Gatineau Power Company

Gatineau Power Company. Registration Statement under Securities Act of 1933, filed with the Securities and Exchange Commission, March 24, 1939.

——— Prospectus filed with the Securities Exchange Commission, June 15, 1946, Amendment No. 3.

Relating to the Montreal Company

Analyses of Montreal Light, Heat & Power Consolidated, by A. D. Watts and Co., stockbrokers, 1926 and 1929.
A Statistical Analysis of Montreal Light, Heat & Power Consolidated, by Geoffrion and Co. (1930).
A Memorandum re the Montreal Tramways and Power Company, of February 27, 1913, prepared by Stone and Webster, stockbrokers.
A Circular Issued by the Public Service Corporation (of Montreal) in 1919.
Report of the Committee of Investigation to the Shareholders of the Montreal Tramways and Power Company Ltd., Montreal; October 24, 1923.
Application by the Montreal Light, Heat & Power Co., for listing on the New York Stock Exchange, May 1, 1902.
Note: The above items will be found in the Corporation Records Collection at Baker Library.
Ellis, C. A. *Report upon the Financial Affairs of Montreal Light, Heat & Power Consolidated and Its Component Companies,* mimeographed, Montreal, November 12, 1946. This report was made in connection with the provincial government's expropriation proceedings in 1944.

Relating to the Saguenay Company

Saguenay Electric Company. Brief Submitted to the Quebec Electricity Commission, 1935.

Relating to the Shawinigan Company

Cadenhead, A. F. S. "The History of the Shawinigan Chemicals, Ltd., 1902–46," unpublished manuscript made available to me by the author.
"Edwin R. Whitney, Appellant, and John Joyce et al., Respondents. Record of Proceedings in the Privy Council on Appeal from the Court of King's Bench for the Province of Quebec." Copy made available to me by Shawinigan Water and Power Company. For a note on the case see *Law Journal Reports,* LXXV (1906), 89–90.
Report of a Speech given by Mr. Aldred in Boston, December 6 (1917). Baker Library, Corporation Records Room (Shawinigan Water and Power Company file).
Letter to Shareholders of Quebec Railway, Light, Heat and Power Co., July 26, 1923. (Quebec Power Co. file).

Relating to the Southern Canada Company

Memorandum Submitted by the Southern Canada Power Company to the Electricity Commission of the Province of Quebec, November 1, 1934.

General

Hamel, P. *Le Trust de l'Electricité,* submission to the Quebec Electricity Commission. Mimeographed, 1935.
Memoire de M. J.-E. Grégoire, Maire de Québec. Submission to the Quebec Electricity Commission. Mimeographed, 1935.
Massue, H. "Memorandum on Rural Electrification," 1943. Unpublished.
——— "Economic Aspects of the Quebec Electric Utility Industry," 1942. Unpublished.
——— "Water Power in Canada," 1949. Unpublished.

Notes

Introduction: Problems and Approaches

1. See J. A. Guthrie, *The Newsprint Paper Industry*, Harvard Economic Studies, Vol. LXVIII (Cambridge, 1941), ch. 4 and pp. 167–172; D. H. Wallace, *Market Control in the Aluminum Industry*, Harvard Economic Studies, Vol. LVIII (Cambridge, 1937), pp. 141–144; H. A. Innis, *Settlement and the Mining Frontier*, Vol. IX of the Canadian Frontiers of Settlement Series (Toronto, 1936), passim. Hydroelectric power is virtually in a monopoly position in Canadian mining because of the location of the mines in northern areas remote from coal supplies (see Innis, pp. 332–334).

2. The Lower St. Lawrence Power Company, a small company serving the Gaspé region, has also been excluded from consideration because of the relative economic insignificance of the area which it serves.

3. A. P. Usher, "Resource Requirements," *Journal of Economic History*, Supplement, VII (1947), 35–46.

4. See, for example, L. Robbins, *An Essay on the Nature and Significance of Economic Science*, 2nd ed. (London, 1949), ch. 2, secs. 4 and 5, especially p. 41.

5. Cf. the following cryptic remarks: "Very large proportions of our use of energy . . . are outright fuel requirements, i.e., requirements in which, for economic or technical reasons, electricity is not now acceptable. But many of these economic and technical limits are not of abiding character, and energy requirements formerly thought to be wholly or mainly direct fuel requirements are increasingly being met with electrical energy" (National Resources Committee, *Energy Resources and National Policy*, Washington, 1939, p. 269).

6. By comparison with hydroelectricity, hydraulic power is so intractable, and so difficult to transport that it may safely be neglected as a major form of industrial power in a modern economy.

7. The pervading diversity of the industry appears between regions as well as between firms. Originally, this study was intended to refer to Canada rather than Quebec. A preliminary survey of the industry throughout Canada, however, made it clear that this plan was impracticable. Regional differences in resources, engineering problems, markets, and forms of business organization have resulted in widely different developments of the industry in different regions; the motley collection of firms af-

forded by the *Canadian* industry beggared contrast, but made comparison all but impossible. It was therefore decided to limit the study to Quebec, which provided a small sample of firms that were roughly comparable as to geographic setting (and therefore engineering problems) and to pecuniary goals—all were private, profit-seeking, enterprises. Fortunately, this drastic reduction in geographic scope did not imply a proportionate reduction in economic significance. Quantitatively, Quebec has long accounted for more than half of Canada's electrical output, while qualitatively the main features of the history of the hydroelectric industry have been reflected in the history of The Shawinigan Water and Power Company, a pioneer Quebec enterprise that has grown to be one of the world's largest electrical companies.

8. The term "price discrimination" is used in a loose sense to include both price discrimination proper (where differences in prices are based solely on different elasticities of demand) and price differentiation (where differences in prices reflect, or may reflect, differences in marginal cost). See W. A. Lewis, *Overhead Costs* (London, 1949), p. 53.

9. A central electric station's diversity factor is increased when it gains a new customer whose peak load is not coincident with the station's peak load. To strive for an increased diversity factor means, roughly, to strive for a variety of industrial customers whose peak loads dovetail with one another. To increase diversity factor is obviously one way to increase a station's load factor.

10. The reader should consult a standard textbook on electricity for a full explanation of this technical concept. See, for example, Chester L. Dawes, *A Course in Electrical Engineering*, 2nd ed. (New York, 1928), II, 367, 369. Roughly, electric *power* (in watts) equals *current* (in amperes) times *pressure* (in volts). In alternating-current electricity both the amperage and the voltage fluctuate in "cycles," a complete cycle being a "sine curve" movement from a maximum positive value to a maximum negative value and back again to the maximum positive value. When the voltage cycle and the amperage cycle coincide, the resulting product (i.e., the power) is always positive and the power factor is unity. Different electrical machines, however, have different characteristics; some "draw" the current ahead of the voltage, some "draw" the voltage ahead of the current. When this happens, during some portions of the cycle a negative voltage is combined with a positive amperage, or vice versa, and the resulting product (i.e., the power) is negative. This means, in effect, that the system is delivering power back to the generator. This "wattless component" of power, as it is called, means that the "apparent power" produced by a generator is greater than the "true power" delivered by the generator, and the ratio of the latter to the former is the "power factor" of the system. A larger generator will be necessary to deliver a given amount of power to a system with a lower power factor than to one with a high power factor. Thus a factory with a low power factor (i.e., with a preponderance of machinery of one characteristic) will either be required by the power company to raise its power factor (i.e., to introduce machinery with the opposite characteristic) or will be required to pay penalty rates for its electricity.

11. Changes in these conditions will be transmitted to the entrepreneur through a change in his cost or revenue curves, but, unlike the situation in perfect competition, they will not always have predictable effects on price and output. For example, an increase in demand for a good produced under conditions of perfect competition will always, at least in the short run, lead to an increase in both the price and output of that good. In monopolistic competition, this may perhaps be considered the "normal" reaction to an increase in demand, but it is not by any means the only one possible. In special cases either price or output may fall or remain constant. It is this inability to predict reactions to changes in cost or demand conditions that led Professor Hicks

to be so despondent about the economics of monopolistic competition. See J. R. Hicks, *Value and Capital* (Oxford, 1939), p. 84.

12. B. W. Lewis, "Public Policy and the Growth of the Power Industry," *The Journal of Economic History*, Supplement, VII (1947), 48.

13. For an example, see Innis, pp. 369, 375–377. It is significant that the question of whether or not capacity has been kept ahead of demand is one of the favorite polemical issues in the public versus private power debate.

14. A careful analysis of price may be indispensable when an author has other ends in view. For example, prices, even when administered, directly affect the allocation of resources, and governmental regulation of electric rates should take this into account. How important a careful analysis of price becomes in the formulation of governmental electrical policy is shown by H. S. Houtthaker in "Electricity Tariffs in Theory and Practice," *Economic Journal* (March 1951), pp. 1–25.

15. See P. S. Florence's remarks on "The Economic Importance of Physical Qualities" in his *The Statistical Method in Economics and Political Science* (New York, 1929), pp. 335–340.

16. J. R. Hicks, "Annual Survey of Economic Theory: The Theory of Monopoly," *Econometrica*, 3 (1935); reprinted in American Economic Association, *Readings in Price Theory* (Chicago, 1952), p. 369.

Chapter 1. The Beginnings of the Central Electric Station

1. This section is a very abbreviated account of early developments based on the secondary sources listed in Section I of the Bibliography. The best modern account of early technology, written, however, from the point of view of the electrical machinery industry rather than the central station, is H. C. Passer, *The Electrical Manufacturers 1875–1900* (Cambridge, Mass., 1953). Passer's work on Edison is particularly good: see especially his "The Electric Light and the Gas Light," *Explorations in Entrepreneurial History*, Vol. 1, No. 3 (March 1949), pp. 1–9.

2. L. W. Taylor, *Physics* (Cambridge, 1941), p. 704.

3. T. C. Martin and S. L. Coles, eds., *The Story of Electricity* (New York, 1919), I, 18.

4. S. Insull, *Central Station Electric Service* (Chicago, 1915), p. 21. This volume contains selected speeches given by Mr. Insull between 1897 and 1914. A second volume of speeches given between 1914 and 1923 was published under the title *Public Utilities in Modern Life* (Chicago, 1924). The two works will be cited subsequently as *Speeches*, I, *and Speeches*, II, respectively.

5. The material in this section is drawn largely from the two-volume history of the project written by its promoter. See E. D. Adams, *Niagara Power*, 2 vols. (New York, 1927).

6. In 1889 Edison proposed an awkward system of electrical generation and transmission by direct current, while Westinghouse was unwilling to recommend electricity at all and proposed instead a system of pneumatic power transmission to Buffalo.

7. It was noted at the time that the younger engineers favored alternating systems, and the older generation of electricians, led by Kelvin and Edison, opposed such plans. The engineers working on the Lauffen-Frankfort line in Germany; de Ferranti who was then establishing an alternating system in London; and Westinghouse in the United States — none of whom had entered the competition — were all advocating alternating-current systems by the latter part of 1890. The experimental line from

Lauffen to Frankfort, built in 1891, on the occasion of the Frankfort Exposition, provided an impressive demonstration of the possibilities of alternating current transmission. This line transmitted 300 horsepower of electricity by means of three-phase current at a tension of 30,000 volts for a distance of over 100 miles. It was much the largest transmission project undertaken up to that time and greatly influenced the decision to use alternating current at Niagara Falls.

8. Two powerhouses were projected, and such was the experimental character of the electrical installation that it was planned to use the second structure for a compressed-air plant. After 1896, however, when electrical transmission to Buffalo was a proved success, the pneumatic plans were scrapped in favor of a second hydroelectric installation.

9. Quoted anonymously in Adams, II, 250.

10. The electrolytic process for the reduction of aluminum ore was developed by Hall in the United States and Héroult in France between 1886 and 1889. Artificial abrasives such as carborundum, alundum, and graphite were produced in electric furnaces at Niagara during the last few years of the century, and calcium carbide was first produced by the Willson Aluminum Works at Spray, North Carolina, in 1891. Major Stassano of Turin began making electric furnaces for the reduction of iron ore in 1896. In 1899 Kjellin in Sweden built the first induction furnace for the production of steel from pig iron, and in 1902 Héroult developed another furnace for the same purpose in France. Not all of these experiments were commercially successful, but they foreshadowed the development of a large market for "process" electricity. On these developments, see *The Story of Electricity*, ch. XIII; J. N. Pring, *Some Electro-Chemical Centres* (Manchester, 1908), passim; J. A. Fleming, *Fifty Years of Electricity* (London, 1921), ch. 4; Wallace, *Market Control in the Aluminum Industry*, Appendix A.

11. Adams, II, 307.

12. Insull, *Speeches*, II, 347, and also 66.

13. Insull's appreciation of the "natural monopoly" character of the electrical business is shown at many points in his writings. See, for example, *Speeches*, I, 75: "The trend of the times is toward concentration of production; it is inevitable that it must come. Ours is a business which is a natural monopoly. It matters not what the legislation of the moment may be, what the opinions of the politicians may be, what our own opinions may be, eventually, all the electrical energy for a given area must be produced by one concern." Insull spoke thus in 1909.

14. This was the burden of many of Insull's addresses. In 1909, for example, after praising the virtues of wholesale, industrial sales of electricity, he commented shrewdly: "In addition, you are in a large way of business, producing your supply on a scale of some magnitude . . . You are starting to get yourselves in a position where you can afford to run your entire small-customer business at a loss, and, gentlemen, you have got to do that eventually, if you expect to remain in the business" (*Speeches*, I, 39). "We should bear in mind, above everything else in the operation of our business, that we cannot afford to place ourselves in opposition to public opinion" (*Speeches*, I, 119). How many private electrical utilities which have since been expropriated could bear witness to the perspicacity of these remarks!

Chapter 2. The Quebec Industry: A Preliminary Survey

1. M. Q. Innis, *An Economic History of Canada*, 2nd ed. (Toronto, 1948), p. viii.

2. Along the St. Lawrence and its northern tributaries is found some 70 per cent of the water-power resources of the province. Most of the remainder is located along

the northern edge of the shield in the watersheds of Hudson, James and Ungava bays. The southern tributaries of the St. Lawrence account for less than 3 per cent of the total. Because of their distance from load centers, the vast resources of the northern shield have not yet been developed or even accurately surveyed. The St. Lawrence and its northern tributaries thus account for roughly 97 per cent of the developed power in the province, while the remainder is located on the rivers that flow into the St. Lawrence from the south. See A. B. Normandin, *Undeveloped Water-Powers in the Province of Quebec* (mimeographed reprint of a paper delivered at the Sixty-seventh Annual meeting of the Engineering Institute of Canada, Quebec, May 12th, 1949), p. 23. The figures he quotes for undeveloped power were derived from the *List of Water Powers in the Province of Quebec*, coöperatively prepared in 1928 by the Dominion Water Power and Reclamation Service, the Quebec Streams Commission, and the Hydraulic Service (Department of Lands and Forests, Quebec). These figures are the latest authoritative estimates available, but are obviously low in the light of present-day techniques of river regulation and of improved (although still very imperfect) knowledge of resources in the more remote areas of the province. Mr. Normandin gives it as his opinion that, with proper regulation by means of storage dams, the potential firm power estimate for the province should be raised from the 1928 figure of 13 million h.p. to 18 million h.p., but recent announcements of power potentials on the Bersimis, Manicouagan, Outardes, and Hamilton Rivers make this estimate likely to be much too small.

3. "Quebec" henceforth refers only to the settled and developed portion of the province, roughly the St. Lawrence Lowlands area.

4. It must be stressed that this question refers to the cost of producing power and *not* to the cost of power to the consumer, i.e., not to electricity rates. Where public regulation of the industry is weak, as it has been in Quebec, there is only the most tenuous relationship between these two magnitudes. In the United States, where regulation has also been ineffective for the most part, it has been noted that the structure of electric rates as a whole "can be understood only as a product of the accidents of utility policy and the strength of industrial bargaining, together with the occasional impact of state regulation or of public power projects" (National Resources Planning Board, *Industrial Location and National Resources*, Washington, 1943, p. 174).

5. Various examples of the actual costs of developing specific sites will be found scattered throughout the chapters which follow. The following quotations may help to support the contention that the cost of developing hydroelectric power in Quebec has been relatively low. "Up to now, the construction cost of the large hydro electric plants on the regulated rivers [in Quebec] has been on an average between $80.00 and $100.00 per horse-power installed" (Normandin, p. 26). My impression is that many important plants in Quebec have been built toward the lower end of this scale, and perhaps at less than $80 per horse power. Compare Mr. Normandin's statement with the following quotation regarding the cost of steam plants in the United States: "The cost of central stations has varied but little since Mr. Edison built the Pearl Street Station in New York City. The writer's records, in more or less detail, cover more than 150 plants built between 1882 and 1936. The average cost of these plants is substantially $75. per h.p. of capacity. Potter quotes figures collected by the F.P.C. for 80 plants built since 1920, which average $80. per h.p. of capacity, while L. W. Morrow lists 16 plants built since 1927 at an average cost of $85. per h.p. installed. The lowest cost of [all] these plants is about $45. per h.p. and the highest approximately $168. per h.p. As a general rule, large plants cost a little less per kw. than small plants" (George A. Orrok, "Progress in the Generation of Energy by Heat Engines," *Proceedings of the American Society of Civil Engineers*, December 1937, p. 1888). I have converted Orrok's

original figures, given in dollars per kilowatt, to dollars per horsepower. For the reference to Potter, see National Resources Committee, *Technological Trends and National Policy* (Washington, 1937), p. 255; for the reference to L. W. Morrow, see *Electrical World*, November 23, 1935. This quotation suggests that the capital cost of *thermal* stations in the United States is but little, if any, lower than the capital cost of *hydro* stations in Quebec; the operating costs of steam stations are of course much higher than those of hydro stations.

6. It might be thought that the cost of building a hydroelectric plant in Quebec could be derived directly from Dominion Bureau of Statistics figures by comparing the series for generating capacity with a series labelled "Investment in Generating Facilities" which was published from 1923 to 1943. (See the annual publication of the Dominion Bureau of Statistics entitled *Central Electric Stations in Canada.*) Unfortunately the vagaries of accounting convention and the mysteries of corporation finance both intervene between actual cost and the book value of investment, which was the magnitude reported by the D.B.S. On the basis of the D.B.S. figures, we would reach the conclusion that the cost per horsepower of developed power was lower in Quebec than in either Ontario or Canada as a whole up until 1929, and considerably higher in Quebec than in the other two areas after 1930. The latter part of this result is absurd. If it means anything, it perhaps reflects a differential financial morality, with respect to such things as watered capital, between Quebec and other areas in Canada. The "Investment" series was discontinued in 1943.

7. Hydroelectric power interests, like other interests whose wealth is derived from the earth, realize the ecological importance of forests. A former president of The Shawinigan Water and Power Company wrote: ". . . in Quebec it is well understood, not only by the Government but also by the wood-using industries directly affected, that the reliability of a river's flow depends upon the forest cover on its watershed and that, therefore, forest conservation is of supreme importance to the hydroelectric industry. There can be no complacency regarding measures for the protection and preservation of the forests" (J. Wilson, "Hydro Development in Province of Quebec," *Electrical News and Engineering*, February 15, 1949, p. 70.) Some of the hydroelectric companies in Quebec have carried out extensive reforestation operations.

8. The spring floods are more violent on the southern than on the northern tributaries of the St. Lawrence; the northern rivers thaw from mouth to source, and flood conditions are thereby mitigated to some extent.

9. On the southern tributaries of the St. Lawrence, however, the spring flood comes about a month earlier and the run-off reaches its maximum in April. This makes interconnection between the Southern Canada Power Company and The Shawinigan Water and Power Company very useful. On the one hand, the south shore company can deliver surplus power to Shawinigan during the period of relatively low stream flow on the north shore just before the spring run-off. On the other hand, the summer flow on the northern tributaries, because of their forest-covered headwaters, is better maintained than on the southern tributaries so that during the summer, Shawinigan can transfer power to the Southern Canada system to correct for this seasonal discrepancy. Unfortunately the plant capacity south of the St. Lawrence is not large enough to make this type of power exchange an important factor in the province as a whole.

10. Pp. 8, 10–12.

11. The capacity of a station is always in excess of the capacity which could be supported at 100 per cent utilization factor by the minimum flow of the river. Throughout Canada it has been found that turbine installation has averaged 30 per cent greater than the theoretical power (at 80 per cent efficiency) ordinarily available for six months of the year.

12. "When a river has its flow regulated by storage the power possibilities of that stream soon become developed to their maximum and the cost of the power is reduced to its possible minimum" (Dr. O. O. Lefebvre, "Storage Reservoirs in Canada," *Engineering Journal*, July 1930, p. 474). The economies of a large plant are very conspicuous in hydroelectric stations, since the major expense of harnessing the river (building the dam and hydraulic works) will usually be substantially the same regardless of the number of generating units installed.

13. Other examples of privately owned storage works, most of them of minor significance, are given in the *Canada Year Book*, 1951, p. 557.

14. On the subject of storage, see the works of Normandin and Lefebvre already cited, and also the annual reports of the Quebec Streams Commission. The first river regulation was undertaken by timber companies, or by the government in their interests, in order to ensure sufficient water to move logs down the rivers. Three of the dams on the upper Ottawa that are now important mainly for the hydroelectric industry were built by the federal government around 1910 in the interests of the lumber industry; in other areas pulp and paper companies have built dams in order to ensure year-round power for their mills and to facilitate the movement of logs. "In certain districts, such as the Saguenay, pulp mills were closed every winter, hundreds of hands being thrown out of work. The Lake Kenogami storage was undertaken with a view to curing the unfortunate situation, and this it has done" (Lefebvre, p. 473). The first real experiment in regulation for hydroelectric purposes was made on the St. Maurice when the Shawinigan company built three small dams on the Manouan River around 1910. This successful experiment was followed by the building of the huge Gouin Dam at the headwaters of the St. Maurice in 1917. A third storage dam for the St. Maurice system was built on the Mattawin River in 1930. The Gatineau dams were built in the latter 1920's; one dam was built on the Lièvre in 1930 and another in 1942. The Saguenay was partly regulated by a combination power and storage dam when the first power development was built in 1926, and two other storage dams were built during the last war. The taming of the Ottawa, a large undertaking, remains for the future.

15. P. 26.

16. Legal rights between Dominion and provincial governments to Canadian water powers have presented a most confused picture, but since 1898, following a decision on the matter by the Privy Council, there has been little doubt that Provincial governments have in most instances been the responsible authorities. A clear summary of the legal aspects of Canadian water powers is included in the article on "Water Powers" by I. Biss in W. Stewart Wallace, general editor, *The Encyclopedia of Canada* (Toronto, 1937), Vol. VI. The use of rivers by power companies is subject to the prior rights of certain other industries. Navigation has first claim on Canadian rivers, and in this connection certain rights over power sites are exercised by the Dominion government under the British North America Act of 1867, and also under subsequent Dominion legislation affecting navigable rivers and international streams. In eastern Canada, it is also recognized that forest industries have river rights prior to those of the power industry, for the purpose of transporting logs. In Quebec, rivers are distinguished on the basis of floatability as well as navigability. If a river is either navigable or floatable by rafts, the water powers on that river belong to the province. The title to the hydraulic power on other rivers may be held privately by the riparian owners if the lands were alienated before 1884, but since that date all powers on any stream have been kept in provincial ownership by the reservation in all land sales of a strip of land along the water's edge. Naturally much litigation has been involved in the attempt to determine whether or not a particular stream was floatable. For two such cases see O. Lefebvre, "Nos Forces

Hydrauliques, Leur Valeur Economique," *Revue Trimestrielle Canadienne* (March 1939), pp. 8–9.

17. Cf. A. Rioux, *L'electrification rurale du Québec* (Sherbrooke, 1942), pp. 67 ff.

18. See *Tableau des Forces Hydrauliques concédées par la Province de Québec du 1er juillet 1867 au 30 juin 1923*, Publication No. 10 of the Service Hydraulique of the Quebec Government (Quebec, 1923); also Publication No. 11 of the same service giving the concessions to August 15, 1934. Figures quoted in the text include, where applicable, fines paid for nonfulfillment of conditions stipulated in the original sale.

19. A. Rioux, p. 67.

20. "In accordance with the provincial Act of 1926 (16 George V. c. 20) no power may be exported to the United States, though on payment of an additional royalty it may be sold to other provinces. Subsequent legislation (25 George V. c. 20) has relaxed the embargo in certain cases" (Biss, p. 271). The federal government has exercised supervision over the export of electricity since 1907, and since 1925 there has been an export tax on electricity. "Electricity is exported from Canada only by license granted by the Electricity and Gas Inspection Services of the Department of Trade and Commerce, and the same branch of the Department has jurisdiction over the export duty which has been imposed since April 1, 1925 . . . The rate is three one-hundreths of one cent per kilowatt hour on electric energy exported" (D.B.S., *Central Electric Stations in Canada*, 1946, p. 3). Reference to the list of water-power concessions in Quebec, cited above, shows that in 1919 and 1920 some large power sites in the Saguenay district were ceded to concerns which had federal licenses to export the power. Nothing came of these projects and the leases were later cancelled.

21. Power companies have benefited not only from ease of access to resources but also from generous charters granted them by provincial authorities. For an abstract of some of the early charters, as well as further information on the cession of power sites, see the Commission of Conservation publication, by L. G. Denis and A. V. White, *Water Powers of Canada* (Ottawa, 1911), pp. 150–154.

22. See *Report of the Electricity Commission of the Province of Quebec*, January 21, 1935. Hereafter this report will be cited as *Electricity Commission.*

23. As the result of an acrimonious dispute over electricity rates in Quebec City between the municipal authorities and the Shawinigan Water and Power Company officials (see Chapter 4), an agitation against the power companies started in Quebec City and "began to spread to other centres, Montreal included, with public ownership of power as its rallying cry. Hence it was that on February 3, 1933, a delegation representing the Confederation of National Catholic Labour Unions of Canada waited on Mr. Taschereau at Quebec and urged him to create a Provincial Hydro Electric system similar to that of Ontario. They were given little encouragement by the Prime Minister, who told them that such a system would cost the Province of Quebec $500,000,000" (J. Castell Hopkins, ed., *Canadian Annual Review*, 1933, p. 185). When the Electricity Commission was appointed and hearings began, "some of the evidence . . . disclosed such a drastic attitude that the Prime Minister (Mr. Taschereau) found it advisable to issue a statement on November 20, 1934 assuring shareholders, bondholders, and all others connected with the power corporations, that their rights would be respected in any reforms eventually decided upon" (*Ibid.*, 1934, p. 198).

24. *Electricity Commission*, p. 29.

25. Officials of two companies have told me that they have kept a comprehensive statistical record of their business only since they were required to produce such figures for the Commission.

The Commission also effected one notable rate reduction: in January 1938, it reduced the domestic service rate of Electric Lights, Ltd., of Gaspé from 36¢ to 25¢ per kilowatt-hour! It was considering a further reduction to 20¢. Provincial Electricity Board, *First Report, 1937–8*, p. 42.

26. *Quebec Electricity Commission.* First Report (1935–36), pp. 9–10.

27. In spite of the weakness of public ownership in Quebec during our period, the private power companies always felt themselves threatened by the success of the publicly-owned system in the neighboring province of Ontario. This feeling they shared in common with the American electrical industry, and the Ontario Hydro-Electric Power Commission became the whipping boy of private power interests both in the United States and Canada. How real the threat was and how much the propaganda of the private concerns succeeded in countering that threat are obscure and perhaps unimportant questions, but it will be interesting here to outline in a few sentences the defensive measures taken by the Canadian industry. The dangers of public ownership were discussed by the Canadian Electrical Association soon after it was founded in 1891, and by 1902 the Association had a "legislative Committee" devoted to fighting a bill by which the Province of Ontario was seeking authority to develop power at Niagara Falls. On the formation of the Hydro-Electric Power Commission in Ontario, the campaign against public ownership was intensified and became more bitter. A private meeting of the executive was held after the 1914 convention in order to develop an offensive. Plans were made to plant articles in English newspapers dealing with "the suicidal policy of the Ontario Government" when it was observed that "Canada being essentially a borrowing community, the various Provincial Governments of Canada often pay to a foreign expression of opinion a deference they withhold from statements appearing in the local press," and a war chest to combat publicly owned utilities was collected. Eventually, of course, the battle was lost in Ontario, and in 1920 the Association moved its headquarters from Toronto to the more congenial atmosphere of Montreal. (The above account is based on material contained in the annual *Proceedings of the Canadian Electrical Association.* See especially the article on the history of the association by its secretary, Mr. B. C. Fairchild, in the 1940 *Proceedings.*) The Canadian Electrical Association had affiliated with the (American) National Electric Light Association in 1911, and in the twenties it was a willing partner in the propaganda campaign which that association waged under the direction of the Messrs. Insull. The crudities and excesses of that campaign in the United States have been frequently told, but perhaps never with such restraint and sadness as by Ernest Gruening in his *The Public Pays* (New York, 1931). The investigations of the Federal Trade Commission, starting in 1928, had revealed the whole unsavory story. The N.E.L.A. dissolved itself in 1933 and changed its name to the Edison Electric Institute. The Canadian Association thereupon resumed its autonomy, although arrangements were made to exchange information with the new American organization. Since then the "public education" campaigns of the power companies have been more restrained but nonetheless persistent. The F.T.C. investigations provided good ammunition for the critics of the private power companies in Quebec. Dr. P. Hamel, in a submission to the Electricity Commission of 1935 entitled *Le Trust de l'Electricité*, attempted to write a Canadian counterpart of the American revelations but in this he had only indifferent success. See also T. D. Bouchard, *La Domination des Trusts Electriques* (St. Hyacinthe, 1934), pp. 22–28. The American investigations had shown that there were definite linkages between the American and Canadian industries, but the Canadian power companies escaped the full glare of publicity since their records were out of reach of the American investigators.

28. For a number of years, the City of Westmount steam station undersold the Montreal Light, Heat and Power Company, a circumstance which put considerable pressure on that organization to reduce its rates. See T. D. Bouchard, *Le Régie Publique*

et L'Exploitation des Forces Hydro-Electriques (St. Hyacinthe, 1928), pp. 2–4. In the early thirties, the city of St. Hyacinthe decided to municipalize its electricity supply and the immediate result was a rate reduction by the Southern Canada Power Company, in spite of the fact that the company "déclarait quinze jours avant le vote [in favor of municipalization in St. Hyacinthe] par le voix de son premier vice-président, que non seulement elle ne pouvait consentir une réduction de taux mais qu'elle serait peut-être obligée de les accroître à cause de la crise que nous traversions" (T. D. Bouchard, *La Domination des Trusts Electriques*, pp. 42–43).

29. The Sherbrooke municipal plant is an exception, having succeeded in debarring the Southern Canada Power Company from the largest city in the Eastern Townships.

30. Provincial Electricity Board, Second Report (Jan.-Oct. 1939), p. 33. See the extended discussion of rural electrification in Quebec in this publication for the type of argument that has been advanced in the past to counter demands for rural electrification. For a refutation of these arguments, see A. Rioux, *passim*.

31. Rioux, pp. 82–93.

32. *Rapport Annuel de l'Office de l'Electrification Rurale* (1949), p. 2. In places this report reads like cheerful blackmail. Electricity has been purchased from private companies at gratifying rates: "A l'automme 1949, la Southern Canada Power accordait un rajustement de tarif qui comporte une réduction importante d'environ un demi-sou le kilowatt-heure, soit le tiers du tarif precedent — la Maclaren-Quebec Power Company, la Quebec North Shore Power Company, et la Saguenay Transmission Company nous ont offert spontanément des conditions acceptables." One company was reluctant: "Plutôt que de modifier ses conditions de vente, la Gatineau Power a laissé soumettre sa cause a la Régie provinciale de l'Electricité qui statuera sur les tarifs applicables aux six coopératives desservies par cette compagnie." And then, two paragraphs further down: "Nous tenons a reconnaître l'excellente co-operation qui nous avons reçue de la Régie provinciale de l'Electricité" (p. 2.). A letter to the author from Mr. Rioux, one of the three members of the Rural Electrification Bureau, points out: "Nous n'avons pas de co-operative d'électricité dans le territoire de la Shawinigan et de la Quebec Power parce que ces compagnies se sont engagées a électrifier toutes les parties rurales de leur territoire dans le plus court délai possible."

33. In this section it will be convenient to compare the development of the industry in Quebec with its development in Ontario — with no polemical intent or any implication that Ontario should be regarded as a yardstick by which Quebec's measurements are to be taken. There is no "normal" hydroelectric development. A comparison of the two provinces is suggested here simply in the hope that it will help to highlight the salient features of the Quebec industry.

34. Throughout, it will frequently be convenient to refer to various power companies by short titles. *Shawinigan*, *Southern Canada*, and *Gatineau* are obvious abbreviations for The Shawinigan Water and Power Company, the Southern Canada Power Company, and the Gatineau Power Company respectively, and there is no difficulty in using the abbreviated form in these cases because the concerns have been known by the same styles throughout their histories. In Montreal, however, the business group responsible for the city's electricity supply changed its corporate name twice during its career, and in 1944 the concern was expropriated by the provincial government. Nevertheless, when we are referring to electricity supply in Montreal, we shall often speak of the *Montreal* company as the concern responsible, regardless of its legal title at the time. By the *Saguenay* company we shall understand the Saguenay Power Company, formerly the Duke-Price Power Company.

35. After 1933 the Maclaren-Quebec company had a capacity equal to about 4.5 per cent of that of the Gatineau Power Company. The businesses of these two concerns are

very similar, so that one might conjecture that Maclaren-Quebec's output was about 45 per cent of Gatineau's output, or close to 1000 million kwhs., in the late 1930's.

The Chute à Caron plant of 280,000 h.p. was completed in 1931. In 1937, however, Wallace wrote: "It appears that energy from [this plant] . . . has found little market as yet" (p. 77), and that it "has not been used for aluminum since its completion in 1931" (p. 299). Since the completion of the aluminum company's Shipshaw station in 1943, the Chute à Caron plant has been used only as stand-by capacity.

The Quebec Power Company buys most of its power from its parent, the Shawinigan company. Figures for its own generation are not available; its production is not included in the Shawinigan figure.

36. In practice, of course, the power companies attempt to notify their customers when a reduction or cessation of such deliveries becomes necessary.

37. Canada, *Report of the Royal Commission on Coal, 1946* (Ottawa, 1947) pp. 388–389.

38. Secondary sales again became very large immediately following the last war, but since then they have again been reduced to small proportions by growth in the demand for firm power.

39. The deductions made here are somewhat larger than the sales to these two industries, since they represent electricity sold to all industries in the industrial classifications of "wood and paper products" and "non-ferrous" metal products respectively. The particular industries mentioned, however, account for the overwhelming majority of electricity sales made to their industrial groups.

40. The "General Manufacturing" series is a residual category. It includes mining and electric railway enterprises, as well as errors and omissions. The category's share of total consumption is based on figures which are directly affected by the very crude estimates made of "Losses." See Appendix, Section 2.

41. We have used the same absolute figure for losses in both calculations. Ideally the losses figures used in the second calculation should have been smaller than those used in the first by the amount of the losses incurred on exports and on secondary power deliveries. The losses figures are crude estimates to begin with and it therefore seemed useless to try to correct them in the way stated above. The losses on exports and secondary sales are in any event disproportionately small as compared with losses on other classes of business, because of the high voltages at which such power is delivered.

In this connection, it should be remembered that the retail markets are responsible for a large proportion of total losses; in the wholesale markets, losses are usually relatively small either because the large customers locate near the power station or because such power is delivered at a high voltage. Thus if we were to apportion losses to the various markets in which they are incurred, we should find that as compared with the figures of Table 2, (1) the "general manufacturing" share of total sales would increase significantly, (2) the retail market's share would increase substantially (perhaps by as much as 3 or 4 percentage points), and (3) the percentages for the other groupings would increase slightly. A table such as is envisioned here would give the percentage distribution of electricity generated to service the various markets — rather than the distribution of electricity consumed by the various markets, presented in Table 2.

42. Since electricity rates are usually in the form of a schedule, with lower charges for higher consumption, there is no simple relationship between "average revenues" and "rates." The relationship depends on the level of consumption: the same "rates" will produce a higher "average revenue" when consumption is low than when it is high. However, *large* differences in average revenues between similar markets in different areas are almost certainly indicative of differences in rates rather than merely differences in average consumption.

43. American statistics are divided into two categories: "Residential" sales (which corresponds fairly closely with the Canadian "Domestic" category), and "Commercial and Industrial Sales." If in the United States rates to commercial customers are about the same as rates to industrial customers, this classification is reasonable, but if, as seems more likely, the rates are different, then the one classification includes two dissimilar groups of data. Even if the average revenue series for industrial sales were somewhat lower than the series for "commercial and industrial" sales, however, it would still be significantly higher than the most closely comparable Canadian series, that for "General Manufactures."

44. To get an average revenue series for the nonferrous industries, we have had to assume that they used no secondary power, since figures available for sales and revenues do not distinguish between firm and secondary power. The nonferrous group, however, did use large quantities of secondary electricity during the 1930's, and this probably accounts for a large part of the hollow in the average revenue series for this market between 1933 and 1937.

No series is given for the wood and paper industries, because the available figures for sales and revenues do not distinguish between firm and secondary power. Figures provided by the Shawinigan Company, however, suggest that firm power sales to the pulp and paper industry were made at average revenues of about 3¢ per kwh.

45. The huge growth of the central Canadian industry in the twenties was in part a response to the American coal strike of April 1922. See *Central Electric Stations in Canada*, 1920, pp. 7–8.

Chapter 3. Early Years of The Shawinigan Water and Power Company, 1898–1914

1. The above account is taken from Gérard Filteau, *L'Epopée de Shawinigan* (Shawinigan Falls, 1944), pp. 87–90.

2. "Edwin R. Whitney, Appellant, and John Joyce et al, Respondents. Record of Proceedings in the Privy Council on Appeal from the Court of King's Bench for the Province of Quebec." Privy Council Case No. 35, 1904. The Shawinigan Water and Power Company kindly allowed me to use their copy of this document. It is hereafter quoted as *Record of Proceedings.*

The appellant was suing the respondents, John Joyce and J. N. Greenshields, in an attempt to prove that he owned a third of the property which these men had sold to the Shawinigan Water and Power Company, and that he was therefore entitled to one-third of the proceeds of that sale. His claim was founded on an alleged verbal agreement which he could not prove, and his suit was refused by the courts. The evidence submitted to the courts was confused and contradictory in character and throws but an oblique light on the pre-history of the Shawinigan company.

3. For the important part played by Joyce in another speculative venture, the promotion of the safety razor, see G. B. Baldwin, "The Invention of the Modern Safety Razor," *Explorations in Entrepreneurial History*, IV (Dec. 1951), pp. 88–93.

4. With Greenshields as his solicitor, Whitney incorporated the Continental Light and Heat Company. This may have been the same company as the Continental Light and Heat Company which later became a subsidiary of the Shawinigan Company. This latter company enjoyed a Dominion charter which gave it the right, among other things, to distribute electricity at any point in the Dominion. See The Shawinigan Water & Power Company, *Annual Report*, 1906.

5. In evidence at the trial, John Forman stated: "I had heard that the Shawinigan Company had not put up the money which was called for in consequence of that sale,

and I asked Mr. Joyce if it were true, and he said yes; why he said 'there is no man around this town would put up forty thousand ($40,000) dollars. I am going to show them that there is one man here who can do it, and I am going back to Boston for the money, but I will make damn sure that when I put up that money on the property (it will be) in such a way that I will get my money first out of the proceeds, the others will have to come in later'" (*Record of Proceedings*, p. 247).

6. Aldred was born at Lawrence, Mass., in 1865. He was the first treasurer of the Shawinigan company, its president from 1909 to 1933, and Chairman of the Board from that time until his death in 1941.

7. Filteau, pp. 91–92, says that Aldred was primarily responsible for getting this group interested in the company. The group was mainly Canadian. Filteau states that Aldred had difficulty in raising money in the United States because of the Spanish-American War then in progress, and because of the inherent riskiness of the enterprise. At the trial previously referred to, however, Aldred said that he did not become active in the company until March 1898. Regardless of what he meant by "active," one can fairly suspect that Aldred, Greenshields, and Joyce all played their parts in the organization of the company.

8. Filteau, pp. 92–93.

9. Filteau reports (p. 124) that in the beginning, "Les banques n'avaient guère confiance [in the Company]; aux débuts, il arriva même que Forget dut endosser un cheque de $50,000 pour qu'il fût honoré." In his evidence of June 18, 1902, given in the court case previously cited, Forget testified that he had, at some earlier time, refused to buy a large block of Shawinigan stock at 15 cents on the dollar, and declared that even then (1902) the stock was only of potential value. Shawinigan had recently been trying to negotiate a contract to sell power at $15 per h.p. to the Lachine Hydraulic Land and Power Company of Montreal, but the deal had fallen through because the Montreal group's terms had been too stiff. Forget, acting for the Montreal company, wanted half of Shawinigan's stock in return for financing the installation of the required generating facilities and the transmission line to Montreal. Shawinigan was willing to part with only one-third of its stock — it was obviously desperate, but not quite ready to capitulate. In 1903 the Lachine Hydraulic Land and Power Company was merged with the Montreal Light, Heat and Power Company. It is interesting to note that in 1902 Shawinigan had first tried to deal with — and perhaps bolster — an independent company, rather than do business with Holt's emerging consolidation.

10. Before the newly organized company could begin construction, one other preliminary difficulty had had to be cleared up. John Forman, although unable to support his claims to certain parcels of land at the Falls, still owned land needed by the Shawinigan company for the construction of its plant. Long negotiations were necessary before Forman consented to sell his land to the company, and it was February 1899 before the sale was completed, at a price of $100,000 and ten thousand dollars' worth of Shawinigan stock. By then, time was running out for one of the conditions under which the province had sold the power site was that $2 million should be spent within 18 months or the purchase price would be forfeited and the sale revoked. To prevent this happening, the company had to pay the province $10,000 in order to gain more time. These annoyances must have seriously depleted the liquid reserves of the company, but they paved the way for more fruitful expenditures.

11. The aluminum company, Shawinigan's first customer, took delivery of its power on July 1, 1901. The parent company of the Northern Aluminum Company, the Pittsburgh Reduction Company, it will be recalled, had been the first customer of the Niagara Falls Power Company a few years earlier.

12. Shawinigan generated 30-cycle current; the Montreal market demanded 60-

cycle current. At Montreal, the 50-kv. 30-cycle current was to be converted to 2400-volt 60-cycle current for delivery to the Montreal Light, Heat and Power Company. Later, some of it was converted to direct current for sale to the Montreal Tramways Company.

13. Willson was born in Woodstock, Ontario. While attempting to develop a process for the electrical reduction of aluminum at Spray, North Carolina, in 1892, he accidentally discovered a process for the manufacture of calcium carbide. He first established a plant in North Carolina, but soon sought a cheap power site in Canada. He investigated Shawinigan Falls in the middle 1890's but "Shawinigan alors était si dépourvu de voies d'accès commodes qu'il chercha ailleurs. Il finit par acquérir la chute à Caron, mais il ne l'exploita pas. Il retourna dans la province d'Ontario, et se fixa à St. Catherines. Il construisit une usine à Merriton et une central electrique sur le canal Welland. Une seconde fabrique s'éléva bientôt à Ottawa" (Filteau, p. 129).

14. This type of development is not unusual in industrial towns in Quebec. See E. C. Hughes, *French Canada in Transition* (Chicago, 1943) ch. V, esp. p. 37.

15. Maintenance of law and order was a problem during the construction period. Before Shawinigan Falls was incorporated as a town, the company erected toll gates at the entrance to its property as a means of keeping undesirables out of its domain — a move that was resented in the suburbs. See Filteau, p. 103.

16. The plan was described by a visitor of that period in the following incredulous tones: "Ces américains ne doutent de rien! Ils ont déjà fait le trace, sur les collines environnantes, d'une ville que s'étendra sur un mille et tiers; traversée d'une extremité à l'autre par un grand boulevard coupant à son tour à angle droit, des avenues numerotées tout comme à New York.

"Le site d'une station est déjà indiqué (bien qu'il n'y ait pas encore de chemin de fer), de même que celui d'un grand hotel. Et puis entre la ville future et les centrales, de vastes terrains ont été réservés pour une quantité d'industries étiquetées comme suit: Coton-Alcali, — Aluminium, — Papier à journal, — Calcium, — Carbure. Ces grands mots de millionaires sont imprimés en grosses lettres sur le plan" (quoted by Filteau, p. 98). The original plan is still in the office of the resident engineer of the company at Shawinigan Falls and Filteau declares: "A peu près rien n'a été modifié. Il n'y a que la partie occupée aujourd'hui par les usines de la 'Shawinigan Chemicals' qui diffère du tracé original" (p. 99).

17. *The Shawinigan Water & Power Company*, a brochure issued by the company, probably about 1905, p. 10. Relationships between the company and the town are described at various places in Filteau's book. One major source of friction resulted from the tax privileges which the three original companies enjoyed: they paid only nominal taxes, and as the town grew, tax receipts proved inadequate to its budget. This, of course, brought about agitation to increase the companies' taxes. In 1920 the matter was settled when the companies agreed to give up their privileges in return for a fixed assessment for a period of 10 years, and an agreement that the town would be administered by a city manager to be chosen equally by the city council and representatives of the companies; also, his salary was to be paid equally by both parties. Since their privileges were about to expire in two or three years anyway, this seems to have been a good bargain from the companies' point of view. The Shawinigan company has done much for the town at various times by donating land for streets, parks, etc. See Filteau, pp. 175–176, 180–182. Aldred personally donated some $175,000 over a period of years to the Aldred Technical Institute, which was opened in 1911.

18. *The Shawinigan Water & Power Company.*

19. For a description of the early electrical plant, see an article written by Wallace C. Johnson, the chief engineer of the Shawinigan company, in the *Montreal Electrical*

Handbook (Montreal, 1904), issued by the American Institute of Electrical Engineers. At that time the plant had three Francis turbines of 6000 h.p. each. The first two were built by I. P. Morris Co. of Philadelphia; the third, with movable guide vanes, was the product of Escher, Wyss and Co. of Zurich, Switzerland. The first two generators were Westinghouse machines, the third had been built in London, England. The I. P. Morris Co. was building a fourth turbine of 10,500 h.p. capacity which was to be equipped with a 6600-kw. Westinghouse generator. These two machines were larger than any that had been built up to that time. For a further description of the plant, also by Johnson, see "Electric Power from Shawinigan Falls, Canada," *Cassier's Magazine* (1904).

20. For the development of markets for aluminum, see D. H. Wallace, *Market Control in the Aluminum Industry* (Cambridge, 1937), ch. 1.

21. Filteau, pp. 105–106, 126.

22. G. Carruthers, *Paper in the Making* (Toronto, 1947), p. 660.

23. *Annual Report*, 1907, p. 12. Subsequent references to annual reports will be abbreviated to A.R., the date, and the page number when available. When a citation refers to an annual report of a company other than the one whose history is the subject-matter of the chapter where the citation appears, the name of the company will also be given.

24. The Niagara Falls Power Co. had expected that its largest market would be in Buffalo, but with the influx of electroprocess industries to Niagara Falls, it soon found that most of its power was sold locally. Mr. Aldred was undoubtedly familiar with this experience, but he wisely decided not to rely on a similar development at Shawinigan Falls. Shawinigan Falls, unlike Niagara Falls, was not then easily accessible to industry, and the electroprocess market at Shawinigan Falls had to be built up by the Shawinigan company itself. Montreal was thus a market of crucial importance to Shawinigan in the early period, and today is still a major market for Shawinigan power.

25. A.R. 1907, p. 10.

26. A.R. 1908, p. 8.

27. A.R. 1910, p. 9.

28. A.R. 1910, p. 7. In 1912 the new allies each purchased a half-interest in the Cedars Rapids Manufacturing and Power Company, which owned a power site on the St. Lawrence River. Work was immediately started on a 160,000-h.p. development to supply power for electroprocess industries at Cedars Rapids and for general demands in the western part of Montreal. The Shawinigan company had thought it wise to participate in this venture "For the purpose of conserving your Company's interest in the Montreal situation, and more closely cementing the relations between your Company and the distributing company in control of that market" (A.R. 1913, p. 8).

29. This station was equipped to produce 60-cycle current, and the frequency changers at Montreal were therefore no longer necessary. Thirty-cycle current was distributed locally and in the area south of the St. Lawrence until the end of the first world war, when the expensive process of changing over to 60-cycle current was begun. Generators at No. 1 powerhouse were converted to 60-cycle at various times, until today only a few machines generate 30-cycle current for delivery to electroprocess industries where it can still be used. Shawinigan thus admitted the obsolescence of its 30-cycle plant and took its loss at a relatively early date. The Hydro-Electric Power Commission of Ontario, built up on the basis of 25-cycle power, postponed the unwelcome chore of changing its frequency until after World War II, by which time the problem had grown to one of enormous proportions.

30. The Shawinigan Carbide Company began production with 12 small furnaces

having an aggregate capacity of about 2000 tons per year. Technological progress was rapid, and a great improvement in the manufacturing process was achieved in 1908 when a new type of furnace was developed which permitted continuous operations. Previously the furnaces had to be dismantled in order to remove the carbide. R. W. Witherspoon, who had joined the company in 1904, was mainly responsible for this innovation. He was a graduate of the University of Rochester and had had experience in the electroprocess industry at Niagara Falls. Larger furnaces were built and power consumption per unit of output was reduced. In 1904 it required one kilowatt-day of electricity to produce 7 pounds of carbide; by 1945 the same power consumption gave an output of 15 to 20 pounds of carbide. Production rose from some 5000 tons in 1906 to 10,000 in 1913, and additional furnaces brought the capacity up to 40,000 tons per year in 1915. (This information, and much of the subsequent data referring to the Shawinigan chemical industries, has been taken from an unpublished manuscript, "The History of the Shawinigan Chemicals, Ltd., 1902–46," by A. F. S. Cadenhead. Mr. Cadenhead, who has been associated with the Shawinigan chemical enterprises since 1916, kindly allowed me to read his work.)

31. See Dr. A. Surveyor, "The White Coal of Quebec," *Industrial Canada*, April 1948, p. 56: "Originally, calcium carbide was regarded as a cheap commercial source of acetylene gas which, in those days, was sold for lighting purposes. The value of acetylene gas for welding and cutting metals had scarcely begun to be realized, and its many present day applications had not yet [been appreciated]. Consequently it was solely on its value as an illuminant that acetylene gas was produced and we had the anomaly of an electric power company fostering the manufacture of a competing product." Gas lighting maintained its position in many small towns and villages well into the twentieth century.

32. A.R. 1908, p. 11.

33. A.R. 1908, pp. 8, 10.

34. The town suffered from inadequate railway facilities, and in the endeavor to improve them the power company played an active part. At first the only railway in the area was the Great Northern, a line running from Quebec City to Hawkesbury, Ontario, with a branch from Joliette to Montreal. In 1904 this railway was bought by Mackenzie and Mann, and became part of their Canadian Northern system. Mackenzie was a director of The Shawinigan Water and Power Company from 1904 to 1916. To provide transportation facilities for the construction of its first powerhouse, the Shawinigan company had built a four-mile spur line from the Great Northern to Shawinigan Falls. After the construction period, this line, the Shawinigan Falls Terminal Railway, continued operations as an electric railway and provided "freight services linking the yards of the Great Northern Railway and the plants of the first power customers, the Aluminum plant, the Paper mill, and the Carbide plant at Shawinigan Falls." (In common with many others in the early years of the century, the promoters of Shawinigan entertained visions of widespread railway electrification. The promoters expected all railways within a hundred miles of Shawinigan Falls to be electrified and to provide a market for 25,000 h.p. of electricity. As early as 1899 the Shawinigan company had planned to build an electric railway to Three Rivers, but the project had been abandoned because of lack of capital. See Filteau, p. 131. In the annual report for 1909 mention is made of a plan whereby all railroads coming into Shawinigan Falls would be electrified, but nothing more is heard of it.) As other steam railways entered the town, agreements were made whereby the Terminal Railway handled both incoming and outgoing freight, and today it still "takes care of the switching of almost all industrial freight for both of the transcontinental railway systems which now serve Shawinigan Falls." See the Shawinigan company's brochure, *Fifty Years of Achievement*, 1948. (In 1913 it

was stated that the Terminal Railway was owned partly by the power company and partly by the C.P.R. and Canadian Northern Railways. The Shawinigan Company, however, had "consistently maintained it position in respect thereof, for the purpose of ensuring the railway situation and making it possible for the factories at Shawinigan Falls to have competing transportation lines." A.R. 1913, p. 9. Later, however, the Terminal railway became a wholly owned subsidiary of the power company.)

The Great Northern Railway was an inconvenient and inadequate means of access to Shawinigan Falls, and a railway to Three Rivers, to connect with the main line of the C.P.R., was completed in December, 1906. This line had been promoted by local interests, both the companies and the town authorities, and it had been financed in part by contributions from Three Rivers and other municipalities. (According to Filteau, p. 131, it was a very popular project and in part was a protest against the policy of Mackenzie and Mann after they acquired the Great Northern. The only rail connection to Three Rivers was via the Great Northern to a junction point with a branch line of the C.P.R. which ran north from Three Rivers to a point on the St. Maurice, Les Piles, above Shawinigan Falls. Mackenzie and Mann, not wanting to coöperate with the C.P.R., discontinued the stop at the junction point, thus cutting Shawinigan Falls off from all direct rail connection to Three Rivers.) The new railway was soon bought by the C.P.R. and it was extended north to Grand' Mère in 1910. It was not until 1929, however, that the Canadian National Railway system was persuaded to rebuild the line of the old Great Northern so that it would pass through Shawinigan Falls.

35. The availability of employment for women probably ensured a more stable male labor force. There are continual references in the annual reports of the Shawinigan company during this period to the beneficial effects which the cotton mill had in "stabilizing" or "strengthening" the labor situation. See A.R. 1913; and for similar developments during the Industrial Revolution in England, see T. S. Ashton, *The Industrial Revolution 1760–1830* (Oxford, 1948), p. 112.

36. See Benoît Brouillette, *Le Développement Industriel de la Vallée du Saint-Maurice* (Trois Rivières, 1932), *passim.*

37. See Raoul Blanchard, *Le Centre du Canada Français* (Montreal, 1947), pp. 156–159.

38. See A.R. 1906.

39. The Canada Paper Company was the chief customer at Windsor Mills. This company was the successor to one of the earliest pulp mills in Canada. Founded in 1866 by Angus Logan and Co., it was the first mill in Canada to produce chemical pulp, using the soda process. *Canada Year Book* (1939), p. 273.

40. At first, the Shawinigan company was humiliated in its own village. A local entrepreneur, J. E. Thibaudeau, seeing how easy it was for the Shawinigan company to produce electricity from water power, installed a 500-h.p. generator on the Shawinigan River in 1903 and offered competition in Shawinigan Falls itself, where the larger company had neglected to secure an exclusive franchise. Mr. Thibaudeau operated his business for some fourteen years, with considerable success, before he exploited his nuisance value by selling out to the Shawinigan company. See Filteau, p. 127, and pp. 165–166.

41. A.R. 1907, p. 9.

42. "The experience of this Company has been that the incidental business along the route of its transmission lines, covers the fixed charge on the entire cost of such lines" (a brochure issued by the company around 1905, p. 8).

43. A.R. 1907, p. 9.

44. Including all power stations and transmission lines, but excluding investment in other companies.

45. In 1907 it is stated that the securities of subsidiary companies are used as security

for the issue of debenture stock of the parent company. Also, ". . . your Directors are pleased to state that the policy of financing on securities sold abroad, has proved advantageous as shown by the fact that while the securities of many Canadian companies have seriously declined during the past year, this Company's securities have held firmly in the market, and notwithstanding the unfavorable market conditions during the past year, this Company was able to dispose of, on a satisfactory basis, its issue of 4½% Debenture Stock as well as the balance of Bonds ($500,000 of Mortgage Bonds) held in the Treasury" (A.R. 1907, p. 9). Investments were made in companies other than subsidiary concerns, such as Shawinigan Cotton Company, Asbestos Corporation of Canada, and, of course, Montreal Light, Heat and Power. By 1913 the total of investments in both subsidiary and other companies amounted to $2.77 million in bonds and $4.55 million in stocks. In the report of that year it is noted that "while it is probable your Company will eventually dispose of its holdings in companies, the operation of which is but contingent to your business, — in the meantime, these investments not only pay a substantial return, but in the aggregate show a substantial profit above cost" (A.R. 1913, p. 9). In 1915 it was stated that there had been no sale of securities during the past two years "owing to market conditions abroad," but money had been raised by sale of stock to stockholders at less than market prices. All finance was channeled through the parent company, subsidiary companies raising money only by selling securities to the parent company. In 1916 the company was selling small amounts of stock to its employees.

46. Up to 1916 the lowest price for Shawinigan stock was 98 in 1910, and for first mortgage bonds was 96 in 1915. After 1910 its common stock usually sold above 100, and reached a premium of 20 percent in 1912 and 1914.

47. A.R. 1915, p. 10.

48. In the case of the pulp company at least, this forecast was much too optimistic. For the first few years, the "cost of production was found to be much higher than previously estimated," and the company was unprofitable. It was forced into paper production after 1903 in an attempt to recoup its losses. Carruthers, p. 660.

49. The Shawinigan Water & Power Company, *Fifty Years of Achievement.*

50. These notes were no doubt those referred to in the Annual Report for 1917. To cover large expenditures for the construction of the La Loutre Dam and the expansion of electroprocess subsidiaries, the company was authorized to issue $4.5 million in two-year, 6 per cent gold notes. "These notes were issued on December 15, 1917. Three million of the notes were sold in the U.S. to a strong group of Bankers and $1.5 million of these notes have been reserved to be offered to the shareholders of the Company. These notes are convertible at any time before maturity into Common stock of the company. . . . It is anticipated, at the maturity of these notes, the money conditions will have so changed that the financing of the Company can be again placed upon a permanent footing" (A.R. 1917, p. 14). Such short-term financing was needed in part because the company had been paid two million dollars for construction of the Gouin Dam in provincial bonds and these were unsalable at the moment except at a sacrifice. A further 2 million dollars was "locked up" in the acetone plant (A.R. 1917.) A previous issue of 2-year, 5 per cent notes had been made in 1916. These transactions perhaps started a trend toward financing in the United States. Many of the holders of the notes exercised the option of converting their holdings to stock before the notes matured. See Annual Reports for 1918 and 1919. In 1921, $4,375,000 worth of bonds were sold in New York.

51. In 1911 the Shawinigan Carbide Company became part of the Canada Carbide Company. This latter company, according to a brochure issued by the power company in 1913, "was formed to take over the properties and plants of the Shawinigan Carbide

Company, the Ottawa Carbide Company and the Willson Carbide Co., of St. Catherines." The new company was controlled by the Shawinigan group. Manufacturing operations in the Ottawa plant were soon discontinued.

52. Many different kinds of "load factors" can be constructed, and these figures probably referred to selected plants. The annual load factor for the Shawinigan system as a whole was around 60 percent in 1917.

53. The discount had presumably reflected the opinion that hydroelectricity, which was subject to the vagaries of stream flow conditions, and which usually had to be transmitted for longer distances than steam electricity, was less reliable than its competitor. In the 1914 Annual Report of the Shawinigan company, it is remarked that steel-tower transmission lines are very reliable and are satisfactory even by comparison with steam electricity generated on the consumer's premises.

54. The following story is perhaps apocryphal, but it serves to suggest a link between the twentieth century and the days of the fur trade. "'We raised as much capital as we could in Montreal' John E. Aldred, first treasurer of the company relates, 'but we were left with many unsold bonds. I went to London to sound out the English money market. On my arrival I went around to see Lord Strathcona. I told him the reason for my trip and had barely started to explain the possibilities of our scheme for the St. Maurice Valley when he interrupted to say: "Show me the map. There's the portage at Shawinigan Falls. I made it dozens of times for the Hudson's Bay Company. Here's what I'll do, Aldred: I'll take a $1,000 bond for every portage I made at the Falls." He took $50,000 of the bonds.' " John Langdon, "Valley of Power," *Industrial Shawinigan, 1941* (published by the Shawinigan *Standard*), p. 27.

Chapter 4. The Shawinigan Water and Power Company, 1915–1940

1. The underestimation of water-power resources in the early days of the company, and the upward revisions necessitated by improved turbines and better hydraulic control, are illustrated by the following. A stock circular of 1900 boasts that the company can develop 100,000 h.p. and perhaps 200,000 h.p. at Shawinigan Falls. By 1929 the capacity of the two powerhouses at this site was 280,000 h.p., with an additional 65,000 hydraulic h.p. A third powerhouse was started in 1946 which will add a further 195,000 h.p. to the capacity at Shawinigan Falls. In 1919 the ultimate capacity of No. 2 Powerhouse was expected to be 75,000 h.p. Its ultimate capacity turned out to be 235,000 h.p.

2. O. O. Lefebvre, "Storage Reservoirs in Canada," *Engineering Journal* (July 1930), p. 472.

3. A.R. 1912, p. 7.

4. A.R. 1918, p. 11. In 1930 Dr. O. O. Lefebvre, chief engineer of the Quebec Streams Commission, wrote that the Gouin Dam had increased the flow of the St. Maurice at Shawinigan Falls from a minimum flow before regulation of 6,000 cubic feet per second, to a flow of 17,000 c.f.s. after regulation.

5. See A.R. 1923.

6. *The Shawinigan Water & Power Company*, a brochure issued by the company in 1919, p. 15.

7. *Ibid.*

8. A.R. 1916, p. 13.

9. A small steam station in Quebec City was included in the property of the Dorchester Electric Company.

10. A.R. 1915, p. 11.

11. A second new company, the Three Rivers Traction Company, was organized by Shawinigan to provide tramway services in Three Rivers whose population, having

doubled in six years, was now over 20,000. In 1923 the tramway was extended to Cap de la Madeleine. The company was reported as a profit-maker and a good customer for Shawinigan power.

12. "H. W. Matheson, a native of Nova Scotia and graduate of Dalhousie University and at that time in the employ of the DuPont Company was retained by Howard Murray [President of the Canada Carbide Company] and brought to Shawinigan Falls to supervise the construction and operation of a projected pilot plant to test out these [German] processes" (A. F. S. Cadenhead, "The History of the Shawinigan Chemicals, Ltd., 1902–46," p. 13. See note 30, Chapter 3.) Matheson was soon joined by H. S. Reid, a graduate of McGill University who had been working with the Consolidated Mining and Smelting Co. at Rossland, B.C., and by Cadenhead, from Queen's University.

13. There were, however, "various accidents and delays" in getting the plant into production. "A new contract, however, has been made with the Imperial Munitions Board, extending the operation of the plant throughout 1918. This contract has been made under such terms and conditions that the results will prove very advantageous to the Company." (A.R. 1917, p. 15). Mr. Cadenhead's manuscript provides a brief history of this period. Great difficulty was experienced in obtaining construction materials, and many chemical and mechanical problems had to be solved before the plant could start production. Aluminum played an important part in the process when it was discovered that unlike steel, it was chemically resistant to acetic acid. At that time, about 50 tons of carbide were needed to produce 25 tons of acetic acid which in turn gave 10 tons of acetone. Acetone was used in the manufacture of cordite, and about 1200 long tons of acetone were shipped to Britain in 1917. Towards the end of that year a great demand arose for acetic acid in the manufacture of airplane dope. The acetone plant was accordingly closed down, and some 10,000 tons of acetic acid was shipped overseas before the Armistice. Construction of an acetic acid plant for the United States government was begun in March 1918, but it had not been completed before the Armistice.

14. Cadenhead, p. 32. The raw material used was a waste liquor from a plant of the Dow Chemical Co. at Midland, Michigan. The product was shipped to the British and French governments.

15. *Ibid.*, p. 34.

16. This plant was organized by Aldred and P. H. Falter of the Aluminum Company, who became a member of the Shawinigan organization after the first world war.

17. A.R. 1915, pp. 11–12.

18. The increase in demand and the rise in the general level of prices probably resulted in some increase in the prices charged for electricity. In 1917 it was stated that no price increases had been charged to normal customers, but that "in some cases where war materials are being manufactured, and where the cost of reaching the customer had to be amortized in a short time, prices have been substantially increased" (A.R. 1917, p. 16). Two years later the annual report stated that "the energy developed by [the Shawinigan] plants has risen in value as the result of the increased cost of its production by other than the Hydro Electric means" (A.R. 1919, p. 12).

19. A.R. 1918. This contract, however, led to a dispute between the company and the United States government which was not settled until 1927, the result of the settlement being that "certain works at Shawinigan Falls built for the supply of chemicals to the U. S. Government reverted in their entirety to the Company, allowing their amalgamation with the other chemical properties of the company" (A.R. 1927, pp. 12–13).

20. A.R. 1919, p. 10.

21. A.R. 1918, p. 11.

22. For the remainder of the chapter, the reader should refer to Table 6 and Chart

4. Figures quoted in the text will not always agree with those in Table 6: the data in this table are grouped in a slightly different manner from the raw data (provided by The Shawinigan Water and Power Company) on which they are based, while the figures in the text are sometimes quoted directly from the raw data themselves. Thus secondary power sales, for example, which are broken down by various markets in the raw data, are in one category in Table 6.

23. See Abbé Albert Tessier, *Trois-Rivières 1535–1935* (Three Rivers, 1935), pp. 158, 166–167.

24. Raoul Blanchard, *Le Centre du Canada Français* (Montreal, 1947), p. 169.

25. Tessier, p. 180.

26. For the early history of this development, see G. Carruthers, *Paper in the Making* (Toronto, 1947), ch. XXVII: Blanchard, pp. 404–405; and A. Desilets, *La Grand' Mère* (Three Rivers, 1933), pp. 36 ff. Forman lost control of the venture in 1887 to American capitalists from New York state who supplied the capital funds that carried the project to completion.

27. See L. E. Ellis, *Reciprocity: 1911* (New Haven, 1939).

28. See G. Carruthers, Part II, chs. XIV and XVIII. For the early history of the mills in the Portneuf area, see his Ch. VI.

29. A.R. 1926, p. 15.

30. With the rapid expansion of capacity after 1921, the need for some market that would absorb temporarily surplus power became very apparent. In the annual report for 1921, it is noted that delivery of the final block of power from the Laurentide Power Company would be taken in July 1922, but that not all of the power which was even then being purchased from Grand'Mère was being used. It was no doubt the pressure of contract purchases from Grand'Mère, taken in conjunction with the postwar slump in demand, that led to the development of the electric steam generator.

31. An earlier, experimental installation had been made at the Shawinigan company's chemical plant, itself a large user of steam.

32. See R. W. Leeper, "Power in the Pulp and Paper Industry," *Engineering Journal* (July 1924).

33. "The heavy demand of the pulp and paper industry for steam will be appreciated when it is realized that for every ton of newsprint manufactured, from 1000 to 1500 pounds of coal and from 10,000 to 13,000 pounds of steam are required. The average coal and steam consumption of seven of the leading mills in Canada is 1400 pounds of coal and 10,700 pounds of steam . . . Coal and the steam generated by it represents not less than 10% and frequently as high as 15% of the total cost of making paper . . . Steam constitutes the second highest single item of cost in the industry" (B. F. Haanel, "Fuel Resources of Canada and their Utilization," *Engineering Journal*, July 1924, pp. 370–371). Cf. John A. Guthrie, *The Newsprint Paper Industry* (Cambridge, 1941), chs. XI and XIII, for cost data in the late 1930's.

34. "The utilization of electric energy for heating is a degrading of energy and is opposed to all principles of efficiency . . ." (B. F. Haanel). One pound of 13,000 B.T.U. coal, burned directly under a boiler at 78 per cent efficiency, will give 10,200 B.T.U.'s of heat. The same coal can produce about 1kwh. of electricity which has a heating value of only 3400 B.T.U.'s. Haanel calculates that "electric energy must be available at not more than 10 dollars per kw. year in order to equal coal at 6 dollars per ton," and R. W. Leeper says that: "As one pound of coal is roughly equal to 3 kwhs. from the heating point of view, it is evident that with coal at $10 a short ton, electricity must be available at ⅓ of a cent per kwhr." The price of coal in Quebec during the thirties was less than $6 per ton (Guthrie, p. 172) so electricity would have had to be priced at less than .1¢ per kwh. to compete with coal. Shawinigan's average revenue from sales

to the pulp and paper industry during this decade, was, for firm power, about .3¢ per kwh., and for secondary power from .07 to .09¢ per kwh. Secondary power, of course, is priced to be just cheaper than coal for steam raising purposes.

35. J. A. Guthrie, p. 173. Dr. Huet Massue, statistician for the Shawinigan company, calculates that at the ratio of 3 kwh. to 1 lb. of coal, electric power during the decade of the thirties obviated the purchase of 6.5 million tons of coal in Quebec. The *Report of the Royal Commission on Coal, 1946* (Ottawa, 1947), p. 390, gives an estimate of 4.9 million tons for 1934 to 1940 inclusive. For a good discussion of the economies of secondary power, see the *Report*, pp. 365–392.

36. A.R. 1924, p. 10.

37. Some of these purchases were simply Shawinigan power that was not delivered. For example, if the Montreal company did not need all the power for which it had contracted, it would sell it back to Shawinigan. The Shawinigan company had to pay for this power, otherwise the Montreal company would use it and shut down some of its own generating facilities.

38. See The Shawinigan Water & Power Company, *A Record of Services Rendered — 1939–45* (Montreal, 1946), pp. 7–8: "Until the Shipshaw power project was brought into production in 1943, the expansion of aluminum production facilities . . . [in Quebec] was predicated principally upon . . . [the power plants] operated by Shawinigan on the St. Maurice River."

39. In 1924 the directors reminded the shareholders that "at the termination of the war, the management decided that, instead of scrapping the chemical plants which had been constructed for war purposes and which now stand in the books of the Company at a value of $2.5 million, it would be possible, by technical research and proper sales management, to develop the production of these plants. Your Directors are able to report that, as a result of several years of effort, these works are now showing a profit, with prospects of substantial further development" (A.R. 1924, p. 10). This happy ending had only just been made possible. The years from 1919 to 1923 were later referred to by the chemical personnel of the company as their "doghouse" days. During these lean years the chemical enterprises were unprofitable and the time was used to carry on extensive research. Mr. Cadenhead gives the late Mr. Julian C. Smith most of the credit for having this policy accepted by the parent concern. The policy paid rich dividends in the later twenties when the chemical business became very profitable and contributed heavily to the profits of the power company.

40. This work led, in 1925, to a linkage with American firms engaged in similar types of industrial chemistry. The Niacet Chemicals Corporation was formed as an electrochemical enterprise and operated a plant at Niagara Falls, N. Y. This corporation represented an association of Shawinigan Chemicals and two American companies, the Carbide and Carbon Chemicals Corporation (a subsidiary of Union Carbide) and the Roessler and Hasslacher Chemical Company. The Niacet company, from Shawinigan's point of view, probably served the dual purpose of providing an outlet for Shawinigan products in the States, and of allowing the company to participate in the control of the part of the American chemical industry which was manufacturing products allied to, or competitive with, Shawinigan products. Shawinigan maintained its interest in this concern until 1945, at which time its holdings were sold out to the United States Vanadium Corporation.

41. These offices were capably managed and are still a part of the Shawinigan organization. In 1923, following the American tariff, the New York company made an arrangement with the United Lead Company whereby it obtained an interest in a small carbide plant at Keokuk, Iowa. Production at this plant was then expanded as a means of avoiding the tariff on imports from Canada.

42. In 1948, "about 80% of the carbide produced by the Carbide Division is used to generate acetylene from which the Chemicals Division manufactures a wide range of industrial chemicals. The Shawinigan Water & Power Company, *Fifty Years of Achievement.*

43. A.R. 1926, p. 10. In 1927 the Shawinigan chemical enterprises were put on a simplified corporate basis by the amalgamation of the Carbide Company and the Electro Products Company into a new concern, "Shawinigan Chemicals Ltd." with a Carbide Division and a Chemical Division. In 1929, a Stainless Steels and Alloys Division was added to the concern. At first, the production of this last division was confined to the manufacture of Duriron under license from the Duriron Company of Dayton, Ohio. Later, the invention of new steel alloys cut into the market for Duriron, and the division entered the wider field of alloy steel production. Markets for its products are found in the pulp and paper and chemical industries of Canada and also in foreign countries.

44. Of an absolute increase of $6.1 million in gross revenue between 1925 and 1929, the pulp and paper industry accounted for a little over $3 million, sales to utility companies and at retail for over $2 million, electroprocess industries for $100,000, and asbestos and textiles together for approximately $800,000. (Asbestos sales may have been included in "utilities" in 1925 since they are not given separately until 1927.)

45. In 1923 the name of Shawinigan's subsidiary in Quebec City, the Public Service Corporation of Quebec, was changed to the Quebec Power Company, which then acquired a controlling interest in the Quebec Railway Light, Heat and Power Company. This latter company was the result of a merger, engineered around 1909 by R. Forget, which had brought together the electrical, tramway, and gas utilities then operating in the Quebec City area. One of the components of this merger, the Quebec Railway Light and Power Company, had been operating in Quebec since 1898, supplying lighting services and power for the small industrial load and the street-railway system. Another had been the Quebec and Saguenay Railway Company which operated a railway between Quebec City and Lake Saguenay that had been built in 1888. This unprofitable line had been a great burden to the 1909 merger, and in spite of the fact that it had been taken over by the government in 1916, its deficits probably contributed heavily to the financial weakness which led to the demise of the Q.R.L.H. and P. Co. In 1922 Montreal interests gained control of the latter company. In the following year Shawinigan, having gained control of the stock, took over its management. According to a letter of July 26, 1923 from the new management to the shareholders of the Q.R.L.H. and P. Co., Shawinigan had brought its stock holdings at 25 per cent of par value, and had bought the bonds of the company at the rate of $27 cash or $30 worth of preferred stock for a $100 bond. The shareholders were also told that the company was then using almost all the power available from its own generating stations and would shortly either have to buy more power or to develop new generating capacity. The company's poor financial position had precluded the latter course; Shawinigan was able to deliver the power and had therefore got the company. At least some of the shareholders in the old company were reluctant to give up their stock, for in the 1923 annual report of the Q.R.L.H. and P. Co., the new Shawinigan management felt it necessary to do some prodding: "It is obvious that the future of your Company is closely linked with that of the Quebec Power Company. Many of your shareholders, recognizing this condition, have deemed it wise to become shareholders in the Quebec Power Company through exchange of their shares." The assets of the Quebec Railway Light, Heat and Power Company were finally purchased by the Quebec Power Company in 1928.

46. In the Annual Report of the Quebec Power Company for 1937, p. 9, it was reported that, "The work of modernizing the Company's part of the street lighting

system in the city of Quebec was completed during the past year, and all arc lamps have now been replaced by modern incandescent units."

47. To maintain a local flavor, the Quebec Power Company actively promoted customer stock ownership and appointed Quebec people to half of the seats on its directorate. The operation of the Quebec Power Company has always been kept separate from that of the parent company, formal relationships being merely those of buyer and seller of power.

48. A.R. 1925.

49. "Retail sales" include sales to domestic, commercial and rural consumers, sales to municipalities for street lighting and other purposes, and contracts for "small power" to small manufacturing establishments. In Table 6 and Chart 4, however, "small power" has been classified with asbestos, textiles, and miscellaneous, in order to give a figure for general industrial sales.

50. A.R. 1930, p. 13.

51. A.R. 1923, p. 10.

52. In 1924 Shawinigan and Montreal Light, Heat and Power Consolidated jointly acquired two utility companies operating in Montreal. One of these companies, in turn, owned the Canadian Light and Power Company, which owned the St. Timothée station. The details of this matter are related in the next chapter. The Shawinigan company operated the St. Timothée plant from 1925 to 1948, at which time it was sold to the Quebec Hydro Electric Commission.

53. Interest in retailing led to greater emphasis on public relations. In the late twenties the annual reports become increasingly cluttered with assurances to shareholders that relations between the company and the municipalities it serves are cordial, and with unctuous remarks like the following: "It has been the policy of the Company to work in harmony with governmental authorities. To the Quebec Public Service Commission your Company has given the heartiest co-operation and assistance" (A.R. 1928, p. 16). The policy of selling small amounts of stock to employees and customers — in essence a rather crude means of building up support for private enterprise — was actively promoted after 1925.

54. A.R. 1932, p. 13.

55. A.R. 1930, p. 13.

56. A.R. 1928, p. 11.

57. The Shawinigan company paid two shares of its stock for each share in the St. Maurice Power Company, and one share of its stock plus $150 cash for each share of the Laurentide Power Company (A.R. 1928, p. 10). The Electricity Commission thought that these prices were high enough to warrant further investigation. See *Report of the Electricity Commission of the Province of Quebec*, 1935, pp. 28–33.

58. The La Tuque site, like the water powers at Shawinigan Falls and Grand'Mère, had been alienated from the Crown before 1907 and were therefore owned in fee simple. After 1907 the province did not sell its water power; instead it rented power rights under the terms of an emphyteutic lease, and it was under this type of arrangement that Shawinigan held its other water powers.

59. From the point of view of the efficient development and utilization of a power river, unitary control is the only defensible form of ownership. Especially is this so when there are storage works and a number of generating stations on the same river. Development must be planned so that the drop in the river is concentrated at points where the available water will do the most work. Where the tail race of one plant is the head race of another, the operation of the plants must be synchronized in order to ensure full utilization of the water. That Shawinigan has developed the St. Maurice to full advantage is indicated by Figure 2 in the text.

60. A.R. 1932, p. 12.

61. A.R. 1931, p. 11.

62. These figures include revenue from sources other than power sales and are therefore not comparable with figures quoted previously. Furthermore, the figures for net revenue after 1933 are not fully comparable with similar figures for previous years, and the extent of the drop between 1930 and 1933 is overstated by something less than half a million dollars. For the change in accounting practice which explains the lack of comparability, see the Annual Report for 1933.

63. In 1932 it was reported that the asbestos industry was suffering from "general over-production and competition. This over-production and competition is largely accounted for by the supply of asbestos from Russia and South Africa. However, in general the asbestos companies south of the St. Lawrence served by your Company have continued during the year to fulfill their contracts for power and present indications are that the situation in this industry is gradually improving" (A.R. 1932, p. 9).

64. A.R. 1931, p. 12.

65. See, for example, V. W. Bladen, *An Introduction to Political Economy* (Toronto, 1951), ch. VII.

66. A.R. 1934, p. 11. Although average revenue figures are to be used very charily, their trend indicates that contract prices stiffened slightly after 1934.

67. Markets for Shawinigan Black, and especially for Vinyl Resins, the group of products which had been developed in the late twenties, grew rapidly after 1930. These latter products were produced at Shawinigan Falls, but because the company licensed its patent rights to others, most of the production was taking place in the plants of the large chemical companies in the United States. A. F. S. Cadenhead comments (p. 27) that "much of the acetic acid business was lost through licensing others to operate our process in more advantageous areas where freight rates were a minor factor, and custom duties did not exist." Shawinigan made coöperative arrangements with American chemical companies later in the decade. In 1937, a new company, the Shawinigan Resins Corporation, jointly owned by Shawinigan Chemicals and the Fiberloid Corporation of Springfield, Massachusetts, was set up to manufacture vinyl resins in a plant at Springfield. (In 1938, the Fiberloid interest in this enterprise was taken over by the Monsanto Chemical Company). In 1941, an arrangement was made with the Union Carbide and Carbon Corporation to produce their patented product, "Vinylite," at Shawinigan Falls: "Canadian Resins which is jointly owned by Shawinigan Chemicals Ltd. and Union Carbide and Carbon Corporation, New York, manufactures in Shawinigan Falls a new plastic material known as 'Vinylite'" (*Fifty Years of Achievement*). This arrangement was the reciprocal of that which had led to the Niacet company at Niagara Falls in 1925 (see note 40, above).

68. A.R. 1930, p. 13. This contract was no doubt made at a reduced price. The average revenue from Shawinigan sales to all utility companies dropped from .475 cents in 1930 to .376 cents in 1931.

69. A.R. 1931, p. 10.

70. The following account is taken from the *Memoire de M. J. E. Gregoire, Maire de Quebec,* in his submission to the Electricity Commission in 1934. The original contract signed with the Quebec Power Company in 1925 was criticized in 1929 by a group of citizens because of what they claimed were excessive rates. In 1930 a municipal commission of enquiry, which was refused access to the company's books, and which was treated uncoöperatively by the Public Service Commission, reported that the rates charged were extravagant and unjust, and recommended municipal ownership of distribution facilities in the city. The city council then planned to denounce the contract at its expiration in 1935. The president of the Shawinigan company, Julian C. Smith,

then began a series of abortive conferences with the council offering new rate schedules which, it was charged, represented a juggling of rates without any real reductions. (At one point, as a *quid pro quo* for moderate rate reductions, the company wanted to be relieved of its obligations for snow removal, to have the payment for its tramway franchise reduced, and to be allowed to provide tramway service on its own schedule!) Legal doubts were raised as to the City's competency to establish its own electrical distribution system and application was made to the provincial legislature to have its charter amended to give it this power. On three successive occasions the city was frustrated in this attempt to get its charter revised. On the second occasion Prime Minister A. Taschereau put them off with the tawdry argument to the effect that "il ne faut pas compromettre mais protéger le capital investi dans le campagnie par les particuliers, les compagnies d'assurances, etc." (p. 12). On the third occasion the representatives of the company were out in force, and the Prime Minister again put off the amendment, on the grounds that a report from a group of engineers studying the situation must first be received. A second report by a group of engineers retained to advise the city said that the city could generate electricity by steam and charge lower rates than those in force, but did not advise public ownership because of the expensive accommodation which would have to be made with the power company. The city council was about to conduct a referendum on the question when a group of its members suddenly voted to renew the contract with the company. "Entre temps," submitted Mayor Gregoire, "Son Honneur Lavigueur, au grand étonnement du public, fait, auprès des officiers superieurs de la compagnie, des demarches personnelles et privées qui demeurent pour tous une énigme fort étrange" (p. 18). In the new contract, prices were not even stated; the company promised only to reduce its rates as its profits rose!

71. A.R. 1937, p. 10.

72. A.R. 1931, p. 10.

73. The information in this paragraph has been taken from an unpublished "Memorandum on Rural Electrification" prepared in 1943 by Dr. Huet Massue. It was made available to me through the courtesy of Dr. Massue.

74. According to Dr. Massue, Shawinigan's rates for farm service were lower than the rates for similar service in Ontario. Consumption in Quebec was nevertheless very low, and the number of electrical appliances in Quebec farmhouses was very small. "Whereas at the end of 1941 the farmers of Ontario were using 10,539 electric ranges and 390 water heaters . . . the farmers served by 'Shawinigan' were only using 37 electric ranges and only 13 water heaters" (ibid., p. 21).

75. At the end of the war, sales at retail rose from 4 per cent of total kilowatt-hour sales in 1945 to 8 per cent in 1949, while the proportion of total gross revenue from such sales jumped from 22 per cent to 32 per cent between the same two years. There has been a continual drop in average revenue per kilowatt hour sold in this market, which reflects both rate reductions and increasing consumption per customer. (Increasing consumption per customer results in a lower average revenue per kilowatt where tariffs provide for reduced prices as consumption increases).

76. The building remained half-empty for years after its completion, and title to it soon passed to the mortgagee.

Chapter 5. The Montreal Light, Heat and Power Company

1. The Montreal Light, Heat and Power Company was formed in 1901. In 1916, along with the Cedars Rapids Manufacturing and Power Company, whose plant was situated on the St. Lawrence west of Montreal, it became the property of a holding company, the Civic Investment and Industrial Company. In 1918 the holding company

was renamed the Montreal Light, Heat and Power Consolidated, a style which was retained thereafter until the property was expropriated by the province in 1944. (The succeeding publicly owned organization is known as Hydro-Québec.) Until 1944, in spite of the changes in name, effective control of the enterprise was exercised by the same group.

2. W. H. Atherton, *Montreal 1535–1914*, 2 vols. (Montreal, 1914), II, 403–404.

3. A. J. Lawson, "Generation, Distribution and Measurement of Electricity for Light and Power," *Transactions of the Canadian Society of Civil Engineers* (1890), p. 182.

4. See J. C. Lamothe, *Histoire de la Corporation de la Cité de Montréal* (Montreal, 1903), pp. 134 ff. Thus even at the reduced price of $60 per arc lamp after 1903, electric lighting was still three and a half times as expensive as gas lighting on a per lamp basis.

5. Montreal Street Railway Company, *Annual Report for 1910*, p. 33. Nevertheless, heavy snowfall and the steep grades on the city streets created many problems for the electric tramway.

6. In 1906 and 1907 the tramway company built two storage battery stations. They were used both for regulating purposes — absorbing the shocks put on the system when cars stopped or started — and for the delivery of power during peak load periods. A.R. 1910.

7. American Institute of Electrical Engineers, *The Montreal Electrical Handbook* (Montreal, 1904), p. 149. This handbook provides descriptions of the plants of important electrical installations in the Montreal and Ottawa regions at that time.

8. *Ibid.*, pp. 156–157.

9. *Ibid.*, pp. 73–84. With the development of the Canadian market, American electrical equipment firms established plants in Canada. The Westinghouse Company, which had supplied much of the electrical apparatus used in Canada, was building a plant at Hamilton in 1904 to manufacture its products in Canada. (The same company had been manufacturing air brakes at Hamilton since 1896; pp. 107–114.) The Canadian General Electric Company, formed in 1891 by an amalgamation of the principal Canadian manufactures of electrical equipment enlarged their Peterboro plant after the turn of the century, and by 1905 had completed "some of the new 15,000 h.p. generators for the Electrical Development Company at Niagara, which are the largest in the world. . . . Never before has machinery of such importance been manufactured in this country . . ." (Annual Report of the Canadian General Electric Company, 1905, p. 9). Allis-Chalmers — Bullock Limited, a company manufacturing a wide range of power and mining equipment, also built a plant near Montreal in the early years of the century. See *Montreal Electrical Handbook*, pp. 143–147. This company was purchased by the Canadian General Electric Company in 1913, and the business continued under the name of Canadian Allis-Chalmers Limited.

10. Of these, the Montreal Gas Company, incorporated under the name of the New City Gas Company in 1847, was itself a merger: in 1894 it had absorbed the Montreal Gas Light Company (founded in 1836), which had been the first gas company in Montreal, and the Consumers Gas Company (founded in 1893), which had been merged before its plant could be brought into operation. In 1901 the Montreal Gas Company was the sole producer and distributor of gas in Montreal and through it the Montreal Light, Heat and Power Company continued to monopolize this business in the city. In 1928, the manufacturing plant of the company was shut down when all gas production was transferred to the Montreal Coke and Manufacturing Company, a new concern jointly owned by the Montreal Light, Heat and Power Consolidated and the Kroppers Company of Delaware. The Montreal Gas Company then became the distributing arm

of the organization and remained as such until 1944 when it, along with the electrical properties of the parent concern, was expropriated by the provincial government.

11. The company also owned the Canadian rights for the manufacture of various lines of electrical equipment. These rights were later sold to the Canadian General Electric Company.

12. Until the Montreal Light, Heat and Power Company took over the operation of this plant in 1902, it had been operated by the Royal Electric Company under an agreement with the Montreal and St. Lawrence Light and Power Company. See C. A. Ellis, *Report upon the Financial Affairs of Montreal Light, Heat and Power Consolidated and its Component Companies* (Montreal, November 12, 1946), p. 38. This report, which will be frequently quoted hereafter, formed part of the investigations which were made into the company's history in connection with the indemnity to be paid the owners of the company after it was expropriated in 1944. It provides a clear and authoritative account of the company's financial history and attempts to give a statement of the amount of money actually invested in the concern. As will become apparent, this was no easy task.

13. The four companies, three electrical and one gas, were bought for 159,728 shares of the new company, being at the rate of (exchange of shares) 2½ for 1 of the Royal Electric and Montreal Gas Companies, 1½ for 1 of the Imperial Electric Light Company, and 1 for 1 of the Montreal and St. Lawrence Light and Power Company. The remainder of the 170,000 issued shares ($17 million par value) were accounted for by 1300 shares subscribed for by the incorporators, 8750 shares paid to J. L. Forget and Co. for their services in incorporating the company, and 222 shares sold to the public (Ellis, p. 37). The purchase price of these properties, as carried on the books of the new concern, represented an amount of over $5 million in excess of the book value of assets as they had been carried on the books of the component electrical companies, and an amount of over $4 million above the former book value of the Montreal Gas Company (pp. 44–45).

14. The three concerns were the Citizens Light and Power Company, the Standard Light and Power Company, and the Temple Electric Company.

15. As noted previously, the Forget firm was interested in the Lachine Company as well as in the Montreal group. See Chapter 3, note 9.

16. Ellis, p. 40. This was made up of a payment of $190 for each $100 share of the Lachine Company, plus the redemption of over a half million dollars' worth of that company's bonds.

17. The above account is based on a conversation with a former executive of the company.

18. It is not known when this station was built. The annual report for 1928 mentions that the company then had a 25,000-h.p. reserve steam station at its gas works at Ville La Salle. The steam capacity of the company in 1942 was given by the Dominion Water and Power Bureau as 22,000 h.p.

19. A.R. 1915.

20. A.R. 1910.

21. The relatively high obsolescence of electrical distribution systems in the early part of the century was undoubtedly one cause of friction between power companies and civic authorities. The companies were naturally reluctant to scrap equipment that would still give service, while the authorities wanted the most modern systems available. Because the utility companies were dependent on municipal franchises to use city streets they were usually in a relatively weak bargaining position, and it was no doubt possible, as a rule, for the city authorities to shift the burden of obsolescence in their lighting systems onto the electrical companies. Costs of obsolescence reflected the prog-

ress of technique, and, sometimes, also decisions to keep the initial costs of an installation as low as possible. The following comments, made by the Commercial Manager of the Southern Canada Power Company, are of interest in this connection: If a company was short of money it was often necessary to build a cheap system with small copper wires and rods — copper accounted for a large part of the cost of distributing system — which made for heavy line losses. The company would hope to be able to rebuild its system properly after it had established its worth and could command capital at lower interest rates. "If one is short of money one has to put in small copper, stand the losses, explain away low voltage, risk transformers, and pray nightly that the god of diversity slumber not [i.e., that peak load would not exceed capacity]. While the equipment in our oldest hydro-electrical developments is in many cases the same as that originally installed, a good example being Chambly power house, where Stanley inductor generators installed in 1897 are still, after 27 years, grinding out their daily kilowatt hours, how much of the distribution equipment originally placed in Montreal is standing today — not one pole or wire; and how much of the equipment, poles, wires, transformers, etc., erected in 1904, 20 years ago, is here to-day, — very little, certainly no transformers, and few poles" (P. T. Davies, "Cost of Electric Power," *Engineering Journal*, August 1925, p. 339).

22. The lease for these water rights ran to 1964. In 1914 the station was expanded to its full capacity of 16,000 h.p., but on completion of the Cedars Rapids project in that year, the Soulanges plant had really become obsolete since the Cedars plant could use the same water more efficiently. (The Soulanges Station was not used much after World War I, although it continued to be operated to a small extent until 1930, when it was shut down and dismantled.) Davis had also arranged that another company, the St. Lawrence Power Company, would not "exercise its charter powers within the Province of Quebec except with consent of the Provincial Light, Heat and Power Company, but that it would exercise such charter power for the use and benefit of the Provincial Light, Heat and Power Company" (Ellis, p. 78; also A.R. 1905, p. 4).

23. It is probable that he was an agent for the Montreal company since no value was entered in the books of that company for the shares it obtained. The payment to Davis, however, a half-million dollars, was capitalized in the accounts of the Provincial company and thus indirectly inflated the financial structure of the Montreal company (Ellis, pp. 79–80).

24. *Electricity Commission*, Exhibit 1-A.

25. One wonders what would have happened had Aldred chosen to hold out a little longer. Montreal's strategic position was very weak as a result of the demand for its power increasing much more rapidly than its own supply. On the other hand, Shawinigan was anxious for markets and perhaps could not afford to wait for five or six years in order to see what would happen. Had the issue been forced, either Shawinigan would have become dominant in the Montreal market or the Montreal company would have had to take strong measures to develop power on its own initiative. In either event, the history of the Quebec industry would have been quite different than it in fact has been.

26. The Cedars Rapids Manufacturing and Power Company, the corporation in which ownership of the power site was vested, had had a long history. Incorporated by Dominion charter in 1904 by a group of Montreal people, the company during the next few years made preliminary arrangements for the development of power. Various parcels of land were acquired and in 1906, according to an undated brochure issued by the company, it was granted the right to use 56,000 c.f.s. of water from the St. Lawrence River at Cedars Rapids, between Lake St. Francis and Lake St. Louis, about 30 miles west of Montreal. With a head of 32 feet this amount of water was sufficient to de-

velop about 160,000 h.p. Developmental plans were drawn up and approved in 1909 by the International Joint Commission. The company was authorized to proceed with its project, and in 1910 the last legal barrier was overcome when a lease on the site was obtained from the Quebec government.

Up until this time, however, adequate financial support for the development seems to have been lacking. The brochure referred to remarks that "because of its magnitude and the fact that the greater proportion of the development would necessarily have to be completed before any power whatsoever could be obtained . . . [the site] . . . stood undeveloped until the control became vested in the joint interests of the Shawinigan Water and Power Company and the Montreal Light, Heat and Power Company." The Montreal and Shawinigan interests obtained control of the company through a Mr. D. L. McGibbon, who had acquired the valuable legal rights mentioned above. In 1912 he sold these rights to the Cedars Rapids company for $9.25 million, paid in stocks and bonds of the company. He then distributed all but two million dollars'-worth of these securities to the Montreal and Shawinigan companies and to Aldred and Holt personally, a small chore for which he was paid $850,000 cash by the transferees. In addition to this amount, Ellis conservatively estimated that McGibbon made a personal profit of nearly a million dollars on the deal, this being the value of the securities he retained less generous estimates for the expenses he incurred (Ellis, pp. 51–54).

The Shawinigan and Montreal companies, having gained control of the Cedars Rapids company, laid plans for the immediate development of the power site. Capital was secured by selling Cedars Rapids bonds, which the partners had bought at 80, to shareholders in the two parent companies at 90, with the added inducement of one gift share of Cedars Rapids stock for each $400 worth of bonds purchased.

27. The water available to the Cedars Rapids company was increased in 1916 when it obtained the right to use an additional 19,000 c.f.s. during the months when navigation was closed, i.e., from November to May.

28. Cedars Rapids Manufacturing and Power Company, Annual Report, 1915.

29. In 1910, again with the Shawinigan company as a partner, the Montreal company set up another concern, the National Hydro-Electric Company, which, according to a former executive of the Montreal Light, Heat and Power Company, was formed with the intention of developing the power of the Carillon rapids on the lower Ottawa River. In terms of our hypothesis as to the strategy of the Montreal company, this looks rather like a defensive manoeuver, and one may doubt whether in fact the Montreal partner was anxious to go ahead with the project. In any event the political difficulties involved in gaining control of this site were sufficient to prevent its exploitation at the time. Since the lower Ottawa is navigable, the federal government had certain rights in the case, and since it is a provincial boundary river, the ownership of its power resources was disputed by Quebec and Ontario. It was the interprovincial conflict which proved insoluble, and though the National Hydro-Electric Company obtained a lease to the site from the Quebec government in 1931 — "les droits, titres et interêts que la Province de Québec peut avoir" — nothing further was done. See Publication No. 11 of the (Quebec) Service Hydraulique, a list of the water powers conceded by the province from October 31, 1923 to August 14, 1934; also a pamphlet by Sir A. Beck, *A Statement by Sir Adam Beck protesting against the Exportation of Electric Power with special reference to the Proposed Lease of the "Carillon" Power Site* (Toronto, 1925). When the Montreal company was taken over by the Quebec government in 1944, the charter of the National company was surrendered, and the lease to the power site was cancelled.

30. This quotation is taken from a Memorandum of February 27, 1913, prepared by Stone and Webster, stockbrokers, for one of their clients. Accuracy of the informa-

tion given out by stockbrokers is never guaranteed. This document is to be found in the file for the Montreal Tramways and Power Company in the Corporation Records Department of the Baker Library at the Harvard Business School. Other documents, to be mentioned presently, are in the same file.

31. The plan was rejected by both companies. See the 1910 Annual Report of the Montreal Street Railway Company.

32. Memorandum by Stone and Webster.

33. This company took over the Saraguay Electric Light and Power Company, the Dominion Light, Heat and Power Company, and the St. Paul Electric Light and Power Company. These companies were powered by small steam stations in Montreal.

34. By this time the Public Service Corporation owned distributing systems in both the east and west ends of Montreal and also in the downtown area. For the corporate history of this concern, see the *Report of the Committee of Investigation to the Shareholders of the Montreal Tramways and Power Company Ltd., Montreal* (Montreal, October 24, 1923). This document is in Baker Library.

35. This document is in Baker Library.

36. This site was owned by the Montreal Hydro-Electric Company Limited, one of the subsidiaries of the Montreal Tramways and Power Company. This company had been incorporated by Dominion charter in 1910, and had bought out the Electric Power Company of Montreal and the Montreal Electric Light Company. (Nothing further is known of the two subsidiaries: they were probably inactive companies.) Its chief asset was the power site referred to in the text. See *Report of the Committee of Investigation to the Shareholders of the Montreal Tramways and Power Company Limited, Montreal.*

37. It controlled all the other subsidiaries but only had "a minority interest in the Montreal Public Service Corporation, now the Quebec-New England Hydro-Electric Corporation" (*Report . . . of the Montreal Tramways and Power Company Limited*). The latter company was about to be acquired by the Shawinigan and Montreal companies. In 1922, by a change in its charter, the Montreal Public Service Corporation had gained the power to acquire the Canadian Light and Power Company, the Beauharnois Electric Light Company, and the National Hydro-Electric Company, the moribund firm controlling the Carillon rapids (see note 29 above). It was forecast that the Quebec-New England Company "with the franchises and rights secured by its Charter, the acquisition of franchises, rights and properties [of its component companies] and those contemplated, will become a powerful factor in the production and distribution of electricity in this Province and elsewhere." But nothing came of this, and the Quebec-New England Company remained inactive.

38. A Shareholders' Investigating Committee explained the failure of the concern as follows:

> It was a very serious task to finance the Company owing to opposition at the outset and later to conditions created by the War and the consequent unsettled conditions of all financial markets. The adverse results shown in the Profit and Loss Statements covering the period of operations for eleven years since the formation of the Company, were due largely to the high cost of short date financing and the high premium paid on United States funds (*Report . . . of the Montreal Tramways and Power Company Limited*).

39. Julian C. Smith, later president of the Shawinigan company, was president of both these companies until his death in 1939.

40. The cash price paid by the Montreal company was about $8.5 million, which was some $4 million in excess of the book value of the concern. See Ellis.

41. A.R. 1924.

42. A.R. 1927. The site was developed to the extent of 45,000 h.p. The water utilized by this plant comes from the Ottawa River, Rivière des Prairies being one of its outlets to the St. Lawrence. The flow of the Ottawa is quite irregular, and because it has three outlets into the St. Lawrence it would be difficult to regulate it so as to increase the minimum flow at the Montreal Island plant. The existing plant of 40,000 h.p. can be operated at full capacity for all but thirty or forty days of the year.

43. The story of the Beauharnois scandal need not concern us here, particularly since it has already been discussed by Professor C. P. Wright. See his *The St. Lawrence Deep Waterway: A Canadian Appraisal* (Toronto, 1935), ch. 6.

44. A.R. 1929.

45. The initial development was 450,000 h.p., rather than the 650,000 h.p. originally planned.

46. Senator Bouchard implied a different interpretation of these events when he wrote: "En 1929, à peu près seul du côté des liberaux, je combattais et votais contre le bill de la Beauharnois Corporation recommandant au gouvernement de conserver à la province le magnifique pouvoir d'eau qui était cédé à cette nouvelle compagnie. On disait dans le temps que la Beauharnois Corporation ferait de la concurrence aux compagnies controlant alors l'électricité; . . . . on m'a demandé comment il se faisait que je combattais les deux parties en cause, et la Montreal Light, Heat and Power qui s'opposait au bill, et les promoteurs de la Beauharnais Corporation, demande à laquelle j'ai repondu en déclarant qu'il ne se serait pas écoulé vingt-quatre mois avant que les deux groupes ne se soient réunis pour continuer à exploiter la province, et c'est qui est arrivé. Quelque temps après l'adoption du bill et la mise en marche des travaux, le principal avocat qui représentait l'opposition siegeait sur le bureau de direction de la Beauharnois Corporation à côté du principal avocat des promoteurs du bill et aujourd'hui la Beauharnois Corporation est la chose du Montreal Light, Heat and Power Consolidated" (T. D. Bouchard, *La Metropole et l'électricité*, St. Hyacinthe, 1934, pp. 48–49).

47. Another threat, not mentioned in the above account, had been that of a municipal generating plant in Montreal, a proposal first made in 1915. The details are obscure. Mr. Bouchard refers to a 100,000-h.p. project which the city proposed to construct in connection with its water-supply canal, and says that after $11 million had been spent on the project it was quietly dropped. Mr. C. J. DesBoillets, the City Engineer, reported to the city on this matter in 1935, and in the following year an Executive Committee Report was drawn up by A. Surveyor et al. I have not seen either of these reports.

48. The smaller and older plants belonging to the company were retired from service at various times. The Soulanges plant was shut down and dismantled in 1930, as was the Lachine plant in 1931. The Chambly plant was retired in 1951 by Hydro Quebec and is to be dismantled. The St. Timothée plant is also to be shut down in the near future.

49. Its new status was evidenced in the following year. "Incident to the power we supply to the Hydro-electric Power Commission of Ontario and the reduction in price thereof under [the] revised contract, it was agreed with the Honourable the Prime Minister of Quebec [sic] that we would make a proportionate reduction to such classes of local consumers as he would designate. Acting upon the advice of the Provincial Electricity Board (to whom the matter was referred for investigation) the Prime Minister has decided that the reduction which will amount to $400,000.00 per annum is to apply to our so-called 'commercial' classification of users" (A.R. 1938, p. 5).

50. Very few details are known about the history of the company, but for our purposes this is perhaps no great loss since details would probably not change the main

view taken here, namely, that the company has been an economically passive firm that has simply grown with its market. The company's management was noted for its secrecy, and legend has it that one of Sir H. Holt's boasts was that he could throw not only the Annual Reports but also the Minute Books of the company into the middle of St. James Street without anyone being the wiser about its affairs. Even the Royal Commissioners investigating the electrical industry in Quebec, who should have been in a position to elicit some information about the company's history, merely protested lamely that "the annual statements submitted to the shareholders have not contained as much information as is desirable" (*Electricity Commission*, p. 32).

51. This document is in the Montreal Light, Heat and Power Consolidated file in the Corporation Records Room of Baker Library.

52. These figures are taken from the Annual Reports of the company, 1902 to 1908. This type of information was not given after 1908. To increase its load factor, the company at first adopted the policy used by the Royal Electric Company: "During the winter months the maximum lighting and power load is not coincident. This is brought about by the Company making a very attractive rate for power which is not used between the hours of 4 p.m. and 7 p.m. of each day during the above months" (*Montreal Electric Handbook*, p. 60). Such conditional power sales, however, were not feasible once electricity became an industrial necessity, and the lapse of this selling policy may explain a drop in the company's load factor from about 54 before World War I to an average of 48 or 49 thereafter.

53. A.R. 1916.

54. See A.R. 1916, and the list of rate reductions in A.R. 1922.

55. No full breakdown of the Montreal company's sales by markets is available. The following figures were provided by Quebec Hydro. Revenue from domestic and commercial sales rose from $4.8 million in 1925 to $7.6 million in 1932, fell to $7.3 million in 1935, and rose to $9.4 million in 1940. As a proportion of total revenue from electricity sales, sales to domestic and commercial customers were 42 per cent in 1925, 43 per cent in 1928, 46 per cent in 1930, 50 per cent in 1932, 49 per cent in 1935, and 49 per cent in 1940. In the 1920's, domestic sales were a growing proportion of the total and seem to have stabilized at about 50 per cent of total revenue in the following decade. In terms of physical sales, domestic and commercial deliveries grew (according to the memory of an official of the company) from about a third of total sales in the early 1920's to about 60 per cent of total sales in the early 1950's.

56. Whether in fact the demand for electricity in Montreal was inelastic is impossible to say. Many would argue on the basis of experience elsewhere that lower rates would have increased consumption sufficiently to increase profits and thus to justify still lower rates: the Montreal company took the view that rates had to be kept high because consumption was low. Between these two arguments there is nothing to choose on logical grounds, and the question of fact as to which view was correct for Montreal during the first four decades of the century cannot now be decided. It must be remembered that Montreal's population was largely French Canadian, and that French Canadians were accustomed to a relatively low standard of living. Perhaps we had better assume that Holt knew pretty well what his market would bear.

57. Bonds outstanding rose from $2.5 million in 1902 to $6.8 million in 1904 after the Lachine Company was purchased, and crept up to $9.44 million in 1916. Bond interest accordingly rose from $112 thousand in 1903 to $321 thousand in 1904 and $442 thousand in 1916. See *Electricity Commission*, Exhibit 1–A.

58. *Ibid.*

59. *Ibid.* Not all of the profits come from electricity sales of course. The Annual Report for 1950 states that in that year about two-thirds of net income was derived

from gas and electricity sales; one third was derived from "extraneous sources"—probably mainly its stock and bond holdings in other companies.

60. The financial ingenuity by which this enormous bonus, amounting to over $32 million, was distributed among the shareholders is carefully analysed in Ellis's report. The cash was raised mainly from a $30 million bond issue which was sold specifically for that purpose. The proceeds of this sale were only $26.4 million however, so that more cash had to be procured. This came mainly from the sale of $5 million of stock to the customers and employees of the company. Even more disgracefully, the stock was sold at $50 per share when even the grossly inflated values on the company's books worked out to an equity of only $28. It had been necessary to raise cash for this distribution, because at the time it was made the retained profits in the company were less than $11 million; in effect the $32 million bonus "was distributed from the inflation of the book values of investments in properties over the capital actually invested therein" (Ellis, p. 14). But instead of the cash bonus wiping out the inflation in the company's assets by writing down the property account, the inflation was maintained simply by writing down the stock account and increasing, as we have seen, the bond account, thus leaving the aggregate liabilities the same as previously. (The book value of the stock account was halved in 1926, and then immediately raised by nearly $11 million, created by additional inflation of securities and transfers from the depreciation reserve, and by $5 million resulting from the sale of stock to employees and customers.) This must surely have been one of the most shameful financial manipulations in the annals of Canadian business.

61. *Electricity Commission.*

62. Over 400,000 shares were sold in this manner at $50 per share, notwithstanding that, as the result of the stock split, the book value of the shares was then in the neighborhood of $17 (Ellis, p. 15). Ellis comments that the selling price "may have been set to discount the generous earnings which consumers were providing to the Company in the bills they paid, and which the Company conserved by its low operating costs" (p. 19).

63. Ellis, p. 17.

Chapter 6. The Southern Canada Power Company

1. See A. R. M. Lower, *Colony to Nation* (New York, 1947), pp. 188 ff.; R. Blanchard, *Le Centre du Canada Français* (Montreal, 1947), pp. 280 ff., 328, 344 ff.; M. L. Hansen, *The Mingling of the Canadian and American Peoples* (New Haven, 1940), pp. 157 ff.

2. In spite of its proximity to the St. Lawrence River, the region was difficult of access in the pre-railway period. It is traversed by three river systems flowing into the St. Lawrence: the Richelieu, the Yamaska, and the St. Francis. Of these, the Richelieu was the most navigable but served only the very western part of the area since it has no large tributaries. Numerous small waterfalls along the other two systems made them all but useless for commercial purposes. As for roads, the settlers "n'avaient à leur disposition que d'horribles chemins, d'ailleurs trop peu nombreux, et sur lesquels on ne pouvait guère circuler qu'en traineaux d'hiver" (Blanchard, p. 279).

3. Towns along the Richelieu River, of course, could get coal by barge from the United States via the Hudson–Lake Champlain route.

4. Blanchard, p. 285.

5. Blanchard, p. 263.

6. The economic stagnation of the area is suggested by population figures. See Jean I. Hunter, "The French Invasion of the Eastern Townships" (M. A. thesis, McGill Uni-

versity, 1951). Most of the population charts (on a county basis) provided by the author show a slight absolute decline in population between 1891 and 1901. The town of Granby was an important exception, its population having grown as the result of the location there of the Granby Rubber Company in 1883 and the Empire Tobacco Company in 1895. Hunter calculates that with the exception of Drummond and Sherbrooke, the counties in the area failed to retain the natural increase of their population from 1901 to 1931 (p. 81).

7. The Shawinigan company also delivered power to the pulp and paper mills at Windsor Mills and East Angus on the St. Francis River itself, thus supplementing the power provided by the mills' own developments.

8. On hearing of the formation of a power company in the Townships, Holt is supposed to have remarked contemptuously that there were no power resources worthy of the name in the area, and that even if there were, no one in the Townships could afford to buy electricity.

9. For the early history of electricity in Sherbrooke, see City of Sherbrooke (Gas and Electricity Department) *Report on the Development of Public Utilities in Sherbrooke from 1880 to Date*, compiled by J. R. McGregor, General Superintendent (Feb. 28, 1928); also Armand Crépeau, *Municipalization of Electricity in Sherbrooke*, an address before the Union of Municipalities of the Province of Quebec at Sherbrooke, November 1929, by the MLA for the City of Sherbrooke.

10. A.R. 1916.

11. The South Shore company had been formed to acquire the power sites mentioned. Plans had been made to establish a paper mill to utilize the power, but these were abandoned when the Southern Canada Power Company was formed. Among the assets the South Shore Power and Paper Company later contributed to the Southern Canada concern was an undertaking by the town of Drummondville to sell its electric plant to the company at cost. See the *Southern Canada Power News*, 25th Anniversary Number (1938), pp. 18–19.

12. A.R. 1916. According to Moody's *Public Utilities* for 1920, contracts had been made to sell 5000 h.p. to Shawinigan from each of the two developments for a fifteen year period. What actually happened was that Shawinigan took no power from the first development and 10,000 h.p. from the second. See below.

13. This process has gone on throughout the company's history. By 1934 the company had purchased 63 local distribution systems (9 of them formerly municipally owned) and had itself built 54 such systems. About two-thirds of the acquisitions came before 1920, many of them through the purchase of the Sherbrooke Railway and Power Company in 1916, and the rest in the following decade. Nine systems were built before 1920, and nearly all the rest between 1924 and 1930.

14. This system was powered by an 800-h.p. hydroelectric station, which continued to be used by the Southern Canada Power Company.

15. See note 12, above.

16. The company's generating capacity, unchanged since 1929, is given as follows by the Dominion Water and Power Bureau. Hemmings Falls, 33,600 h.p.; Drummondville, 18,400 h.p.; Sherbrooke, 4,000 h.p.; Burroughs Falls, 2,000 h.p.; Farnham (on the Yamaska river), 800 h.p.; total, 58,800 h.p. With the exception of the station at Farnham, the small power plants acquired by the company when it purchased other systems have been retired from service.

17. No information relating to the cost of developing power sites on the St. Francis River is available, but it is clear that the cost per developed horsepower would be much higher than it would be on the St. Maurice. In the first place, the flow of the St. Francis is so irregular that the average utilization factor of a plant using the river is

quite low. (In its submission to the Provincial Electricity Commission the Southern Canada Power Company stated that one horsepower of its installed capacity produced only 2700 kwh. per year as an average for a five-year period. This represents a capacity ratio of only 40 per cent. Only part of this undercapacity, of course, would be caused by flow conditions; the figure also reflects load factor conditions. In recent years, the company has been able to generate an average of 204 million kwhs. per year. High water in 1947 permitted the output to be raised to 252 million kwhs., while in 1948 low-water conditions forced the output down to 150 million kwhs. The former figure represents the highest output which the company has yet achieved, while the latter is the lowest since 1931 when drought conditions reduced output to 134 million kwhs.) Secondly, land that has to be acquired to allow for flooding behind power dams in the Townships is expensive relative to the cost of land in the nonagricultural Laurentian areas. Also, the geological structure is less suitable for dam and powerhouse foundations in the Townships than in the Laurentian areas of the St. Maurice.

18. The company also owned and operated the transportation system in Sherbrooke. This business became unprofitable at the outset of the depression and the service was discontinued at the end of 1931.

19. See *Electricity Commission*, p. 36.

20. As would be expected, the importance of its small domestic business has resulted in the Southern Canada Power Company's being very "public relations" conscious, and its leaders have played a prominent role in the fight to defend private ownership of electrical utilities. Profiting from the familiarization of the public with securities during the war, the company early in the twenties launched an aggressive campaign to sell preferred stock to its customers and employees. It prides itself on being one of the first companies in Canada to adopt this practice, and has adopted the motto "Owned by those it serves." Maintaining harmonious relations with the many municipalities in which the company sold electricity was a trying business, and diplomacy sometimes broke down. See, for instance, the note in the Annual Report for 1934: "Notwithstanding the low rates now in effect, the City of St. Hyacinthe is installing a Diesel engine operated municipal system to compete with your Company for a part of its business in the City of St. Hyacinthe." The city in fact expropriated the company's distribution system and bought power from the company at wholesale. In 1947 the municipality resold the system to the company.

21. A.R. 1921.

22. The rapid growth in the company's business since the end of the second world war suggests that a further great increase in the domestic use of electricity is taking place in the Townships. As we have already noted, the Shawinigan company is experiencing a similar upsurge in its retail business in other parts of the province.

23. A.R. 1931 and 1932.

24. A.R. 1918.

25. *Southern Canada Power News*, 25th Anniversary Number (1938), p. 9. Mr. Burnie, now retired, was the director of the Industrial Development department of the Southern Canada Power Company. He joined the company in 1926, after having been engaged in similar work for the C.P.R. in Ontario. I am indebted to Mr. Burnie for a stimulating discussion on the industrial development aspects of the company's business, and many of his ideas are incorporated in the paragraphs which follow.

26. A.R. 1933 and 1938.

27. The manufactures of the Eastern Townships are mainly valuable in relation to their bulk. Because of the freight rate "arbitrary" at Montreal, manufacturers in the Townships are at a disadvantage compared with manufacturers in Ontario when their products are shipped west of Montreal. On the freight rate arbitrary, see Canada, *Report*

of the Royal Commission on Transportation 1951 (Ottawa, 1951), pp. 149–151.

28. These figures have been drawn from information given in R. Blanchard, pp. 290–312, and relate to a region which includes (a) most of the territory served by the Southern Canada Power Company, excluding, however, the important industrial towns of St. Hyacinthe and St. John; and (b) the territory between the St. Francis and Chaudière Rivers served by the Shawinigan company including the asbestos district of the province. Most of the industrial development, however, has taken place in the first part of this region, and with the modifications noted in the text the figures give a fair indication of the manufacturing activity in the Southern Canada Power Company's territory in the late thirties. Much of this industry obtains its power from the Southern Canada Power Company; but it must be remembered that Sherbrooke, the largest manufacturing city in the area, provides most of its own power from a municipally owned system, and that the large plant of the Dominion Textile Company at Magog, employing over 1800 workers in 1936, develops its own hydroelectric power.

Together with those engaged in woods operations, sawmilling, mining (about 3200 in the asbestos district), central electric stations, and various small establishments such as printing shops, Blanchard estimates that there were about 30,000 industrial workers in the Eastern Townships in 1936. To this figure should be added about 4000 employees in St. John and St. Hyacinthe. A figure of 25,000 to 30,000 employees would be a reasonable estimate of the industrial workers in the territory served by the Southern Canada Power Company. Because of the large amount of female labor employed in the textile industries, the figure for the "heads of families employed" would be significantly smaller.

29. Like other industrial revolutions, this one has had interesting demographic aspects. Once the Townships had become well settled, around 1900, they began to contribute their own quota of young French Canadians to the stream which, especially from the older regions of the province, was flowing to New England. The pressure on the land became more serious after 1930 with changes in the American immigration laws which made emigration much more difficult. The growth of industry in the Townships provided an outlet for a growing population; it tended to reduce emigration to the United States in the 1920's and provided employment for those who were unable to emigrate in the 1930's.

30. The material and the quotations in the remainder of this paragraph have been taken from the *Memorandum submitted by the Southern Canada Power Company to the Electricity Commission of the Province of Quebec, November 1, 1934*, pp. 5–6. The figures for population, payrolls, etc., which are used in the *Memorandum* came from Canadian Government publications. See also E. C. Hughes, "Industry and the Rural System in Quebec," *The Canadian Journal of Economics and Political Science*, Vol. 4, No. 3 (August 1938), pp. 341–349, esp. pp. 346–347.

Industrial growth in the Townships should be placed against the background of industrial growth in Quebec as a whole. Manufacturing statistics on a county basis in Canada are available for only a few years, but from the figures available, I have made the following rough comparisons between the number of employees in manufacturing industry in Quebec and in the thirteen counties in which the Southern Canada company operates. (Manufacturing statistics were collected on a different basis after 1917 in Canada, so that the absolute figures given below for 1910 are not comparable with those for later years.) Employment in manufacturing in Quebec rose from 158,207 in 1910 to 197,207 in 1930, an increase of 24.6 per cent; but fell to 155,025 in 1932, or less than the 1910 figure. Employment in the thirteen counties in which we are interested rose from 17,397 in 1910 to 21,469 in 1932 (the 1930 figure is not available) or by 23.4 per cent. From 1932 to 1939 the increase in Quebec was 42 per cent, and that in the selected counties 48.6 per cent. These comparisons suggest that the rate of industrial growth in the Townships during the interwar period was at least as rapid as that in the province as a whole, and probably significantly larger than that in the province as a whole during the decade of the thirties. The rate of growth in the Townships during the quarter century before the first world war was probably considerably less than that in the province generally (see the early part of this Chapter), so that there can be little doubt that the Townships have greatly improved their relative industrial position in the province during this century. Comparing 1939 with 1910, our figures give an increase in employment of 39 per cent for Quebec and 83 per cent for the selected counties. For the county figures, see Canada, Department of Trade and Commerce, *Geographic Distribution of Manufacturers*, for the years 1932 to 1939.

31. W. H. Carter, Jr., "American Branch Plants in Canada," unpublished doctoral dissertation, Harvard University, 1932, p. 226.

32. With regard to the concentration of industry in the St. Francis valley, Blanchard comments, p. 310–311: "Influence évident d'un bon système de voies de communication et d'une heureuse utilisation des ressources hydrauliques: peut-être aussi, pour le sud, action de l'exemple Américain. L'esprit Américain est très perceptible à Sherbrooke."

33. The sample is admittedly crude. It leaves out Sherbrooke, the premier city of the area. There is no indication of the mortality of firms in the group included. Reporting may have varied from year to year. There is no adequate indication of the size of the firms listed so that large and small count equally as one. Moreover, some firms are listed twice, once when the decision to locate in the area has been made, or when construction has started on a new plant, and again when the plant is in operation. In the statistics given in the text an attempt has been made to eliminate these duplications and also to ignore firms that are obviously picayune.

34. H. Marshall, P. A. Southard, and K. W. Taylor, *Canadian-American Industry* (New Haven, 1936). American branch plants had, of course, been an important part of the movement of industry into the area before 1932. The American firms are not usually specifically indicated in the Southern Canada Power Company's Annual Reports, although it was noted that all five of the new plants established in the area in 1921 and 1922 were subsidiaries of American concerns.

35. The reciprocal trade arrangements between Canada and the United States in 1935, and between the United States, Great Britain, and Canada in 1938, reduced somewhat the incentive for the migration.

Chapter 7. The Ottawa Valley and the Saguenay River

1. This concern was the pioneer electrical enterprise in Ottawa, succeeding the Chaudière Electric Company, founded in 1887, which first introduced incandescent lighting to the city. (An older arc-lighting concern had been founded in 1881.) The company's plants at Chaudière Falls gave unreliable service because of their susceptibility to ice problems and because of the variable flow of the river, and a steam plant was built as a reserve in 1893. From 1905 on the company was subjected to the competition of a municipal system which bought its power from the Hydro-Electric Power Commission of Ontario. In 1909 the company became a subsidiary of the Ottawa Light, Heat and Power Company. This latter company was finally taken over by the H.-E.P.C. of Ontario after the end of the second world war.

2. One of these plants, of 4000 h.p., was owned and operated by the Ottawa Power Company until 1920, at which time it was sold to the Ottawa Light, Heat and Power Company.

3. For a description of these early plants see *Water Resources Paper No. 33* (Ottawa,

1923), a publication of the Dominion Water Power Branch of the Department of the Interior. These plants were constructed in the latter years of the nineteenth century and the early years of the twentieth. With the exception of the Hull Electric Company, which was controlled by the Canadian Pacific Railway, all of the enterprises seem to have been owned by local capital. See also Leo G. Denis, *Electric Generation and Distribution in Canada* (Ottawa, 1918), pp. 47, 145–146; "Water Power Resources of Canada and their Development" by J. T. Johnston, *Engineering Journal* (July 1930), p. 148; "The Water Power Resources of Canada" by M. J. Patton, *Economic Geography* (1926). Annual Reports for most of the companies are available in the Corporation Records Room at the Harvard Business School library.

4. Following the 1943 agreement, the Ontario Hydro immediately made plans for the exploitation of three sites on the upper river with an aggregate designed capacity of over 800,000 h.p., and the largest of these, the Des Joachims development of 480,000 h.p., was brought into operation in 1950. The immense water power of the lower river at the Carillon Rapids and also the smaller site at Hawkesbury are under the jurisdiction of Quebec; they are not to be developed immediately since, unlike Ontario, Quebec is not short of power at the present time. See T. H. Hogg and O. O. Lefebvre, "Ottawa River Power Sites Agreement," *Engineering Journal* (June 1943), pp. 334–336.

5. Besides these small central electric stations, there were two industrial concerns with power developments on the Lièvre river at Buckingham. The James Maclaren Company, an old lumber firm in the Ottawa valley, had built up, by 1930, a 19,250–h.p. development to supply its pulp and paper mill in the town; and in 1914 the Electric Reduction Company started a development, also at Buckingham, which was completed to 10,500 h.p. in 1938.

6. Earlier, the Shawinigan and Montreal companies had apparently had designs on the lower Ottawa, but nothing came of the project. See Chapter 5, note 29.

7. I am indebted to Mr. G. G. Gale for this information. Mr. Gale has been associated with the Gatineau Power Company since its formation and has been president of the company since 1934.

8. *Moody's Public Utilities*, 1924.

9. *Water Resources Paper No. 33*, p. 365.

10. *Moody's Public Utilities*, 1924.

11. The development was extended to 54,000 h.p. by the Gatineau company in 1929.

12. *Moody's Public Utilities*, 1924. Moody's also states that the company had a long-term contract with the Montreal Light, Heat and Power Company. No further information on this matter is available.

13. Annual Reports of the Ottawa-Montreal Power Company, 1925 and 1926.

14. For the history of the Riordon firm, see G. Carruthers, *Paper in the Making* (Toronto, 1947), pp. 483–522.

15. In 1927 the Gatineau Company formed a subsidiary, the Gatineau Electric Light Company, which was to operate all the transmission and distribution properties of the Gatineau Power Company, but this arrangement was discontinued in 1930, when all the generating, transmission, and distribution properties in Quebec were returned to the parent company. The Gatineau Electric Light Company now owns and operates only a small distribution system in Ontario. In 1940 the Gatineau Power Company also owned the following properties: (a) The Gatineau Transmission Company, operating 55 miles of high-tension line by which power deliveries are made to the Ontario Hydro-Electric Power Commission system; (b) The Gatineau Bus Company Limited, operating motor buses in and about Hull; (c) the St. John River Storage Company, which owns a storage dam on the Madawaska River in the province of Quebec, the dam being used to regulate the flow of water to the St. John River plant of the Canadian Interna-

tional Paper Company in New Brunswick. Also, in 1932, the Gatineau Company had purchased 49 per cent of the stock of the E. B. Eddy Company. This stock had formerly been owned by Canadian International Paper Company. (Annual Report of the International Hydro-Electric Company, 1932.) In 1943 it was reported that the Gatineau Company had sold its interest in the E. B. Eddy Company to a nonaffiliated purchaser. (Annual Report of the International Hydro-Electric Corporation, 1943.)

16. Except for the years 1936–1937 when it paid no dividends on its common stock. the Gatineau Company was the mainstay of the International Hydro-Electric System throughout the thirties. The system's holdings in the New England Power Association, which accounted for nearly 75 per cent of its portfolio, yielded no dividends. See Annual Reports of the International Hydro-Electric Corporation, especially those for 1941 and 1943. The system disposed of most of its New England holdings and today owns only a small fraction of the stock of the New England Power Association. It still controls the Gatineau Company through stock ownership, and owns all the stock of the Eastern New York Power Corporation.

17. Annual Report of the Canadian Hydro-Electric Corporation, 1930.

18. First Annual Report of the Canadian Hydro-Electric Corporation, 1928. The Annual Review of the Gatineau properties was included in the annual reports of this corporation until 1936. Since 1937 the Gatineau Power Company has issued its own annual reports.

19. This isolated line, serving half a dozen small towns, may possibly have represented an attempt on the part of the Gatineau company to gain a foothold in the area south of Montreal at a time when neither the Shawinigan nor the Southern Canada companies had established themselves firmly in the territory. However that may be, the line, though still owned by the Gatineau company, was soon firmly hemmed in by Shawinigan to the west and the Southern Canada network to the east. (The Shawinigan lines in this area drew their power from the St. Timothée generating plant on the St. Lawrence River.)

20. See Table 9. This table also shows how secondary power sales were increased to take up the slack during the suspension of the Ontario power contracts in 1936 and 1937.

21. Canadian Hydro-Electric Corporation, Annual Report 1931.

22. See the Gatineau Power Company's *Registration Statement under Securities Act of 1933*, filed with the Securities and Exchange Commission, March 24, 1939, p. 41. The statement is available in the Baker Library at the Harvard Business School.

23. *Prospectus filed with the Securities Exchange Commission, June 15, 1946, Amendment No. 3.* This document is also available at Baker Library.

24. For a list of Beck's speeches and pamphlets, see *Contributions to Canadian Economics*, Vol. III, p. 83. See also A. Brady "The Ontario Hydro-Electric Power Commission," in the *Canadian Journal of Economics and Political Science* (August 1936), especially pp. 339–341.

25. The people of Ontario were reluctant to admit that their "inexhaustible" supply of water power was in fact finite. They were perhaps still more reluctant to become dependent on American coal for their power supplies, particularly since the Hydro had been called into being, in part, as a means of reducing dependence on coal imports and thus mitigating the industrial consequences of those disruptions in the supply which were a result of the unsettled labour conditions in the American coal industry early in this century. Only in the last few years, with the power supply much tighter than it was in the 1920's, has Ontario brought itself to build steam electric stations.

26. J. Castell Hopkins (ed.), *Canadian Annual Review* (1930–1931), p. 114.

27. The Maclaren-Quebec Power Company was incorporated in Quebec in 1930 as the Buckingham Power Company, its present style being adopted by Supplementary

Letters Patent later in the same year. The firm owns three power plants on the Lièvre River (a tributary of the Ottawa River between Montreal and Ottawa), the High Falls plant of 120,000 h.p. built in 1930, the Masson plant of 136,000 h.p. built in 1933, and a 19,250–h.p. plant at Buckingham, at which site a small 550–h.p. station had been built in 1913. The firm is controlled by the Maclaren family which has been active in the lumber industry of the Ottawa valley for the past eighty years. Besides its sales to the Hydro, it provides power (some 66,000 h.p.) to the James Maclaren Company, the family newsprint concern, sells electricity at retail in Masson, and supplies the distribution systems of the Town of Buckingham and the Papineau West Co-operative. During the war it also sold power to the Electric Reduction Company, which itself owns a 10,500–h.p. development in Buckingham.

28. I. M. Biss, "Recent Power Legislation in Ontario," *Canadian Journal of Economics and Political Science* (May 1936), p. 212.

29. The Hydro's expenditure for purchased power dropped from $7,936,923 in 1935 to $2,824,228 in 1936. *Canadian Annual Review* (1935–1936), p. 265.

30. For an outline of this dispute see the *Canadian Annual Review* (1935–1936), pp. 196–200, 211–212, 217–220; and 1937–1938, pp. 152–155, 171–173.

31. *Moody's Public Utilities* (1936), p. 318.

32. See E. E. Free "The New Empire of the Saguenay," pp. 28–9 in *Le Saguenay Industriel* (Aubin and Grenou, 1929).

33. See Chapter 3, note 13.

34. For the negotiations between Price, Duke, George D. Haskell (who was interested in producing aluminum), and the Aluminum Company of America, see D. H. Wallace, *Market Control in the Aluminum Industry* (Cambridge, 1937), pp. 73–74 and 132–135. Cf. also C. C. Carr, *Alcoa, an American Enterprise* (New York, 1952), pp. 103–104 and 212–213.

35. During World War II, regulating dams were built on two of the rivers flowing into Lake St. John. These dams further improved the regulation of the river.

36. See note 35, Chapter 2.

Chapter 8. Hydroelectricity and Industrial Development

1. Popular notions tend to become wishful thinking, and in Canada wishful thinking is often conducted in terms of "vast natural resources." Especially in Ontario and Quebec, where no coal is mined, water power is very apt to be the symbol of future hopes, and one could easily compile quite an amusing collection of economic forecasts based on hydroelectric development that are almost lyrical in their optimism. Thus in 1910, an engineer writing on the virtues of storage reservoirs for hydroelectric plants: "The ultimate result will be that the territory from Labrador to Port William must become a great power centre, and, by improved transmission, distribute power to great distances. Indeed, by the end of the twentieth century, the Ottawa Valley may be the power heart of the world and the centre of a delightful district unsullied by coal smoke and beautified by reservoirs of unrivalled natural beauty" (Commission of Conservation, *First Annual Report*, 1910, p. 169).

And in 1947, the anonymous civil servant who prepared the text of a government publication: "Figuratively, nearly every Canadian has the miracle of an 'electric horse' at his command to help him do his work, to light his way, to chill or cook his food, to heat his water, to drive his tram or train, to bring him music and entertainment, to turn night into day, and do a thousand and one things with incredible speed and efficiency. This magic horse is willing and able to work 24 hours a day the year long — ever at the call of his master's finger tip [*sic*] — and in reserve, thundering down the white-maned falls and rapids of the hinterland, many millions of magic Centaurs await the harness of this and future generations" (*Central Electric Stations in Canada, 1947*, p. 5).

Then, too, there was the engineer who in 1916 envisioned a vast industrial development in western Canada: Electrical fixation of atmospheric nitrogen would provide for the perpetual replenishment of prairie soils, and "by electrometallurgy the iron ores of Lake Winnipeg will assume a commercial value, and the future market of the West for iron and steel will find considerable locally manufactured . . . It is not out of the way to predict that the Prairie Provinces will be served with transmission lines joining the Eastern, Northern and Western powers, augmented by steam driven plants at the coal mines and serving the transcontinental railways, the municipalities, the rural population, electrochemical works, electrometallurgical works and widespread industries. . . ." (P. H. Mitchell, "Water Powers of the Prairie Provinces," *Water Resources Paper No. 16*, Ottawa, 1916, issued by the Dominion Water Power Branch of the Department of the Interior). In the present chapter we take a more sober approach to the subject of hydroelectricity and its relation to industrial development.

2. E. W. Zimmerman, *World Resources and Industries* first ed. (New York, 1933). Chapters XXVIII and XXIX provide a thoughtful discussion of the economic significance of electricity.

3. In a few cases, it is true, notably in the growth of electroprocess industries in Norway, hydroelectric development has led to the establishment of new industries, unknown in the age of coal, in areas previously untouched by industrialism. An industrial development of this sort, however, consists mainly of a highly specialized group of industries which for technological reasons require very large amounts of electricity, and is therefore too narrowly specialized to conform to the common meaning of "an industrialized area." In our discussion of electricity and industry we shall ignore, for the most part, the electroprocess industries (such as the aluminum reduction industry in Quebec) on the grounds that such industries are special cases and that the relationship of electricity to their development is an obvious one.

4. An earlier version of much of the material in Sections II and III appeared in J. H. Dales, "Fuel, Power, and Industrial Development in Central Canada," *American Economic Review, Papers and Proceedings* (May 1953), pp. 181–198.

5. To use *thermal* electricity for heating purposes requires two energy transformations (the heat of coal to electricity and electricity to heat) which wastes energy in the physical sense and is therefore expensive in the economic sense, as compared with the single process of burning coal (or some other fuel) to produce heat. It will also normally be uneconomic to use *hydro*electricity for heating purposes because the price of hydroelectricity, being monopolistically determined, will be set in relation to the price of thermal electricity in all areas where the two processes are in actual or potential competition. Thus the price of hydroelectricity probably renders it uneconomic for most heating purposes wherever it is sold today. Certainly this has been the case in Quebec. See Canada *Royal Commission on Coal, 1946* (Ottawa, 1947), p. 388. (This report is hereafter cited as *Carroll Commission*.) It is possible, of course, to imagine an area where hydroelectricity is so plentiful and cheap that it could undersell fuels in the market for heat even when fuels are available at reasonable prices. Slightly more realistically, it is possible, in an area where water power is plentiful and cheap but fuels scarce and expensive, that a government might wish to subsidize the production of hydroelectricity for heating purposes in the interests of developing manufacturing industry.

6. For an alternative explanation of this important proposition, see *Carroll Commission*, pp. 383–388.

7. The range of processes in which electric heating is used has been increasing over the last fifteen or twenty years, and enthusiasts argue that just as electricity has tri-

umphed over the steam engine in power production, so it will eventually capture much of the heating market from fuels. A recent advertisement by the Massey-Harris Company of Canada states that it has developed a new process of electric forging. If this process can be generalized to all types of forging operations, it will relax significantly the present limitations on electric heating. Electric heating is now used extensively in the automobile industry. It appears probable, though, that the use of electric heating will be confined to special situations where heat has to be applied in small quantities to a specific area and where temperature control is important. Where large amounts of heat are required it is unlikely that electricity will compete with coal. Electrical heating may very well provide an important market for central electric stations in the next decade or so, but it is unlikely that the total amount of heat so generated will be large enough to replace any significant amount of fuel in the industrial market for heat.

The heating market was first explored by the General Electric Company in the United States during the depression of the 1930's in an attempt to bolster sagging sales of power appliances with a new line of electrical heating apparatus. Power companies were alive to the potentialities of the market, and a subcommittee of the Canadian Electrical Association was set up to promote the use of electric heating in Canada. This subcommittee was active during the later thirties but the booming market of the war years led to a reduced interest in its activities. After the war, attention was again directed to the market for electrical heating. See the report of the Industrial Power and Heating Committee in the Canadian Electrical Association's Annual Report for 1950. (I am indebted to Mr. C. H. Talbot of The Shawinigan Water and Power Company for some of the information presented in this footnote.)

8. *Carroll Commission*, p. 388.

9. See National Resources Planning Board, *Industrial Location and National Resources* (Washington, 1943), p. 180.

10. *Ibid.*, p. 166.

11. In the United States the industrial consumption of coal fell sharply in 1930, remained at low levels during the depressed thirties, and increased only modestly during the war years; the industrial consumption of electricity, on the other hand, increased steadily from 1932 on. In Quebec, in contrast to the American experience there was a marked upward trend in the industrial sales of *both* electricity and coal after 1932.

12. Of course some products, for instance some chemicals, can be manufactured by two or more quite different processes, and the same product could then be economically manufactured in countries with widely different resource patterns. Electricity itself provides a good example, since it is produced by the thermal process in areas with good fuel supplies and by the hydraulic process in areas with good water-power resources.

13. The size of the price differential for bituminous coal as between three American cities and two American lake ports may be gauged by reference to figures given in the *Carroll Commission*, pp. 339 and 344. The cost of American coal in Quebec will be higher than in Ontario by at least the cost of transporting it through the St. Lawrence canals from Lake Ontario to Montreal. Quebec also uses Nova Scotian coal. This coal, however, is high cost at the mine, and in order for it to compete in the Montreal market its price has to be kept down to the price of American supplies by Dominion government subsidies. In some years, subsidies are also necessary in Quebec markets east of Montreal. For details on the subsidies, see the annual reports published by the Dominion Coal Board. Nova Scotian coal is also of inferior quality for many industrial uses. See *Carroll Commission*, pp. 434–435, 488–489.

14. In view of the general similarity of the fuel-power resources patterns in Ontario and Quebec, it seems rather surprising that our statistical evidence should show such a marked difference in the proportion of heat to power used by industry in the two prov-

inces. An American investigation, however, showed that the locational pattern of manufacturing industry is quite sensitive to fuel and power costs. The cost and consumption of fuel in 47 states were correlated, yielding a regression of .712. "The slope of this line, which is 1.67 is an indication of the elasticity of demand for fuels for all industries taken as a whole. Since in any given industry, however, the elasticity of demand for fuels is likely to be quite small, fuel generally being required for technological reasons in approximately fixed proportions to other factors, this correlation is in fact occasioned by the concentration of more intensive fuel consuming industries in the lower-cost area. While the correlation is far from perfect, and the use of States as units conceals a wide variation in cost within each State, the analysis none the less suggests a very far-reaching degree of general fuel orientation." The same study indicated that "the degree of power orientation . . . , while considerably less than with fuels, is none the less very substantial" (*Industrial Location and National Resources*, pp. 166 and 174).

15. Further evidence of the difference in the relative use of heat and power in Ontario and Quebec is given in the following table. Figures published in the Canada Year Book make it possible to derive the expenditures of manufacturing industries on fuel and electricity, by provinces, from 1926 on. From these figures the ratios of expenditure on heat to the expenditure on power in each province have been calculated for five representative years. The figures used in the calculation are revenue figures and thus the resulting ratios will be affected by the differential prices of fuel and electricity as between the two provinces. However, since the evidence of the table is so strong, we need not attempt to correct for this factor.

Ratios of Expenditures on Fuel to Expenditure on Electricity by Industry in Quebec and Ontario

	Quebec	*Ontario*
1926	1.45	2.4
1930	.83	1.8
1933	.61	1.4
1939	.65	1.8
1944	1.05	2.2

16. This section has been written after an inspection of the detailed manufacturing statistics for Quebec (published annually in the *Statistical Year Book for Quebec*) and the ranking of selected American industries by their physical consumption, per dollar's-worth of product, of various fuels and of electric energy, given in tables published in *Industrial Location and National Resources*, pp. 167, 168, 177.

17. The gaps could no doubt be seen much more clearly by comparing Quebec with the United States, a prime example of coal-based industry, but the non-comparability of industrial classifications between the United States and Canada makes it difficult to construct a fair comparison between these two regions.

18. The aggregate net value product for the thirty leading industries was, in Ontario, $521.2 million, and in Quebec, $341.6 million.

19. At least until recently, when Ontario has been able to draw on Albertan oil, Quebec has had easier access to petroleum supplies than Ontario. Quebec was able to import her supplies by tanker, mainly from South America, while Ontario drew her supplies from American fields, either by pipeline to Sarnia or pipeline and lake tanker to other ports on the Great Lakes. The ratio of petroleum to coal used in Quebec is higher than in Ontario for both industrial and domestic uses. See Canada, *Petroleum Fuels in Canada* (Bureau of Mines Publication No. 808), p. 4.

20. Again it must be emphasized that our purpose is not to give a one-factor explanation of the industrial patterns in Quebec and Ontario; these examples have been quoted to show that the facts are consistent with our hypothesis that the fuel-power situation has had a noticeable influence on the industrial composition of the two provinces.

21. See G. J. Stigler, "Production and Distribution in the Short Run" in American Economic Association, *Readings in the Theory of Income Distribution* (Philadelphia, 1946) pp. 119–142. The "divisibility" of modern production, of which Professor Stigler speaks, results largely from electric drive.

22. See D. B. Creamer, *Is Industry Decentralizing?* (Philadelphia, 1935) p. 10. This study showed that, between 1899 and 1933, the proportion of wage earners in manufacturing in the "principal cities" of the United States and their "satellites" (cities of over 100,000 population in the same area) declined from 43.2 per cent in 1899 to 39.7 per cent in 1919 and 35.7 per cent in 1933. The industrial "peripheries" of these cities grew from 15.7 per cent in 1899 to 20.2 per cent in 1919 and 20.3 per cent in 1933. "Important industrial counties" (i.e., industrial areas which included no principal cities) accounted for 8.4 per cent of the wage earners in 1899, 8.3 per cent in 1919, and 10.3 per cent in 1933. The changes, especially in the interwar period are small. Professor C. Goodrich, who contributed the Preface to Creamer's study, summarized the situation as follows: "The concentration of employment in the principal industrial cities has steadily diminished. There is thus evidence of a moderate amount of decentralization . . . The recorded changes represent for the most part not a scattering of factories up and down the length of the land, but a gradual and limited spreading and filling out of the industrial pattern within the major manufacturing regions" (p. vii).

23. See E. M. Hoover, *The Location of Economic Activity* (New York, 1948), pp. 208–209.

24. Hugh MacLennan, "City of Two Souls," *Holiday* (August 1951), p. 78.

25. A study of the United States in 1939 showed that though only 23 per cent of all employed workers were engaged in manufacturing, the coefficient of association between wage earners in manufacturing and total population on a geographic basis was .78 (*Industrial Location and National Resources*, pp. 107 and 119). As a result of the large movement of people from the farm to industry during the last dozen years, the coefficient will undoubtedly have risen since 1939.

26. Dr. William H. Dean Jr., in his *The Theory of the Geographical Location of Economic Activities* (a doctoral dissertation submitted to Harvard University in 1938) shows clearly the importance of food supplies in the location of manufacturing activity. This very important work represents one of the few attempts to treat the problem of the location of industrial structures among different regions. Dr. Dean treats "the market" as a separate variable in his analysis, arguing that the market is located at "nodal points" of commerce (p. 46) which are geographically fixed from the point of view of industry. This clear distinction between commercial areas and industrial areas may well be justified in a discussion of medieval or early modern industry, but today the greater part of trade and commerce is closely associated with industry and therefore it seems better, as we have argued in the text, to view "commerce" and "the market" as results rather than determinants of the regional location of industry.

27. By the term "industrial structure," we mean simply a manufacturing development sufficiently large and diversified to correspond to the ordinary meaning of "an industrial economy."

28. This statement of the proposition is crude and incomplete, but we believe it to be sufficiently accurate and realistic to support the empirical analysis which appears later

in this section. Here three comments are in order by way of elucidation and amplification.

a. The proposition assumes that the economic "region" is a meaningful concept which can be defined, if necessary, for the purposes in hand.

b. We are implicitly assuming that an "industrial structure" has some minimum size, that there is some "critical volume" of industry above which a region will have a viable industrialized economy and below which there can be no industrialization in the common sense meaning of that word, though there may be isolated manufacturing establishments. This assumption is largely a matter of "hunch," but it may be supported positively by reference to "external economies," about which we really know very little, and negatively by the observation that industry *is* concentrated regionally, not spread evenly over the earth. In industrial development feast or famine seems to be the rule, moderation the exception. It should be noted that different industrial structures may have different compositions (as illustrated in Section III of this chapter) and therefore different materials requirements. The elaboration of our theory would require, as a preliminary step, a description and classification of industrial structures according to inputs or outputs.

c. The 50 per cent rule applies when only one of the two or more regions under consideration has 50 per cent or more of the materials requirements. More generally, when (a) two or more regions equidistant from one another have more than 50 per cent of the requirements, or when none has 50 per cent of the requirements, and when (b) the aggregate of resources is sufficient for one industrial structure but less than sufficient for two, industrial development, if it occurs at all, will take place in the region that has the largest fraction of the materials requirements. When two or more regions have more than 50 per cent of the requirements and when the aggregate of resources is sufficient to support two or more industrial structures, industrial development may take place in two or more regions. The proposition could be further complicated by assuming regions at different distances from one another and by taking account of different mobilities of different materials.

29. The ratio of the cost of a factor to total costs of production is frequently taken as a measure of the locational attraction of that factor. This "measure" has no merit. It is an *ex post* measure when what is needed is clearly an *ex ante* concept. As Professor Florence remarks when discussing the use of a cost-ratio measurement to indicate the importance of transport costs to the location of an industry, "It should . . . not be forgotten that cost of transport may be low for the very reason that in choosing a location . . . care was taken to make it low" (P. Sargent Florence, *Investment, Location, and Size of Plant*, Cambridge, England, 1948, p. 128). Location theorists, although perfectly well aware of the shortcomings of the cost-ratio measurement, nevertheless make frequent use of it and thereby involve themselves in contradictions and statements that seem to confound common sense. Thus Professor Hoover, co-author of an article in which the defects of the cost-ratio measurement were clearly set out (*Industrial Location and National Resources*, p. 331), argues elsewhere that although atomic energy may soon make it possible for "any region on earth . . . to generate electric energy . . . at costs comparable to present costs [in thermal stations in the United States]" this prospect "does not seem to portend . . . any revolutionary locational changes" because energy costs "are small in proportion to other items of procurement, distribution, and processing costs" (E. M. Hoover, *The Location of Economic Activity*, New York, 1948, pp. 183–184). Although W. Isard and V. Whitney, in their *Atomic Power* (New York, 1952), reject any rigorous application of the cost-ratio measure of locational significance (pp. 72–75), they minimize the probable locational effects of atomic power largely on the basis of the relative unimportance of power costs in industrial location

and the unlikelihood that atomic power will be much, if any, cheaper than thermal electricity or hydroelectricity (pp. 60–71). These expectations are no doubt sound with respect to areas which already have good energy resources and are already industrialized. But the probable significance of atomic power to the industrialization of underdeveloped areas is still an open question. Another author, L. Gordon, uses the cost-ratio measurement against his better judgment, and on the basis of it concludes that "in the great majority of industries, fuel and power are locationally insignificant" (*Industrial Location and National Resources*, p. 159). Yet a few pages later, working with empirical data, Gordon carries through a correlation analysis which "suggests a very far-reaching degree of general fuel orientation" (p. 166) and which shows that "the degree of power orientation . . . is . . . very substantial" (p. 174).

30. But see note 12 of this chapter. The assumption of variable proportions is usually supported by the example of capital and labor and it is frequently argued that in "backward areas" as compared with industrialized areas more labor and less capital will be used in production. This may be a realistic assumption in some areas of economic activity, for instance in construction, agriculture, and perhaps in commerce. To a certain extent also, of course, labor may be substituted for machines in some manufacturing processes, as where seamstresses are used rather than sewing machines. But where this is general the economy is likely to be a "crafts" or "putting-out" economy, and not an "industrialized" economy in the modern sense of the word. A steel mill, an oil refinery, a pulp and paper plant, an automobile factory, a cotton-spinning factory or a radio works — all are likely to be much the same the world over. The more elaborate the technology, it seems to me, the more rigid it is likely to be, and the more appropriate the assumption of fixed proportions becomes.

31. For an estimate of annual per capita materials consumption in the United States, see the *Report of the President's Materials Policy Commission* (Washington, 1952), Vol. I, p. 4.

32. There are still some candidates left. The exclusion of domestic fuel requirements from our reckoning would not be restrictive in warm climates. It is also a justifiable exclusion insofar as some sort of domestic fuel, such as peat, lignite, or wood, is ubiquitous. A housing census in Canada in 1941 showed that 46 per cent of Canadian homes used firewood for heating, while only 42 per cent burned coal (*Canada Year Book*, 1945, p. 255). The exclusion of transportation fuel requirements is probably a good deal more restrictive; but railways (the main consumers) usually pass through *some* regions that have fuel supplies, and can, of course, transport their requirements from one region to another at cost, by using their own facilities.

33. The only mineral fuels produced in central Canada are quantitatively insignificant and declining amounts of oil and natural gas in southwestern Ontario.

34. *Canada Year Book* (1952–53), p. 485.

35. See Chapter 2, note 20.

36. See H. A. Innis, "Economic Nationalism," *Proceedings, Canadian Political Science Association* (1934), pp. 17–31.

37. *Industrial Location and National Resources*, p. 157.

38. Isard and Whitney, pp. 58, 71, 158–159, come to the opposite conclusion as a result of conducting their argument in terms of individual industries.

39. Dean, chapter VII. Dr. Dean believed, however, that nineteenth-century industry was never so decisively oriented to coal as early modern industry had been to food (pp. 236 and 392).

40. See E. W. Gilboy, "Demand as a Factor in the Industrial Revolution," *Facts and Factors in Economic History* (Cambridge, 1932), pp. 620–639; and also her *Wages in Eighteenth Century England* (Cambridge, 1934).

41. "The electrical industry represents one of the greatest achievements of applied science which man has yet attained. Only the chemical industry among basic industries can be placed on the same level" (E. W. Zimmerman, *World Resources and Industries*, p. 561).

42. A copy of this document is available in the Library of the School of Commerce, McGill University.

43. See the annual publication of the Dominion Bureau of Statistics, *Report on Index Numbers of Electric Light Rates*, which includes tables of typical monthly bills for different electrical consumptions in different towns and cities of Canada.

Chapter 9. Summary

1. Export to Ontario provides a third type of market important to that section of the Quebec industry located on the Ottawa and St. Lawrence Rivers. In this case, Quebec power supports industrialism in Ontario. Its role here has been that of servicing rather than developing a market, although it can be argued that the growth of that market itself owes much to hydroelectric development in Ontario.

2. The railway and the power industries required similar enterpreneurial capabilities, and it is interesting to note the number of cases of ex-railway personnel who became associated with hydroelectric enterprises. Sir William Mackenzie of the Canadian Northern Railway was the promoter of an early project at Niagara Falls designed to provide power for his Toronto Street Railway, and was at one time a director of the Shawinigan Company. This latter company numbered among its original investors the manager of the Grand Trunk Railway, a promoter of a railway in the Eastern Townships, and a vice-president of the (Quebec) Great Northern Railroad. Sir Herbert Holt, architect of the Montreal Light, Heat and Power Company, had been an engineer with the C. P. R. and had also been associated with Mackenzie and Mann, the builders of the Canadian Northern. In two other cases early power companies were closely associated with street-railway enterprises, and curiously, in each instance, contributed a president to a modern power company. Mr. Gale of the Gatineau Power Company started his career in the Hull Electric Company (then owned by the C. P. R.) which owned the street railway in Hull; and Mr. Woodyatt of the Southern Canada Power Company started as an electrical engineer with the Sherbrooke Railway and Power Company.

3. Until 1930, the Quebec companies customarily made their bonds payable in Canadian or American dollars or sterling at the holder's option, and these gold bonds involved the companies in large exchange losses when Canadian and British currency depreciated against the American dollar in the early thirties. Nearly all the subsequent bond issues of the industry have been made payable in Canadian funds only, a policy rendered feasible by the growing marketability of Canadian securities both at home and abroad.

4. In addition to the industrial development work of the Southern Canada Power Company, town officials and Chambers of Commerce have been active in attracting firms to the area. Sherbrooke, with its publicly owned hydroelectric system, has also succeded in maintaining its position as the premier manufacturing city in the Eastern Townships.

5. Cf. the following comments on the American electrical industry: "Low rates for electric energy, if accompanied by that increased consumption which experience indicates would be the result, is not an appalling prospect for the industry . . . The industry has been timid in its policy of extension of service and increase of consumption through lowering the rates. It is noteworthy that the profits of the industry have been increased where, as on the Pacific coast, extensions, lower rates, and increased consumption have been forced by well-managed municipal plants; and where, as in the area of

the Tennessee Valley Authority, lower rates and increased use have been forced by activities of that Authority. . ." (H. S. Person, "Economic and Social Significance," *Transactions Third World Power Conference*, Washington, 1938, Vol. II, p. 683). An executive meeting of the Canadian Electrical Association was held in 1914 to develop a strategy for fighting public ownership in Ontario. An Ottawa man spoke: "I have had a very long experience in electric lighting. I suppose I am one of the earliest pioneers in Canada, having commenced about 1880 and have been at it ever since . . . There has been no respect in Ontario for our vested rights, none whatsoever. It is simply because we have been able to fight them successfully in our own district that we exist to-day. I do not know how it is we have continued to pay good dividends in face of the way we have been reducing rates, but we have been doing it nevertheless. I do not know how long it is going to go on. I hope it will go on indefinitely." This gentleman's long experience had taught him nothing about the elasticity of demand.

INDEX

Bei Fragen zur Produktsicherheit wenden Sie sich bitte an:
If you have any questions regarding product safety,
please contact:

Walter de Gruyter GmbH
Genthiner Straße 13
10785 Berlin
productsafety@degruyterbrill.com